Gendered States: Women, Unemployment Insurance, and the Political
Economy of the Welfare State in Canada, 1945–1997

In the period since the Second World War there has been both a massive
influx of women into the Canadian job market and substantive changes
to the welfare state as early expansion gave way by the 1970s to a
prolonged period of retrenchment and restructuring. Through a detailed historical account of the unemployment insurance program from
1945 to 1997, Ann Porter demonstrates how gender was central to both
the construction of the postwar welfare state and its subsequent crisis
and restructuring. Drawing on a wide range of sources including archival material, UI appeal court decisions, and documents from the government, labour, and women's groups, she examines women's treatment
within the UI program, the implications of restructuring for women's
equality, and how women's groups, labour, and the state interacted in
efforts to shape the policy agenda. She suggests new analytic approaches
with the view to further developing a feminist political economy of
welfare s'                                                      ess and
nature o                                                      new,
neoliber

Porter                                                   based
on a fam                                                 e that
assumes                                                  ty for
both m                                                   ty for
women                                                    nefits
have u                                                   asing-
ly diffi                                                 homy,
feminis                                                  disci-
plines.

(Comp

ANN P                                                    litical
Science

Studies in Comparative Political Economy and Public Policy

Editors: Michael Howlett, David Laycock, Stephen McBride, Simon Fraser University. *Studies in Comparative Political Economy and Public Policy* is designed to showcase innovative approaches to political economy and public policy from a comparative perspective. While originating in Canada, the series will provide attractive offerings to a wide international audience, featuring studies with local, subnational, cross-national, and international empirical bases and theoretical frameworks.

For a list of books published in the series, see p. 357.

# GENDERED STATES

Women, Unemployment Insurance,
and the Political Economy of the
Welfare State in Canada, 1945–1997

*Ann Porter*

UNIVERSITY OF TORONTO PRESS
Toronto Buffalo London

© University of Toronto Press Incorporated 2003
Toronto Buffalo London
Printed in Canada

ISBN 0-8020-3523-X (cloth)
ISBN 0-8020-8408-7 (paper)

Printed on acid-free paper

---

**National Library of Canada Cataloguing in Publication**

Porter, Ann
  Gendered states : women, unemployment insurance, and the
  political economy of the welfare state in Canada, 1945–1997 / Ann
  Porter.

  Includes bibliographical references and index.
  ISBN 0-8020-3523-X (bound)    ISBN 0-8020-8408-7 (pbk.)

  1. Insurance, Unemployment – Canada – History – 20th century.
  2. Women – Employment – Canada – History – 20th century.   3. Canada –
  Economic policy – 1945–   4. Canada – Social policy.   I. Title.

  HD7096.C3P67 2003       368.4'4'0971       C2003-902020-7

---

This book has been published with the help of a grant from the Canadian
Federation for the Humanities and Social Sciences, though the Aid to
Scholarly Publications Programme, using funds provided by the Social
Sciences and Humanities Research Council of Canada.

University of Toronto Press acknowledges the financial assistance to its
publishing program of the Canada Council for the Arts and the Ontario
Arts Council.

University of Toronto Press acknowledges the financial support for its
publishing activities of the Government of Canada through the Book
Publishing Industry Development Program (BPIDP).

To the memory of John and Marion Porter
and to Nicolas Ewen

# Contents

Conclusion   231

# Preface

I first became interested in the question of gender and income security policies in the late 1980s. The Canada–U.S. Free Trade Agreement had been signed not too many years earlier and the Macdonald Royal Commission on the Economic Union and Development Prospects for Canada had by then released its report, which called not only for a 'leap of faith' with respect to free trade, but also for a far-reaching restructuring of social programs. This was a time of extensive lay-offs in industries such as clothing and textiles, when contingent, 'flexible' work was growing, and when many women were faced with a great deal of job insecurity and with difficulty juggling workplace and family responsibilities. Debate over the future of social policy became sharply polarized as two very different dialogues unfolded. Official commissions of inquiry, a number of 'think tanks,' and the Conservative government, followed by the Liberal government, were articulating the view that the state needed to reduce expenditures, that greater emphasis needed to be placed on market forces, and, in addition, that welfare state programs needed to be restructured in ways that would, for example, break 'dependencies' on them. At the same time, popular sector groups, including women's organizations and labour unions, were drawing attention to the increasing insecurity that people were experiencing and were calling for more comprehensive programs that would address the impact that large-scale economic and social transformations were having on people's lives. As these divisions became sharper in the 1990s, a series of reforms to UI and other social programs effectively implemented the vision articulated by the former group.

The present study focuses on the UI/EI program and is concerned with how social, political, and economic forces came together to construct and reconstruct the welfare state and its entitlements in particular ways. It now seems that for only a relatively brief time did the state assume a major responsibility for addressing the problem of market-generated unemployment, and did the idea take hold that there should be some form of income security for those who become unemployed as a result of market forces. It seems ironic now that just as women gained a greater presence in the labour force and obtained greater formal equality, this form of 'citizenship right' was eroded. This book provides an historical examination of the gendered basis of the postwar welfare state, its crisis, and neoliberal restructuring. The focus is on the policy of a single state – the Canadian state. The title 'gendered states' refers to two different time periods: the postwar regime and the subsequent neoliberal one. Although gender relations and women's rights and entitlements were very different in these two periods, both regimes were, I argue, structured around and based in fundamental ways on gender differences and inequalities.

A number of people made it possible for me to undertake and complete this project. In the initial stages of the study, which began as a doctoral dissertation at York University, I received invaluable critical feedback and support from Pat Armstrong, Judy Fudge, Ken McRoberts, and especially Leo Panitch. Stephen McBride generously commented on an early version of the manuscript. During a year I spent in Ottawa, a number of people provided encouragement and helpful insights. I would like to thank Pat Armstrong, Hugh Armstrong, Caroline Andrew, Wallace Clement, Wendy McKeen, and Rianne Mahon. Particular thanks to Viviane Guenette and Claude Danik both for their encouragement and for making the year in Ottawa possible. York University has continued to provide a stimulating work environment. I would like to thank my colleagues there for ongoing and valuable discussions. Greg Albo, George Comninel, Judy Fudge, and Leo Panitch should be thanked in particular. I would like to thank Tanya Dubar for her help with the tables and bibliography. I gratefully acknowledge the assistance of Virgil Duff, Barb Porter, and Matthew Kudelka of U of T Press in shepherding the manuscript through the various stages.

A number of friends, colleagues, and family members have provided me with intellectual and personal support and engaged political discussions over the years. I would especially like to thank Ann Ball, Nancy Bayly, Cathy Blacklock, Emily Brown, Marcy Cohen, George Comninel,

Jan Kainer, Ross Sutherland, Marion Pollack, Chris Gabriel, and Tony Porter. Special thanks to Margaret White for her support in many forms. Finally, I would like to thank Nicolas Ewen for helping me keep things in perspective, and Geoffrey Ewen for his ongoing support and encouragement to see the project through. I dedicate this book to the memory of my parents, John and Marion Porter, strong voices for social justice through many of the years covered in this book, and to my son, Nicolas, with hope for the future.

# GENDERED STATES

# Introduction

In December 1995 one of the most sweeping overhauls ever to an income security program in Canada was announced. The unemployment insurance program was to be renamed 'employment insurance,' its costs were to be reduced by $2 billion a year, and it was to be based on a new approach to the unemployed. The goal was to move from 'passive' income support to an 'active' labour market program, one that would reduce the disincentives to work that were said to be found within the program, reinforce the 'value of work,' and offer 'unemployed Canadians the tools to lift themselves up and find new opportunities.'[1] In the discussions that had preceded its introduction it was argued that the social programs of the postwar era were no longer appropriate and that a redesigned program was necessary to meet the challenges of globalization, technological change, trade liberalization, and changing labour market and demographic structures.

The employment insurance legislation, introduced the following year, represented one possible response to globalization and the large-scale social, economic, and political shifts that had occurred in the last decades of the twentieth century. It was a response that represented, if not the consolidation, certainly a new stage in a market-oriented or neoliberal approach to welfare state reform. The UI program as it was restructured in the 1990s constitutes a form of privatization of unemployment in that it has involved a downloading of both costs and responsibilities to individuals and households, and also further reduced the state's responsibility for maintaining relatively high levels of employment and for providing income security for those unable to provide for themselves. It is based on the notion that unemployment is to a large extent voluntary, a consequence of individual attributes, behaviours, and/or skills, and that care must be taken to prevent individuals from developing patterns of dependency on state benefits. It is a market-based solution in its emphasis on encouraging the 'employability' of all adults and in its assumption that the unemployed must adapt to the marketplace. It is a state-based program in its support for low-wage industries through the use of wage subsidies and income supplements within an income security program. It represents the erosion of universality and of a rights-based social safety net. The new program is a two-tier system whose benefits go mainly to a core of full-time, full-year workers, with only limited benefits for the growing number of contingent, part-time, and temporary workers who fall outside this model.

All of this represents a profound restructuring of the UI program. This book is concerned with what this restructuring has meant for women and with how changes in women's roles and activities form part of the larger process of welfare state development and restructuring. The book emphasizes how state policy with regard to income security for the unemployed takes shape within a broader welfare state regime. Such a regime involves the coming together of a number of forces and factors, including shifting ideologies, political struggles, the structure of domestic and international economies, and the ways in which work is organized, services are provided, and 'social reproduction' activities are addressed (including childrearing, caring, and other activities necessary for daily survival and individual growth and development). Central to all of this has been a shift in the relationship between the state, the market, and the family in organizing and undertaking these activities. The book describes and discusses two periods of development and restructuring in the UI program, as well as in the larger welfare state regime. The first period, from 1940 to 1971, was shaped by postwar conceptions of social welfare and influenced by Keynesian notions of the role of the state in the economy. The second, from 1971 to the late 1990s, was marked by a prolonged economic crisis, by a restructuring of the economy both domestically and globally, and by the introduction of widespread social policy reforms.

One of the key premises of the book is that gender has been key to both these periods of welfare state reform: it was central not only to the construction of the postwar welfare state regime, but also to its subsequent crisis and to the restructuring process that occurred from the 1970s onwards. The term 'gender' has become something of a contested concept. The term was developed to emphasize that relations between men and women are socially constructed and not simply based on biological differences. Yet more recently it has been argued that sex or 'nature' is itself socially constructed; thus, as Joan Scott points out, the distinction between the physical and the social, between nature and culture, is difficult in practice to maintain.[2] Furthermore, as the universal or essentialist categories of women as delineated in the early second wave of feminism were challenged, it became apparent that the term gender similarly carried the danger of suggesting a universal experience and thereby obscuring differences between women. Feminists have increasingly emphasized that gender, race, and class are closely intertwined and mutually constituted systems and that gender is constituted in race- and class-specific ways.[3]

Gender in this study is understood broadly as incorporating the social relations that help define women's condition and that structure relations between men and women. The emphasis is on women's concrete, historically grounded experience; on their efforts to find income, to organize, and to form alliances; and on the often contested ideologies that structure women's activities and around which capitalist economic or welfare state restructuring has taken shape. Gender, then, has to do not only with ideology, meaning, and representation, but also with power, institutional structures, the allocation of material resources, and efforts to contest visions of the world and the ways that material resources that shape women's lives have been distributed. Gender, in all these senses, needs to be examined in order for us to understand development and change within welfare state regimes. While I use the terms 'woman' and 'gender,' it is with the recognition of the multitude of differences that separate women on the basis of race, region, age, sexuality, disabilities, and so on. At the same time, there is also a recognition of some commonalities, both material and in the categories used by those making laws, recording and undertaking studies, and gathering data over the decades on which this study is based.[4]

I explore the interconnections between gender and political economy in the shift from the postwar to a neoliberal welfare state by examining the unemployment insurance (UI) program. Instituted in 1940, UI was the first major federal income-security initiative. It has remained an especially critical federal public policy, tied closely to both general macroeconomic and labour market policies. Thus, shifts in orientation with respect to UI reflect larger debates about the direction of these other policy areas. The program is also critical in that it has touched many people's lives and because having employment – or the income to support oneself and one's household if unable to find suitable work – is one of the basic conditions of survival and well-being. As the House of Commons Committee responsible for hearings during the 1994 social security review noted: 'Few issues aroused as much concern and concentrated passion ... as the questions surrounding the reform of unemployment insurance.'[5] The UI program, then, has been one of the most important programs and also one of the most contested. Questions regarding what constitutes an acceptable level of unemployment, how responsible the state is for ensuring work or income security, what measures are to be undertaken to achieve this end, and even the definition of an 'unemployed person' and what constitutes 'suitable work' have all been very much subject to debate.

An examination of UI is also important from the perspective of women. Studies analysing women and the welfare state initially drew attention to women's position in needs-based social assistance programs, where they tended to be overrepresented. It was commonly argued, for example, that there was a two-track system of benefits, with women largely confined to a second tier where benefits were based on need and where they were excluded from insurance-based programs contingent on labour market participation.[6] This approach shed important light on women's experience within social assistance programs and highlighted how women, defined predominantly by their role as mothers, were often marginal to the labour market and to labour market–based programs. This perspective, however, tended in the long run to underestimate the importance for women of programs such as UI, under which entitlement was considered a right based on participation in the labour force.[7] As women's labour force participation increased in the postwar period, the rights-based UI program formed an increasingly important part of women's lives; it helped shape women's employment opportunities, their access to independent sources of income, the conditions under which they had children, and family structures and consumption patterns, as well as the overall structure of the labour market.

An examination of UI policy also reveals the tensions that have existed between women's roles in the home and in the labour market, and the difficulty that state policies have had addressing these tensions. This is evident, for example, in discussions of whether women with domestic responsibilities should be considered legitimately 'unemployed' and whether benefits should be available for maternity and parental purposes. Maternity provisions are often seen as something of an anomaly in the UI plan, yet it is not coincidental that in 1971 maternity was included as part of the program. The UI program is, in essence, about how people participate – or are unable at times to participate – in the labour market. One of the defining conditions of women's labour force participation has been their role in bearing and rearing children. An examination of the UI program's treatment of pregnancy and maternity reveals how women's labour force participation, and the conditions under which they find work, or cannot find work, is tied to and constrained by their role in reproduction and by the nature of state programs and policies.

This study addresses three main underlying questions. First, at a theoretical level, the work is situated within a feminist political economy framework. It is concerned about understanding how gender interconnects with other political economic forces in the formation and restructuring of the welfare state. While the political economy literature on the welfare state has demonstrated important links between changing economic and state forms, it has only recently and to a limited extent incorporated considerations of the family and gender, and these elements have rarely figured as central organizing or conceptual principles.[8] Yet the gender transformations that have taken place in the past fifty years, especially as women have left the home for the paid labour force, have profoundly altered the nature of paid work, family structures, and political activity; indeed, they constitute one of the central sources of tension, contradiction, and change in the postwar period. The present study argues that a reconsideration of feminist political economy is especially important in the current era, during which global economic restructuring has highlighted the importance of thinking again about the interconnections between capitalist relations of production, gender, other forms of inequality and oppression, and state policies.

Second, at a more concrete level, this book is concerned with what UI policy has meant for women. To what extent have the influx of women into the labour force and the mobilization for women's rights changed assumptions about family models and work patterns on which welfare state programs are based? How have conflicting tensions between working in the paid labour force and in the home, and between women's roles as mothers and as workers, been addressed? Are women more able or less able to provide for themselves and their families? Have the changes led to more or less gender equality? This study attempts to answer these questions and to suggest how the UI program over the years has affected women – the conditions under which women and families have struggled to cope with the effects of unemployment, with inability to work because of pregnancy or family responsibilities – and how women have often found it difficult to gain access to UI income security benefits. The notion that UI creates dependency and the fear that workers simply want to cheat the system have been consistent themes among policymakers since the program was launched, and have often focused on women in particular. By providing a sense of the difficult conditions that women and families often confront as they try to work out survival strategies in the face of unemployment, I hope this study will somewhat counterbalance this view.

A third concern is to better understand how and under what conditions changes in state policy come about. While the welfare state literature refers often to the shift from a Keynesian welfare state to a neoliberal or post-Fordist state, my concern here is to address the *process* through which this shift occurred. This change did not arise out of an abrupt reversal of policy that the Fordist/post-Fordist, Keynesian/neoliberal welfare state dichotomies often imply; rather, many of the elements of neoliberal restructuring arose from tensions and contradictions that were a part of the postwar model from its inception and, indeed, that were articulated as proposals for welfare state reform as early as the 1960s. The book begins from the perspective that it is important to identify how contradictions and pressures developed as the postwar welfare state rose, became consolidated and gave way to the neoliberal state, and to understand how various forces and political actors have interacted to shape public policy in the past half-century.

There have been two major eras in the history of unemployment insurance policy in Canada since the Second World War, parallel to the two periods in the gendered political economy of welfare state development noted earlier. The first era, from the inception of the UI program until 1971, was one of welfare state growth and expansion and culminated in the introduction of what was viewed as one of the most generous programs ever for the unemployed. This was also a time of growing female entry into the workforce and increasing mobilization around women's rights. The second era, from 1971 to the end of the 1990s, was dominated by a prolonged economic crisis and by the slow acceptance of a market-driven agenda of privatization, fiscal restraint, and global economic competitiveness. Accompanying this period of sustained crisis, re-evaluation, and retrenchment was the continued entry of women – especially women with young children – into the labour market and the ongoing mobilization of women around a rights-based discourse.

These shifts in state policy and in women's activities formed part of a more general shift in the relationship between the family, the market, and the state, and in the contribution of each to the organization and provision of the goods, services, and activities necessary for individual survival and growth. The postwar welfare state, viewed by some as the 'golden age' of the welfare state,[9] was based on the assumption that there was a primary male breadwinner, a dependent wife at home, and a state that would provide income security essentially as a supplement where needed to the male wage. Within welfare state programs, women's dependent position was often reinforced by formal juridical inequalities. A labour market divided by race/ethnicity and region further reinforced inequalities in access to welfare state programs. By the early 1970s this state–family–market nexus had been significantly altered. An expanded welfare state, with modified family wage notions at its base, was now linked to an increasingly feminized service-sector workplace and to families where the norm was to have more than one earner. By the 1990s a different type of shift had taken place. More responsibility for income maintenance, unemployment, and social welfare was being placed on individuals and households; at the same time, women were continuing to enter the labour market to seek paid employment. The welfare state was moving definitively away from the male breadwinner model toward a model based on formal equality and on the existence of multi-earner families in which each individual was 'employable.'

The two parts of this book follow these broad historical developments. Chapter 1 introduces the theoretical issues that inform the study, drawing on both feminist and political economy literature, and proposes a model in which a complex ensemble of variables – including ideology, juridical norms, political struggles, race and ethnicity, and production and consumption patterns – shape the direction of a particular regime. Of central importance within this ensemble, is the relationship between production and social reproduction and, in particular, how this relationship has manifested itself since the Second World War in the nexus between family, state, and work. In analysing the welfare state we must consider how women's entry into the labour force is changing that nexus – its contradictions, tensions, and limitations – and how various actors have attempted to change that relationship.

Part I (chapters 2 to 4) traces the gendered development of the welfare state from the Second World War until the 1971 overhaul of the UI program. It examines how pressures in a range of areas – including economic, ideological, legal/juridical, and political – reinforced one another over twenty-five years to create the momentum that led to substantive changes in the UI program, in the welfare state regime as a whole, and in women's status. Women achieved greater formal equality as well as recognition for their rights as both workers and mothers.

Chapter 2 discusses how the welfare state (including the UI program) of the years 1945 to 1960 was constructed on a gendered model which assumed that women would be primarily in the home and which was based often on formal juridical inequalities. It argues that the family wage model of this period was not monolithic; rather, tensions and contradictions were apparent as early as the 1950s. Challenges brought by both women and unions helped build pressure for change.

Attitudes and policies with respect to pregnancy and maternity formed a key part of the development of a gendered labour market and welfare state regime. In the initial postwar years, pregnant women were expected to return to the home and had very restricted access to UI income security. By 1971, rights-based maternity benefits (albeit limited in scope) were available to working women through the UI program. Chapter 3 examines the shift from a program that essentially excluded pregnant women workers to one in which maternity benefits were made available (as part of the 1971 revised UI program).

The 1960s were dominated by discussions of 'manpower' planning and welfare state growth. In the case of UI, this led eventually to a much expanded program in 1971. The same decade was also a time of unprecedented female entry into the labour market and growing mobilization around women's rights. Chapter 4 argues that while there was little awareness within discussions of 'manpower' planning of the significance of a feminized, contingent work force, income security considerations reflected concerns about the growth of part-time work and the possibility that women's increased labour force participation could result in a drain on UI funds. While these contradictions became more apparent in subsequent decades, the response in the 1960s to these already emerging trends was critical in reinforcing gender inequalities and in laying the groundwork for subsequent reforms, including neoliberal reforms.

Part II (chapters 5 to 8) outlines the contentious process of restructuring that began in the 1970s but that was enacted in a more far-reaching way in the 1990s. The 1970s and 1980s were a time of prolonged crisis and of debate over possible new directions. Shifting gender roles and new political forces were central to attempts to redefine the regime. There was pressure for restructuring from two sides: as a result of the growing mobilization of women organized around a rights-based discourse, and as a result of the economic crisis, globalization and growing demands for fiscal restraint. This section examines how shifts in political forces, in ideology, in gender relations, and in the relationship between the domestic and the international economy led to the consolidation of a particular type of neoliberal model.

Chapter 5 returns to the question of maternity benefits. It examines the limitations and benefits of the 1971 maternity provisions, the challenges that were mounted to them, the expansion in benefits that occurred with the 1983 amendments to the UI Act, and how, in the process, conceptions of equality also came to be challenged.

Chapter 6 discusses the gender dimensions of the economic crisis, as well as the beginning of welfare state restructuring in the 1970s as it manifested itself in debates about unemployment and UI. It points to the gendered nature of the response to the crisis – in particular, the representation of women as 'secondary workers' taking advantage of the UI system and driving up the unemployment rate.

Chapter 7 examines the direction of welfare state reform during the 1980s and early 1990s. It considers the ideological groundwork for and subsequent efforts at UI restructuring initiated by the Mulroney Conservatives. It discusses the move throughout this period both toward increased recognition of gender equity issues, and toward subordinating UI reform proposals to a broader agenda encompassing deficit reduction, increased international competitiveness, and the fostering of a good climate for business.

Chapter 8 discusses the consolidation of a neoliberal welfare state under the Chrétien Liberals in the 1990s. A number of elements came together in this decade and resulted in far-reaching changes. These elements included growing pressure from economic globalization, the continuing growth of a contingent workforce, and pressures to address the deficit and the debt. Also critical was a shift in the relative power of various social actors.

One of the arguments I present in this book is that a key contradiction of the postwar regime was between a welfare state based on the notion of male, full-time, full-year workers and the actuality that the labour force was increasingly short-term, contingent, and feminized. With the restructuring of the 1990s, this contradiction was largely addressed. It was in large part resolved by allowing greater formal equality, but by also reducing entitlements so that income security was now primarily for a core of full-time workers. This approach has addressed immediate fiscal pressures and has created a more business-friendly climate. At the same time, however, it has created new forms of inequality and a growing polarization between those with relatively stable jobs *and* access to UI/EI income security and those with access to neither. Overall, gender gains have been undermined by the large-scale withdrawal of state support for the unemployed and by the increased emphasis on individual responsibility for unemployment, combined with more general welfare state restructuring and social service reductions that have made the conditions of women's *and* of men's lives increasingly difficult.

The inequalities and shortcomings of the new neoliberal model mean there are likely to be ongoing challenges. One of my underlying concerns, then, is to better understand the attempts by various groups to influence the direction of welfare state reform, the structural contradictions and the constraints faced by these groups, and the possibilities for restructuring in other directions.

# CHAPTER 1

# Gender and the Political Economy of the Welfare State: Theoretical Considerations

This work aims to help further a feminist political economy. In an era when global economic restructuring is combining with neoliberal state initiatives to define so many of the conditions of women's lives, a reconsideration of the ways that both state policies and capitalism have historically built on, and are structured around, different forms of oppression and inequality is particularly pressing. For this project it is important to draw not only on political-economy and early socialist feminist work, but also on the insights of more recent feminist analyses. These analyses have emphasized the importance of women's struggles, of historical specificity, and of considering how global capitalism is structured around particular ideologies and hierarchies, as well as how class interacts with other variables or axes of domination, including gender, race, and sexuality.

In this work I put forward a model in which the relationship between numerous variables – labour markets, unpaid work in the home, family work/life patterns, race and ethnicity, political struggles, gender ideology, juridical norms, state policies – can be considered as part of a dynamic whole in which there are 'multiple strands of determination'[1] and complex processes of interaction and change. A key concern is to understand those processes of interaction and change: how various forces and factors come together to create tensions and pressures, and do so in cumulative patterns that bring about or forestall more substantive changes. These changes occur in many arenas, including gender relations, state policies, and economic and welfare state regimes. While the complex ensemble of variables noted above shapes the direction of

particular regimes, of central concern within that ensemble is the relationship between production and social reproduction. Of particular
interest for our purposes is how that relationship has manifested itself
in the postwar period in the nexus between the institutions of the
family, the state, and the market. So we must consider how women's
entry into the labour force changed that nexus, as well as the contradictions, tensions, and limitations in the way that nexus has been defined
and how various actors – individual women, women's groups, labour,
business, and the state – have attempted to influence the relative responsibilities and powers of those various institutions. This book is a
historical study of political, social, and economic forces as they have
manifested themselves through particular state policies. It is also concerned, then, with a model for policy analysis; with a framework that
can help shed light on how particular policies come about, the constraints faced by various groups as they attempt to influence policy
directions, and the possibilities for and limitations on new forms of
restructuring. In this chapter, I discuss the socialist feminist literature as
it developed in the 1970s and 1980s, its limitations, and possible new
directions for analysis. Then, I examine the feminist literature on women
and the welfare state, focusing in particular on the changing nature of
women's citizenship entitlements. After that I discuss the political
economy literature on economic and welfare state restructuring. Finally, I draw on each of these bodies of work to consider a gendered
political economy of the welfare state involving a complex interaction
of variables with the state, the market, and the family as its nexus.

## Women and the State

### Socialist Feminism and Its Critics

In the past twenty-five years a considerable body of feminist literature
has addressed the relationship between women and the state. Socialist
feminists provided some of the earliest theoretical work on the subject.
This work, which first appeared in the late 1970s, was situated within
larger debates that raised such questions as these: What is the relationship between the production of goods in the formal economy and the
reproduction of labour taking place in the family? Is the 'root' cause of
women's oppression located in the biological fact that it is women who
bear children, or in the psychological and sexual relations between men

and women? Or does it, rather, have to do with ideology and the construction of notions of what constitutes the 'proper' sphere for women? How are these biological, psychological, social, and ideological factors connected to the class oppression found in capitalism? What, in other words, is the relationship between capitalism and patriarchy? Attempts were then made to determine the role of the state in creating and maintaining these structures of capitalism and patriarchy.

A number of different elements were emphasized in examining the relationship between these factors. The early 'domestic labour debate' focused on women's role within the home and emphasized how women's domestic labour helped create economic value.[2] Heidi Hartmann adopted a 'dual systems' approach, arguing that capitalism and patriarchy constituted two separate but interrelated systems.[3] Others emphasized the role of the state, for the most part arguing that the state has contributed to women's oppression through its support for family households characterized by a male breadwinner and a dependent wife responsible for domestic duties.[4] Authors such as Mary McIntosh, for example, argued that the state has contributed both to women's oppression and to the long-term functioning of capitalism through its support for family households characterized by a male breadwinner and a dependent wife responsible for domestic duties.[5] Zillah Eisenstein and Jane Ursel, following a dual systems approach, argued that the state's role is to mediate between the needs of the separate but interdependent systems of capitalism and patriarchy (or production and reproduction).[6]

For their part, Dorothy Smith and Wally Seccombe explored the relationship between family forms and capitalist development.[7] Smith argued that the capitalist economic relations to which particular families are articulated are critical in determining the nature of women's work in the home, as well as power relations between husband and wife. Thus, for example, in the nineteenth century the position of women differed significantly depending on the extent to which farm families were self-sufficient (as opposed to integrated with the market economy). In the twentieth century, she suggested, working-class women were more likely to have paid work and thus to have more power within the family than middle-class women, whose domestic labour became organized as a personal service to an individual man.[8]

One of the strengths of this socialist feminist work was that it conceptualized the relationship between production, reproduction, and the state – or between class, gender, and the state – as centrally important to the development of the structures of capitalism and to defining the condition of women. It situated women within a political-economic framework based on the notion that in the structures of capitalism there were inherent contradictions and exploitative features. Furthermore, it concerned itself with the links between activities in the home, capitalist development – including the structuring of labour markets – and the development of state policies. However, these variables were examined at that time in what proved to be limited ways. Influenced by the renewed interest in Marxism and by attempts to develop a Marxist analysis of the state, it largely attempted to 'fit' women into the categories developed by Marxist analyses.[9] This work tended to present economic factors as ultimately determinant[10] and to posit the determining relationships as *separate from* and *external to* the family and gender relations. This obscured how family and gender dimensions can influence, and form part of, the development of economic structures and class relations. The emphasis on structures and functions, with state activity being explained in terms of meeting the needs and ensuring the long-run maintenance of capitalism and/or patriarchy, meant that contradictions, tensions, and struggles for change were obscured. Many critical questions concerning the operation of the state itself were not addressed. The analyses, for example, provided little discussion either about pressures from outside the state or about divisions and struggles within the state that may have either influenced the direction of state policy or provided possibilities for advancing women's interests. Finally, the focus of this early work was on women's position of dependency and subordination within the home; much of it concentrated on explaining the consolidation of women's position as unwaged housewives within the nuclear family in the nineteenth and early twentieth centuries.[11] As such, it had little to say about the enormous changes occurring in families, in women's position, and in women's relationship with the state as from the 1950s onwards more and more married women sought work in the paid labour market.

By the mid-1980s, feminists were developing critiques of this work and indicating new directions for analysis. The emphasis on the position of the housewife was counterbalanced by Armstrong and Armstrong, Connelly, MacDonald, Luxton, and others, who contended that women's work in the labour market, as well as in the home, was important to capitalist economic development and to the nature of class relations.[12] Feminists began to assert the need to *reconceptualize* various categories in ways that not only added on new subject matter but also forced 'a critical re-examination of the premises and standards of existing scholarly work.'[13] Thus it became apparent that it was not enough simply to add gender to already existing conceptions of class – such basic conceptual categories needed to be rethought. Feminist literature shifted its emphasis away from structures and functions to examine the role of women as subjects and political actors helping, for example, to shape the direction of welfare state policies.[14]

Probably, though, the most significant challenges to feminist thought came from women of colour and others who had been marginalized by the second wave of the women's movement. These authors insisted that the universal categories of 'woman' in these analyses did not apply to *all* women's experience and that it was crucial, therefore, to recognize differences *between* women based on race, ethnicity, sexuality, and other forms of identity. It was pointed out that attempts at universal theorizing at high levels of abstraction tended to posit an essential category of 'woman' at the expense of both historical accuracy and sensitivity to particular national and group differences. A number of authors pointed out that the male-breadwinner family model at the centre of much of the early feminist critiques was derived from the experience of Britain in a particular era and could not be taken as a universal model of women's oppression.[15] It was also argued that even within countries such as Britain, this family form has not applied to all ethnic groups, nor has the state supported such a model for all sectors of society. It was argued, for example, that for Blacks the family is not necessarily the major agency of women's oppression, especially given the role of state coercion and violence.[16]

Responding to these criticisms, feminist work shifted its emphasis to the need to recognize that women face multiple oppressions and that there is not a single determinant relationship between these factors. The predominant response has been a turn to postmodernism and a new emphasis on a multiplicity of different identities.[17] Other authors, however, have retained class as an important analytic category and considered the ways that class intersects with gender, race, and other systems of domination. Armstrong and Connelly, for example, suggested that 'gender, race/ethnicity and regionality/nationality interact with class in various ways with one being more salient than another at different points in time.'[18] Seccombe and Livingstone argued for 'a more fluid, multidimensional perspective' in which inequalities of class, gender, and race 'are not fixed in a hierarchy of personal worth,' but at the same time insisted on maintaining a materialist basis to their analysis.[19] Joan Acker emphasized the need to rethink conceptions of class in order to

18

incorporate relations of distribution[20] and to do so in a way that would incorporate an understanding of the processes of class formation, including how 'class is formed in and through processes that also create and re-create racial and gender formations.'[21] Similarly, authors such as Evelyn Nakano Glenn called for an integrative framework in which 'race and gender are defined as mutually constituted systems of relationships.'[22] Others continued to examine the ways in which economic concepts – including the concept of class – could be expanded to include unpaid domestic or reproductive labour.[23] Another avenue of investigation has involved examining the ways in which global capitalism has been structured around inequalities of gender, race, ethnicity, and sexuality.[24]

One of most influential efforts to rethink the relationship between gender, class, race, and other oppressions has come from feminists of colour and Third World feminists examining the intersections of multiple oppressions as experienced by women in their everyday lives. The notion of an 'intersectional' paradigm has been developed to analyse the ways in which race, class, gender, sexuality, and other axes of domination constitute mutually constructing systems of oppression, manifested through a variety of institutions including schools, housing, and government bodies.[25] This paradigm starts from the perspective that people's lives cannot be separated out into discrete oppressions that can be understood in an additive way; rather, multiple oppressions can come together in powerful systems of domination. Intersecting oppressions are organized through diverse local realities, and the specific 'matrix of domination' will vary with the particular individual or group and the local and historical circumstances.

Joanna Brenner suggests that an analysis of intersectionality (or 'class as social location') is of importance to understanding how people interpret and make sense of their lives, form identities, and organize and develop resistance strategies; but additionally, she undertakes an analysis of capitalist relations of production ('class as social relations of production'), including the dynamics of the capitalist economy, the expansion of markets and production, the nature of capitalist restructuring, the powers of the capitalist class, and so on.[26] She suggests that the latter sets the context within which multiple oppressions are experienced and political movements develop. Brenner's approach suggests the importance of analyses that are something more than the experience from an individual or group standpoint; nevertheless, she leaves open the question of the relationship between what she identifies as two forms of class. In what ways, for example, does capitalist restructuring draw groups and individuals into particular processes of accumulation in ways that both build on and re-create hierarchies based on gender, race, class, or sexuality? In what concrete ways does capitalist and state restructuring contribute to or create new matrices of domination? And how has the resistance of women and others resulting from their class location affected the restructuring process itself?

I would like here to build further on that work which views global capitalist restructuring and the institutions supporting it as powerful forces with enormous influence over women's lives, but which also recognizes that the forms restructuring takes involve a complex relationship between multiple forces and sites of oppression, resistance, and efforts to bring about change. In doing so, I will argue that greater attention needs to be paid to two aspects. First, greater consideration must be given to the *historical* dynamic of capitalist accumulation and political economic development – including the tensions, contradictions, pressures, and other social forces that can become sources for change – and to how all of this plays out in particular situations. Second, it is important to consider further the role of the *state* not only in shaping the form that restructuring has taken but also in responding to pressures to address various concerns – including gender and other equity demands – and in helping shape restructuring in ways that can build on or attenuate various inequalities. Recent work considering the relationship between class, gender, and diversity has paid less attention to the role of the state than some of the earlier socialist feminist work. A particular theme in this study is the ways that state policies vis-à-vis the family have changed – indeed, how the erosion rather than the maintenance of the male-breadwinner family forms part of the dynamic of the restructuring process. We must consider how changes in the nature of welfare state regimes, in women's state entitlements, and more generally in the relationship between the state, the family, and the market form part of the restructuring of both production and social reproduction.

*Women and the Welfare State: National and Comparative Studies*

As feminist analyses moved away from universal theorizing, one focus of study became national and comparative analyses, including those with respect to women and the welfare state. Some of these examined the gendered nature of women's welfare state entitlements and the extent to which the state has supported particular family 'models.' In Britain and the United States, until recently the predominant argument in the feminist welfare state literature was that women have received welfare state benefits mainly on the basis of being 'wives' and 'mothers' rather than workers. Like the early socialist feminist work, this literature emphasized how the state, through its welfare provisions, reinforced a position of dependency for women within male breadwinner families. For example, Carole Pateman's ground-breaking work pointed out that the notion (found within traditional liberal theory) that women belong to the sphere of the family rather than to the public sphere of work and citizenship was reflected both in a gendered understanding of citizenship and in patriarchal welfare state structures. She argued that women have been incorporated into those structures as dependants of male breadwinners and that the unpaid caring work performed by women in the home has gone unrecognized.[27]

Similarly, Gillian Pascall, Hilary Land, and Jane Lewis looked at the British welfare state and found state support for a family model based on the assumption that men are breadwinners and that women provide care in the home.[28] In the United States, feminists noted that welfare state provisions are based on these same assumptions. Authors such as Barbara Nelson, Nancy Fraser, and Diana Pearce further argued that there is a two-track welfare state structure, with women tending to be excluded from insurance-based programs in which eligibility is based on wage work and instead receiving benefits based on their role within the family. The consequence, they contended, is that rather than rights-based benefits, women tend to receive benefits such as mothers' allowance, which are means-based and in the 'poor law' tradition.[29]

Yet the literature focusing on other countries questioned the universality of these Anglo-American theoretical frameworks. These international studies found considerable variation both in the nature of women's welfare state entitlements and in the family models on which they were based. Borschorst, Siim, Lewis, and Astrom, for example, pointed to the erosion of the male breadwinner model in the Scandinavian countries[30] and to state efforts beginning in the 1960s to encourage married women's participation in the labour force through such measures as increased childcare provisions. Lewis and Astrom suggested that in Sweden there had been a conscious political decision to shift the basis of women's welfare state entitlements from mother to worker.[31] Borschorst and Siim argued that in both Denmark and Sweden, state policies now recognize women's role as mothers *and* workers.[32] They suggested that in the 1960s a new partnership developed between the state and the family in relation to human reproduction, especially regarding care for children, the sick, the elderly, and the handicapped. Siim argued that in Denmark a new understanding of citizenship developed that accepted motherhood and care work as part of the social responsibilities of the state, and that this type of work thus became part of social citizenship.[33]

For their part, feminists undertaking comparative studies found considerable variation in the strength of the male breadwinner model. For example, in a four-country comparative analysis Jane Lewis found that Britain and Ireland were 'strong' male breadwinner states where women received benefits primarily as wives and mothers.[34] France was classified as a 'modified male breadwinner country' where women's labour market participation was to some extent encouraged by the state and where the emphasis in family policy was on pronatalist concerns and on children rather than women. Finally, Sweden was described as a 'dual breadwinner model' where women's entitlements were based on their role as workers. Similarly, Diane Sainsbury in a comparative study of Britain, the United States, the Netherlands, and Sweden found that 'although social rights in all four countries were influenced by a traditional familial ideology in the 1960s, the Netherlands approximated most closely the breadwinner model, while Sweden least resembled it. The UK and the US occupied middle positions, but the policies of both countries bore much stronger similarities to those of the Netherlands than to those of Sweden.'[35]

In Canada a number of authors have taken up the issue of women's welfare state entitlements, addressing such questions as whether they have received benefits on the basis of being mothers, or workers, or both. Focusing on Ontario's mothers' allowance program, Pat Evans found that from the 1920s until the 1960s the emphasis with respect to benefit eligibility was on single mothers as mothers rather than as workers; from the 1960s until the mid-1980s they were viewed as mothers *and* workers; and finally, since the mid-1980s single mothers have increasingly been viewed as workers rather than as mothers.[36] Katherine Scott similarly argues that within Ontario's social assistance program, single mothers have increasingly been redefined as employable and that a new vision has developed of a 'gender-neutral worker-citizen,' with social entitlements linked to one's status as an independent wage earner.[37] Jane Pulkingham and Leah Vosko have noted that within the UI/EI system women are increasingly being viewed as workers, even

as new forms of *de facto* dependency are being created.[38] Janine Brodie
has argued that restructuring has entailed a new form of citizenship
with a shift away from the construction of 'mothers as gendered citizens' toward the targetting of benefits on the basis of whether citizens
are 'deserving' or 'undeserving.'[39]

Other feminists have attempted to build on and reconceptualize Gosta
Esping-Andersen's power resource model in ways that take gender into
account.[40] Ann Orloff, Jane Lewis, Julia O'Connor, and Sheila Shaver
have all argued that greater recognition needs to be given to families
and to women's unpaid caring and domestic work in the categorization
of welfare state regimes, as well as in the conceptions of citizenship on
which welfare state models are based.[41] In the same vein, they suggest
that it is important to examine not only the division of labour between
states and markets – the primary emphasis of the power resource
model – but also the division between families, states, and markets in
the provision of caring activities, welfare services, and goods.

In evaluating welfare state regimes, Orloff and O'Connor have both
argued that while the emphasis in the power resource model has been
on decommodification and on welfare state entitlements that provide
*insulation* from market forces, for many women the critical issue is
commodification – that is the means of gaining *access* to paid employment.[42] In this sense, policies such as childcare, maternity leave, and
flexible work hours, which make employment possible, are also important social rights. Both stress that critical for women are policies that
allow for 'personal autonomy'[43] or the 'capacity to form and maintain
an autonomous household.'[44] These would allow individuals 'freedom
from compulsion to enter into potentially oppressive relationships in a
number of spheres.'

This literature on women and the welfare state has made a vital
contribution. It has pointed to the traditional lack of recognition for
women's contributions in the home, and to the gendered nature of
entitlements in various countries, and it has emphasized the importance, when evaluating welfare state regimes, of the relationship not
simply between the state and the market, but between the state, the
market, *and the family*. These are important elements to consider when
we are evaluating welfare state regimes and considering the social
forces and contradictions that are creating pressure for new welfare
state models and propelling the direction of change. An understanding
of formal equality and juridical norms and of the extent to which there
may be inequalities in entitlement to state benefits is an important

element of the complex ensemble that delineates welfare state regimes and gender relations.

In addition, there are four other elements that should be highlighted further. First, while women's increased role in the labour force has been recognized, particularly with respect to the shifting basis of women's welfare state benefits, the significance for the welfare state regime as a whole of the transformations taking place as women have entered the labour force needs to be analysed more extensively. One issue of concern is how women's increased labour market participation rendered obsolete and contradictory a welfare state model based on the assumption that women were in the home, and how these contradictions have created pressures for a new welfare state model.

Second, with the emphasis on citizenship entitlements and country-specific analyses, the links between the changing nature of women's position and the larger political and economic forces and structures that are shaping both state policy and women's lives have tended to be lost. For example, the gendering of the power resource model has provided important criteria for evaluating welfare states, yet there is a tendency to look at states, families, and markets at a particular point in time and to leave unanswered questions about the dynamic relationship between gender and other political-economic forces in the development of economic and welfare state regimes. This again points to the need to further develop a feminist political economy that would analyse more fully the dynamic of interaction and change between relations and activities within the household, labour market changes, and welfare state development and restructuring – including changes in welfare state entitlements. Equally important, and related to this, would be to look closely at the role of women as political actors within welfare state regimes,[45] the better to understand how women, both on their own and in conjunction with other groups and actors, have acted to alter their position of dependence within the family, to achieve greater equality, and to influence the direction of state policies.

Third, as noted earlier, it is important to develop a framework that is sufficiently open that it can incorporate the ways in which race and ethnicity intersect with gender and class in the development of particular welfare state and economic regimes. Fiona Williams, among others, has argued that analyses of welfare states need to take into account not only the development of capital/class relations and divisions between the public and the private family spheres, but also the development of nation-states including, for example, the nature of postwar migration and settlement within particular countries.[46] As noted earlier, feminists of colour have made important contributions in pointing to how welfare state policies are not simply gendered but involve the intersection of gender, race, and other variables.

Finally, we must consider more closely our criteria for evaluating welfare state regimes. Orloff and O'Connor suggest the 'ability to maintain an autonomous household' as a critical measure of the extent to which welfare states promote or encourage gender equality. The major emphasis here is on freedom from oppressive gender relations within the nuclear family. The ability to be economically independent and to receive benefits on an individual basis is critical for women, but on its own is a somewhat limited goal. I would rather see potential economic independence as a necessary criterion – though insufficient in itself – for the alternative arrangements we might wish to work toward. In this respect, for example, developing social solidarity, community networks, and a shared concern for the welfare of others is equally important.

## Gender, Economic, and Welfare State Restructuring

The political economy literature on the welfare state has suggested close ties between the economic restructuring that has occurred since the mid-1970s – including, most recently, economic restructuring at a global level – and welfare state reforms. This literature is now large,[47] but I would like to point to two examples that indicated early on important characteristics of the new forms of welfare state restructuring. John Myles and Bob Jessop both argued that new welfare state structures developed as the system of production shifted away from a Fordist regime based on the mass production of consumer goods toward a post-Fordist regime characterized by flexible production and (as Myles points out) a service-based economy.[48] As Myles noted, the 'social security' state of the Keynesian era was based on the principles of universality (with benefits considered an entitlement, not targetted at the poor) and on ensuring levels of demand in markets for *consumer* goods; in contrast, the new welfare state, as earlier in the century, is concerned with creating or maintaining appropriate *labour* markets. This is reflected in the establishment of programs designed to provide only a minimum level of subsistence and in attempts to eliminate work disincentives – for example, by allowing benefit recipients to retain more of their earnings from paid work. The income security system thus becomes both a system of wage subsidies for low-wage earners and a component of an industrial strategy encouraging low-wage employers, especially in the service sector. Bob Jessop, for his part, described the new post-Fordist state as a 'Schumpeterian Workfare State' (SWS).[49] The new regime that accompanied this state, he argued, is characterized by a 'hollowing out' or loss of capacity of the nation-state as the role of 'supra-national' state systems and local states has increased,[50] by a concern with encouraging market innovation (hence the reference to Schumpeter), by flexibility, and by international economic competitiveness. Social welfare policies, he pointed out, have been cut back and restructured in attempts to subordinate them to market forces. There is some suggestion, particularly in Myles, that large numbers – especially women and minorities – were left *out* of the postwar Fordist arrangements;[51] however, the analyses provide little sense of what women were actually doing or of how their activities contributed to the formation of particular regimes.

Linda McDowell also focuses on the transition from a Fordist to a post-Fordist regime, but argues that a central characteristic of the transition has been the erosion of the 'old gender order' based on family wage assumptions and the emergence of a new gender order in which women's work in the labour force (often part-time and flexible) plays a central role.[52] She suggests further that the reduced concern of states with the social reproduction of working-class families can be seen, for example, in lowered social welfare expenditures. Many other authors have similarly pointed out that economic restructuring at both global and local levels has been fundamentally gendered.[53] Restructuring, for example, has involved not only an expansion of the private realm in terms of market relations, but also the reprivatization of social welfare responsibilities to the home.[54] In this sense, then, the shift to a new regime has not simply involved changes in the relationship between the state and the economy; it has at its base a restructured relationship between the state, the market, and the family.

### Gender and the Political Economy of the Welfare State: Production–Social Reproduction, a Complex Ensemble, and the Family–Market–State Nexus

Building on this work, we need, first, to explore in greater detail how women, the family, and other gender relations were constituted both as a part of the postwar regime and in its subsequent restructuring, and second, to consider more closely the *processes* through which the transition from one regime to another takes place and how gender interacts with other political-economic forces in those processes. This can be addressed through a broader political economy in which we consider the relationship between numerous variables as part of a dynamic whole. Key to consider are changes in the relationship between production and social reproduction, and how these are manifested through changes in family work/life patterns, class structures, and state policies (including the shifting nature of welfare state entitlements and related citizenship rights). Also important is how these changes interact with the shifting dynamics of race and ethnicity, gender ideology and practices, and political struggles.

In developing such a political economy it is useful to draw on the work of one of the early exponents of the regulation school, Michel Aglietta.[55] Aglietta developed the notion of an 'ensemble' of factors characterizing a regime of accumulation. This approach looked at a wide range of variables defining a regime; it also accorded a central place within the ensemble to the relationship between the mode of production and the mode of consumption. Others have generally interpreted the 'mode of consumption' in a narrow sense, simply in terms of levels of consumer demand[56] (examining, for example, the relationship between Fordist production and the relatively high wages in that sector that allowed certain consumption patterns). Aglietta, in contrast, treated it much more broadly and included a discussion – albeit with unequal weight – of a number of elements contributing to the definition of what he referred to as the 'conditions of existence of the working class.'[57] This included consumption norms, the structure of the family household, wage scales, collective bargaining procedures, and social security provisions. Thus, more than most who subsequently followed in this school, Aglietta integrated a discussion of family structures and consumption patterns and posed as central to his analysis of both regime stability and change the question of the relationship between the processes of capital accumulation and the mode of consumption.

While Agrietta's emphasis on an 'ensemble' of factors and on the relationship between production and consumption (including family structures) is useful, in his analysis the reproduction of labour power and the formation of norms of social consumption are still dealt with in quite a restricted way. As feminists have pointed out, social reproduction and the reproduction of labour power entail a complex array of relationships and activities, and these are not adequately captured in his model. Women's work in the home, it has been pointed out, has involved a variety of unpaid work, including caring activities such as childrearing, looking after other adult family members, cooking, shopping, and cleaning, and attempts to stretch the family budget, as well as, at particular times, a variety of non-market income-generating activities such as taking in boarders and doing other people's laundry.[58] Feminist historians, for example, examining the links between the sphere of reproduction and that of production, have provided rich details of the multiple ways in which the work women undertook in the home was shaped by, and contributed to, the development of the larger structures of capitalism.[59] We can draw on and extend the work of these feminists in order to understand, in a more dynamic sense, the interaction of women's unpaid labour, the capitalist production process, and state policies, and how through the processes of interaction and development all three have been transformed.

The notion that an ensemble of factors defines a regime can be reconceptualized, then, first, so that it centres not so much around the modes of production and consumption, but has at its core the relationship between production and social reproduction. In highlighting this relationship we are also highlighting the interconnectedness – in people's lives and in the system as a whole – of the processes by which people earn a living in the paid labour market and the processes through which caring activity takes place and intergenerational development and maintenance are ensured. The notion of an 'ensemble' of factors can further be reconceptualized so that the many 'axes of domination' present within particular regimes, including race, sexuality, and gender ideology, can be seen as helping shape the particular forms that production and social reproduction take. The organization and activities of women as political actors and their relationship to other political forces also must be considered as part of the ensemble. Finally, also important to include is the question of formal rights and juridical equalities (long a focus for the mobilization of women's groups), and the nature of welfare state entitlements and of related democratic citizenship rights enjoyed by different groups on the basis of race, gender, or region. In this sense, some of the recent feminist work on citizenship entitlement can be useful for broadening the notion of an ensemble.

In a particular era, certain variables within a complex network may assume more importance than others. Similarly, in order to analyse certain policies or trends, a smaller range (or particular intersections) may be of particular relevance. Looking historically, the needs of social reproduction have been ensured by a range of institutions including not simply the family but in addition the state, religious organizations, trade union benevolent associations, charities and food banks, and private-for-profit entities in the marketplace.[60] An important area for investigation, then, is the relative responsibility assumed by these various institutions in different eras. I would argue that in the period after the Second World War the central nexus – not only in terms of social reproduction but also for the ensemble of factors as a whole – has been the relationship between family, market, and state. One of the most significant changes during this era was that women began entering the labour force in massive numbers. A central question, then, is how this changed the nexus between family, market, and state. The change in the welfare state regime has not simply been a function of a changed production regime or economic base, as suggested by Myles and Jessop; rather, it is part of a much more complex web of changes, including – quite centrally – changes in the family and in women's position in the home and in the labour force.

The 'family,' it should be noted, is best not approached as a single entity; rather (like the state and marketplace), it is itself a site imbued with power relations and tensions. Struggles to change the terms of those power relations are often individualized and isolated, but they can sometimes take on a more collective dimension and themselves become a force for change. In the past fifty years we have seen a proliferation of dual-earner families, single-parent families, same-sex families, 'cluttered nests' of returned adult children (in the 1980s and 1990s),[61] and so on. Thus, the forces both within and outside households bringing about these changes, and the responses to them, form part of the analysis.

A second important component of the model is that it ought to shed light on the complex processes through which the interaction of these variables actually brings about change. In other words, we need to consider how and why the *transition* from one regime to the next occurred. This would involve less of a counterposing of a Fordist/post-Fordist or Keynesian welfare/Schumpeterian workfare state, and more of an understanding of the *processes* by which the shift from one regime to another occurred.[62] McDowell has suggested that the Fordist regime was characterized by relative harmony between the mode of accumulation and the institutions of social regulation, including the male-breadwinner/dependent-female nuclear family and the Keynesian welfare state.[63] In this book I attempt to demonstrate that there was not so much *harmony* between the mode of accumulation and forms of social regulation, as contradictions and pressure for change. While the male bread-winner model remained important in the postwar period, especially as an ideology, by early in the Fordist period cracks were appearing as women began playing an increasingly important role in the paid labour force. Pressures mounted for changes in women's entitlement to state benefits and for their right to equal treatment within state programs. Women were also becoming increasingly visible as political actors, and the state itself was beginning to become aware of women's equality issues.

## Conclusion

This work is situated within a feminist political-economy framework. A central concern is to better understand how gender interacts with other political-economic forces in the development and restructuring of wel-fare state regimes. I have argued that in undertaking such an analysis, we can analyse welfare state regimes as complex webs of forces in which the relationship between numerous variables – labour markets, unpaid work in the home, family structures, race and ethnicity, political struggles, state policies – can be considered as part of a dynamic whole in which the process of interaction and change is critical. While this complex ensemble can be seen as shaping the direction of a regime, key is the relationship between production and social reproduction and, especially in the postwar era, as this has been manifested through the nexus between the family, the market, and the state. A central question here is the nature of the tensions and contradictions within that nexus, how women on their own and in conjunction with others attempted to change that relationship, and how a combination of political-economic forces led eventually to a restructuring of the family–market–state rela-tionship in a neoliberal direction.

# Contradictions and Transformations in Families, Markets, and the Welfare State, 1940–1971

The welfare state established in the decades following the Second World War was not simply a 'Keynesian' welfare state compatible with notions of state involvement in stimulating demand; it also had as a key characteristic that it was based on a family wage model. In the decades following the war, women were encouraged to return to the home and the cult of domesticity was at its height. The welfare state programs of the era were based on the assumption that men were the primary breadwinners and that women were dependants in the home. The reality for many was, of course, quite different: many families depended on the income brought in by married women. The labour market of this period was divided not only by gender but also by race, ethnicity, and region, and there was considerable variation in the extent to which the male breadwinner arrangement actually prevailed.[1] Despite all this, the ideology of the period strongly portrayed the male-breadwinner family as both the norm and the desired family arrangement, and this ideology dominated when policy was being shaped. This division between family and market was often reinforced by formal juridical inequalities and by state administrative practices that made both jobs and welfare state benefits more difficult for women to receive – especially married women and women with children. The lack of state provision in certain areas of social reproduction, particularly with respect to early childcare, and the virtual exclusion of women from UI income security benefits in the period around pregnancy and childbirth further reinforced an unequal labour market and women's dependency within the home.

By 1971 enormous changes had taken place in this family–market–state arrangement. A massive influx of women into the labour market signalled a major shift in family work/life patterns and resulted in an increasing feminization of the labour force. Women were filling positions – often part-time or temporary – in the growing service sector of the economy. In addition, a significantly expanded welfare state provided greater income security. In introducing maternity benefits the system for the first time recognized that women were likely to remain in the labour force for extended periods, including around childbirth.

Part I traces the shifts that occurred between 1940 and 1971. It identifies how contradictions and pressures in a range of areas, including the economic, familial, juridical, and political spheres, built on one another to bring about far-reaching changes. In terms of economic and material conditions, notwithstanding the ideal of the single-earner male breadwinner, economic growth and consumption patterns (also important to postwar ideology) and family living standards could not be sustained with this type of family/workplace arrangement. Family incomes had to be supplemented both by state programs and by the increased employment of married women. Tensions were also evident within the nuclear family itself. Many women did not accept the male-breadwinner model. As a result, attempts to achieve greater financial security and independence and to reconcile women's new role in the labour force with their continued domestic responsibilities, became a powerful force at the root of the second wave of the women's movement. As women began to enter the labour force, there was a further contradiction between their status as individual workers and juridical norms and a welfare state structure which assumed that women were in the home and which was often explicitly discriminatory. Pressures began to mount for women's right to equal treatment within state programs. Women began to form new organizations, to mobilize in different ways, and to make new types of demands. These included the demand not just for equality of treatment, but for special programs, such as maternity leave, as a precondition for achieving equality.

By the early 1970s these contradictions and pressures – economic and other pressures within households, a growing presence of women in the labour force, the increased militancy of women's groups and labour, pressures for change through the courts and administrative tribunals – had combined with a period of economic growth to create the basis for a substantially different welfare state regime and family–work–state nexus. The new model involved an expanded welfare state with a modified family wage notion at its base, with increased state responsibility for social reproduction, and with links to an increasingly feminized service-sector workplace and to families where the norm was now to have more than one earner. While this period was one of some optimism, of growing mobilization around a rights-based discourse, and one in which an expanding economy and state seemed to provide some resources for equality goals, by the 1960s other contradictions were already apparent. The distinction between those with a 'major' and a 'minor' labour force attachment and the proposal for a two-tier system based on those distinctions first emerged at this time. Discussions in this period about how to address the changing labour force structure built on gendered assumptions and in important ways laid the groundwork for subsequent reforms, including those in a neoliberal direction.

In the next three chapters I examine how these new pressures and contradictions combined to build momentum for an expanded welfare state, for greater equality for women, and for a new family–market–state arrangement. Chapter 2 examines the construction of a gendered labour market and welfare state regime in the period from 1940 to 1960, focusing in particular on women within the UI plan. Chapter 3 discusses how the treatment of pregnant working women within the UI program formed a key component of a labour market and welfare state structured around gender inequalities. It discusses the pressures that led to the enactment of maternity benefits (albeit limited in form) in 1971. Chapter 4 examines discussions within the state leading to an expanded UI program, focusing in particular on the response within 'manpower' discussions to the growing female, contingent labour force.

# CHAPTER 2

# Gender and the Construction of the Postwar Welfare State

The welfare state and economic regime established in Canada during the Second World War and in the immediate postwar period was fundamentally gendered. It was assumed that men would be the primary breadwinners, that women would look after the home front, and that the state would step in to provide for such contingencies as the temporary unemployment of the male breadwinner. It was based on a particular family–market–state arrangement whereby women performed certain types of labour in the home and did not perform certain types of work in the paid workforce. While there was considerable variation between women, and while many women's lives did not fit the postwar ideal, these gendered assumptions were integral to welfare state programs. In the immediate postwar period, from approximately 1945 to 1960, both UI provisions and the ways in which they were administered were often explicitly discriminatory, and were based on the assumption that women's primary role was in the home. Decisions by UI administrators about benefit eligibility often steered women toward jobs in particular sectors, and this also helped to create a gendered and unequal labour market. In these ways the UI program often denied women, especially married women, an independent source of income and reinforced their dependence on the family and on the male breadwinner.

But this was not a stable order. This period was not one of relative harmony between the mode of accumulation and the institutions of social regulation (including the family and welfare state);[1] it was, instead, one of underlying tensions and contradictions – including, quite centrally, with respect to women. Almost as soon as the act was implemented, concerns were expressed about the nature of the benefits women would receive.[2] After the war many women showed a reluctance to return to the home and to give up the relatively well-paid jobs they had occupied. Their willingness to appeal UI decisions suggests that they did not agree with the unequal nature of their entitlements. By the 1950s tensions were becoming apparent between a postwar welfare state model, which assumed that women were primarily in the home, and emerging labour market trends, which suggested that women would be growing more important in the formal economy. By the mid-1950s women were entering the labour force in increasing numbers; furthermore, women's organizations and trade unions were becoming increasingly concerned about equality rights for female workers and were making stronger efforts to change this gendered welfare state arrangement.

This chapter examines the construction of the gendered labour market and the welfare state regime between 1945 and 1960; it also examines how the efforts of women and unions to change certain provisions began to call this regime into question. The first section examines how women were viewed in the documents that laid the basis for the postwar welfare state and how the UI program helped establish a gendered labour market in the postwar years. The second section discusses formal gender inequalities in UI entitlements. Especially important in this regard was the 'married women's regulation' – a special regulation in effect from 1950 to 1957 that required married women to meet extra conditions in order to obtain benefits. The third section examines the beginning of mobilization to change these formal inequalities.

## The Construction of a Gendered Labour Market and Welfare State Regime

During the Second World War women entered the labour force in unprecedented numbers, their participation rate increasing from 24.4 per cent in 1939 to a high of 33.5 per cent in 1944.[3] Before this they had worked mainly in low-wage jobs in domestic service and in unskilled occupations now, in increasing numbers, they were taking up higher paid, skilled positions, most notably in manufacturing. As a consequence, their average weekly earnings increased dramatically,[4] from an average of $12.78 per week in 1939 to $20.89 per week in 1944.[5]

Despite the upheavals brought about by the war, the federal government documents that helped shape the postwar period viewed women's role in much the same way as in the prewar period: women's place was considered to be primarily in the domestic sphere, with the husband as the chief wage earner.[6] Notions about women's citizenship rights, duties, and entitlements reflected this view. Women's claims to welfare state benefits were seen to be based not so much on their status as individuals or as workers in the labour force (as it was for men), but rather on their role as wives and mothers. This view can be seen, for example, in the documents that attempted to lay the groundwork for a Canadian welfare state in the postwar period. In Leonard Marsh's 1943 *Report on Social Security for Canada*,[7] the family was viewed as the basic unit for social security purposes. Marsh proposed a social security program based on the 'two-person unit,' with children covered separately through children's allowances. He regarded the typical 'contributor unit' as being 'the single man who, in all probability, in the course of time will become a married man.'[8] A man's contributions were thus regarded as 'providing for himself and for his wife, actual or potential.'[9] A woman, on the other hand, was to be covered primarily 'in her capacity as housewife.'[10] Marsh seems to have been giving the woman in the labour force some status as an autonomous individual vis-à-vis the welfare state; he recognized, for example, that women were included in the 1940 UI scheme as wage earners rather than as dependants. Yet he also believed that 'the duration of her earning life may be anticipated as comparatively short.'[11] It was proposed that women, once married, would still have a right to social security with regard, for example, to disability, widowhood, and old age; however, they would enjoy this right as dependants, through their husbands.[12]

The report of the 1943 Sub-Committee on the Post-War Problems of Women (a subcommittee of the federally appointed Advisory Committee on Reconstruction)[13] contained a number of contradictory notions about the position of women in the postwar world. On the one hand, subcommittee members strongly expressed the view that women should be treated equally as 'full members of a free community,' in part, in recognition of their role in the war years.[14] They suggested that a woman's rights as a citizen should include 'the right to choose what occupation she will follow' as well as 'the right to equality of remuneration, working conditions, and opportunity for advancement.'[15] The subcommittee members also expressed concern that many women were earning extremely low wages; their UI benefits, as a result, 'would not amount to a bare subsistence minimum.' Furthermore, they had concerns about the levels of benefit compensation for single women supporting adult dependants – usually a parent or parents.[16]

At the same time, however, the subcommittee clearly saw women's primary role as being in the domestic sphere. While strongly endorsing women's right to choose, they nevertheless believed that most women would choose marriage. Women's contribution to the building of democracy was seen as largely being through the establishment of 'happy homes,' the foundation of a 'true democracy.'[17] In terms of social security provisions, the subcommittee members expressed concern about benefit levels for single women, but they also declared their 'definite support' of the 'two-person' unit as proposed by Beveridge and advocated in Marsh's report.[18] They quoted with approval from Beveridge that 'the plan for social security ... treats a man's contribution as made on behalf of himself and his wife as a team, each of whose partner is equally essential and it gives benefits as for the team.'[19]

Postwar notions about entitlement to work and about what constituted 'full employment' or 'unemployment' were also highly gendered. Postwar policies were motivated in part by a concern to ensure jobs for men at the end of the war and by a fear of returning to the high levels of unemployment that had characterized the Depression, or to the unrest that had followed the First World War.[20] Both Marsh and the 1945 *White Paper on Employment and Income* expressed the view that a large number of women employed during the war would voluntarily retire from the labour market to either resume or take up their domestic role.[21] The Sub-Committee on the Post-War Problems of Women also believed that after the war, marriage or settlement on farms would be the best solution to the problem of large numbers of unemployed single women.[22]

The federal government policies of the postwar reconstruction period reflected these views. The government took a variety of steps to reduce women's – especially married women's – attachment to the labour force. These included the closing of daycares,[23] the renewal of civil service regulations preventing married women from working for the federal government,[24] and changes in income tax regulations that amounted to a disincentive for married women to work for pay.[25] Other measures tended to steer women away from the relatively well-paid jobs they had occupied during the war toward the low-wage service sector; for instance, women who had been laid off after the war were encouraged to take training courses in such areas as domestic service, household management, waitressing, and hairdressing.[26]

The labour market reconstructed after the war was divided not only by gender but also by race and region. Dionne Brand estimates that until the Second World War, some 80 per cent of Black women in Canadian cities worked in domestic service.[27] During the war they began entering factory work, but after the war they returned to domestic labour. The racialized nature of this work was further reinforced as they were joined in the 1950s by women from the Caribbean, who were being recruited as domestics through a special federal program.[28] In addition, Black women began to find work in such service industry positions as nursing assistant, hotel cleaner, and maid.[29] In the decades following the Second World War some occupations, including clerical, secretarial, and sales, were perceived as white women's work, and Black women were virtually excluded from them.[30] In a discussion of the British Columbia labour market, Gillian Crease notes that Asian Canadians and First Nations people were excluded from these same occupations.[31] Furthermore, the labour market was very much divided by region, with employment opportunities and work situations varying widely from one part of the country to another.

The federal government's measures to reduce women's labour force participation were indicative of its gendered approach to employment questions. The postwar notion of full employment was limited in Canada not only by the modest goal of a 'high and stable' level,[32] but also by  being applied mainly to men. A government document of the period noted: 'Women are encouraged only to enter the labour market when economic activity is at such a level that their employment will not prevent men from obtaining positions.'[33] This meant that for women there was no attempt to ensure either employment or income; indeed, these were achievable for men only if large numbers of women left the labour force. The result of these policies, combined with a renewed emphasis on an ideology of domesticity, was that women's labour force  participation dropped from its 1944 high of 33.5 to 25.3 per cent in 1946. It remained at 23 to 24 per cent for the next nine years before beginning to increase again.[34]

Thus the state was involved in reconstructing a particular type of labour market, one divided by gender, race, and region. The postwar regime was based on a particular type of family–market–state nexus, one that involved women moving back into the home and leaving relatively highly paid and highly skilled wartime manufacturing jobs to take part-time and insecure jobs in the poorly paid manufacturing and service sectors. In sum, women were being marginalized in the economy and placed in a position of economic dependence in the family.

The welfare state being constructed in the postwar years reinforced *unemployment insurance.*

these divisions. In the years following the war both the provisions and the administration of the UI scheme reflected the notion that women's primary role was in the home, and that in the labour force they were to occupy only certain types of mainly low-wage positions. As a result, women did not have equal access to benefits. Furthermore, the UI plan was administered in a way that contributed to the building of a gendered labour market. And since it was assumed that women were available in the home to look after much of the caring work, there was relatively limited state involvement in the caring aspects of social reproduction.

*insurance different men & women*

The UI Act was introduced in 1940, just as the war was starting. This act was significant in that it introduced, for the first time, an income security program for the unemployed in which benefits were a right based on participation in the labour force.[35] According to the act, benefits were to be paid to unemployed workers who had made contributions for at least 180 days during the two years immediately preceding the claim and who showed they were capable of and available for work but unable to find suitable employment.[36] Benefits were calculated as a proportion of contributions, which in turn were dependent on earnings. At first, the amount of benefits paid was 34 times the average weekly contribution paid by the claimant for those without dependants, and 40 times the average contribution for those with dependants.[37] Throughout the 1950s, benefits were adjusted somewhat by amendments, so that by 1960 the benefit rate for those with dependants was about 50 per cent of earnings and for those without, about 37 per cent of earnings.[38]

Many occupations, both male and female, were initially excluded from coverage. In the first year of operation only 42 per cent of the labour force was in insured employment. Excluded occupations included transportation by water or by air, stevedoring, most lumbering and logging, domestic work, hospital work, teaching, and government employment. Also excluded were employees with yearly salaries over $2,000. Coverage increased to about 50 per cent of the labour force by the end of the 1940s and was extended even further in the 1950s.[39] The UI plan was financed through the tripartite contributions of employees, employers, and the government. Employees and employers paid equal shares; the government contributed an amount equal to one-fifth the aggregate contributions of the other two, as well as administrative costs. Contributions were paid into the UI Fund, a special account of the Consolidated Revenue Fund.

Overall responsibility for administering the UI program was in the hands of the Unemployment Insurance Commission, made up of a chief commissioner, a commissioner representing employees, and another representing employers. UI insurance officers were to follow the UI Act and regulations in determining eligibility. In reality, they enjoyed considerable discretion in deciding individual cases. Structures were established to allow for the appeal of UI officers' decisions. An individual whose claim was disallowed had the right to appeal to a tripartite Board of Referees,[40] again made up of representatives of employers, employees, and the government. Under certain conditions the decision of a board could be appealed to a UI Umpire, who was chosen from among the judges of the Exchequer Court and the Superior Courts of the provinces.[41] The decisions of the UI Umpire formed a body of jurisprudence that was to guide UI insurance officers in future decisions.

For women, the UI program was important in that formally working women were now entitled to benefits as individuals in their own right, rather than indirectly as dependent wives or mothers. Women now had access to an insurance plan based on labour market participation and were not simply confined to a lower tier of means-tested benefits. Women's access to this form of income security allowed them a degree of financial independence they did not previously have. Nevertheless, views about women's role, about the type of work they should do, and about what constituted legitimate unemployment meant that even here, women did not have access on the same terms and conditions as men.

How women fared in the UI plan was influenced greatly by postwar views about the role of women. Just as notions of full employment were gendered, so too were notions of unemployment. Because women were defined primarily by their activities and position in the home, even those who had been engaged in wage work were not really considered unemployed when they lost their jobs. It was assumed that they would take up or intensify their activities within the home and that they would be supported by their husbands or fathers. As a corollary, married women's claims to UI benefits were often similarly regarded as not legitimate, and there was a deep-rooted fear that they would try to defraud the UI system. In addition to making administrative and judicial decisions that limited pregnant women's access to benefits (discussed in chapter 3), the UI program helped create dependencies and inequalities in access to both benefits and jobs. This was evident in a number of respects: in the special provisions for those with dependants, through evaluations of whether women were really 'available' for work and of what was considered 'suitable employment'; in the encouragement of women to accept work in low-wage job ghettos; and finally, in

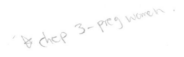

& chep 3 - preg women .

the enactment in 1950 of a regulation requiring married women to fulfil additional requirements as a condition of eligibility. These elements are discussed below.

## Gender Inequality in UI Entitlements

*Dependency Rates*

Ruth Roach Pierson examined the origins of the UI program and found that 'gender pervaded the 1934–40 debate on UI, and was inscribed in every clause of the resulting legislation.'[42] As she describes, when the first UI Act was drafted by the Bennett government in 1935 (an act declared *ultra vires* the federal government and never implemented), both contribution and benefit rates (which were based on flat rates) were lower for women than for men; the rationale was that a man needed a higher rate in order to provide for his family.[43] When the 1940 act was finally instituted, sex-based differences in rates were eliminated. It seems that this was partly attributable to pressure for equal treatment for women.[44] There was little resistance to this on the part of state administrators, as they believed that the same outcome – lower rates for women – would be achieved through a benefit structure based on income rather than flat rates. Even among those favouring equal treatment for women, the concern was about single women wage earners (who, as Pierson points out, were considered more like males)[45] rather than married women, who were still seen as dependants. Thus, despite the lack of explicit sex-based differentials, the ideology of the male as the breadwinner who thus required a higher income was in no way called into question.

In addition, Pierson pointed out, the family wage ideology which assumed that married women would be supported by their husbands was incorporated in the UI program through a 'dependents' allowance.'[46] According to the 1940 act a higher dependency rate was payable to '(i) a man whose wife is being maintained wholly or mainly by him, (ii) a married woman who has a husband dependent on her or (iii) a married person, widow or widower who maintains wholly or mainly one or more children under 16.'[47] While the provision for dependants was articulated in basically gender-neutral terms, there was certainly the assumption that the higher rate was for married men. Gender inequalities in benefit rates did, in fact, result; in the 1945–8 period approximately 56 per cent of men drawing UI were classified as having dependants and received the higher rate, compared to only about 5 per cent of women.[48] By 1960 these differences were even greater. For men drawing UI, 60 per cent were classified as having dependants, compared to only about 7 per cent of women.[49]

*'Suitable Employment' and the Reconstruction of a Gendered*
*Labour Market*

To qualify for benefits, unemployed workers had to show they were 'capable of and available for work but unable to find suitable employment.' If they refused to accept employment considered 'suitable,' they would be disqualified. What was considered 'suitable,' however, was highly subjective and gendered. Evaluations of this criterion as the war industries wound down and as men returned from the war resulted in inequality in access to benefits for women; it also resulted in women being steered – clearly with some resistance – into low-wage sectors. Many of the decisions made by UI officers were appealed, both to Boards of Referees and to the UI Umpire. The decisions of the umpire in the immediate postwar period reveal that women were often disqualified from receiving benefits for a certain period when they refused to accept work at a fraction of the pay they had received during the war. Women were often expected to accept work in either the service sector or low-wage female-dominated manufacturing sectors, when they had previously been employed either in the more highly paid manufacturing sectors or by the government. For instance, in 1946 a woman who had been working as a radio examiner doing war work at 74.58 cents per hour, was disqualified from receiving UI for four weeks after she refused to accept general factory work at 45 cents per hour.[50] A woman who had been employed as a packer in a brewery during the war at $33.15 a week was disqualified for six weeks for not accepting a job as a confectionery packer at the prevailing wage in that industry of $15.40 a week.[51] A woman employed by the Dominion government from 1940 to 1947 at $152 per month was notified after almost six months of unemployment of a job as a ward aide at a local hospital for $75 per month plus one meal a day for a forty-eight hour week. When she refused to apply on the basis that she knew nothing about the work and that she had spent time and a considerable amount of money obtaining mechanical drafting training, she was disqualified for six weeks because she had refused to apply for work in a suitable employment.[52] The four- or six-week disqualification in these cases was significant not only for the immediate loss of benefits, but also because it indicated the expectations concerning appropriate work for women and held out the threat of further disqualification should similar work be refused in the future.

The issue of women being expected to accept work at low rates of pay was raised in the House of Commons by CCF members Stanley Knowles (Winnipeg North Centre) and Angus MacInnis (Vancouver East). Knowles noted that initially women who were laid off from wartime jobs were granted UI when they met the usual conditions – that is, they were available for work similar in character, and work was unavailable for them. Yet, he added, women who applied somewhat later were offered jobs not at all similar in character and at much lower rates of pay. When they were unwilling to take these jobs, they were told they were thereby disqualified from receiving benefits. Knowles referred to stories of

> married women who had become grade 2 or grade 3 stenographers and who were offered such positions as charwomen, assistants in laundries, ironers, work at slicing bread, icing cakes, baby sitting, housekeeping and so on. When they report that they are unwilling to take positions of this kind and feel that they should not be asked to take them within the meaning of the words 'suitable employment,' they are simply told by the people in the offices to whom they appeal that nothing can be done about the matter.[53]

MacInnis noted that a directive sent to him from the UI office in 1946 stated that an offer at a wage rate of 5 cents an hour lower than the former rate might be considered suitable after three weeks of unemployment, and that 10 cents an hour lower (the equivalent of about $16/month) might be suitable after four weeks.[54] It appeared, however, that this directive did not apply to women. MacInnis cited the example of a woman who had been earning $160 a month who was disqualified because she refused to accept a job at $100 – a drop of $60 per month. She appealed to the Board of Referees, which sustained the disqualification because she had placed a restriction of $125 per month on her services. The employment officer who gave evidence swore that no positions for 'girls' that had been listed at the office carried a salary of $125 a month.[55] To some extent, private industry clearly played an important role in the reconstruction of a gendered labour market through its reluctance to retain or advertise more highly paid positions for women once the war was over.[56] However, state policy – including the UI system – also had a role to play in this regard.

*Instituting Formal Inequality: The Married Women's Regulation*

While the UI Act as initially framed did not explicitly differentiate between men and women, in the five years after the war momentum built for more formally entrenched gender differences. By 1950 an explicitly discriminatory regulation was introduced that required married women to work an additional period of time in order to prove attachment to the labour force. The regulation was not revoked until 1957. While it was in effect, 12,000 to 14,000 women annually were disqualified. According to the UI Commissioner, this saved the UI Fund an estimated $2,500,000 per year.[57]

Discussions of special UI provisions for married women had taken place as early as the 1930s. Pierson noted that it was assumed at the time that married women would be provided for by their husbands. Therefore, for married women to claim UI was 'a contradiction in terms or, what was greatly feared, a way to defraud the system.'[58] The 1940 act, however, did not contain a special provision for married women,[59] although similar regulations were established under the British UI Act of 1935 and in a number of American states.[60]

Pressure to enact a married women's regulation came in the context of a renewed emphasis on the male-breadwinner ideology. A policy restricting the right of married women to UI was in keeping with the notion that married women did not belong in the labour force and that their status as dependants meant that they had less need for income security. The view was put forward that the war being over, women should once again choose between employment and marriage, and that it was improper for those choosing the latter to also collect UI benefits. This was the view expressed in 1946 in an Edmonton newspaper: 'It was never intended, surely, that a young woman quitting work in order to get married should thereupon become eligible to draw unemployment benefits. In such a case, the employe [sic] makes her choice between employment and marriage. If she choses [sic] the latter, she can hardly be said to be unemployed, in fact or theory.'[61]

The pressure to enact a regulation for married women came mainly from two sources. First, business associations such as the Canadian Manufacturers Association and the Canadian Construction Association actively called for such a regulation. These two groups pointed to the high amount of unemployment benefits paid out in 1948 and 1949 and attributed this in part to the abuse of the UI Fund by married women and pensioners who, they argued, did not really wish to find work.[62] Second, the UI Commission, the UI Advisory Committee* (UIAC), and the actuarial adviser responsible for assessing the fund's finances, all took the view that married women – especially young married women – were draining the fund and that a special regulation should be enacted.[63] Between 1947 and 1949 the UIAC drew attention to the amount of benefits that were being paid to recently married women – women who, they suggested, were representing themselves as unemployed when they had actually withdrawn from the labour market, had no serious intention of working, and were not obliged by economic circumstances to find employment.[64] In July 1949 the UI Commission proposed – and the UIAC endorsed in principle – a regulation stipulating that married women would be entitled to benefits only if they contributed to the fund for an additional period of time following marriage to prove their commitment to the labour force.[65] This was given further weight by the actuarial advisor, A.D. Watson, who in December 1949 expressed concerns that virtually mirrored those of the two business associations. He pointed to the amount paid out in claims in 1947 and 1948 (two years, he argued, with extremely low levels of unemployment), suggested that married women and pensioners may have been guilty of drawing on the fund when they had really left the labour force, and declared emphatically that 'persons who are not available for insurable employment on account of some necessary work about the home ... or on account of illness, personal or in the family, or on account of a birth, marriage or death in the family ... have no right to benefit.'[66] Watson was also concerned about possible abuses arising from the extension of benefits to the seasonally employed. Here again, women were singled out; as he put it, 'this is an area where married women may prove to be very effective claimants unless controlled by sound regulations.'[67]

---

*An Unemployment Insurance Advisory Committee (UIAC) was established to advise the Commission and to make recommendations regarding the Insurance Fund and the coverage of those not insured under the Act. It was made up of a chairperson and from four to six other members with an equal number of representatives of employers and employees, appointed by the Governor-in-Council after consultation with their respective organizations.

State officials outside the commission and the UIAC had somewhat mixed views, although they were generally supportive of the regulation. One state official called it an 'unjustifiable discrimination.'[68] However, the Deputy Minister of Labour, A. MacNamara, sounded both amused and dismissive, and generally did not take very seriously any harm that the regulation would do to women. Fraudena Eaton – one of the few people whom the government might have considered a spokesperson on women's employment issues[69] – expressed concern about the regulation. In his reply to her, MacNamara stated: 'I suppose that there are quite a number of girls who have no intention of working after they get married who will be glad to have Unemployment Insurance Benefits to pay the instalment on the Washing Machine – or is it a new Television set?'[70]

Labour representatives took a somewhat ambiguous position with regard to a regulation for married women. At the UIAC meeting where the regulation was approved in principle, none of the three labour representatives objected.[71] At a subsequent meeting, when a draft of the regulation was approved, the representatives of the Canadian Congress of Labour (CCL) and the Trades and Labor Congress of Canada (TLC) were absent.[72] In contrast, there was strong and unequivocal opposition from labour on a similar proposal with respect to pensioners and older workers, and the UIAC did *not* endorse a special regulation for this group of workers.[73] The labour representatives on the UIAC opposed to this latter type of regulation, and the Railway Brotherhoods showed up to present a brief expressing strong opposition. They argued that it would be unfair to pensioned railway workers if, following compulsory retirement from the railway, they would be required to work fifteen weeks in order to prove their attachment to the labour force so as to qualify for UI benefits. They decried 'the destruction of the equity and right of the potential claimant,'[74] yet their statement referred only to pensioners. In sum, neither the Railway Brotherhoods nor the labour representatives on the UIAC showed similar concern about the situation of married women.

Following the announcement of a possible regulation for married women, despite the silence of the CCL representative on the UIAC, the CCL as a whole quickly took a position of strong opposition. This was evident in the recommendations passed at CCL conventions in 1949 and 1950,[75] in statements made by individual staff members,[76] and in the 1950 CCL brief to the federal government.[77] Yet from the CCL's discussion of the issue it is clear that the group's real worry was that a regulation discriminating against married women might be the thin edge of the wedge: that it might pave the way for similar regulations targetting other groups – especially pensioners – and the act as a whole might be undermined.[78]

The TLC took a more ambiguous position. At its September 1950 convention a resolution was passed expressing concern about the possible restriction of benefits for pensioners and married women.[79] Nevertheless, Percy Bengough (president of the TLC), a month later, in a memo to the deputy labour minister, MacNamara, stated that the married women's regulation was 'both necessary and well thought out.'[80] It seems that considerable weight was given to this latter position, with MacNamara stating that 'in view of his attitude I think there should be no hesitation about putting through the regulations.'[81]

Married working women at this time were not well represented by women's organizations. As will be seen later, the largely middle-class women's groups of the period did not at first speak out in opposition to the regulation. Furthermore, when the UIAC was first established in 1940 there was a 'woman's representative,'[82] but in 1947 this position was dropped.[83] This meant that the interests of women workers were not represented by the groups pressuring the state to enact particular policies, nor were they represented within the institutions of the state itself that were responsible for implementing UI. All of this reflects the relatively weak position of women at this time. Most women in the labour force were not organized. As the Conservative MP Ellen Fairclough (Hamilton West) later pointed out, women were working as clerks in stores and in small places that were not unionized, and most did not have a voice in the administration of the act through labour unions, or management, or as individuals. So it was 'comparatively easy for the administration to legislate against them for the purpose of disqualification, whether justified or not.'[84]

Regulation 5A, the 'married women's regulation,' was brought into force by Order-in-Council P.C. 5090 effective 15 November 1950, following an amendment by the House of Commons to the UI Act specifying that the commission was empowered to make regulations with regard to married women. The regulation provided that a married woman would be disqualified from receiving UI benefits for a period of two years following her marriage unless she fulfilled certain conditions proving her attachment to the labour force. Specifically, beyond the general requirement of being unemployed, and capable of and available for work but unable to find employment, a married woman had to work for at least ninety days (a) after her marriage if she was not employed at the date of her marriage or (b) after her first separation from work after her marriage if she was working at the time of her marriage. She was exempted from the regulation, however, if her separation from work was due to a shortage of work or to an employer's rule against retaining married women, if her husband had died, become incapacitated, or had deserted her, or if she had become permanently separated from him.[85]

The introduction of the special UI regulation made it even more difficult for women to acquire an independent income. During the first two-and-a-half months that the regulation was in force, 10,808 women were disqualified.[86] The regulation meant that women who were recently married and lost their jobs had to find *another* employment for ninety days (later amended to sixty days) before being able to collect benefits, even if they had been working and paying contributions for many years. CCF member Clarence Gillis (Cape Breton South) provided an example of what this meant in his region:

> For example, the Maritime Telephone and Telegraph Company put in a dial system. When that happened a lot of women were let out. Many of them were married, and had gone back to work. Some of them had been working for as long as four or five years. But when they registered for unemployment insurance they were told that since this was their first separation after being married, they must go back and take employment for 60 days in order to qualify. That is the way it was administered. For many, many months we wrestled with that particular problem and it was never cleared up.[87]

Although women who became unemployed because of a shortage of work were exempt from the regulation, this appears to have been broadly interpreted, and there were many other situations in which women who lost their jobs were disqualified for two years after marriage. The umpire's decisions, for example, record the case of a woman in the garment industry whose employer claimed that she had been dismissed because her work was not satisfactory and who was disqualified for the two-year period.[88] Another involved eighty women 'who refused to accept the role of strikebreaking by returning to employment under the employer's terms.' In this case, two women who were recently married were disqualified from receiving UI for the two years following marriage, while the other seventy-eight were able to claim benefits.[89] In another case, a woman wrote to Stanley Knowles explaining that she lost her job at the T. Eaton Co. when she got married because the policy of the department she was working in was not to employ married women. However, she did not qualify for an exemption to the married women's regulation since Eaton's stated that they had no *overall* store policy with regard to married women. She was therefore disqualified from receiving UI for two years from the date of her marriage.[90] In her letter to Knowles she noted:

> The cost of living is so high that my husband and I find it very difficult to get along with only one of us working. For the past three months I have tried to get a job but have been unable to do so. An Insurance Officer told me in an interview that it was almost impossible to place me now that I was married and this same person also told me that I would have to work 90 days before I could claim benefits. When I appealed my case I asked the court how they expected me to work for 90 days if I was unable to find a job and they said 'That is the $64.00 question. We can't answer that.'[91]

Many such cases involved women who had their left employment or been laid off because of pregnancy.[92] In these cases also, married women were disqualified for a period of two years following marriage. Women who left their jobs in order to follow their husbands to another city were also disqualified for two years following marriage for voluntarily leaving their jobs for personal reasons.[93] A 1955 amendment did allow women moving to another city to qualify for benefits, but only provided there were 'reasonable opportunities for her to obtain suitable employment' in that area. The latter phrase meant that many women were still disqualified.[94]

While the UI Commission's concern focused on married women as likely to 'abuse' the UI plan, evidence indicated that for many women it was an economic necessity to work and that married women were facing considerable difficulty in finding employment. For example, the Women's Division of the National Employment Service (the section of the UI Commission that referred people to jobs) reported that during 1950 there was a steady increase in the number of female applicants registered at local offices of the commission for whom it was not possible to find suitable employment. They noted that the increase was due at least in part to the rising cost of living in Canada and to the necessity for married women to find work in order to augment the family income.[95] In both 1951 and 1952, they had difficulty filling orders for secretaries, stenographers, and typists, but this was not because of a

lack of qualified women looking for work: 'It was generally the experience of placement officers that most of these applicants were married or
in the older age brackets, and thus could not meet requirements of
employers' orders in many instances. Despite efforts of employment
officers to persuade employers to consider such applicants, the general
trend was for single women well under thirty years of age.'[96]

Referring to both married and single women, in 1954 the Women's
Division reported that the number of unplaced female job applicants
had steadily increased, whereas the number of job vacancies had decreased.[97] Women also seem to have represented a disproportionate
number of those placed in casual jobs by the UI employment service,
and therefore would be more likely to have renewed claims for benefits.
In 1952 women represented 36.3 per cent of regular placements but 63
per cent of casual placements.[98]

By the early 1950s, then, the UI program was actively contributing to
the creation of a family–market–state arrangement and of a welfare
state regime in which women's dependency was both encouraged and
assumed. Furthermore, this regime was based on juridical inequalities.
In effect, the regulation was denying an independent source of income
security to married women who were otherwise entitled to benefits. As
Stanley Knowles pointed out, women not only had to be unemployed,
but also had to *find* work in order to be eligible for benefits: 'You require
of married women ... not only that they be available and not only that
they report once a week; you require that they actually be at work. If a
married woman needs work, wants it, and tries her best to get it but
cannot get it then you deny her unemployment insurance benefits to
which she is otherwise entitled because she has not proven her attachment to the labour market by actually being at work.'[99]

As others pointed out, the regulation, which implied that married
women did not really need the money and therefore should not be
entitled to UI, was contrary to the basis of the scheme, according to
which benefits were a right, not something for which a means test
should be applied.[100] Married women were presumed guilty of abuse
until they were able to prove otherwise, by finding employment subsequent to marriage.[101]

## Growing Pressure for Change

By the mid-1950s, objections to the married women's regulation were
being strongly voiced by labour organizations, by women's groups, and
by various members of the House of Commons. The CCL took the lead

(along with a number of MPs) in calling for its repeal. The regulation's repeal was clearly not at the top of the CCL's list of concerns about UI in the 1950s (it generally was listed after such issues as the extension of coverage to other occupations, an increase in benefit rates, and so on); nevertheless, at its annual conventions, in its briefs to the federal government, and in its submissions to the UIAC and to the UI Commission, the CCL repeatedly expressed its opposition to the discriminatory treatment of married women claimants and called for the regulation to be eliminated.[102] Protests against the regulation were also registered at meetings of the labour representatives on the Boards of Referees (attended by the CCL, the TLC, and the Quebec-based Canadian and Catholic Confederation of Labour [CCCL]). In 1951 a major joint submission to the UI Umpire by the three labour bodies (the CCL, TLC, and CCCL) was undertaken at the initiative of the CCL, with the labour representatives arguing that the regulation had resulted in 'unjustifiably discriminatory action against certain married women' and urging its elimination.[103]

In Quebec, the CCCL also clearly voiced its opposition to the married women's regulation. Besides participating with the other labour bodies in presentations to the UI Umpire and the UI Commission, the CCCL, in its annual brief to Cabinet, regularly requested the abolition of those sections of the UI Act and the Regulations which placed married women in a special category.[104] Indeed, in 1951 the CCCL devoted an entire section of its brief to the federal government (considerably more than the other labour bodies) to the married women's regulation, declaring that it could not agree to 'the disqualification in advance of a whole category of insured persons simply because it is more difficult to verify their good faith.'[105]

The TLC opposed the regulation less actively. Resolutions continued to be brought forward and passed at TLC conventions urging the repeal of the married women's regulation,[106] but the TLC executive seemed at best lukewarm in its opposition. The Executive Council in its annual report to the convention regularly recommended changes to the UI Act, but it was only in 1955 that it urged the removal of the married women's regulation.[107] Similarly, each year in its brief to the federal government the TLC recommended changes to the UI provisions, but it was not until 1952 that this included changes to the married women's regulation, and even then it was simply stated that the regulations 'should be given more sympathetic consideration' and that the ninety days required to establish benefit rights should be reduced to sixty.[108] It was only in 1954 and 1955 that the TLC's brief called for the abolition of the married women's regulation altogether.[109] Unlike the CCL, it did not raise the issue in submissions to the UIAC.[110]

The Canadian Labour Congress, formed after the merger of the CCL and the TLC in 1956, took up the former CCL's strong opposition to the married women's regulation.[111] Individual union locals also played a role in representing their members before the Boards of Referees and the umpire and urging that the regulation be rescinded.[112]

As noted earlier, women's organizations had a much less institutionalized forum for expressing their views on unemployment insurance. Not only did labour groups have representation on the UIAC and the UIC, but they often made additional submissions to the UIAC. It seems that women's organizations, on the other hand, were not usually notified of hearings on the subject of UI or invited to attend.[113] Nevertheless, both individual women and women's organizations as a whole eventually came to play an important role in urging the repeal of the regulation. For example, both the National Council of Women of Canada (NCW) and the Canadian Federation of Business and Professional Women's Clubs (BPW) took a stand on the issue.

The NCW was an umbrella group for a range of organizations – church-based, professional, and other.[114] Their meetings to some extent were concerned with arranging social functions, but they also discussed and passed resolutions on important matters of the day, ranging from the guaranteed annual wage to international peace. They supported equal rights and greater opportunities for women in many fields, including the appointment of women to the Civil Service Commission, the Senate, and the UI Board of Referees; the right of women to serve on juries; and equal pay legislation.[115] On labour issues, however, their positions often reflected the middle-class biases of their members. For example, the Economics and Taxation Committee of the NCW suggested that 'women of Canada might use their influence to discourage wage demands.'[116] On the question of the married women's regulation, there was little recorded discussion by women's groups until the mid-1950s. At the 1954 annual NCW meeting a resolution was brought forward that Regulation 5A be rescinded and that the 'UI Commission take the same action to protect the Unemployment Insurance Fund against unjust claims from married women as is taken with other categories of claimants.'[117] The resolution, however, was *defeated* by 139 to 41,[118] and it was not until two years later, at a subsequent convention, that the same resolution passed.[119] Once it was passed, the

NCW then made representations to the Minister of Labour and to Prime Minister St Laurent requesting that the married women's regulation be rescinded.[120]

The BPW brought together women in business and the professions and thus tended to focus more specifically on the issue of women's employment. This group also passed resolutions on a variety of issues that would improve the position of women; for example, it called for the introduction of equal pay legislation, the removal of discrimination against married women in the federal civil service, the appointment of women to the Senate, the establishment of a women's bureau within the federal government, and so on.[121] On many occasions the BPW passed resolutions urging the federal government to appoint a woman to the UI Commission[122] and for the UI Act to be amended to include 'sex' as a basis for non-discrimination in referring applicants to employers (this was already the case with respect to 'race, creed, colour, ancestry and origin').[123] At the 1954 and 1956 biennial conventions, a resolution was passed urging the revocation of the married women's regulation.[124] Representations on the subject were subsequently made to the federal labour minister, the Industrial Relations Committee examining the 1955 revisions to the UI Act, and prime ministers St Laurent and Diefenbaker.[125]

A number of MPs also tried to have the regulation repealed. Ellen Fairclough, elected as a Conservative MP in Hamilton West and one of a very small handful of women in the House of Commons in the 1950s, to some extent acted as a spokesperson for women's organizations in the House. She was probably the most persistent of the MPs in calling for its elimination. She also urged many times that women be represented on both the UI Commission and the UIAC.[126] As noted earlier, Stanley Knowles and Clarence Gillis of the CCF also played an important role in urging that 'this discrimination against married women ... be eliminated.'[127]

By the mid to late 1950s, then, pressure was growing to revoke the regulation. Labour was the first and most consistent of the organized groups in urging the abolition of the regulation, but by the mid-1950s the voice of women's organizations was also critical.[128] The position of women's groups was given added weight by the fact that Ellen Fairclough, a member of the BPW who for many years had spoken out against the discrimination of women in this regulation, had become a cabinet minister (although not directly responsible for UI) in the new Diefenbaker government.[129] More fundamentally, however, this shift in policy was a reflection of the changing position of women, and of charges in family/workplace relations as more and more women entered the labour force and as outright discrimination came to be seen as less and less acceptable. The married women's regulation was revoked on 15 November 1957 by P.C. 1957–1477, shortly after Diefenbaker's Conservative government came to power.[130]

The question of a special regulation for married women remained a contentious issue into the early 1960s. Business groups continued to call for the re-enactment of a married women's or similar legislation, arguing, for example, that 'abuses must be eliminated ... or the Fund will be drained by special minority groups at the expense of the majority of contributors.'[131] At the urging of one of the employer representatives, the issue came up again in the UIAC,[132] but unlike a decade earlier, the labour representatives were opposed to such a regulation. No agreement was reached, and thus in the end no recommendation was forthcoming.[133] The question of the status of unemployed married women and their use of UI was also a subject of discussion in the 1960 hearings of the Special Committee of the Senate on Manpower and Employment. Studies undertaken for this committee indicated a continued concern about the motives of married women claiming UI.[134] The committee's report, drawing on these studies, argued that 'many of the married women who present themselves at the offices of the Unemployment Insurance Commission have only an intermittent, temporary or tenuous attachment to the labour force ... There is a real question as to whether the present provisions of the unemployment insurance system are appropriate in these cases.'[135]

The subject of married women's regulations came up a final time at the 1961 hearings of the Committee of Inquiry into UI, chaired by Ernest C. Gill. The Gill Committee was appointed by the Conservative government in the early 1960s in the context of rising unemployment and concern about a possible depletion of the UI Fund. Its terms of reference included determining 'the means of correcting any abuses or deficiencies that might be found to exist.' A long list of business organizations presented briefs arguing that married women (again, along with older workers and seasonal workers) were draining the fund and urging the reinstatement of married women's regulations.[136] But a number of other organizations now categorically rejected the reinstatement of such regulations. Women, both as individuals and as members of organizations, by this time had a much stronger presence. The NCW declared emphatically that they were 'unalterably opposed to any change in regulations which would be prejudicial to the rights and interests of women, whether married or single.'[137] The BPW brief contained no specific reference to the question of a married women's regulation; it did, however, recommend the inclusion of 'sex' in clauses preventing discrimination in employment.[138] In addition, the CLC, the International Railway Brotherhood, and others also now expressed strong and unequivocal opposition to the reinstatement of regulations restricting benefits to married women.[139]

Despite the various studies and the requests from business groups, the married women's regulation was not reinstated. The Gill Committee recommended that no special regulations be enacted relating to married women (although it did suggest more active claims supervision).[140] This change in state policy was indicative of a shift in the position of working women. Married working women were entering the labour force in growing numbers and were becoming an increasingly important source of labour for both the growing service sector and the state. This development entailed changes in the prevailing ideology. The idea that women only worked for a short time before marriage and then belonged in the home no longer corresponded to the reality of women's lives, and it was becoming more and more unconscionable for state policy to be based on such a notion.

In addition, changes were occurring in the representation of women's interests in the political arena. As women came to play an increasingly important role in the paid labour force, their interests came to be better represented both by labour and by women's organizations. This increased concern about women workers on the part of labour by the late 1950s can be seen in the growing number of discussions on the role of women in trade unions and the formation of white-collar organizing committees, as well as in the establishment of women's committees in some of the central labour bodies.[141] Women's organizations also had a renewed interest in equality rights for women workers, as evidenced not only by their actions with respect to UI, but also through their efforts, for example, to have equal pay legislation introduced and to have a woman's bureau established within the federal Department of Labour.[142] Particularly important, on some issues labour and women's organizations now shared the same point of view. The result was that whereas in 1950 it was possible to enact a regulation disqualifying a large number of married women from receiving UI benefits, by 1960 this was no longer possible.

## Conclusion

The years 1945 to 1960 marked the consolidation of a gendered and unequal welfare state and labour market. This was encouraged in part by a state that feared a renewal of the high unemployment of the Depression years, in the context of a return to the prewar ideology of domesticity that had never really been abandoned. The enactment of policies encouraging the withdrawal of women from the labour force, and the creation of a gendered and unequal welfare state structure, also must be seen in the context of the constraints of the postwar economy, in which only limited employment opportunities were available. All of this reflects how gender ideology can be applied in constructing policies to overcome basic structural limitations in the economy.

The postwar regime was based on a certain relationship between work, family structures and state programs: that paid work would principally be undertaken by a male breadwinner, that the basic work involved in the daily maintenance and reproduction of the labour force would be undertaken by women in the home, and that the state would step in to provide continuity of income when, for example, the male breadwinner was unemployed. Social insurance programs, such as for unemployment, were important in establishing a 'social security' welfare state; this state, however, was based on fundamental inequalities in the home, in the labour force and in state entitlements.

The UI scheme of this period restricted both employment possibilities and income security for women. The provision of dependants' allowances meant that women tended to receive a lower rate than men. The expectation placed on women that they accept work in low-wage sectors helped in the reconstruction of a gendered and unequal labour market and further encouraged women's dependence on the male head of household. Finally, the introduction in 1950 of a regulation imposing additional conditions on married women formally entrenched inequalities in the UI scheme. These policies together disqualified many women from receiving benefits to which they would otherwise have been entitled, and denied many married women an independent source of income, and contributed to the concentration of women in low-wage job ghettos.

This postwar regime did, however, contain many points of tension. Contradictions in the family–work–state nexus and pressures from a range of sources provided the momentum to bring about changes. In terms of economic and material conditions, a major contradiction of the postwar period was the *inability* of most Canadians in single-earner, male-breadwinner families to buy the new consumer goods or even, by the 1960s, to maintain family living standards. Dennis Guest has noted that in the early 1940s 'only 43.7 per cent of families of wage earners, outside of agriculture, had sufficient income to guarantee them a satis-factory nutritional diet.'[143] Family income had to be supplemented on the one hand by state income support programs such as family allow-ances and UI (which by the 1950s was providing regular additional yearly income in critical seasonal industries), and on the other hand by the increased employment of women, including married women. By the mid-1950s, then, the balance between women's domestic and labour market work was shifting, with women increasingly taking jobs outside the home for at least part of their married life. Between 1951 and 1961 the labour force participation of married women doubled from 11 to 22 per cent. This represented a fivefold increase over 1941, when mar-ried women's participation rate was approximately 4 per cent.[144]

There were also tensions and contradictions within the structure of the nuclear family itself. Women were experiencing these contradic-tions in their daily lives and were beginning to mobilize against the isolation and inequalities of the nuclear family structure. Attempts to achieve greater financial security, to break out of the confines of the nuclear family, and to reconcile women's new role in the labour force with their continued domestic responsibilities did much to propel the second wave of the women's movement.

As women began to enter the labour force, the contradiction grew between their status as individual workers entering into contract in the labour force, and juridical norms and a welfare state structure which assumed that women were in the home and which were often explicitly discriminatory. Pressures began to mount, then, for changes in women's entitlement to state benefits, and for their right to equal treatment.

As the 1950s progressed, there were considerable changes in the prevailing ideology, in women's activities, and in the ways working women were represented. The entry of married women into the labour force also began to erode the ideology of domesticity. The idea that women belonged exclusively in the home no longer corresponded to the reality of their lives, and it became more and more difficult to justify a policy such as the married women's regulation, which was based on such an assumption. In addition, in the late 1940s, working women, who constituted a relatively small part of the labour force, were not well represented either by labour or by women's organizations. By the late 1950s, however, both groups were beginning to more actively take up the issue of equal rights for women workers. The combined opposition of these groups to policies that discriminated against certain women was key both to the revocation of the married women's regulation and to ensuring that a similar one was not later reinstated. It also meant that as the 1960s commenced, the debate about welfare state programs and the place of women within them had evolved considerably.

Thus, economic and familial pressures, contradictions with respect to the legal/juridical apparatus, and shifts in ideology meant that welfare state policies that were discriminatory and based on the assumption that women were in the home were no longer appropriate. Also, the changing character of political actors – including both labour and women's groups – their growing concern with equality issues, and changes in the relationship between them meant a shifting complex of forces and a substantial change in the regime. Clearly women were in the labour force on a permanent basis, cracks were appearing in the male-breadwinner model, and discriminatory legislation was no longer acceptable.

CHAPTER 3

# From Exclusion to Entitlement: Pregnancy, Maternity, and the Canadian State

Attitudes and policies with respect to pregnancy and maternity formed a key part of the construction of the postwar gendered labour market and welfare state regime. The ideology of domesticity involved not only the notion that men should be the primary breadwinners, but also that women during pregnancy and early childrearing should withdraw out of sight and into the private sphere of the home. These views very much influenced women's access to UI income security. In the immediate postwar years, UI officials were reluctant to consider those who were visibly pregnant as available for work, and unemployed women who were pregnant had great difficulty obtaining either work or UI benefits. The UI program helped both to sustain the view that pregnant women did not belong in the public sphere and to create a labour market in which pregnant women were, at best, granted a marginal place. This, then, was a further way in which state policies reinforced women's dependency on a male breadwinner and perpetuated gender inequalities.

The ideology of the dependent wife at home remained well entrenched throughout the 1950s; however, as noted in chapter 2, tensions in and challenges to this model were also apparent throughout this time. Attitudes toward pregnant women in the labour force changed much more slowly than toward married women in general.[1] But, as married women entered the labour force in growing numbers and showed reluctance to leave work at the first indication they were to have children, they began to challenge existing norms and practices concerning pregnancy and to make claims for state benefits. One of the key challenges to the treatment of pregnant workers within the UI plan, and to the prevailing family welfare state model, came, then, from working women themselves as they attempted to work out strategies for financial survival.

Much of the discussion in feminist literature concerning attitudes and strategies with respect to pregnancy and maternity has focused on the distinction between emphasizing women's 'equality' and women's 'difference.'[2] One can argue that women are 'different' from men and that special considerations such as maternity benefits are necessary to recognize their particular needs; or one can argue that such special treatment would reinforce assumptions about women's biological role that can ultimately be used against them, and that the necessary approach to take, then, is that women are 'equal' to men and therefore require identical treatment. This debate played an especially prominent role in the United States, where judicial battles have been key in women's equality struggles and where, as Carole Pateman has pointed out, 'an extremely individualist political culture combined for long periods with a conservative Supreme Court has meant that a choice between equality and difference is often posed more sharply [than in other countries].'[3]

In Canada, debates about the extent to which benefits should be available to women in the maternity period were not posed to the same extent as in the United States as a stark dichotomy between equality and difference. Rather, there were a series of sometimes overlapping struggles during which both elements were emphasized at different times and in different forums and the two approaches were not treated as necessarily mutually exclusive. Strategies and arguments shifted with the actors and the particular context.[4] Initially, as a counter to exclusion, individual pregnant women, supported at times by local trade unions, asserted their right to claim UI benefits if unemployed. Essentially, they were demanding equality of treatment in the administration of UI: that pregnant women who were 'capable of and available for work' should have access to benefits on the same terms and conditions as others. The existence of the rights-based UI program that women had access to – even if on somewhat uncertain terms – was significant in that it provided women with access to *some* sort of income if unemployed, as well as a forum, eventually, for questioning the terms on which that income was provided.

In the late 1940s and 1950s the UI Commission and the administrative tribunals hearing UI appeals (the Board of Referees and the UI

Umpire) played a key role in defining the conditions under which pregnant women could receive benefits. Initially the adjudicating authorities reinforced both the view of women as dependants and the exclusion of women from the workforce during pregnancy and maternity. These tribunals were, however, confronted sooner than other parts of the state both with the contradiction between prevailing notions and the realities of women's lives, and with challenges arising from the inequality of treatment that restricted pregnant women's access to benefits. By eventually granting pregnant women the right to receive UI in certain circumstances, the administrative tribunals themselves became a force for change. Their decisions pointed to some of the program's contradictions, and this created further anomalies – for example, that pregnant women could receive benefits under certain conditions but not others. These anomalies, in turn, created pressure within the state to address the question of unequal treatment and pointed to the need for a plan that addressed the specific question of maternity. At the same time, other social actors began increasingly to demand that formal maternity leave and benefits be provided as a more positive entitlement recognizing women's differences. At first neither the central labour bodies nor women's groups were much interested in a maternity program; but by the mid-1960s both these groups had begun taking up the issue. In addition, other parts of the state, in particular the Women's Bureau of the Department of Labour, became interested in the maternity question.

Once maternity benefits were on the state agenda, the formulation of specific provisions was the result of two parallel processes within the state: discussions about the UI program centred in the UI Commission and undertaken in the context of an expansion of that program; and discussions within the Department of Labour, where the Women's Bureau played an important role. The policy as finally implemented contained contradictory elements. Policy rationale and directions reflected both fears that pregnant women would abuse the UI system and views from earlier in the century regarding the need to 'protect' women and infants during the period around childbirth. Overlaid on this were the beginnings of a more rights-based discourse that was being put forward by the emerging second wave of the women's movement – women's right to a job and income security and to take leave when they (in consultation with their doctors) judged best. The clash between these two approaches was evident in the legislation that was finally introduced in 1971. Specific provisions in this act reflected policy options that developed at a time when the overriding concern was with infant health and well-being; they were introduced, however, in a climate of increasing mobilization around a discourse based on women's rights and equality. This provided the basis for subsequent challenges to the legislation.

In this chapter I first examine how in the 1950s the exclusion of women from benefits during pregnancy and early maternity formed part of a gendered postwar welfare state regime. I then discuss the growing pressures for equal treatment and for special maternity provisions. Finally I examine the nature of the policy process within the state that led to the eventual implementation of maternity benefits within the UI program.

## Pregnancy, Maternity, and Working Women: Exclusion from Benefits

In the late 1940s and during the 1950s little was available in the way of maternity-related state benefits for women. Mothers' allowances had been introduced in five provinces between 1916 and 1920[5] but were quite limited. They were needs-based benefits that provided assistance to 'deserving' mothers in cases, such as for widows, where a male breadwinner was unable to provide for the family. Universal family allowances, introduced in 1944, paid a small sum to all mothers. However, they were considered essentially a supplement to the male wage and a way to stave off possible large wage increases.[6] Both consisted of relatively small amounts directed to women in the home and were based on the notion that a male breadwinner would provide, to the greatest extent possible, a family wage. By the end of the Second World War there were no programs providing either security of income or employment for women through pregnancy and early childrearing.[7]

One source of income security that *was* available to working women after 1940 was the UI plan. The UI program, however, had clearly been designed with the male worker as a model. There were no provisions either in the 1940 act or in the regulations introduced in subsequent years that dealt with pregnancy. By the 1950s, however, as more and more married women entered the labour force, in the absence of other programs, women who lost their jobs or were laid off during pregnancy were beginning to make claims on the UI program. UI officials were confronted with such questions as whether and under what conditions pregnant women leaving their jobs should be eligible for UI, whether women should be able to collect benefits immediately before and after birth, and whether women with young children should be eligible.

The UI plan thus became a site of contestation over the place of pregnant women in society and over women's entitlement to state benefits in the period around pregnancy and maternity. The guiding factor in these decisions was ostensibly whether such women met the conditions of the UI program, which required that individuals show themselves 'capable of and available for work but unable to obtain suitable employment.' In practice, however, pregnant women were viewed with great suspicion; again it was feared that they might be especially likely to abuse the system. Moral judgments about women's proper role and duties, and about the place of pregnant women in society, often entered into decisions about eligibility. In addition, even though UI was a rights-based program, the criterion of need – such as whether, for example, the woman was the family's breadwinner – constantly arose in evaluations of women's eligibility for benefits.

## UI Adjudication and the Exclusion of Pregnant Women Workers

In the absence of provisions in either the act or the regulations, the guidelines followed by insurance officers and Boards of Referees were based largely on rulings by the UI Umpire. The representations to the Umpire and his eventual rulings on these issues point to the ways in which gender ideology can be created and sustained, to class differences in approaches to pregnant women in different workplaces, and to the varying ability of different actors to successfully win appeals. These discussions also shed light on women's employment in this period. Those who argued that pregnant women were simply trying to abuse the UI system were implying that these were middle-class women working for a little extra; yet many of the cases concern women working in extremely arduous conditions, who were far from the middle-class life portrayed by the ideology of the time.[8]

Pregnant women wishing to continue work, seeking new work, or simply trying to qualify for benefits faced many obstacles. The idea that women could continue working after marriage was slowly becoming more widely accepted, yet it was still assumed that once children were expected they would return to the home. As Joan Sangster has shown, strong social disapproval of visibly pregnant women forced many to resign.[9] Furthermore, many employers had explicit policies against retaining pregnant women. In other cases women left their jobs while pregnant because they found that the work they were engaged in was too physically demanding to undertake while pregnant. Still others found themselves laid off during pregnancy simply because they worked in occupations, such as in clothing or electrical assembly, where frequent layoffs were the norm. Those trying to find new employment had an extremely difficult time persuading employers to take them on, and when they approached the UI office for benefits they encountered further barriers. Women filing a claim for UI, and those already receiving benefits, were required to inform the local office immediately of a pregnancy and the expected date of confinement,[10] and were then treated in an altogether different way from other claimants. As one woman stated:

> There appears to be a prejudicial and discriminatory attitude on the part of employers towards hiring a pregnant woman regardless of her capability and willingness to work. Although I was available for work ... the Unemployment Insurance office made not a single attempt to send me to a job, and when I asked why, a member of the [Board of Referees] stated they had a responsibility to their employers, who objected to a pregnant woman being sent to them as a prospective employee (even a temporary worker) and even though she may hold a bona fide medical certificate.[11]

One guideline for insurance officers established early on by the UI Umpire was that pregnant women should be considered not capable of or available for work, and therefore ineligible for benefits, for a period six weeks before the expected date of 'confinement' and for six weeks after it.[12] In 1946 the umpire noted that 'a woman suffers on account of childbirth a total temporary incapacity ... Generally speaking, medical and legislative authorities have determined the normal period of incapacity as being approximately six weeks prior and subsequent to the event.'[13]

The assumption that women were not capable of or available for work during this twelve-week period was reaffirmed in numerous rulings in the 1950s and 1960s.[14] An amendment to the UI Act in 1953 meant that those already on claim who became incapable of work 'by reason of illness, injury or quarantine' could continue to receive benefits, but this did not apply to pregnant women. The umpire, ruling on the issue in October 1954, stated: 'It is obvious that pregnancy cannot in any way be assimilated to injury or quarantine ... It is a natural condition for a woman and, notwithstanding the fact that for a certain period of time a pregnant woman ordinarily becomes incapacitated for work, her incapacity cannot be recognized as being due to illness within the meaning of [the UI Act].'[15]

Only in highly exceptional circumstances was the six-week disqualification prior to confinement reduced. The strength of the view that pregnant women should not be in the workforce and the lengths that women had to go to prove entitlement to benefits are clear in one case from 1953. Here it was decided that since the woman was the bread-winner of the family, had shown a willingness to work, and had produced a medical statement that she was capable of work, and since the 'advanced stage of pregnancy [was] not too obvious,' and since it appeared that she was capable of carrying out the duties of her normal occupation, stenography, 'without undue embarrassment to any employer,' she could be considered available for work and therefore receive benefits until two weeks before the birth.[16]

There were three other main types of pregnancy and maternity-related claims that the umpire was asked to rule on. The first involved 'involuntary layoffs,' that is, the termination of women for reasons such as a shortage of work or an employer policy against retaining married or pregnant women. The second involved women who had 'voluntarily' left work because of pregnancy. The third concerned the availability of women after childbirth.

In the first type of case, where 'involuntary' layoff was involved, a key factor in determining eligibility for benefits in the 1950s was the *appearance* of the claimant – in particular whether she was 'obviously pregnant.' One of the first cases of this type, coming before the umpire in 1952 (CUB 819), involved a stenographer who had been employed by a barrister. She was already receiving benefits when the local office submitted a report stating that 'the claimant was in an advanced stage of pregnancy which was so obvious that she could not possibly be referred to any employer; that her chances of obtaining employment were practically nil and that she had not been looking for work for the past six weeks.'[17] The insurance officer disqualified her 'because, in his opinion, the claimant's physical condition had so restricted her sphere of employment as to render her not available for work.' The umpire upheld the decision, ruling that 'a claimant whose obvious condition makes it impossible to place her in employment but who is apparently physically able to do the kind of work for which she had applied' cannot be considered as available for work and therefore was not entitled to insurance benefits.[18]

This ruling was challenged a year later in the case of a bobbin packer laid off because of a shortage of work.[19] The insurance officer disqualified her after receiving a report that the 'claimant is obviously pregnant and from appearance it is doubtful whether she is capable of work.' The Board of Referees upheld this decision based on the previous ruling in CUB 819. The Textile Workers' Union, which was representing the woman, appealed to the umpire as follows:

> In the case of CUB 819, the employee was laid off on the grounds of an obvious pregnancy condition. In the case of our claimant she was laid off on grounds of lack of work ... In the case of CUB 819, the employee was a stenographer to a barrister, therefore her condition would be exhibited publically. Our claimant is a factory worker. In all our mills women in pregnant condition usually work until a few weeks before child birth. The decision on whether they continue working depends upon their physical condition and not their physical appearance ... [The employment officer] admitted she had not referred the claimant to any employment. Therefore what grounds and on whose opinion was she deciding that the claimant could not be placed in employment?[20]

These arguments apparently convinced the umpire, who eventually decided in the woman's favour. All of this suggested a benefit entitlement based not only on appearance but also on a rather different understanding of the notions of 'public' and 'private.' The distinction presented here was not so much between the public realm of work and the private sphere of the family, but rather had to do with pregnant women's visibility, and whether the work took place in a factory or in a more 'middle-class' occupation such as secretary to a barrister (where being visibly pregnant was less acceptable).

Despite this ruling, pregnant women's eligibility for benefits in the case of layoffs was far from clearly established. The umpire, attempting to rule further on the issue, argued that a number of factors were involved in determining availability, including 'the stage of the claimant's pregnancy; the extent of her capability for work; her appearance as the result of pregnancy; the nature of the work for which she is qualified; her intention and mental attitude towards accepting employment and her domestic circumstances.'[21] A few weeks later, in attempting to further clarify the issue, the umpire reiterated that 'in cases dealing with the availability for work of pregnant women, one of the determining factors is the claimant's eagerness to look for employment ...

Another factor is the appearance of the claimant resulting from pregnancy.' He noted the 'general principle' that 'the availability of a claimant may be determined objectively by her chances of obtaining employment in relation to a set of circumstances beyond her control or which she has deliberately created.'[22]

The second type of case the umpire ruled on involved women who 'voluntarily' left their employment because of pregnancy. Generally, in situations not involving pregnancy, those voluntarily leaving their work faced a six-week disqualification penalty. Pregnant women, however, were considered ineligible for benefits from the time they left their job, even if early in their pregnancy, until six weeks after the birth; thus they were disqualified in some cases for months. Social and employer pressure for visibly pregnant women to remain at home forced many women to leave their positions, so it was often difficult to determine whether the woman had resigned voluntarily or whether the employer 'had taken the initiative in causing unemployment.' There was a deep-rooted assumption, however, that pregnant women did not want to work or that they should be at home. Thus, where there was not a clear shortage of work, it was generally assumed pregnant women left work voluntarily and that those who then applied for UI were attempting to defraud the system.

The practice of disqualifying those who voluntarily left their work until six weeks after the birth was a result of guidelines first laid down by the umpire in 1949. The case involved a woman working as a punch press operator in a radio manufacturing company. She had left her job because the work was too heavy, but she had submitted a medical certificate stating that she was capable of part-time work. The umpire decided that it would be unlikely that an employer would want to take on a woman in her condition and noted that 'she should be more considerate of her health and of the future of the child that she is carrying.'[23] He added that the UI Act 'only provides insurance against forced unemployment, when a person is available for work, but cannot find employment. It does not provide insurance against ... the inability of a woman to work due to the fact that she is expecting a baby.' He went on to rule:

> From the date that a woman leaves her employment for health reasons brought about by pregnancy she fails to prove that she is capable of and available for work and cannot do so until six weeks after the birth of her child or until she has recovered to such an extent that she can resume

employment. Unless there are special distressed circumstances where the claimant is the breadwinner of the family and reasonable opportunities of part-time work prevail, benefit should not be allowed.[24]

The umpire later clarified that 'recovery to such an extent that she can resume employment' meant recovery *after* confinement; essentially, he was disqualifying women voluntarily leaving work due to pregnancy until at least six weeks after the birth.[25]

Though rulings sometimes went in a woman's favour,[26] these principles were regularly reaffirmed in throughout the 1950s. Also denied benefits were, for example, a woman who had left work in the early stages of pregnancy due to nausea, but was looking for work later in her pregnancy when she was once again in good health;[27] a woman who had left her job as a checker in a laundry because, given her pregnancy, she found it too difficult to stand all day, and who had stated that she wanted to find lighter work;[28] a woman who had left her work because she had felt ill due to pregnancy, who had presented a medical certificate that she was later in good health, and who wished to find a temporary stenographic position;[29] a bank teller who left her employment and who stated that she would 'take office work where she would not meet the public' (the umpire in this case ruled that 'the embarrassment of having to meet the public in her condition was a matter for the employer, and not her, to decide');[30] a telephone operator who left work when two months pregnant because the job 'was too hard on her nerves';[31] a cowl assembler, about three months pregnant, whose job involved 'heavy work ... where intense heat and strong odours of rubber prevailed';[32] and a welder, a laundress, and a waitress, all wishing to find lighter work.[33]

On many occasions the referees clearly disagreed with the principles outlined by the umpire, arguing that the woman *should* be considered eligible for benefits, but they were almost always overturned by the umpire. For example, in the case of the telephone operator, the cowl assembler, and the waitress, the Boards of Referees all argued that they should be eligible for benefits, arguing that 'an indefinite disqualification to a person pregnant only two months is not, in our opinion, reasonable.'[34] In the case of the waitress, they contended 'that the claimant had proved her intention to continue work ... that the claimant had good grounds for leaving her employment in order to avoid a possible miscarriage and that she had proved her intention to continue in the labour market.'[35] The umpire, however, overturned the boards' rulings in all these cases.

A final issue concerning pregnancy and maternity that the umpire was called to rule on concerned the availability of women after childbirth. As noted earlier, women were automatically disqualified for six weeks after the birth. In addition, women with young children were required to show they had satisfactory childcare arrangements when proving their eligibility for benefits.[36] Women with very young children were viewed with particular suspicion. Thus, for example, in 1958 a woman who registered for employment and who filed an application for benefits shortly after her baby was born, was able to show that she had satisfactory childcare arrangements, but was disqualified by the insurance officer as not being available for work because her baby was not bottle-fed. This was upheld by the Board of Referees, although eventually overturned by the umpire when she was able to show that she could switch the baby to bottle feeding within a day.[37]

During the 1950s, then, state policies, as revealed in the decisions of the umpire and the actions of UI officers, helped sustain a particular gender ideology according to which women during pregnancy and early childrearing belonged in the home. It also helped create a type of labour market where pregnant women and women with children had little place – a labour market that was based on and that helped sustain fundamental gender inequalities. UI was a rights-based program, yet for a pregnant woman, entitlement was based on myriad factors including appearance, public visibility, attitude to work, and family circumstances. By limiting women's access to income security at a critical period in their lives (i.e., during pregnancy and childbirth), UI policies further reinforced women's dependence on the family and on the male breadwinner. To some extent, these policies reflected a desire to comply with the wishes of employers and reinforced gender ideologies already present in the workplace.

### The UI Adjudicators: From Reinforcing Exclusion to Limited Equality of Treatment

By the late 1950s and early 1960s the UI adjudicators had begun making different decisions. The UI administrative tribunals, though initially upholding traditional views, found themselves having to respond to the everyday life situations of women and men as they struggled to find the financial means to survive. They were confronted sooner than other levels of the state with the contradictions between prevailing notions and the realities of women's lives. As decisions involving pregnancy continued to be appealed, and as challenges to the inequitable treatment that pregnant women were receiving continued, the umpire began modifying his approach. This, then, suggested a very different role for the state than earlier in the decade. It seemed at first as if the umpire had been working in concert with employers, accepting and enforcing the view that pregnant women should not be in the workforce. Now the state to some extent had become an agent of change.

Regarding 'involuntary' layoffs, the shift in umpire rulings can be seen in a 1958 case involving an assembler for an electric company who was laid off due to a shortage of work. The umpire ruled that she *should* be able to receive benefits since there was no evidence that her inability to find work 'was due to any reason other than because no employment was available.' The umpire went on to state the important principle that a placement officer's comment that because of pregnancy a claimant was not acceptable to employers did not constitute a basis for disqualification, since there was no evidence that she was not acceptable to *any* employer.[38] In 1960 the umpire went further, stating that 'a lenient view can usually be taken in those cases where pregnancy is found to have had nothing to do with the claimant's unemployment or where it is the employer who has taken the initiative in causing unemployment.'[39] This principle seems to have been applied throughout the 1960s.[40] Generally, pregnant women who did not leave work of their own accord were allowed to collect benefits until six weeks prior to the birth, providing they met the normal requirements – for example, by showing a willingness to work by registering regularly for work.

By 1960 the umpire had also begun making different rulings in cases involving pregnant women 'voluntarily' leaving their work. A case came before the umpire in 1960 involving a woman whose work as a machine operator required lifting heavy articles. She had had a number of miscarriages and on her doctor's advice had left work when two-and-a-half months pregnant to look for lighter work.[41] The Guelph Labour Council and the Textile Workers' Union made strong arguments on her behalf. The umpire, unlike in earlier cases, decided that because the claimant was in the early stages of pregnancy, because there was a good chance of her obtaining lighter work, and because she had not refused to accept any such work, she should be eligible up until the time she was about six months pregnant (when the UIC received a medical statement that she should do work of an 'exceedingly light character').[42]

The notion that a pregnant woman voluntarily leaving her job should be presumed to be unavailable for employment was further challenged in 1960 by a secretary in a Vancouver law firm.[43] In her appeal to the umpire she took strong exception to the established rulings which presumed that a woman leaving her work because of pregnancy was not available for other types of work. The umpire made this important statement:

> It is impossible for me, in the absence of a refusal of suitable employment or without other reliable indications that a claimant's declared willingness to work is not genuine, to assess the probability of a claimant's accepting or obtaining work of the desired kind ... The adjudicating authorities cannot in law, arbitrarily presume that a claimant will automatically refuse suitable employment nor assume that the conditions of the labour market are unfavourable to a claimant ... non availability cannot be inferred solely from a claimant's omission to make a personal search for work or from the reluctance of certain employers to hire pregnant women.

He ruled that a city the size of Vancouver could provide temporary work of the type the claimant desired and therefore that she should be considered as having been available for work until six weeks before the date of confinement. This ruling represented a significant departure from earlier cases: factors such as appearance clearly were absent from evaluations of availability, and it was no longer simply assumed, without any proof, that pregnant women were not interested in work and that employers would not hire them. This ruling set a precedent. For example, in subsequent cases of women leaving their jobs to look for lighter work[44] or because of early nausea,[45] the umpire ultimately decided they should be considered available for work and therefore eligible for benefits.

The right of pregnant women to UI was much more clearly established by 1960, but it was still far from guaranteed. Insurance officers enjoyed a great deal of discretion, and there was considerable variation in their decisions about whether to allow benefits, in the rulings of the Boards of Referees, and even in the umpire's rulings. For example, a spinner in a Quebec textile mill who left her work when two-and-a-half months pregnant and registered for lighter work where she could sit down[46] was not as lucky as the Vancouver legal secretary, whose case had been heard only a few months earlier. In the spinner's case the insurance officer disqualified her from receiving benefits and the Board of Referees upheld this decision, referring to the standard argument that it 'doubt[ed] very much whether any employer would be interested in hiring her in her condition.' It offered the further justification that 'the claimant is not supporting a family.' The umpire, in turn, upheld the decision of the Board of Referees. It seems, then, that the criteria of appearance and need both continued to influence decisions.

In addition, it was still often assumed that a woman leaving her job for any reason, who also happened to be pregnant, was in fact leaving her job *because* of her pregnancy. When pregnancy was involved, the benefit of the doubt was still rarely extended to the woman. This was the situation, for example, in the 1961 case of a stenographer who left her job, stating that she was unable to find a housekeeper to care for her young children. When it came to light some time later that she was pregnant, the insurance officer disqualified her, retroactively and for an indefinite period, on the grounds that she had voluntarily left because of pregnancy.[47] It was also the situation in a 1963 case involving a woman who left her work as an 'egg candler' at Loblaws when twenty-two weeks pregnant, wishing to find lighter work.[48] The board upheld the insurance officer's disqualification, stating that 'we cannot conceive of lighter work for her.' It then became clear that the work involved standing in a cold room (63 to 64 degrees) for eight and a half hours a day inspecting and culling eggs, and at times lifting crates weighing 20 to 30 pounds. In the end, however, the disqualification was retained because, it was stated, 'basically the claimant terminated her employment because of an advanced stage of pregnancy.'[49]

Overall, however, by 1960 an important shift had occurred in the approach of UI adjudicators toward pregnant women. There was an implicit questioning of the view that visibly pregnant women should be excluded from the public sphere; the criterion of appearance was no longer a decisive factor; and in cases where the claimant's unemployment was through 'no fault of their own,' a 'lenient view' was taken in the granting of benefits. Pregnant women thus achieved greater (although far from complete) equality of treatment within the UI program and began to have greater access to income security benefits. The decisions of the UI umpire to allow pregnant women, under certain conditions, to receive benefits pointed to some of the contradictions and inadequacies within the program and helped create pressure for further change. While women were provided with some income if they were laid off and left work relatively early in their pregnancy and were looking for new work, by late pregnancy, when they were most in need of benefits, they had no income security. Other women found themselves having to stretch the limits of the UI qualifying conditions in order to find some income. It was becoming apparent that a program was needed that would address women's specific needs around maternity. It would be some time, however, before such a program was introduced.

*The Strength of the Male-Breadwinner Norm: The State, Labour, and the Women's Movement*

By the early 1960s there was greater leniency in the umpire's decisions with respect to pregnant women. Nevertheless, the strength of the male-breadwinner norm precluded many calls for maternity benefits as a positive state entitlement. The continuing pervasiveness of the male-breadwinner norm can be seen not only in the pronouncements of other parts of the state, but also in discussions within the labour and women's movements.

Many branches of the state, including the UI Commission, expressed alarm that the leniency extended by the umpire to pregnant women was resulting in greater abuses and a drain on the UI fund. For example, the 1962 report of the Gill Committee of Inquiry into the UI Act expressed concern that married women laid off because of pregnancy were able to draw benefits 'although their availability for employment is extremely doubtful.'[50] They recommended that such women be excluded from UI until eight weeks after confinement and that pregnant women laid off for other reasons be considered unavailable for eight weeks before and eight weeks after the birth.[51] This would have constituted considerably harsher treatment of those laid off because of pregnancy; it also would have extended the period when pregnant women were automatically ineligible by an additional two weeks before and two weeks after the birth. The same committee recommended that women with children below school age be considered unavailable for employment, and therefore ineligible for UI, unless they could prove they had satisfactory childcare arrangements.[52] As noted earlier, this practice was already being followed by insurance officers. The Gill Committee felt that a reassertion of insurance-based principles could be achieved in part by excluding those, such as pregnant women and mothers of young children, whom they considered not really available for employment.[53] Significantly, as an alternative the committee suggested a maternity-related program, arguing that if maternity benefits for employed women were desired, this would be better addressed through another social security program instead of being 'swept in as part of an unemployment insurance plan.'[54] In subsequent years, commentaries within the state on the Gill Committee's report generally offered few objections to these recommendations. For example, a 1963 interdepartmental committee indicated support for the proposals with respect both to pregnant women and women with young children and suggested that these proposals be put on a statutory basis in order to prevent alteration by future umpire decisions.[55] Proposals by the Department of Labour in 1964 did not differ significantly from existing practices. This department argued that women's eligibility before confinement should be left to the discretion of employment officers; after confinement, it should depend on medical statements about the woman's physical condition. In the early 1960s, within the bureaucracy, no serious consideration was yet being given to the possibility of maternity leave.

At this point, neither was there support for a maternity program from the labour movement. The labour movement as a whole was ambivalent to married women in the workforce and to pregnant women's entitlement to UI. This reflected the continuing strength of family wage notions. As seen earlier, trade unions representing members before Boards of Referees, and labour representatives sitting as members of those boards, did question the practices of UI insurance officers and the rulings of the UI umpire. Individual trade unions and locals provided critical support to unemployed pregnant women in calling essentially for equality of treatment within the UI program, in the sense that pregnant women who were available for and capable of work should be entitled to benefits on the same basis as others.

A discussion of women's entitlement to UI benefits during pregnancy and immediately after the birth of the child at the 1954 TLC convention reveals the divisions and conflicting approaches within the labour movement on the issue. A resolution calling for the continuance of UI benefits during pregnancy and for six weeks after the birth of the child was brought forward by the Winnipeg and District Trades and Labour Council.[56] A Toronto delegate, speaking in favour of the resolution, pointed to several cases where the employer, knowing the employee was pregnant, 'summarily dismiss[ed] her due to the fact that she could not complete the season.'[57] Another pointed out that the TLC had gone on record 'as being in favour of men who lose their employment as a result of illness' and argued that pregnant women were in exactly the same situation.[58]

But not all the delegates supported the idea of benefits for pregnant women. Some argued that the male wage should be sufficient to support a wife at home and that while single women were entitled to both jobs and UI, this was not the case for married women. One delegate, from Windsor, stated that 'when a woman gets married, her husband is supposed to earn enough money to keep her ... We are supposed to keep the husbands working so that they will have a pay cheque to take home. In the case of single or widowed women, I don't think we have this trouble.'[59] A similar point of view was expressed by a Toronto delegate: 'There are far too many married women in certain industries today keeping single women walking the streets, who can never qualify for unemployment insurance ... Married women should have no need to work in a country of this kind ... Let's ... get the wages and conditions so that we can keep our wives at home and not ask them to do two jobs, to keep their husbands instead of us being responsible for keeping them.'[60]

Others' support for married and pregnant women's right to jobs and to UI was qualified by indications that there were exceptional circumstances (such as women having to 'support their injured husbands from the Korean War')[61] or that women would really prefer to be at home.[62] The TLC did pass the resolution, and in its memorandum to the federal government a few months later it included a request not to deny benefits to married women who become pregnant,[63] but the issue did not come up again. Furthermore, the TLC made few demands for state-provided maternity benefits. To the extent that it made demands for maternity-related state support, it was not for rights-based benefits that would include women in the labour force, but rather for 'greater [governmental] responsibility for the maintenance of mothers and widows through mothers' and widows' allowances.'[64] Essentially, it was calling for the extension of a needs-based benefit which assumed that women's place was in the home.

In 1954 the CCL also passed a resolution supporting the idea of unemployed pregnant women's right to UI. The convention proceedings suggest general agreement that the treatment of pregnant claimants was 'inconsistent and unsatisfactory' and that 'proper evidence as to capability, such as a medical certificate, should be sufficient to protect such claimants from disqualification.'[65] Nevertheless, they suggested that the situation could be dealt with without amending the act and recommended instead that the congress make representations to the UI Commission in this regard.[66] As with the TLC, the issue did not come up again. The CCL also did not demand specific maternity-related benefits. In the 1950s it demanded simply the adoption of 'a national social security program covering the whole field of health, invalidity and old age pensions'; at the same time, it recommended the abolition of means-tested benefits.[67] The TLC, CCL, and later the Canadian Labour Congress all consistently passed resolutions calling for a sickness insurance plan, or an extension of the UI Act to include those who became unemployed due to illness,[68] but this did not include a demand for pregnancy-related benefits.

With the merger of the two labour bodies in 1956 to form the Canadian Labour Congress, the TLC's demand for mothers' and widows' allowances was folded into a general call for a comprehensive national social security system; yet even then no demand was made for maternity-related benefits.[69] While commenting that it found the Gill Committee's recommendation of eight weeks before and after the birth 'unduly restrictive,' the CLC voiced its support instead for the existing system, 'which allows for individual assessment of capability and availability, assisted by the interpretations which the umpire has established.'[70] During the 1960s the CLC's demands for social security sometimes listed maternity as one area among many where provisions were required,[71] but this was not done consistently, and clearly such leave was not a high priority for the congress.[72]

The major women's groups of the 1950s and early 1960s also did not express much concern about the treatment of pregnant workers within the UI plan; in fact they seemed far from considering the possibility of maternity leave. The National Council of Women (NCW), the largest of the women's organizations, was composed mainly of middle-class women, many of whom did not themselves work for pay outside the home. Many recognized that more and more married women were entering the paid labour force, often out of necessity, and stressed that women should be free to choose whether to seek paid employment or to remain in the home.[73] But, for the most part the NCW's members accepted the male-breadwinner model and saw women as having an essential role and duty as mothers and wives. The NCW's solutions to the difficulties for employed women with domestic responsibilities tended to be privatized ones: it was up to individual families and working women to find their own solutions, to defray the costs, and to work out arrangements that to the greatest extent possible left family structures and relationships intact. For example, when asked to comment on the issue, the NCW noted that while most women would spend the large part of their lives working outside the home,

these same women, of course, by reason of their biological function, will
be responsible for the continued life and health of the human race. It is
important, therefore, that the maternity function of working women be
safeguarded by all possible means. Every effort should be made to provide that women may, without serious disadvantage to their position,
withdraw from the labour force during the childbirth period ... and, if
they so desire, during the years in which their children are young. Un-
doubtedly one of the most effective means to this end is to ensure that
they may find satisfactory employment again when their maternal responsibilities permit them to seek it.[74]

This group's solution for working women having children was not
security of employment or maternity leave, but rather assistance through
counselling and retraining in finding new employment, income tax
deductions for those requiring domestic help,[75] and part-time employment for 'the woman who must supplement the family income but
whose time and strength do not permit her to accept full time employment outside her home.'[76]

In 1964, one of the NCW's committees undertook a discussion on the
employment of women with family responsibilities. The views expressed
included that those who work from choice 'need no special consideration,' that 'efforts should be made to bring the income of the wage
earner more in line with the needs of a family so that women would not
be forced out into the business world,'[77] and that 'if we wish to have
emancipation in choice of jobs and in recognition for work well done,
we must be willing to forgo the special privileges which attend our
being female.'[78] While there was some suggestion that good daycare
should be available to employed mothers, the only financial aid suggested was a continuation of the needs-tested benefits already available
through mothers' allowances and through other provisions of provincial social assistance acts. Pregnancy and maternity were seen as an
individual and familial responsibility rather than a social one: 'The
decision re the dutiful handling of family responsibilities is a problem
to be faced within the home. Only when acute financial difficulties arise
may outside help be welcomed; then the services of trained Social
Service or Staff Worker should be available.'[79]

In the 1950s and early 1960s the Canadian Federation of Business and
Professional Women's Clubs (BPW) showed little interest in maternity
leave. The BPW brought together employed women. It saw a role for

women in the public sphere, but its views on income security benefits were constrained both by its membership – many were single, middle-class professionals and businesswomen – and by its acceptance of the notion that maternity and childrearing were an individual and family responsibility. In 1963 the BPW did voice its opposition to the Gill Committee's recommendations with respect to pregnant women and women with preschool children, and to the notion that such women were trying to cheat the UI Fund.[80] Yet, the following year the BPW's convention *defeated* a resolution that included a recommendation that no discriminatory regulations relating to UI benefits be enacted against married women and women with children.[81] Like the NCW, the BPW generally saw the solutions to the problem of working women with domestic responsibilities as these: part-time work, vocational guidance and training for women once they decided to re-enter the labour force, and income tax deductions for working women employing domestic help.[82] In response to a 1963 questionnaire, the BPW commented: 'While we would agree that certain leave of absence be given opinion varies greatly on the length of time. It is felt that it would be difficult to guarantee re-employment at the end of one year in an economic complex such as exists in this country.'[83] Certainly there was no question of providing benefits to maintain income during the period around childbirth.

Thus, in the early 1960s there was little support from either labour or the women's movement for a maternity-related program. The pressure to move on the issue, and the challenges to a family work model according to which women in the maternity period did not belong in the labour force, came rather from pregnant women trying to work out strategies for financial survival, choosing to remain in the labour force, and if unemployed, making claims for state benefits. The claims they were making forced the UI adjudicators to reconsider their approach until eventually they began granting pregnant working women some degree of equality of treatment in access to UI benefits. In this respect these women were supported at times by individual trade union locals. By the mid-1960s, however, more serious challenges to prevailing conceptions of the place of pregnant women, and to their right to benefits, began rising from within the state, from the emerging second wave of the women's movement, and finally, from the labour movement. These cumulative challenges would eventually result in demands not only for equality of treatment but also for the recognition of women's specific needs with respect to pregnancy and maternity.

## Toward the Implementation of Maternity Benefits and the Recognition of Difference

Within the state, beginning in the mid-1960s, questions began to be raised about whether benefits should be provided explicitly for maternity purposes. Some suggested that since pregnant women were collecting UI benefits anyway, it might be appropriate to simply legitimize this, and to reduce any abuses, by allowing women to receive benefits for maternity purposes.[84] Others suggested that maternity benefits could be included as a possible extension of the sickness benefits that were, by the mid-1960s, being considered for inclusion in the UI program.[85] A 1966 interdepartmental committee, for example, noted that while 'it might be objected that pregnancy is to some extent voluntary,' it would 'probably be difficult to exclude pregnant women if unemployment resulting from sickness is covered.'[86]

The presentation, within the state, of maternity benefits as a positive right or benefit for women was made, at least initially, from the Women's Bureau of the Department of Labour. Sandra Burt has argued that the policymaking which resulted in 1971 in the introduction of maternity benefits was state-directed – in particular, that women's groups played little role and that 'the most consistent and best-informed pressure came from the Women's Bureau, lobbying the federal government from within.'[87] Certainly the bureau played an important early role in raising awareness of the maternity issue by disseminating information, commissioning a study, and encouraging discussion among women's groups.[88] By 1966 the bureau had also begun to make the case, in discussions within the state, for a more comprehensive maternity plan. It did so, however, with considerable caution. Marion Royce, the bureau's director, pointed to the problems inherent in linking pregnancy to sickness benefits, as some had suggested, and instead proposed consideration specifically of maternity benefits:

> While [pregnant women's] situation is comparable to that of sick persons, the analogy can be overworked since obviously a normal pregnancy is not an illness. At the same time, just as in the case of sickness, workers would be better served by a sickness insurance plan, so women who have had to leave gainful employment because of pregnancy would be more appropriately covered through the social provision of maternity benefits.[89]

In other policy recommendations, the bureau urged both that maternity leave and maternity-related financial benefits be seriously considered.[90]

These requests were tempered by the suggestion that financial benefits were not really feasible and that it would therefore be best to focus on the question of maternity *leave*, involving only such issues as protection against dismissal because of pregnancy and the right to reinstatement in the former job or an equivalent.[91] The Women's Bureau's cautiousness can also be seen in its efforts to avoid suggesting measures that could be viewed as discriminating in favour of women. Royce, for example, argued that 'proposals for special provisions for women workers need to be weighed very carefully in order to ensure that in the long run they do not become a handicap in that they tend to create a privileged class within the labour force.'[92]

The Women's Bureau was not the only body to raise the issue. The bureau had ongoing contact with other groups, including women's organizations and employer and employee organizations, and was aware of the concerns and issues arising from those quarters.[93] Other parts of the state also began to support the notion of maternity leave. For example, in 1966 a UIC subcommittee recommended that a study be made of the need for maternity protection for women 'with a view to determining whether amendments to federal legislation are appropriate.'[94] Between 1968 and 1970, NDP member Grace MacInnis introduced three private members' bills designed to provide maternity leave for women employed in the federal jurisdiction.[95] MacInnis's private member's bills did not pass, but they did raise awareness of the importance of maternity leave, create pressure for the government to act on the issue, and present the view that special arrangements *would* be necessary for working women with domestic responsibilities.[96] MacInnis argued that dealing with the issue of pregnancy was necessary in order to achieve equality for women in employment and that 'this is not merely a woman's problem ... It is a family problem and a community problem and must be met as such.'[97]

Most significantly, by the mid-1960s, widespread social, economic, and political changes were provoking a shift in the perception of women's issues, and important new actors with respect to women's issues were beginning to make their presence felt. As described more fully in chapter 4, women were entering the labour force in massive numbers. As they did, groups such as the NCW became less representative of women and found it harder and harder to play a significant role in the political arena.[98] On the issue of maternity leave, the NCW remained ambivalent, at times reiterating its belief that mothers of young children should be at home,[99] and at other times suggesting that maternity legislation and benefits should be provided for working women, although not at public expense 'except in cases of need.'[100] The BPW, although oriented to working women, was also falling out of step with the times. It eventually did recommend maternity legislation, but not until 1968 did it pass a resolution urging the federal government 'to provide for adequate maternity leave, maternity benefits, protection of employment both in seniority and reinstatement and protection of the health of women workers during the maternity period.'[101]

The strongest impetus for a maternity program recognizing women's particular needs came from new spokespeople on women's issues. Internationally there was a growing mobilization around women's rights. A number of countries, including the United States, were undertaking studies on the status of women, the UN had issued a declaration on the rights of women,[102] and the ILO was sponsoring activities on the subject of working women. In Canada, in 1967, the federal government appointed the Royal Commission on the Status of Women after extensive lobbying from newly formed women's groups.[103] Cerise Morris and Monique Bégin have emphasized that the establishment of the commission was not a response to a groundswell of unrest among Canadian women[104] and that despite its creation, 'women as a constituency were simply not part of the political agenda of the Canadian state.'[105] Nevertheless, the creation of the Commission, and the hearings it conducted were critical in helping raise the profile of women's issues generally, encouraging the articulation of a new, rights-based discourse, and stimulating a number of organizations to formulate legislative demands.

The commission did not issue its report until September 1970, well after discussions within the federal government on maternity leave proposals were under way, yet its impact on the maternity issue is clear. Its terms of reference included consideration of 'the special problems of married women in employment and measures that might be taken under federal jurisdiction to help in meeting them.'[106] The issue of job protection during pregnancy and maternity came up in many briefs and discussions at the public hearings.[107] It became clear that an issue of concern was that pregnant women had no job protection, that many were required to leave their jobs when they were no longer able to work, and that women rarely received any kind of income protection during the maternity period.[108] The NCW and the BPW held that maternity was essentially an individual and family responsibility, and both these groups as well as the Women's Bureau shared the concern that there be no call for special 'privileges' for women. In contrast to all this, one of the four principles adopted by the commission was that 'society has a responsibility for women because of pregnancy and childbirth, and special treatment related to maternity will always be necessary.'[109] The commission recommended, among other things, an eighteen-week maternity leave, with dismissal being prohibited during that leave, and that the UI Act be amended to provide eighteen weeks of maternity benefits.[110]

Finally, within the CLC, despite the lack of official pronouncements, there was growing awareness about women's issues. As the 1960s progressed, for example, *Canadian Labour* began publishing articles discussing difficulties in achieving women's equality.[111] OFL Women's Conferences were addressing a range of issues including equal pay, daycare, maternity leave, and job training.[112] In part as a response to the establishment of the Royal Commission on the Status of Women, women within the CLC began articulating demands concerning working women. The OFL and CLC briefs to the Royal Commission both called for a range of measures to improve the position of women including equal pay, maternity leave, daycare, and training.[113] While these proposals would not be incorporated into the CLC's overall demands for social security,[114] they did represent an important development within the labour movement, and they added to the growing pressure for legislative changes on women's issues. In addition, by 1967, individual unions such as the FWTAO were expressing interest in the issue of maternity leave.[115]

### The Formulation of Maternity Provisions: The Policy Process within the State

By the latter part of the 1960s, as demands increased from a variety of sources, concrete proposals for legislative amendments with respect to maternity benefits were being formulated within the state. Once these benefits were accepted as part of the state's agenda, maternity provisions were the result of two parallel processes within the state. On the one hand, discussions took place within the Department of Labour, where the Women's Bureau played an important, role, albeit not an exclusive one or even the most progressive one. On the other hand, the provisions resulted from developments and discussions about the UI program centred mainly on the UI Commission, where discussions about expanding the UI program were taking place. Here, control of abuses and the health of the UI Fund remained central concerns.

Within the Department of Labour, a Working Party Committee with representatives from different branches was established in July 1968 'to recommend a course of action that might be followed by the government in coming to grips with Maternity Leave.' This broader committee laid the groundwork within the state for maternity leave legislation.[116] It was decided that maternity leave provisions – including such things as job security during the maternity period – could best be established through an amendment to the Canada Labour (Standards) Code. One of the committee's main concerns was the ratification of the ILO Convention on Maternity Protection, first passed in 1919 and revised in 1952.[117] This convention, drawn up at a time when the concern was to protect maternal and infant health, called among other things for a maternity leave of six weeks before and a *compulsory* leave of six weeks after confinement, as well as benefits sufficient to maintain the mother and her children.[118] The 1952 revision stipulated that cash benefits should be not less than two-thirds of previous earnings.

Within the committee there was considerable disagreement over maternity entitlement. Some felt it was important to adhere to the convention, including the requirement of a twelve-week leave with a six-week compulsory postnatal component.[119] The view was expressed that the state had a role to play in maternal *protection* and that workers needed to be protected 'not only against employers, but also against themselves,' and further, that it was important to adhere to international standards in this regard.[120] Other committee members, however, articulated a view based on the notion of women's *entitlement* to leave and benefits. For example, Eileen Sufrin argued that if the employee chose to, she should be able to request *less* than six weeks of prenatal leave and, with a doctor's recommendation, less than six weeks of postnatal leave.[121] Some pointed out that specifying a compulsory leave – especially when there was no provision for cash benefits – could create considerable hardship.[122] The major issue, then, was not whether the leave period was adequate, but whether or not it should be compulsory and whether women should be entitled to take *less* leave. This, again, reflected an equality-based argument: the right of women to work in the period around maternity. It sought to establish that in the immediate prenatal and postnatal periods, women could be 'available for and capable of work.'

Even those who questioned the notion of compulsory leave were concerned about getting medical advice on the most desirable amount of time for women to be off work. Maternal and infant protection as determined by the medical profession and enforced by the state was thus still an issue. Accordingly, the committee sought medical opinion on the 'minimum period of pre and postnatal leave from the standpoint of the mother and/or mother and child.'[123] Weight seems to have been given to the opinion of the Maternal Mortality Committee of the Canadian Medical Association, which came down on the side of a compulsory postnatal leave of six weeks. For prenatal leave, they declared that the optimum time was ten weeks, the minimum time six weeks. Furthermore, 'pregnant women in the workforce should be permitted time off from work to afford adequate medical surveillance and to attend prenatal classes.'[124]

These recommendations were incorporated into the Report of the Working Party Committee, issued in 1969. This committee recommended that the Canada Labour Code be amended so that an employee with six months' service would be permitted a maternity leave of six weeks prior to the date of confinement and a compulsory leave of six weeks following the date of delivery; this could be extended by application of the employee but was not to exceed twenty-six weeks. It also made a number of recommendations regarding maternity-related job security.[125] With respect to cash benefits, again, there was a concern not to suggest legislation that would be seen as 'discriminating' in favour of women only – a view put forward quite strongly by Sylva Gelber, the new director of the Women's Bureau.[126] The committee argued that cash benefits for women on maternity leave should not be proposed unless there was a general fund paying disability benefits to women *and* men. They recommended either that the UI Fund be broadened to cover benefits during disability, or that a special social insurance fund be created for that purpose.[127]

The role of the Women's Bureau within this committee was one of caution. It seemed afraid to push for legislation that would be seen as providing privileges to women; it was unwilling, despite the 'fluid situation with regard to social programs,' to push for a program requiring additional funding; and it suggested that the government would not be prepared 'to launch a new venture with regard to maternity protection.'[128] Gelber argued that extensions of the six-week postnatal leave should only be allowed on medical grounds[129] and that in the event of other needs, 'welfare programmes are more appropriate and the employer can not be asked in justice indefinitely to extend leave guarantees on so broad a basis as "the mother's need" to make suitable arrangements for the care of the child.'[130] In addition, she suggested that matters such as retention of seniority during maternity leave should not be included in the proposed legislation[131] and that anything beyond a basic minimum should be left to employer/employee negotiations.[132] Challenges to the status quo and pressure for more extensive measures from within the bureaucracy came rather from those in the Department of Labour with previous links to the labour movement, such as Eileen Sufrin and Harry J. Waisglass.[133] Waisglass, for example, supported incorporating the principle of seniority or reinstatement in a former position within the Labour Code, and pointed out the difficulties of leaving the maternity issue to collective bargaining 'since the vast majority, probably more than 85 per cent, of women in the labour force are not covered by collective agreements.'[134]

By the fall of 1970, discussions on maternity leave were taking place in Cabinet. In the Social Policy Committee, questions were raised, again, about whether postnatal leave should be compulsory. Representations by Treasury Board pointed out that this would mean a perhaps unwelcome change to existing and more flexible public service employment regulations.[135] Officials within the bureaucracy questioned the advisability of compulsory leave; they also had worries about contravening both medical advice and the ILO recommendations on the subject.[136] In the end, Cabinet decided to introduce legislation providing those with at least one year of service with a maternity leave not exceeding eleven weeks before the estimated date of delivery, and a period of six weeks following delivery, which could be *shortened* with the consent of the employer and the approval of the doctor. In addition, the legislation, finally introduced in 1971, made it illegal to dismiss or lay off an employee because of pregnancy.[137]

Parallel with the discussions within the Department of Labour, which focused on changes to the Canada Labour (Standards) Code to ensure maternity-related job protection, proposals were being developed for cash maternity benefits within the UI Commission in the context of more general discussions about the reform and expansion of the UI Act. The 1968 *Report of the Study for Updating the Unemployment Insurance Programme* was the first UI program review to recommend maternity benefits. To some extent this was seen as an extension of proposed sickness benefits. The view was expressed that since pregnant women were collecting UI benefits anyway, it might simply be appropriate to legitimize this, and to reduce abuses by introducing maternity benefits.[138] There was also, however, some indication that there could be a case for maternity benefits on equity grounds, especially given the increase in female labour force participation.[139]

In February 1970 the UIC came forward with the set of proposals, which would form the basis of a White Paper, *Unemployment Insurance in the 70s*,[140] which was tabled in the House of Commons on 17 June 1970 and would be incorporated essentially unchanged in the 1971 legislation. These proposals included the payment of benefits to those whose income had been interrupted due to either sickness or pregnancy, at 66⅔ per cent of previous earnings for a total period of fifteen weeks. The White Paper and the ensuing UI legislation reflected contradictory approaches to pregnant women. On the one hand, both expressed a fairly positive view of working women's contributions to the economy and of the need for special benefits around maternity. The White Paper noted that the introduction of pregnancy-related benefits 'recognizes the particular status of women in the labour force and is a step toward eliminating some of the hardships they experience.'[141] Similarly, Labour Minister Bryce Mackasey, in presenting the new proposals, noted the importance of women's earnings to family income and that past treatment of pregnant workers had been 'unfair to the female population.'[142]

At the same time, however, UI Commission officials continued to emphasize maternity benefits as a way to reduce program abuses.[143] For his part, Mackasey referred to pregnant women as causing 'one of the greatest unintentional abuses under the present plan.'[144] The legislation itself reflected both continuing suspicion of pregnant women workers and notions from earlier in the century about maternal protection. Concern about abuses was evident, for example, in the provision that maternity claimants must demonstrate a 'major attachment' to the labour force by having worked twenty weeks within the last fifty-two, compared to the eight required by those applying for regular benefits. Concern that women would abuse the system by becoming pregnant and then entering the labour force simply in order to claim benefits was reflected in what became known as the 'magic ten' rule. This specified that a minimum of ten of the weeks worked had to be between the thirty-first and the fiftieth weeks before the expected date of birth.[145] Also, women claiming maternity benefits were to be subject to a two-week waiting period, which was now to be required of all UI claimants. (Department of Labour officials objected to this provision, arguing that 'there is no way in which a pregnant woman can minimize the termination of her condition'[146] and that it would penalize women working until confinement, who would then only be eligible for benefits for four of the six weeks postnatal leave.)[147] Concerns about maternal and infant health and about women's capacity to work around childbirth were reflected in the provision that benefits be taken during the period starting with the ninth week before the estimated date of confinement until six weeks after. They were also reflected in the provision that a pregnant claimant who did not qualify for maternity benefits would be 'disentitled' from regular benefits for eight weeks before the expected week of birth until six weeks after the birth.[148]

## Conclusion

In the late 1940s and 1950s the Canadian state helped sustain a gender ideology where pregnant women did not belong in the public sphere; in this way it helped reinforce a gendered and unequal labour market. These gender inequalities were further encouraged by the exclusion of women from UI through much of the pregnancy and maternity period. As more and more married women entered the labour force, however, they challenged both the notion that pregnant women did not belong in the workforce and the restricted conditions under which they could receive UI. Much of the initial challenge came from individual pregnant women, who in working out strategies for financial survival – supported in this at times by labour unions – took claims to UI administrative tribunals. Essentially, they were asserting the right to equal treatment within the UI program: that pregnant women who were unemployed but capable of and available for work should also have the right to receive benefits. This was partially achieved when around 1960 the UI umpire began taking a more lenient view of pregnant women. Yet women were still excluded from benefits in the immediate childbirth period, and no program was in place providing benefits specifically for maternity purposes.

By the mid-1960s, pressures were beginning to increase for a program that would address women's particular maternity needs. The combined pressure from women searching for some kind of income security, from UI adjudicative decisions, from the UI Commission, and from other parts of the state concerned about reducing UI misuse, as well as from the emerging new wave of the women's movement and others demanding maternity leave as a positive entitlement, resulted in 1971 in a provision for maternity benefits within the UI plan. These provisions marked a significant change in women's relationship to the state and suggested a different family–work–state model from that which had previously existed. Earlier welfare state measures with respect to mothers consisted of needs-based benefits which assumed that women's role was in the home; now, maternity benefits were provided as a right to women employed in the labour force provided they met certain conditions. There was increased recognition that women were both workers and mothers and that maternity was not simply an individual and familial responsibility. This both allowed women greater continuity of work experience and somewhat greater economic independence.

The policy finally implemented contained contradictory elements. The inclusion of maternity benefits as part of the UI program had the advantage of ensuring such benefits within a rights-based, nationwide program. But it also tied benefits to an insurance program based on notions of a particular type of male worker, and concern with preventing abuses and a drain on the fund remained determining factors. It had the effect of excluding those women who were not in the labour force, or who were not able to find the stable kinds of jobs needed to meet the qualifications of an insurance-based program. At no point was the creation of a separate maternity program seriously considered. To some extent this may have been a reflection of concerns about entering provincial areas of jurisdiction, and certainly the UI program had the attraction of being a nationwide program already in place. It was also, however, a reflection that the voice for working women was still weak at this point. Contradictions also resulted from the dual origins of the maternity leave, which was coming out of (a) the UI program, where pregnant women were viewed with much suspicion, and (b) the demands of social groups for benefits as more positive rights. A disjunction was evident between on the one hand legislation framed according to notions from early in the century about maternal and child health, pregnant women's capacity to work, and pregnant women as abusers of the UI system, and on the other the growing mobilization of women around a rights-based discourse – the right of women to a job and income security, and the right to take leave when women judged best. This clash between legislation framed according to past notions of women's role and the growing movement for women's rights, in turn, provided the basis for a confrontation over the legislation almost as soon as it was introduced. This is examined in more detail in chapter 5.

# CHAPTER 4

# Women into the Labour Force, UI Review, and Expansion

The period from 1960 to the early 1970s was one of economic expansion, growing female employment, increased labour militancy, and a renewed mobilization for women's rights. In the context of three minority governments, new welfare state programs were introduced. A series of UI program reviews culminated in the introduction in 1971 of the most comprehensive income security program to date.[1] The 1971 legislation was significant for women, not only because it introduced maternity benefits for the first time but also because the greatly extended coverage and lower qualifying conditions embodied in the provision for 'regular' benefits meant that many more working women had access to UI.

But these gains, achieved through a more comprehensive safety net, were tempered both by the context in which they were introduced and by the approach that underpinned the scheme as a whole. The state's response during this period to the massive influx of women into the labour force reflected continuing gender biases. Assumptions about the role of women helped structure approaches to the new income security program. In particular, there were ongoing fears that given women's primary position in the home, they were in a position to choose to work part-time or not at all, and that this might result in abuses of, or too great a drain on, the UI program. In the mid-1960s these concerns were manifested in attempts to redefine the basis of entitlement by distinguishing between two tiers of benefits: one tier to fit the Fordist model of workers employed on a full-time, year-round basis, but subject to periodic layoffs; and a second tier for those not perceived as having such a clear 'attachment to the labour force.'

Discussions of UI in this period focused strongly on ways to link UI to a comprehensive 'manpower' program. Despite the massive influx of women into the labour force, state officials showed little awareness of the significance either of the increasingly contingent nature of work or the growing feminization of the labour force. Explicitly discriminatory measures were by then seen as less and less acceptable, yet there was still little recognition that there might be a need for a different approach to manpower planning as a result of women's entry into the labour market and the questions this posed for reconciling domestic responsibilities with workplace demands. Besides all this, the gains made by women as a result of the extended coverage and greater accessibility to benefits were a result not so much of efforts to explicitly include women, or to reduce gender inequality; rather, they were a consequence of the general expansionary trend in welfare state provisions in the late 1960s. There was no explicit concern for gender equality, which meant that once the expansionary period was over, those gains were more easily eroded.

A central argument in this chapter is that there was a growing and fundamental structural contradiction between the nature of the labour market and the workforce on the one hand and the type of welfare state program in place on the other. The model of income security developed during the Second World War was based on the notion of a Fordist full-year, full-time worker. By the 1950s, part-time and 'contingent' work were already growing more important. Furthermore, income security provisions had been developed with the industrial male worker as a model, yet the economy was increasingly drawing on a female labour force with other work/life patterns and whose income security needs were not being met. These contradictions are key to understanding the subsequent crisis of the welfare state and the nature of the responses to that crisis. To the extent that the growing contingent work force was addressed, it was to express fears that women were 'abusing' UI and to attempt to create a two-tier system of benefits. While these contradictions became more apparent in subsequent decades, the response in the 1960s to these already emerging trends reinforced gender inequalities and laid the groundwork for subsequent reforms, including those in a neoliberal direction.

## Women, Work, and Family

By the 1960s, women were entering the labour force in growing numbers. Women's labour force participation had increased from 23.5 per cent in 1951 to 28 per cent in 1960 and to 36 per cent in 1970.[2] The influx of women meant a change in the workforce composition. In 1951 women made up 22 per cent of the labour force. By 1960 this had increased to 25.8 per cent, and by 1970 women constituted almost one-third (32 per cent) of the labour force.[3] Especially significant was the increase in the number of married women. Between 1960 and 1970 their labour force participation rate increased from 19 to 32 per cent,[4] and their incomes were becoming ever more critical as a means of supporting the living standards of families. A survey of married women working for pay conducted in the late 1950s found that economic factors were the most important in the decisions women made to work outside the home.[5] Sylvia Ostry further found that in the early 1960s wives were making a significant contribution to family income – a contribution that was especially important when the husband had a very low income.[6] The Armstrongs similarly provided evidence that during the 1960s, as individual wage disparities grew, the entry of married women into the labour market prevented an erosion in the economic position of families. They pointed out that in 1951 most families (57 per cent) had only one income recipient, but by 1971 this had been reversed, with 64.9 per cent of families having more than one income recipient.[7] Both these trends indicated that women were contributing more and more to the family's economic survival, and that their doing so was becoming more and more necessary.

By the 1960s, then, a significant evolution had taken place in the family/work model. It was still widely assumed that married women's primary responsibility was in the home; at the same time, marriage and having children no longer involved a permanent withdrawal from the labour market, as the postwar ideology of domesticity suggested. As Ostry noted, between 1951 and 1961 the greatest increase in labour force activity had been among women thirty-five to fifty-four. This had resulted by 1960 in a 'two-phase working life cycle' for women.[8] Women's labour force participation reached an initial peak in the years before they were married; large numbers then withdrew from the labour market during the early years of child bearing, and rearing; later, a substantial number re-entered the labour force when their children were somewhat older.[9] While much of the increase in women's participation was due to married women returning to employment once their children reached school age or older, significant increases were also occurring in the participation rate of married women in their childbearing years. For example, the participation rate of married women aged twenty-five to thirty-four increased from 18.7 per cent in 1961 to 32.8 per cent in 1970, while that of married women aged twenty to twenty-four increased from 25.8 to 43.7 per cent in the same period.[10]

Women entering the labour market were concentrated in jobs in the growing service and public sectors, often in temporary or part-time positions. Between 1953 and 1964 over one-third of the increase in total employment was in part-time work (less than thirty-five hours per week), and women workers made up 70 per cent of the growth in this labour sector.[11] In 1960, 17 per cent of the women in the labour force worked part-time,[12] by 1965, 22 per cent of women in the labour force were in this category; by 1970 this had increased to 25 per cent. For men, too, the percentage working part-time was increasing (from 3.1 per cent in 1960 to 6.3 per cent in 1970), although this was still far less than for women.[13] Thus, the Fordist work pattern, never firmly established in Canada, had been further eroded by the 1960s. Part-time and casual work, later to be identified as a prime characteristic of 'post-Fordist' flexible work patterns, was already growing in importance.[14] Women, who were the majority of these 'contingent' workers, were thus joining seasonal workers as being outside the ideal Fordist worker model.

In much of the discussion among policymakers in this period it was assumed that women were working part-time out of choice. Part-time work was commonly put forward as an ideal way for women 'to add to family income without neglecting essential duties of the home.'[15] Ostry defined as voluntary part-time all those who 'usually' worked fewer than thirty-five hours per week and 'economic part-time' as those who usually worked more than thirty-five, but were working less during the reference week due to short-time and turnover.[16] How much 'choice' was actually involved for those working fewer than thirty-five hours per week is far from clear. Certainly, part-time work *was* welcomed by many women.[17] Their choices, however, were constrained by the continuing assumptions and realities of women's primary familial responsibilities, by financial considerations, and by the lack of alternative arrangements for childcare and for care of other family members.

In addition, part-time work was also clearly to the advantage of employers in the growing service sector.[18] The Women's Bureau expressed concern that part-time workers were often forced to take jobs with low wages and poor working conditions and that this 'could undermine the conditions in jobs set by other workers.'[19] Women's groups such as the NCW suggested that while part-time work might be the preferred option of some women, it also had disadvantages and that many might prefer full-time work.[20] It urged that women working part-time 'should have the same protection and assistance in all possible respects as the full-time worker and should be regarded as a bona fide member of the labour force ... Care should be taken to see that women are not by reason of their sex compelled to accept part-time employment in lieu of the full time employment they might prefer.'[21]

For many women, finding any work at all was difficult. The 1960s was a period of economic growth and expansion, yet the labour market for women was uneven and unstable. Through the first half of the 1960s the women's employment division of the UIC's National Employment Service reported shortages of skilled female personnel in some growing state and service sector occupations such as nurse, librarian, medical technician, and dietician. At the same time, however, it reported a 'surplus' in manufacturing and in areas requiring fewer skills.[22] In 1960, for example, it noted that 'the over-all situation for women ... was that vacancies generally called for women with education, training, and experience in specific occupations, whereas a great many applicants lacked these attributes.'[23] Even in the retail area, it was consistently reported that there was a demand for women 'with suitable qualifications and experience' but that 'comparatively few women could meet the employers' specifications.' Overall there was 'a surplus of women interested in obtaining employment in retail stores.'[24] Similarly, while skilled stenographers, typists, and specialized business machine operators were in short supply, there was a surplus of female applicants for unskilled office clerk positions.[25] Furthermore, many women looking for work through the National Employment Offices were being placed in 'casual' jobs of six days or less.[26]

Both the NCW and the BPW raised concerns about the issue of counselling and retraining for 'mature' women re-entering the labour force. At a 1961 meeting with Prime Minister Diefenbaker, the BPW emphasized the need for training for older women, pointing out that 'many older women, now listed as unemployed, had been out of the working force for some years but are now compelled by family circumstances to seek employment or wish to return to work after being free from family responsibilities.'[27] The NCW passed resolutions calling for the NES to expand its counselling and testing services.[28] In February 1965 a consultation under the auspices of the Women's Bureau similarly urged that more counselling and guidance be available for women: 'The work of the NES in this respect should be strengthened.'[29]

Academics and state officials responded to these shifting patterns of female employment with the argument that women's unemployment was of a different nature than men's because women could 'choose' whether to work. Studies at the time noted that whereas in most advanced industrialized countries, between 1946 and 1966 the unemployment rate for women was higher than for men, in Canada the reverse was the case[30] (see table 4.1). In what became the official interpretation of this trend, Ostry argued that it was not simply that women were concentrated in the growing sectors of the economy where they were less likely to experience unemployment, but also that Canadian women were not fully committed to the labour force:

> Canadian women are less fully 'committed' to labour force activity than are women in these other countries. Thus, when they lose a job they are less likely to remain in the labour market looking for work, but instead return to some non-labour force activity. Many desire only intermittent work and will take a suitable or convenient job when it becomes available ... Canadian women tend to 'by-pass' unemployment when both entering and leaving employment.[31]

Ostry found that nearly one-third of women with labour force experience in 1964 worked only part of the year and did not look for work when they were not employed. Only 10 per cent of men were in a similar position.[32] She further argued that while the working life of most men is characterized by continuity, in contrast,

> The working life of most women is characterized by discontinuity: they may enter and leave the labour force several times over the course of their lives. The reason for this is that most women, unlike most men, are free to choose among many different types of activity: paid employment, leisure, volunteer work, work in the home ... The element of choice in the labour market behaviour of women in our culture is significant and it is this element which accounts for the characteristic variability – over time and space – of female labour force activity.[33]

Even though women were withdrawing from the labour market rather than registering as unemployed, these views on the nature of female unemployment helped foster the notion among state officials that women might claim to be unemployed when they were not really looking for work. Significantly, UI statistics continued to show that women were paying considerably *more* in contributions than they were receiving in

Table 4.1   Unemployment rate, Canada, 1946–66

| Year | Males | Females | Total |
| --- | --- | --- | --- |
| 1946 | 4.2 | 2.4 | 3.8 |
| 1947 | 2.9 | 1.7 | 2.6 |
| 1948 | 2.8 | 1.8 | 2.6 |
| 1949 | 3.6 | 1.9 | 3.3 |
| 1950 | 4.2 | 2.4 | 3.8 |
| 1951 | 2.8 | 2.1 | 2.6 |
| 1952 | 3.2 | 2.2 | 3.0 |
| 1953 | 3.4 | 1.6 | 3.0 |
| 1954 | 5.1 | 2.6 | 4.6 |
| 1955 | 4.9 | 2.6 | 4.4 |
| 1956 | 3.9 | 1.9 | 3.4 |
| 1957 | 5.3 | 2.3 | 4.6 |
| 1958 | 8.1 | 3.6 | 7.0 |
| 1959 | 6.9 | 3.0 | 6.0 |
| 1960 | 8.1 | 3.6 | 7.0 |
| 1961 | 8.4 | 3.7 | 7.1 |
| 1962 | 6.9 | 3.3 | 5.9 |
| 1963 | 6.4 | 3.3 | 5.5 |
| 1964 | 5.3 | 3.1 | 4.7 |
| 1965 | 4.4 | 2.7 | 3.9 |
| 1966 | 4.0 | 2.6 | 3.6 |

Source: Sylvia Ostry, *Unemployment in Canada*
(Ottawa: Dominion Bureau of Statistics, 1968),
tables 1 and 2.

benefits.[34] It was estimated, for example, that in 1965 and 1966 women as a whole paid $8 million more in contributions than they received in benefits; for men it was the reverse. In 1963 women constituted 27.6 per cent of the labour force[35] but accounted for only 24.6 per cent of the regular UI benefit periods established and 20.1 per cent of the seasonal benefit periods established.[36]

These views about women's lack of commitment to the labour force, about their ability to choose whether to work, and about part-time work were recurring themes throughout the 1960s as the UI program underwent a series of reviews. They were also reflected in the structure of the UI program that was finally implemented in 1971.

## UI Review, Manpower Planning, and the Female Labour Force

In the 1960s a series of reviews of the UI program were undertaken. The first of these, the Gill Committee of Inquiry[37] (see chapters 2 and 3), was appointed by the Conservative government in 1961. The 1960s began with the highest rate of overall unemployment in the postwar period. Between 1957 and 1958 the unemployment rate had increased from 4.6 to 7.0 per cent; although it dipped slightly in 1959, it remained at about 7 per cent in 1960 and 1961 (Table 4.1). (There was a wide gap in the official male and female unemployment rates. In 1960, for example, the male rate was 8.1 per cent and the female rate was 3.6 per cent.) There was considerable concern that these high levels of unemployment, combined with the changes that had occurred in the UI program in the 1950s, were resulting in a drain on the UI Fund.

While the Gill Committee was concerned about abuses of the UI program, and the maintenance of sound insurance principles (as noted with respect to both married women and pregnant women), its report was also indicative of a change in approach to the UI program. The report argued that a plan based on insurance principles was needed in order to 'absorb the first impact of unemployment,' but that this could not solve either the problems of unemployment or address the needs of all the unemployed. For that reason it recommended a plan of extended benefits financed from general revenues for those who had exhausted their insurance benefits. This new plan would be designed to address the longer-term unemployment that could result from such factors as an economic recession, the closing down of an industry in a single-industry area, and technological changes.[38] At the same time, the report argued that there was a need for a comprehensive employment and manpower policy involving monetary and fiscal policies, the retraining and relocation of workers, the development of winter works, and so on.[39]

With respect to women the Gill Committee's report took the view that unemployment for married women was of a different nature than for men, so they should be treated differently. As noted in chapter 2, this committee did not recommend special regulations for married women. However, it did propose restricting eligibility both for pregnant women and for women with preschool children.[40] It also suggested that married women in general were in an especially favourable position to abuse the UI system because they were able choose whether to work. Married women, the committee contended, 'have a unique ability to move into and out of the labour force at will.'[41] It suggested that the growth of the service sector 'with [its] special demand for women has made this type of employment pattern more readily available.' It argued that abuses by married women (as for others) could be controlled not by enacting special regulations that might be viewed as discriminatory, but rather by other means, including 'more active claims supervi-

sion and more vigorous follow-up of cases where referrals to job opportunities have been made without successful placement.'[42] The committee also suggested that its recommendations to increase qualifying
conditions and to shorten the duration of benefits would reduce abuses
by those who were employed in an 'intermittent fashion' or who had
withdrawn from the labour force.[43]

The Gill Committee further recommended that married women be
excluded from the proposed extended benefit program unless they
were the sole support of their household: 'The community may reason-
ably undertake to assist the head of a household after he or she has been
subjected to a period of unemployment beyond the duration of insurance benefits but we do not think there is the same obligation to a
married woman who is not the sole support of the household, at least
without proof of need.'[44] Here, the committee was reflecting and reinforcing the view that married women were not committed to the labour
force and that their earnings were of little importance to their own
survival or that of their family. It was also suggesting that married
women were not likely to be affected by the factors causing the longer-
term unemployment that the extended benefits were supposed to address, such as the closing of an industry in a single-industry town, or
the lack of particular skills. Concomitantly, it was implying that women
did not need the benefit of the 'comprehensive manpower and employment programs' that were to accompany extended benefits. The implication was that married women were not unemployed because of such
factors as lack of skills, but rather due to other causes, such as a voluntary withdrawal from the labour force. In addition, once again, for
married women, the criterion for eligibility was not to be past contributions to the UI plan, but rather need as the program assessed it.

The release of the Gill Committee's report sparked considerable debate. At first, there was substantial support from within the state for the
report's recommendations, including those with respect to women. The
UIC, for example, indicated its general agreement, including with the
recommended exclusions from extended benefits (although noting that
there might be administrative difficulties with this).[45] A 1963 interdepartmental committee, set up within the federal government to review
the Gill Report, also was generally supportive of its recommendations,
including the proposed exclusion of some married women from the
extended benefit plan.[46] The reason for this, they argued, was that 'the
concept of extended benefit, payable out of general taxes is that it
should be limited to persons still in the regular labour market, unem

ployed for a considerable time, and presumed to be in need.'[47] Presumably, like the Gill Committee, they considered that married women would not be in that category.[48] On the other hand, others within the state, particularly from the Department of Labour, raised a number of concerns, including that proposals to restrict benefits to mothers with young children and to exclude some married women from extended benefits could be considered discriminatory. It was pointed out, for example, that this could especially be a problem since there was no similar proposed exclusion of a second or third male breadwinner in the household.[49]

Women's groups raised further objections. The NCW argued that the requirement that married women prove they had childcare arrangements was discriminatory and 'would trespass seriously upon the rights of women.' It also pointed out that the exclusion of married women from extended benefits not only was discriminatory but also would cause considerable hardship in cases, for example, where it might be difficult to prove 'need,' but where the married woman's income was nevertheless essential to the household.[50] The Canadian Federation of Business and Professional Women's Clubs (BPW) took a fairly hard business line that the UI plan must be restored as an insurance scheme, that 'recognized abuses' must be prevented, and that the plan should be maintained on a 'sound actuarial basis.'[51] But at the same time, it argued that women should receive fair treatment within the program. Thus, it opposed the Gill proposals 'which singled out, or appeared to single out, classes of women as targets for arbitrary and discriminatory action.' This included the recommendations that would 'penalize' pregnant women and women with preschool children, that would exclude some married women from extended benefits, and that suggested that married women in particular were abusing the act.[52]

For its part, the CLC objected to the Gill Report's recommendation that some married women be excluded from extended benefits. It did so on the grounds that this would introduce a means test into the UI Act and that no distinction should be made between men and women or between married and single women.[53] Yet the CLC did not object to married women being required to prove childcare arrangements, nor (as noted earlier), did it object to the principle that pregnant women should be disqualified from receiving UI for a certain period before and after the birth of the child, although it did find the report's recommendations 'unduly restrictive.'[54]

The Gill Committee recommendations were, for the most part, not acted upon. While there are indications that Diefenbaker was interested in implementing them,[55] the Liberal government elected in April 1963 chose to develop its own proposals.[56] In the following years the federal government undertook further UI program reviews, which, as Leslie Pal points out, were 'largely internal to the federal government.'[57] Women's groups expressed their reluctance to comment on the UI plan while the internal government review was being conducted.[58] The CLC made recommendations with respect to UI in the 1960s, focusing on such issues as the extension of coverage to a wider range of occupations and an increase in benefit rates.[59] Labour groups had significant influence throughout the 1960s as a result of increased labour militancy in an era of minority governments, but they did not participate directly in the detailed UI program reviews. Significantly, in this period the UI Advisory Committee, with labour and employer representatives, was largely pushed to one side; discussions took place mainly at the level of the executive and within the bureaucracy.[60]

By 1963, when the new Liberal government came to power, the political and economic climate had changed considerably. The unemployment rate had dropped from a high of 7.1 per cent in 1961 to 5.5 per cent in 1963 (see Table 4.1). The Department of Labour, headed by Allan MacEachen, was now concerned with developing new proposals for an unemployment compensation program.[61] In particular, there was a concern to 'get away from the so-called insurance principles and [to] strongly stress a positive approach to remove persons from unemployment.'[62]

The Department of Labour's alternative proposal for an income maintenance and employment adjustment program,[63] completed in February 1964, constituted a significant re-evaluation of compensation for the unemployed. It stated that such compensation 'should not be regarded as an insurance problem,' where the primary concern was keeping the plan solvent; rather, it should be seen 'as an unavoidable responsibility of the Government.'[64] The report recommended a move away from an insurance plan because it 'fail[s] to cover many types of unemployment.'[65] It also argued that an excessive concern with insurance aspects 'led the [Gill] Committee to propose a number of measures in regard to seasonal workers, workers who voluntarily leave their employment, married female workers, severance pay and supplementary unemployment benefits: which could, if applied, have harmful effects on labour force development, on labour market functioning, or on industrial relations.'[66]

The Department of Labour proposal, did, however, also incorporate the idea of a two-stage system of benefits: a regular benefit to provide for relatively short periods of unemployment, and an extended benefit available on exhaustion of the regular benefit. The latter would allow income maintenance during periods of prolonged unemployment; it would also be 'a strategic tool in a program of efforts on many fronts to adjust and re-establish the unemployed as productive members of the labour force.'[67] The major emphasis in these new proposals was on the linking of income maintenance to adjustment programs such as training, counselling, and rehabilitation – programs that would constitute an 'investment in the development of the nation's human resources.'[68] The report recognized governmental responsibility for dealing with unemployment, yet it offered no specific policy proposal for how high overall levels of employment were to be maintained. To some extent, high levels of employment were simply assumed; but more generally, in keeping with the supply-side focus of employment policy in the early 1960s,[69] the emphasis was on dealing with unemployment by shifting the unemployed into appropriate adjustment programs.

The report gave little consideration to part-time work or to the training, counselling, and other adjustment problems faced by women as they entered or re-entered the labour force in massive numbers; this despite the attention drawn to these issues both by women's groups and by the Women's Bureau. Rather, the assumption remained that women were not fully committed to the workplace, and the concern was with the possible costs this type of labour might involve. While not explicitly discriminating against married women,[70] these proposals were significant in that for the first time distinctions were being introduced between those perceived as 'bona fide' members of the labour force and those with 'a minimal labour market attachment.' The former included industrial workers and those in the male-dominated seasonal industries, and it was recommended that these groups be provided with more generous benefits.

In designing a formula for benefit duration, the department argued that it was important 'to make relatively more generous provision for those with a prolonged past record of insured employment, but who have recently encountered recurrent cyclical or technological unemployment,'[71] and to reduce benefits for those with fewer weeks of work.[72] It seems that the group being targeted for these more generous provisions was the 'typical' industrial worker, or, as the department put it, 'bona fide members of the labour force who have had full-time employment for most of the preceding two years.'[73] On the other hand, the department argued that those who 'would go for any considerable part of the year without income, have such a minimal labour market attachment that they require more than merely income maintenance.'[74] Although women were not specifically mentioned, it seems that they were probably whom the department had in mind for a reduced benefit, since most seasonal workers were not included in this category. On the contrary, the department recommended more generous provisions for seasonal workers 'who have bona-fide off-seasons, as in the construction industry or in lake and river shipping.'[75] On the issue of part-time workers, the major concern, again, was with costs to the UI program. The department recommended that a minimum of two full days be required for a week to be counted as a contribution week. This would have made qualification more difficult for those working part-time or with many broken weeks of employment. In addition, the department recommended an increase in the number of weeks needed to qualify for UI. This would have favoured those with more stable and long-term work patterns, while making the plan less open to relatively new entrants and to those working irregularly – categories more typical of the growing female labour force.

The Department of Labour proposals did not receive governmental approval, and in 1965 yet another interdepartmental committee was established to 'start afresh ... to look at the total adequacy and needs of our Unemployment Insurance Programme.'[76] Its report, issued in March 1966, followed the direction of earlier reports in recommending extended coverage, a new benefit formula (including an increase in benefit rates), and a greater emphasis on the possible linking of UI to manpower and vocational training programs. Like the 1964 report, its major emphasis in dealing with the problems of unemployment was on the better utilization of human resources through various adjustment programs including technical and vocational training, manpower mobility, winter employment, and the economic development of 'depressed areas.'

Again, there was little consideration of the growing female labour force, even though women *were* taking up vocational retraining courses in growing numbers,[77] and even though women's groups and the Women's Bureau were still drawing attention to the need for retraining programs for women.[78] To the extent that the influx of female labour was taken into consideration, again, it was to express concerns about women's possible overuse of the UI program. The 1966 interdepartmental committee did recommend reduced work requirements for UI and an increased length of time that benefits could be collected.[79] (This would have made it easier for new entrants to qualify and also provided them with a longer benefit period.) Along with these proposals for more generous benefits, however, came continued proposals to restrict benefits for those considered 'marginal members of the labour force.' A distinction was being made between those with a 'major' attachment to the labour force and those with a 'minor' one. Here an explicit connection was being made between the latter group and women.[80] Specifically, the report recommended a minimum earning requirement both during the total qualifying period and for each week. As the report stated, these requirements were to

> set limits to the collection of benefits by persons having insufficient attachment to the labour force. [They] are likely to be marginal members of the labour force, who do not desire full-time, year-round employment. Such a person is likely to be a secondary earner in the family, and perhaps a housewife, student or retired person. It seems questionable whether these people should be eligible to draw benefit on the basis of a relatively small amount of employment. It does not seem feasible, however, to identify these individuals and subject them to special regulations. They should, therefore, be eligible to draw benefit whenever they are qualified under the general regulations. These general regulations, however, should be so drawn as to require convincing evidence of attachment to the labour force to qualify a person for benefit.[81]

By the mid-1960s, then, discriminatory measures had clearly become unacceptable.[82] Yet at the same time, a difference between groups in benefit entitlement (discrimination in effect) was being created by distinguishing between those with a 'major' as opposed to a 'minor' attachment to the labour force. Also, while there was some awareness that the labour market was being transformed by the entry of women, the prevailing assumption continued to be that women would continue to see their primary role within the home – that they could choose to work or not, and that many chose to work intermittently.

After almost six years of review and several throne speeches promising reform of the UI program,[83] the government was still reluctant to introduce legislative changes. Women's issues were not the contentious ones. Those related more to benefit formulas, provisions for seasonal workers and fishers, and the possible encroachment of employment adjustment programs onto provincial areas of jurisdiction.[84] In addition, by the middle of the decade unemployment rates had dropped significantly. By 1966, unemployment was at 3.6 per cent (Table 4.1) and reform of the UI system no longer seemed as pressing an issue. Moreover, the UI Fund deficits of 1963 and 1964 had vanished and the fund balance was once again high.[85] In addition, the government of the mid-1960s had a full legislative agenda of social reforms including the introduction of pension provisions, medicare and federal involvement in social assistance. Not only was a consensus on UI – targeted as it was to working people – more difficult to obtain, but given the low unemployment rates, reform of the plan no doubt seemed less pressing.

A decision to reform the UI Act seemed difficult to reach. In the meantime, however, certain UI provisions – especially those dealing with benefit rates and exclusions because of income level – needed to be dealt with. Benefits under the revised 1955 UI Act were approximately 50 per cent of earnings for claimants with dependants and 37 per cent for those without. These were adjusted periodically by amendments until 1959, when the maximum weekly amounts payable were set at $36 and $27 respectively. By 1967, in effect, the benefit rates had fallen significantly below the 50 per cent and 37 per cent levels.[86] In addition, since 1959 the income ceiling above which salaried workers were not covered had been set at $5,460, and as salaries increased a growing proportion of workers were being excluded from the plan. Accordingly, in May 1967 the UIC submitted proposals to Cabinet to provide for higher benefit rates, the collection of higher contributions, and an extension of coverage.[87] Both the Department of Labour and the Cabinet Committee on Manpower, Social Development and Employment had a number of reservations about these proposals. The UIC, for example, had proposed that 'contributions should be charged which would be sufficient to keep the Fund in balance at an assumed 5% unemployment,'[88] but the Department of Labour felt that this was too pessimistic and designed simply to build up the UI Fund (they felt it was unlikely that unemployment would rise above 4 per cent). In addition, the department argued that the proposed income ceiling (of $104 per week) was too low and that the UI Commission had ignored a number of the department's suggestions.[89] As a result, the Cabinet committee decided that a new committee of interdepartmental officials should review the UIC proposals[90] and develop recommendations for legislative amendments, which would be considered by Parliament in the fall of 1967.[91]

The entire structure of the UI program was thus once again opened up for review. Issues discussed by this new interdepartmental committee included not only benefit rates and coverage but also some new issues, including possible coverage in the event of illness or pregnancy and governmental contributions to the cost of unemployment.[92] It seems, for example, that the proposal that the government assume the costs for UI once unemployment reached a certain level (in this case 3 per cent) originated in these meetings. The originator of this idea was Tom Kent, then with the Department of Manpower and Immigration. It was seen as a means not only of allowing the federal government a clearly defined role in UI, but also as a way of 'making a firm commitment to reach the target of 3 per cent unemployment by 1970, suggested by the Economic Council of Canada.'[93]

Problems clearly remained, however, in reaching agreement.[94] Legislation was passed in March 1968 that addressed the immediate need for an increase in the coverage ceiling and in benefit rates (so they would be at 50 per cent of earnings for those with dependants and at 40 per cent for those without),[95] but at the same time it was agreed that 'a full-scale revision of the UI program' was needed.[96] The first step in this revision was the preparation, under the direction of the UI Commission, of the five-volume *Report of the Study for Updating the Unemployment Insurance Programme*,[97] issued in 1968. This would form the basis of the 1970 White Paper on Unemployment Insurance in the 70s and the subsequent legislation to amend the UI Act, introduced in 1971.

The UI review process within the federal government had been ongoing since the early 1960s. For a number of reasons, including an inability to reach decisions on contentious issues such as coverage for fishers and seasonal workers, benefit rates and eligibility criteria, priority given to other legislation, and concern about encroachment on provincial jurisdiction, the government did not move on UI reform. By the close of the decade, however, pressure having accumulated from a variety of sources, the government finally acted on the issue and undertook a more far-reaching re-evaluation of the program.

Economic changes exerted some pressure to finally introduce UI changes. By the middle of 1967 and through 1968 unemployment rates were once again rising (see Table 4.2). (The female rate was now very similar to the male rate, with the former at 4.4 per cent and the latter at 4.6 per cent. By 1969 the female rate, at 4.7 per cent, was higher than the male rate of 4.3 per cent.) No doubt this rising unemployment rate provided some impetus both for the short-term increase in benefit rates and for a larger-scale revision of the UI program.[98] In addition, by the late 1960s the Canadian economy was for the first time experiencing the

Table 4.2   Unemployment Rate, Canada, 1967–71

|      | Men 15 years and over | Women 15 years and over | Total 15 years and over |
| --- | --- | --- | --- |
| 1967 | 3.9 | 3.7 | 3.8 |
| 1968 | 4.6 | 4.4 | 4.5 |
| 1969 | 4.3 | 4.7 | 4.4 |
| 1970 | 5.6 | 5.8 | 5.7 |
| 1971 | 6.0 | 6.6 | 6.2 |

Source: Statistics Canada, cat. 71-201, *Historical Labour Force Statistics 1983* (Jan. 1984), pp. 181, 186, 191

simultaneous pressures of rising inflation and unemployment, although mild by comparison with what was to come in the 1970s. The government chose to make its major priority combating inflation, and realized this could entail continuing increases in unemployment levels, although it was expected that unemployment would rise only marginally.[99] One argument that was advanced by some in the Department of Labour was that a generous UI scheme could help reduce the conflict between unemployment and inflation – in particular, that it could 'do much to offset the criticism of an unemployment level of say 4% rather than 3% that may be required to maintain a more stable price structure.'[100] At the same time, it was felt that a more generous scheme might require the government to assume a larger share of the contribution, otherwise 'there might well be undue opposition to the scheme.'[101]

The government was also under considerable pressure from labour, the result of an unprecedented rise in industrial militancy and a series of minority governments. Trudeau's 1968 election on the theme of a 'Just Society' increased still more the expectation of new social policy initiatives.[102] The 1960s was also a decade during which poverty was rediscovered. While the major focus of government efforts to wage a 'war on poverty' was not the UI program, an increase in and extension of UI benefits was certainly in keeping with this concern. As labour militancy continued, and as unemployment began to rise again in the late 1960s, UI reform became more pressing.

Significant changes were also occurring in the position and activities of women. Women – especially married women – were continuing to enter the labour force in growing numbers; furthermore, social attitudes were evolving rapidly and women were expressing more clearly their dissatisfaction with their role and position within the family. As noted in chapter 3, the major actors with respect to women, and the

ways in which women's issues were presented, were also being radi-
cally transformed. In particular, the appointment of the Royal Commission on the Status of Women in 1967 raised awareness of women's
issues – including those facing women as they entered the labour force
– and further encouraged a new, rights-based discourse.[103] As noted
earlier, within the CLC there was growing awareness of the changing
position of women, and the OFL and CLC briefs to the Royal Commission both called for a number of measures to improve the position of
women, including equal pay, training, daycare, and maternity leave.[104]
Public attitudes with respect to married women's employment also
seemed to be changing. More and more people had come to view
married women as wage-earning individuals in their own right. For
example, a 1968 survey of attitudes to UI found that 62 per cent of
Canadians felt that a married woman's benefits should be calculated on
the basis of her own income, while only 14 per cent felt that total family
earnings should be taken into account.[105]

## Toward an Expanded UI Program and a New
## Family–Market–State Arrangement

The 1968 *Report of the Study for Updating the Unemployment Insurance
Programme* reflected many of the themes developed throughout the 1960s
review process. A major emphasis was on the need to move away from
strict regimes of income maintenance toward a combination of income
maintenance and 'developmental' measures, such as counselling and
training.[106] Training programs were seen as benefiting the individual by
'providing more effective human development' and the economy by
increasing productivity.[107] It was argued that the UI program needed to
be integrated with a more comprehensive manpower and social development program, so that in the short run it would provide 'alleviation
of hardship due to interruption of earnings' and in the long run 'a contribution to manpower adjustments mainly through a careful sorting out
of the needs for such adjustments in the population experiencing unemployment.'[108] It was believed that through rational planning and 'social
engineering,' it would be possible to move from a welfare state stamped
by an 'aura of charity and philanthropy' to a 'service state' designed to
allow for the greater development of human potential. This, in turn,
would benefit both individuals and the economy.[109]

Framed at a time when unemployment rates were still not expected
to exceed 4 or 5 per cent, the report proposed a much more generous

compensation scheme involving virtually universal coverage, low eligibility requirements, and higher benefit rates. (It was thought that extending coverage to low-risk sectors such as teachers and government employees would help finance the scheme.) The report proposed that benefits be paid according to a complex three-stage process that would allow for income maintenance and enable the UI program to be integrated with a broader manpower program. It was recommended that benefit duration depend not only on employment history but also on a willingness to participate in adjustment programs and on the regional unemployment rate. Apart from an initial three weeks of benefits, available only to those with a 'substantial' attachment to the labour force (twenty weeks or more of employment in the past fifty-two), it was suggested that only eight weeks of work would be needed to qualify for benefits. The benefit rate would be 66⅔ per cent of earnings for those without dependants and, in the last stage, 75 per cent for those with dependants.[110] In addition, the report recommended that sickness and maternity benefits be introduced.[111] It was proposed that the plan be made self-financing from employer and employee contributions at what was considered to be a full employment level of 4 per cent unemployment. (When the unemployment rate rose above 4 per cent, the federal government would assume responsibility for the extra costs of providing regular unemployment benefits.)[112]

In the initial three-week stage, the individual was to be 'left to himself in his search for a job.'[113] In stage 2 (twelve weeks) there would be increased monitoring of the claimant, entailing interviewing and counselling to detect abuses and identify particular problems, such as the need for skills training or relocation. Initially there would be 'no compulsion' for the individual to enter a particular program. Near the end of this stage, however, there would be a more intensive interview, during which it would be determined whether the claimant needed some type of employment adjustment program.[114] Depending on the diagnosis, the claimant would either have his or her benefits terminated, or enter stage 3, which involved referral to a Manpower program for retraining and/or relocation. If the claimant lived in a high-unemployment region, he or she could be eligible for extended benefits for up to another thirty weeks, depending on labour market conditions.

Women as a group had little visibility in this new scheme of things. The authors of the *Updating* report were clearly concerned that as female labour force participation increased, part-time and part-year work, as well as voluntary withdrawal from the labour force, were also growing. Again, they felt that caution needed to be taken when revising the UI plan so that compensation was not provided to those who were not sufficiently 'attached to the labour force.'[115] Concretely, the report suggested that to reduce the use of the UI plan by part-time workers, those earning less than $25 per week in a particular employment be excluded.[116] The report also proposed excluding those who had dropped out of the labour force 'or who have been considered so automatically.' The latter, they suggested, referred in particular to 'the young mother who will be regarded as detached from the labour force after child-birth.'[117] They proposed that rather than using the UI system, these cases 'will have to be handled by a welfare system which will keep open its connections with the information and placement service and with the proposed [UI] schema.'

The White Paper *Unemployment Insurance in the 70s* took up many of the themes of the 1968 report, including the need for an integrated approach to social policy and for UI to concern itself more with human development. It reiterated the view that the UI program needed to reflect the shift in thinking from the welfare state to the service state, and that the new reoriented program should not only provide financial support but also 'provide an efficient pipeline to vocational counsel-ling, job opportunities and other manpower programs.'[118] Like the 1968 report, the White Paper proposed virtually universal coverage, an increase in benefit rates to 66⅔ per cent of earnings (which would increase to 75 per cent of earnings in the later stages for those with dependants), lower eligibility requirements, and the introduction of sickness and maternity benefits. It also proposed that the federal gov-ernment assume responsibility for the extra costs of unemployment insurance when the national unemployment rate was over 4 per cent (as well as for the additional benefits to regions when the regional unemployment rate was above 4 per cent and exceeded the national rate by over 1 per cent).

The White Paper further proposed a complex benefit structure. This was now increased to five phases, with the length of time on benefits depending on the national rate of unemployment, the length of time spent in the labour force, and the regional rate of unemployment.[119] Like the 1968 report, the White Paper emphasized that claimant inter-views would provide links with Manpower services. Ever more inten-sive interviews would be conducted as the claimant passed through the various phases; these would determine how well the individual had 'taken advantage of the services and whether they were effective.' A refusal to participate could result in ineligibility for future benefits.

Most of the recommendations of the White Paper were incorporated into Bill C-229, which was passed in 1971. Coverage was extended to all those who worked in an employer–employee relationship (96 per cent of the paid labour force excluding the self-employed, compared to 68 per cent labour force coverage in 1968).[120] A somewhat different five-phase benefit structure was introduced,[121] although again, the length of benefits depended on employment history and on regional and national unemployment levels. The first phase provided (after a two-week waiting period) between eight and fifteen weeks of benefits, including a three-week lump sum payment for those who had been laid off due to a shortage of work and who were not expected to be recalled for at least five weeks. (It was argued, in part, that this would reduce administrative costs.) In phase 2, benefits were automatically extended for another ten weeks. In phase 3, 'major attachment claimants' (i.e., those having twenty or more weeks of employment) were entitled to up to eighteen weeks of benefit, depending on the number of weeks of previous employment.[122] Phase 4 provided additional weeks of benefits depending on the national rate of unemployment, while phase 5 could extend benefits further depending on the regional unemployment level.[123] Overall, this represented far more extensive income security. Under the old plan, those with thirty weeks of work in the previous two years could receive fifteen weeks of benefits, with additional seasonal benefits provided in some cases. Under the new plan, those with eight weeks of work in the previous year could receive at least eighteen weeks of benefits,[124] while those with twenty weeks could receive a maximum of fifty-one weeks of benefits. The federal government assumed the costs of regular benefits in the initial benefit periods attributed to a national unemployment rate over 4 per cent and all benefits in phases 3, 4, and 5.[125] The 1971 legislation also incorporated a proposal in the 1968 report (taken up in the White Paper) to restrict benefits for some part-time workers.[126]

The benefit rate was substantially increased. The basic rate was increased to 66⅔ per cent of earnings. In addition, for the first time since the introduction of the legislation in 1940, the division between benefits for those with and for those without dependants was substantially altered. Previously the dependency rate applied from the beginning of the claim and for those at all income levels; the new scheme provided a higher rate of 75 per cent of earnings, but only to claimants who were low earners (earning less than one-third the maximum weekly insurable earnings) or who were in the 'extended benefit period' and had been unemployed for eighteen to twenty-five weeks.[127] The definition

of dependency remained basically unchanged.[128] The rationale for providing a higher rate after a considerable period of unemployment was
that certain expenditures – for example, 'mortgages, insurance payments, car payments' – become more critical at this point, especially for
those with families.[129] When pressed on the matter during committee
hearings, Desroches, from the UIC, also suggested that the motivation
for starting the dependency rate at a later point was partly financial –
that there was a trade-off between having a dependency rate start at
the beginning of the claim, and having a regular benefit rate as high as
66⅔ per cent: 'If you are going to put dependency back in then you
would not pay 66⅔. You would have to re-examine the whole basis
of 66⅔.'[130] Clearly, this suggested a shift in government priorities away
from providing differing levels depending on family status in favour of
a higher overall individual rate. Nevertheless, evaluations of need in
the context of family situations where the male was still considered the
primary breadwinner did remain a significant part of the deliberations
and of the legislation as it was introduced.[131]

## Conclusion

Overall, the 1971 legislation offered unprecedented income security for
the unemployed. It provided virtually universal coverage against the
risk of unemployment, much more accessible benefits available for a
longer period of time, and at a rate that would come much closer to
maintaining living standards. In addition, the new plan also meant
greater access to income security for many women. The extension of
coverage to include hospital workers, government employees, and teachers brought far more women under the plan (although teachers, for one,
were opposed to being covered). The lowering of eligibility requirements to eight weeks in the previous year, although intended more to
allow new labour force entrants such as high school graduates to gain
access to the plan,[132] also benefited women, both older women re-
entering the labour force and those only able to find work for short
periods of time.[133] A further significant change, as noted in chapter 3,
was that for the first time maternity benefits were provided to women
in the workforce. Finally, the modification in the dependency rate provided for greater equality in benefit rates; overall, many more women
than before had access to a higher benefit rate (66⅔ per cent).
    At the same time, the plan contained new sets of contradictions and
limitations. Most notably, the program was based on two underlying

assumptions: unemployment would stay low, and the state would need to do little to maintain this low level beyond implementing some type of 'active manpower policy,' mostly involving retraining and relocation programs.[134] There was no serious commitment to low unemployment; in fact, there was a suggestion that a more generous UI scheme might make somewhat *higher* levels of unemployment more acceptable. In other words, UI was to be used as a tool, not to stimulate demand in a Keynesian sense, but rather to make it acceptable to fight inflation more strenuously than unemployment. The more generous UI program, combined with a lack of commitment to low levels of unemployment, meant that by the mid-1970s, when the economic crisis took hold and unemployment mounted, the program came under unsustainable financial pressures (see chapter 6).

The new UI plan was further limited in the extent to which it incorporated notions of redistribution and equality. The proposals and subsequent legislation did clearly entail a redistribution – in particular, from the stably employed, including salaried workers and teachers, to the more intermittently employed, including women and resource workers.[135] Redistribution, however, was not explicitly discussed as one of the goals; rather, the emphasis was on the establishment of the structures 'to help each individual to make the highest and best use of the human capital embodied in him.'[136] While the proposals also contained for the first time provisions for regional variation in the length of benefits, this was not discussed in terms of income redistribution. On the contrary, where it was most clearly elaborated – in the 1968 report – it was assumed that high unemployment in any one region would be temporary and that the proposed system would actually reduce the regional redistributive effects of the UI program.[137]

With respect to women, while provisions were of overall benefit, the changes were certainly not introduced with the specific intention of allowing women greater equality or greater access to benefits. The gains, rather, were a consequence of the general expansionary trends in welfare state provisions in the late 1960s. Indeed, considerable suspicion remained about the nature of women's labour force activity and their ability to 'choose' whether to work. Essentially, the only response to the growing female contingent workforce was in terms of women potentially abusing the UI system. The 1971 legislation, like the 1968 report and the 1970 White Paper, was concerned about limiting access to UI for those without 'sufficient' attachment to the labour force. The end result was measures that although not explicitly discriminatory, were what later came to be described as 'discriminatory in effect.' All three of these documents proposed to restrict benefits to part-time workers. All three also distinguished between those with a 'major' attachment (twenty weeks or more of employment in the previous year) and those with a 'minor' attachment to the labour force (eight to nineteen weeks of employment in the previous year). A number of benefits, such as UI sickness and maternity benefits, the initial three-week lump-sum payment, and some additional weeks of 'extended' benefits, were available only to those with a 'major' labour force attachment.

The growing female contingent workforce was dealt with only through measures designed to contain potential abuses, yet the issue itself reflected a growing structural contradiction between the nature of the economy and labour force and the types of welfare state programs in place to support them. The model of income security that had been in place since the 1940s was based on the notion of a Fordist full-year, full-time worker, yet part-time and casual work had been growing in importance at least since the 1950s. In addition, there was a growing contradiction between a welfare state income security plan organized as if the labour force was male and the reality that work was increasingly being performed by a female labour force with other work/life patterns. A two-tier system, with one tier for those employed on a full-time, year-round basis, but experiencing short-term layoffs, and a second tier for those who did not have a major 'attachment' to the labour force, was not a major defining feature of the program at this point. Nevertheless, the trend was significant, both in terms of what was to become a widening structural contradiction and in terms of the response taken up much later by those instituting reforms in a more conservative direction.

Similarly, contradictions were also incorporated into the plan in that, while providing for more generous benefits, there was at the same time a continued concern with abuses. The notion of 'social engineering' involved submitting a claimant 'to an ever more intensive probing' to identify problems such as a lack of skills. While espousing an optimistic view of the possibility of rational planning, the proposals also involved a coercive element and a concern with intensifying control; these make it misleading to speak of a 'liberalization' of the UI program in this period. Furthermore, such measures, even in a period of low unemployment, could seem heavy-handed. In a period when unemployment was being allowed to rise to high levels, such measures ran the risk that monitoring might be conducted, not to better identify particular needs but rather to reduce the amount of benefits to be paid; and that as a result unemployed workers, especially those unemployed on a longer-term basis, might be harassed.

The reviews and reforms of the 1960s were especially significant, in that while providing an expanded welfare state in the short term, they also laid the groundwork for what was later to be a restructuring in a neoliberal direction. This was evident not only in the emphasis on dealing with economic problems by focusing on individual attributes and behaviour and other aspects of the supply side of the equation, but also in that it provided solutions to structural problems in ways that reinforced inequalities. In particular, the distinction between benefits for those with a 'major' and a 'minor' labour force attachment marked the beginning of a two-tier solution to demographic and economic changes. In addition, there was limited positive consideration of women's particular needs with respect, for example, to manpower planning and other programs that might affect their labour force participation. Differences were treated negatively, as a possible source of a drain on the system, rather than positively in the sense of the need to create special programs for women because of their particular situation and responsibilities.

In the thirty years since the UI Act had been introduced a substantially new regime involving a different family–market–state relationship had been established. The influx of women into the labour force meant that most families now had more than one income earner; furthermore, the nature of work had changed as women entering the labour market were concentrated in the growing service and public sectors, often in temporary or part-time positions. Overall, there was greater formal equality for women. That the state was playing a new and expanded role was visible not only in the 1971 UI amendments but also in the introduction in the 1960s of the core programs of the Canadian welfare state, including medicare, the Canada Pension Plan, the Guaranteed Income Supplement, and the Canada Assistance Plan. Some of the pressures within the postwar model had been addressed but other contradictions were growing more apparent, especially as the economic crisis developed and a restructuring of the welfare state became more necessary. The nature of these contradictions, the debates about possible directions for reform, and the solutions finally adopted are the subject of Part II.

# PART II

# On the Path to Neoliberalism:
# Gender, Crisis, and Restructuring

As noted in chapter 4, by the early 1970s a substantially new regime involving a restructured family–market–state relationship had been established. Some of the tensions in the larger network of variables had been at least partially resolved. For example, state benefits allowed for higher standards of living, and many explicitly discriminatory provisions had been removed, which eased some of the legal/juridical contradictions noted earlier. Women's labour force participation had grown, providing both more economic independence for women and increased family incomes. The new model, then, involved an expanded welfare state with modified family wage notions at its base and with links to an increasingly feminized service-sector workplace and to families where the norm was now to have more than one earner.

Some of the tensions had been resolved; others, however, were exacerbated, and as the model was put in place new pressures developed. The shift from Keynesianism to neoliberalism is often presented as an abrupt policy reversal; in fact, the establishment of neoliberalism as a hegemonic paradigm involved a long ideological and political struggle. The 1970s can be seen as a critical moment, *une époque charnière*: the old model had clearly reached its limits, and the new direction was very much open to contestation. Shifts in the regime involved not only changes in production and in the relationship between state and the economy, but also in social reproduction – in the division of responsibility between families, markets, and the state for such things as childrearing, caring activities, and health care. Shifting gender roles and new political forces were thus central to attempts to redefine the regime. Gender ideology, changes in women's work patterns and in family structures, and shifts in women's state entitlements and political activities were all important factors in the transition to a new economic and state form.

As the 1970s unfolded, a new complex of forces came to drive welfare state development. First, this period was shaped by the emerging economic crisis and by growing fiscal pressures on the state. With respect to UI, as noted earlier, this was partly due to the implementation of a more generous income security program at a time when unemployment was rising. The growth of the service sector and of a part-time, contingent workforce further increased pressures on state programs, which had assumed that Canadians would be working on a full-time, year-round basis. Finally, the growing internationalization of economic activity placed new constraints on the state while at the same time limiting the effectiveness of a model based on stimulating domestic demand.

Second, contradictions remained between women's new role in the labour force and the legal/juridical structures. Outright discrimination was now generally unacceptable, but other juridical barriers limited women's full participation in the labour force. This was especially the case with respect to pregnancy and maternity; consider here, for example, court rulings that discrimination on the basis of pregnancy did not constitute sex discrimination. Furthermore, contention developed over whether legislation could be considered 'discriminatory in effect' if it targeted not women but rather areas such as part-time work, where women predominated.

Third, the contradiction between state–market–family relations (or between production and social reproduction) was taking on new dimensions. The introduction of maternity benefits marked a recognition that women were now both mothers and workers; but the very partial and limited nature of these benefits meant that tensions remained both in women's ability to maintain workforce continuity and in their ability to adequately address the needs of social reproduction. This tension was felt by individual women (and was manifested in ongoing attempts to change the terms and conditions of these benefits), and more generally in terms of the structures of the workplace and home (manifested in high turnover rates, inadequacy of child care provisions, and so on).

Fourth, major changes in political forces were taking place. By the mid-1970s increasingly vocal forces were pushing for change in the direction of fiscal restraint, monetarism, free markets, welfare state retrenchment, and increased global competitiveness. This involved not only an ideological re-evaluation within traditional political parties and within the state, but also the emergence of new political voices, including the Fraser Institute and newly formed business lobby groups such as the Business Council on National Issues (BCNI).[1] By the 1990s the political terrain had shifted considerably, not only domestically with the creation of new political parties – most notably the Reform/Alliance – but also internationally. Forums such as the G7/G8 and trade agreements such as NAFTA and the WTO were playing an increasingly prominent role in setting policy agendas and promoting neoliberalism as a solution to the widespread economic, social, demographic, and other changes that were taking place.[2]

The period from the early 1970s to the late 1990s was also marked by the rise – and by the 1990s, the weakening – of women's advocacy inside and outside the state. In the 1970s and into the 1980s there had been a growing mobilization for women's rights. Especially critical had been the formation of the National Action Committee on the Status of Women (NAC) in 1971–2. The original intent of this group had been to lobby for the implementation of the recommendations of the Royal Commission on the Status of Women. Although there was some continuity between NAC and the earlier women's groups,[3] NAC drew under its umbrella and came to eclipse groups such as the BPW and the NCW, which in past decades had tended to be the voice for women in Ottawa. In addition, the Liberal government, after the Status of Women report was released, established a network of advisory positions within the state to represent women's interests. This network provided an avenue for women outside the state to raise concerns and complaints; it also played an important role in raising awareness of women's issues and in lobbying for change from within. The Women's Bureau of the Department of Labour had been established in the mid-1950s; women's advisors had also been appointed in a number of departments including Justice, Health and Welfare, Employment and Immigration, and the Secretary of State.[4] In 1973 the Canadian Advisory Council on the Status of Women (CACSW) was created, and given two broad responsibilities: to advise the federal government with respect to the status of women in Canada, and to inform the general public on 'matters of interest and concern to women.'[5] After the Canadian Human Rights Commission (CHRC) was established in 1978 and the Charter of Rights and Freedoms was introduced in 1982, further avenues opened up for individual women and women's groups to redress inequalities.

Finally, the labour movement was also changing. The growth of public sector unions and increases in their female membership meant that by the end of the 1970s, new issues were being raised and new demands formulated. As a result, by the late 1970s the sites of struggle both inside and outside the state with regard to women's issues had become numerous and the environment within which policy was determined had grown increasingly complex.

But by the 1990s this policy arena had shifted considerably. Funding for women's groups was reduced, beginning under the Conservatives in the late 1980s. NAC, undergoing internal changes and subject to external pressures, lost visibility as the national voice of Canadian women. The CACSW was closed in 1995. Within the state there was a shift away from special programs for women toward a less activist 'gender-based analysis.'[6] Finally, in policymaking circles, the Department of Finance with its connections to the international arena was assuming growing importance, while popular sector groups, despite a proliferation of consultations, were effectively losing influence. Overall, then, there was a shift in the balance of forces, with an international, market-driven agenda gaining greater prominence.

How these forces played out, leading eventually to the replacement of 'unemployment insurance' by 'employment insurance' and to the restructuring of one of the most important income security programs in Canada, will be explored in the next three chapters. Chapter 5 discusses the challenges to maternity, pregnancy, and equality as evidenced in the mobilization for improved maternity benefits and for a changed definition of sex discrimination between 1971 and 1983. Issues with respect to gender and social reproduction were critical to the redefinition of the regime. Chapter 6 focuses on the gender dimensions of the economic crisis and on the response to it in the 1970s as manifested through early attempts to restructure UI 'regular' benefits between 1975 and 1978. Chapter 7 discusses the laying of the groundwork for a new, market-oriented paradigm both at an ideological level and at a political level, and how this paradigm took hold by the end of the 1980s through a more substantial UI restructuring. Chapter 8 examines the Liberal government's far-reaching reforms in the 1990s. Overall, women have achieved greater formal equality and some improvement to maternity benefits, but this has been undermined by the massive downsizing of the UI program and by the entrenchment of a two-tier system that effectively excludes many women.

# Social Reproduction in a Transition Period: Maternity, Rights, and Conceptions of Equality

As noted in chapter 3, the maternity provisions incorporated in the 1971 legislation contained contradictory features. For first time, working women had access to rights-based benefits around childbirth. This represented a significant expansion of the state's responsibility for social reproduction and helped establish a new family–market–state relationship in which women were recognized as both workers and mothers. At the same time, however, the inclusion of maternity as part of the insurance-based UI program meant that concerns about abuses, about a possible drain on the fund, and about women meeting criteria that had been established with 'regular' workers in mind, remained central to the benefit scheme. Furthermore, despite the growing mobilization of women around a rights-based discourse, much of the legislation was framed according to notions from early in the century about maternal and child health and about pregnant women's capacity to work.

The contradictions and inadequacies of the UI maternity program became evident as soon as women attempted to make use of it. Women did, however, achieve some success in changing both the terms of the debate and specific program provisions. In particular, legal challenges questioned both notions of equality and the exclusion of women from regular UI benefits in the period around childbirth. Amendments introduced in 1983 significantly increased accessibility to maternity benefits, while overall amendments made the plan more consistent with a rights-based framework. These were important gains; even so, the extent of the reform was limited. The courts in this period ruled that discrimination on the basis of pregnancy did *not* constitute sex discrimination.

Only to a very limited extent did the state assume collective responsibility for issues around childbirth and childrearing. Some attempts were made to promote a more comprehensive maternity or parental plan that would be available to both men and women and separate from the UI program, but such a plan was never discussed in detail and was never on the state agenda in any serious way. Reforms, therefore, remained limited both by the context of the debate and by the maternity plan's location within the UI program. This became especially serious because retrenchments to the 'regular' UI program also applied to maternity benefits. The result was that though some of the anomalies were worked out, and though the program became based more on notions of women's rights than on maternal health, overall the provision of benefits to women around social reproduction remained tenuous. In this chapter I examine what the 1971 maternity provisions meant for women, the challenges that were mounted to these provisions, and, finally, how by 1983 both more accessible and rights-based benefits were incorporated into the UI Act.

## The 1971 Maternity Provisions: Implications for Women

The inclusion of maternity benefits as part of the UI program in 1971 resulted in a complex and convoluted set of regulations and requirements that incorporated conflicting concerns – not only to provide some sort of benefit but also to control abuses, maintain insurance principles, and to protect women and children in the period around childbirth. The maternity provisions were contained in Sections 30 and 46 of the act. (See Chart 5.1 for an outline of the maternity provisions and amendments.) Two provisions in particular were intended to address the concern that women were simply entering the labour force once pregnant in order to obtain benefits. The legislation specified that a woman had to be a 'major attachment' claimant with twenty weeks of insured employment rather than the eight required for regular benefits. In addition, to ensure that the woman was working at the time of conception, what became known as the 'magic ten' rule stated that ten of those weeks had to be between the fiftieth and the thirtieth week before her expected date of 'confinement.'

Other provisions specified that maternity benefits had to fall within the 'initial benefit period' – that is, the first eight to fifteen weeks of benefits. This meant that a woman who, for example, had been unemployed for a period of time and was collecting regular benefits could

Chart 5.1    Maternity Legislation and Amendments, 1971–83

| | | |
|---|---|---|
| 1971 | Bill C-229 | *Eligibility* |
| | | • 20 weeks insured employment during previous 52 |
| | | • 'Magic Ten': a minimum of 10 weeks worked between the 30th and the 50th week before the expected date of birth |
| | | • Benefits had to fall within the first 15-weeks of a claim |
| | | *Entitlement* |
| | | • 15 weeks of benefits |
| | | • Benefits had to be taken in the 15-week period starting 8 weeks before the expected week of birth and ending 6 weeks after the week of birth |
| | | *Section 46* |
| | | • Regular benefits could not be claimed in the 15-week period starting 8 weeks before the expected week of birth and ending 6 weeks after the week of birth |
| 1975 | Bill C-69 | • Those who had claimed some regular or sickness benefits and gone back to work for at least 20 weeks were able to voluntarily terminate their initial benefit period and establish a new maternity claim |
| 1975 | Bill C-16 | • Benefits could be drawn at any time between the 8th week before the expected week of birth and the 17th week after the expected week |
| 1983 | Bill C-156 | • Section 46 eliminated |
| | | • 'Magic Ten' eliminated |
| | | • Benefits could be paid at any time during a 25-week period, rather than in first 15 weeks only |
| | | • 15 weeks of benefits available for adoptive parents, either mother or father |

not then switch to maternity benefits. If the woman qualified, after a two-week waiting period she could receive fifteen weeks of maternity benefits. These benefits, however, had to be taken in the period eight weeks before the expected date of confinement, the week of confinement and six weeks after it. Section 46 specified that a claimant was not entitled to receive regular benefits in the period around childbirth, now defined as the fifteen weeks that started eight weeks before the expected week of confinement and that ended six weeks after the week of confinement. This meant that if a claimant did not qualify for maternity benefits, she also could not receive regular benefits during this period.

Questions about a number of these provisions had been raised as early as the hearings preceding the implementation of the 1971 legislation. For example, both Ed Broadbent and Stanley Knowles from the NDP suggested that rather than a rigid division of the benefit period into a set number of weeks before and after the birth, the timing of the fifteen weeks should be left to the discretion of the woman herself.[1] The UI Commission had some difficulty in explaining the rationale for this provision. It argued that this was the period in which it had already been established that women were not capable of or available for work, and that the maternity provisions simply waived this requirement and instead provided benefits for this same time period. When pressed further, it fell back on medical explanations, stating, for example, that the provision 'is intended to cover both sides of a particular event on the basis of the knowledge we have and medical experience has that this is a good thing to have before and after,' and that 'it is just a plain fact of life that some women should not work after so many months, you know, because of their awkwardness or whatever you want to call it.'[2]

Almost as soon as the legislation was implemented, individual women, women's groups, and women within the state pointed out that this very specific allocation of benefit weeks, which required that the bulk of the leave be taken before rather than after the birth, did not suit most women. The commission's position reflected the persistence of medical views about when women should stop work and societal views about when it was appropriate for pregnant women to withdraw from sight into the private sphere. Women themselves, however, pointed out that they generally felt better before the birth of the child than after, that often women needed more than six weeks to feel ready to return to work after childbirth,[3] and that besides, it was extremely difficult for women to breastfeed their infants if they had to return to work after six weeks.[4] Further problems arose for women whose babies arrived prematurely, or whose doctor did not accurately predict the date of birth; these women would be faced with a considerable reduction in benefits.[5] By extension, women whose babies arrived late would find that most of their fifteen weeks of benefits had already been used up.

A second provision of the act that made it difficult for many women to qualify for maternity benefits was the requirement that these benefits be taken in the 'initial benefit period.' For pregnant women, this meant that if they were already receiving regular benefits because they had been laid off (possibly because of pregnancy or a shortage of work), or if they had left their work early in their pregnancy due to illness and received sickness benefits, their maternity benefits were either greatly reduced or eliminated entirely.[6] Once they had used up fifteen weeks worth of benefits (whether regular, sickness, or maternity benefits, or some combination of these), they would no longer be in the initial benefit period and could not receive maternity benefits.[7]

The 'magic ten' rule that required women to have at least ten weeks of insured employment, or to be receiving UI benefits, between the fiftieth and thirtieth week prior to the expected date of confinement also greatly restricted women's access to benefits. Many women were disqualified because they were not able to prove they had these weeks. This included women who for any number of reasons had to look for work somewhat after the estimated time of conception; those who worked intermittently or were subject to periodic layoffs and who were not fortunate enough to have ten weeks of employment around the estimated time of conception; those who may have shown attachment to the labour force by working at the time of conception but who did not have ten weeks of *insured* employment;[8] and a number of teachers who worked regularly on contract from September to May and who were not eligible if the ten weeks around the time of conception occurred during the summer months.[9] The accuracy of the assessment as to the expected date of confinement also became critical. There were cases, for example, of women who were ineligible because they did not have enough weeks before the *expected* date of confinement, although they would have had the necessary weeks if those weeks had been calculated from the *actual* date of birth.[10]

There were other difficulties besides these. Many women found not only that they were ineligible for maternity benefits for one of the reasons noted above, but also that they were 'disentitled' from regular benefits for almost four months under Section 46 on the basis that they were not capable of or available for work during this period. The disqualification of women in the period around childbirth was no longer, as in pre-1971 cases, simply based on judicial precedent that could be altered by future umpire decisions; it had been placed on a statutory basis, with the term of disqualification lengthened to coincide with the period of maternity benefits. This meant that the disqualification period was defined as from eight weeks before the expected week of confinement until six weeks after the week of confinement. The umpire stated that the act was 'categorical' on this issue; thus, no matter what the situation, or what the medical evidence as to their availability or capacity for work, women who did not qualify for maternity benefits would be disentitled for those fifteen weeks around childbirth.[11] In addition, mothers attempting to claim regular benefits after the maternity benefits were over continued to have difficulties because they were expected to prove they had childcare arrangements. Finally, problems arose with the implementation of the UI Act in the case of adoptive parents. Many objections were raised about the fact that adoptive parents, even though they were usually required by adoption agencies to stay home for some six months, were ineligible for benefits.

## Challenges to the Maternity Leave Legislation

The Canadian political landscape of the 1970s was deeply marked by a surge of activity around women's issues. Women were more and more drawing on a rights-based discourse to challenge prevailing views about women in society and to demand changes on a range of specific policy fronts. In the case of maternity leave, complaints and challenges arose almost as soon as the 1971 provisions were introduced. Questions were raised in the legislature, especially by the NDP. Objections came from women's groups and from individual women both inside and outside the state. Cases were brought before the UI Umpire, the Federal Court of Appeal, and the Supreme Court of Canada. Labour bodies, within which women's participation continued to grow, also increasingly took up the issue.

### Early Challenges: Women within the State

Initially, it was women within the state who played the most critical role in raising awareness of the problems with the maternity leave legislation. As Vickers and colleagues describe it, in the early 1970s, notwithstanding the important role played by trade unionists Grace Hartman and Madeleine Parent, NAC was dominated by the liberal feminists who had pushed for the Royal Commission.[12] That organization was concerned primarily with overt discrimination and with issues such as equal pay, daycare, and law reform.[13] NAC would eventually play an important role in the maternity debate, but in the early 1970s it expressed little concern about the issue.

As noted earlier, in the 1970s a network of women's advisors was established within the state. Sue Findlay has argued that during those years women's representation within the state was constructed 'in a way that controlled women's demands and limited reforms.'[14] It was no doubt true that vis-à-vis a woman's movement impatient for change, the state as a whole seemed to put up considerable resistance to women's demands; nevertheless, the importance of the presence of a network of 'femocrats' within the state should not be underestimated. Through this network, to a much greater extent than before, women successfully placed women's issues on the agenda of the Canadian state. And in policy areas such as UI, the presence of women within the state pushing for equality of opportunity and opposing discriminatory measures did play an important role in bringing about changes that made a real difference to women's lives. With respect to UI in the early 1970s, the CACSW, women within the state, and the NDP at the legislative level took the lead in challenging discriminatory provisions.

One of the first aspects of the maternity program to be called into question was the division of the leave period into a set time before and after the birth. Individual women raised the issue with MPs and with the new women's and human rights advisors, arguing that the individual should be able to decide how the fifteen weeks should be allocated.[15] In March 1972 the NDP introduced a number of bills to liberalize the new UI plan, including one that would permit women applying for maternity benefits 'to decide how many of the 15 weeks of benefits to which they are entitled will be taken before confinement and how many afterwards.'[16] In 1974 the CACSW issued a report criticizing the requirement that benefits be taken in a set period before and after 'confinement,' the magic ten rule, and the eligibility requirement of twenty weeks employment.[17] The CACSW also launched an appeal to women's groups to urge passage of a number of bills, including one that would make the maternity leave period more flexible.

In 1975, following 'recommendations made by the Advisory Council on the Status of Women, many agencies and individuals,' the maternity leave provisions were amended so that women were able to draw the fifteen weeks of maternity benefits at any time beginning in the eighth week before the expected week of birth and ending with the seventeenth week after the week of birth.[18] In introducing the bill, Marc Lalonde, Minister of National Health and Welfare, noted that the amendment would 'permit women who prefer it this way, either for health or any other reason, to reserve most of their maternity leave for after the child is born.'[19] This not only vastly improved the benefit entitlement, but was important in that the terms of debate had been redefined. It was no longer simply a question of 'expert' evaluations of women's physical capacities. Rather, the debate now centred around women's right to control their own lives and to themselves determine the best time to take leave.

A second aspect of the program that was called into question early on was the requirement that when claiming regular benefits, women – but not men – with young children had to prove they had childcare arrangements. Here, again, women in advisory positions within the state played a critical role. In 1973, for example, both Sylva Gelber of the Women's Bureau and Martha Hynna, the Coordinator of the Status of Women in the Privy Council Office, raised the issue.[20] While the UI Commission firmly maintained that the greater domestic responsibilities of new mothers made it reasonable to require evidence of childcare arrangements as proof of availability for employment,[21] Hynna pointed out that the practice was discriminatory.[22] She further argued that it was unreasonable to expect women to make babysitting arrangements before they had actually been offered a job, or had an income to pay for those arrangements:[23]

> In my opinion until people stop making assumptions that women with children are *not* available for work there will continue to be discrimination against women in employment ... The Unemployment Insurance Commission does not demand of every one applying for benefits that they indicate their personal circumstances, ie, whether they have children, whether they have dependant parents at home, whether they have a spouse who is attending university or even whether their spouse is working ... Why, just because a claimant is a woman who has a child should they assume that she is not available for work?[24]

The solution that the UIC arrived at in 1975 was to demand that *both* men and women prove childcare arrangements.[25] A UIC internal bulletin in April 1975 stated that the requirement to prove childcare arrangements applied 'equally to the male spouse or single male parent' as to the female.[26] Nevertheless, a survey of UIC staff two years later found that 'female claimants were invariably questioned regarding domestic obligations (e.g. childcare) while male claimants were not.' It was suggested that either staff might not have been aware of the new guidelines or that they might have had 'inhibitions which make it difficult for them to question male claimants regarding domestic responsibilities and childcare obligations, especially when this involves face to face interviews.'[27] Women's representatives at a variety of levels made repeated attempts to bring attention to the problems the childcare requirement posed for women trying to qualify for UI. In September 1976, for example, the CACSW recommended that 'a simple statement by a claimant that suitable child care arrangements have or can be made should suffice for UIC requirements of a claimant's availability for work. It is unrealistic to expect persons to have made firm commitments without a firm job offer, since it is in many cases financially unfeasible to have day care unless a person is employed.'[28] The following year the CACSW again protested the practice of questioning women in detail about childcare arrangements, which included requiring them to submit the names and addresses of babysitters, or Manpower asking them 'to appear within hours or less for job interviews.'[29]

In 1976 the CACSW, based on a study by Elsie Robindaine-Saumure, provided a comprehensive analysis of the maternity provisions and recommended extensive changes to the maternity leave program.[30] Besides recommending changes with respect to required childcare arrangements, the council urged that the two-week waiting period be eliminated and that the UI Act be amended to allow employers to top up maternity benefits to the level of the employee's regular salary. It also recommended that consideration be given to a special maternity or parental allowance for women who are not in the paid labour force (and therefore not eligible for UI).[31] The council further recommended that fifteen weeks of benefits be extended to adoptive parents. It also expressed concern that 'by and large, pregnancy is still looked upon as an illness, parenting is still considered a maternal responsibility rather than a parental one, and the economic contribution of the homemaker is not recognized.'[32] Robindaine-Saumure noted the contradictory attitudes toward pregnant working women:

According to employers – and they might be right – the public would feel uncomfortable when confronted by a waitress, salesgirl or secretary whose swollen stomach leaves no doubt as to her condition. However, in beauty parlors where customers are exclusively female, there is no sign of malaise at the sight of pregnant hairdressers who spend long hours on their feet, handling dye and sprays that are sometimes toxic ... Are these reservations regarding pregnant women who work during the final months of their pregnancies only the result of a desire to protect them against themselves, even when these women insist they feel fine? Or are they the result of deep-rooted atavistic thinking, which impels people to protect not so much the health of the mother but rather the life of the child she is bearing? Isn't it possible to detect a residue of puritanism behind the facade of these undeniably noble sentiments? Is pregnancy an obscene phenomenon to be hidden from sight by strictly confining future mothers to their homes?[33]

Thus, the CACSW as well as women's advisors within the state played an important role in challenging conceptions of pregnancy and maternity, whether pregnant women should be confined to the private sphere, and the extent to which mothers can or should participate in the labour market. They also pointed to discriminatory practices and suggested important amendments to improve maternity leave provisions.

## Pregnancy, Equality, and Court Challenges

The 1970s also saw an unprecedented extension of challenges concerning pregnancy, maternity, and sexual equality to the level of the courts. As discussed earlier, individual women and union locals had been taking cases before the umpire since the 1940s; by the late 1970s the Bill of Rights, human rights legislation, and, by the 1980s, the Charter were all being used to challenge conceptions of equality and to assert rights with respect to pregnancy and parental care. In addition, for the first time, women's organizations had become major actors.

Challenges invoking the Bill of Rights initially focused on Section 46, which prohibited women who did not qualify for maternity benefits from receiving regular benefits for a period from eight weeks before the expected date of birth until six weeks after. Insurance officers for a long time had followed the practice of disqualifying women for a number of weeks around childbirth; but after 1971 that disqualification was placed on a statutory basis. In 1975 a case came before the umpire involving a woman who had been laid off and was collecting regular benefits. She was disentitled from benefits from eight weeks before the expected date of confinement until six weeks after the birth, on the basis that she had passed the initial benefit period and was therefore not eligible for maternity benefits.[34] The commission also stated that she was not eligible for any other benefits in the period around childbirth. She argued that she never at any time had applied for maternity benefits, yet the UI Commission took the view that her rights must be determined on the basis of her pregnancy. The woman appealed to the umpire, citing the Bill of Rights to argue that Section 46 discriminated against women by reason of their sex. The umpire disagreed, ruling that 'if there is discrimination in Section 46 (and I am not convinced there is) it is not discrimination by reason of sex, it is discrimination only among members of the same sex. In that situation, I do not think the Canadian Bill of Rights has any application.'[35]

A few years later the validity of this section was again challenged. This case reached the Supreme Court of Canada. It involved Stella Bliss, a clerical worker in Vancouver. When she was about seven months pregnant she was fired from her job because of pregnancy. She applied for UI but was told she did not qualify for maternity benefits because she did not have the 'magic ten' weeks of employment around the time of conception; furthermore, she was disqualified from other benefits because of Section 46. She then lodged a complaint with the B.C. Human Rights Commission regarding the termination of her employment. As a result she was reinstated, and worked until four days before her child was born. Six days after the birth she again applied for UI. The commission agreed that she was capable of and available for work and unable to obtain suitable employment, but added that Section 46 was an absolute prohibition: 'Even though the claimant has proved herself capable of and available for work (except for a few days) during the six weeks after the week of delivery, the section bars any payments.'[36]

When the Board of Referees rejected her appeal, she launched a further appeal to the umpire.[37] Bliss, now represented by the Service Office and Retail Workers' Union (SORWUC), argued that Section 46 contravened the Canadian Bill of Rights and constituted discrimination on the basis of sex (males were obviously not affected). She further argued that it constituted discrimination among classes of the same sex, since the 'available and capable' pregnant (or post-pregnant) female was forbidden benefits whereas a 'non-pregnant' female was not. Finally, she argued that Section 46 created 'inequality before the law, or deprives individuals such as the claimant of due process of the law.'[38] This time the umpire accepted the argument that Section 46 constituted sex discrimination and that it denied certain women equality before the law:[39]

[Section 46] plainly denies benefits to certain claimants, who might otherwise be covered by the entitlement provisions, even though those claimants prove themselves separated from employment, capable of and available for work, but unable to obtain suitable employment. The denial is predicated, firstly, on the biological difference between the sexes. The section then goes further and differentiates between pregnant women, others who have recently given birth, and those women who do not fall within those descriptions.[40]

The UI Commission appealed the decision to the Federal Court of Appeal, which overturned the umpire's decision. Mr Justice Pratte, writing the decision for the Federal Court in June 1977, argued that Section 46 did *not* constitute discrimination on the basis of sex: 'Assuming the respondent to have been 'discriminated against,' it would not have been by reason of her sex ... If section 46 treats unemployed pregnant women differently from other unemployed persons, be they male or female, it is, it seems to me, because they are pregnant and not because they are women.'[41] Pratte's argument was in keeping with U.S. Supreme Court rulings in 1974 and 1976 that exclusion of pregnancy from income protection insurance did not constitute discrimination on the basis of sex and therefore that pregnancy-related conditions could be excluded from disability plans.[42] Pratte, however, also argued that the Canadian Bill of Rights itself did not expressly prohibit discrimination and that the real question to be determined was whether Bliss had been deprived of 'the right to equality before the law' as declared by s. 1(b) of the bill.[43]

Pratte argued, first, that Section 46 did not contravene equality before the law in the sense of 'equality in the administration or application of the law,' which was the interpretation of the phrase that Justice Ritchie had given in an earlier decision, *A.G. Canada v. Lavell*. Second, however, he offered a 'wider' interpretation of 'equality before the law.' He argued that this expression did not mean 'that all persons must have, under all statutes, exactly the same rights and obligations.'[44] Rather, the right to equality before the law should be determined according to whether the distinction between persons made in the statute is 'relevant' or 'irrelevant.'[45] He suggested that Section 46 was based on a relevant distinction – specifically that unemployment caused by pregnancy was different from other types of unemployment because it is 'usually the result of a voluntary act,' and moreover, that 'Parliament possibly considered it desirable that pregnant women refrain from work for 14 weeks on the occasion of their confinement.'[46] He also argued that Section 46 had to be read with Section 30 and other provisions of the act. Since Parliament had created a new kind of benefit in favour of pregnant women, it was reasonable for it to determine the conditions according to which it would be payable. Finally, he argued that the maternity legislation was 'enacted for the purpose of achieving a valid federal objective.'[47] Pratte did not specify what exactly he meant by this, although one interpretation is that the 'federal objective' was considered 'valid' because it was thought to be 'beneficial' – that is, part of a scheme to provide special maternity benefits.[48] Another interpretation suggests that the phrase referred to the division of powers in the BNA Act and that an objective was 'valid' if it was within the federal area of jurisdiction.[49] For all the above reasons, Pratte stated that Section 46 did not contravene the Canadian Bill of Rights.

In 1978 the case went to the Supreme Court of Canada. By this point a range of women's and labour organizations, including SORWUC, the Vancouver Status of Women, the B.C. Federation of Women, the B.C. Government Employee's Union, and the B.C. Federation of Labour, as well as a group of activist lawyers, had become actively involved in supporting and funding *Bliss*.[50] Representatives of women and women's organizations at a national level had also taken up the issue. In June 1977 the CACSW issued a recommendation that women not be automatically disentitled from regular benefits under Section 46.[51] NAC, which had also begun to look at the issue of UI and maternity benefits, passed resolutions at its March 1977 annual meeting calling for the deletion of the 'magic 10' requirements.[52]

In October 1978 the Supreme Court, in a 7 to 0 ruling, upheld the Federal Court decision that Section 46 did not discriminate on the basis of sex and did not deny women equality before the law.[53] Justice Ritchie, who delivered the judgment, followed Pratte in arguing that Section 46 had to be understood in conjunction with Section 30, which provided special benefits to pregnant women. Section 46, he argued, simply constituted a 'limitation of entitlement' with regard to these special benefits. Furthermore, he argued, Parliament was fulfilling a necessary role in prescribing these conditions of entitlement, and 'the fact that this involved treating claimants who fulfill the conditions differently from those who do not, cannot, in my opinion, be said to invalidate such legislation.'[54]

Ritchie went on to distinguish this case from the Supreme Court ruling in *Drybones*, where the Supreme Court had ruled that a section of the Indian Act involving 'intoxication off a reserve' and applicable only to Indians was contrary to the Canadian Bill of Rights:

There is a wide difference between legislation which treats one section of the population more harshly than all others by reason of race as in the case of *Regina v Drybones* ... and the legislation providing additional benefits to one class of woman, specifying the conditions which entitle a claimant to such benefits and defining a period during which no benefits are available. The one case involves the imposition of a penalty on a racial group to which other citizens are not subjected; the other involves a definition of the qualifications required for entitlement to benefits, and in my view, the enforcement of the limitation provided by s.46 does not involve denial of equality of treatment in the administration and enforcement of the law before the ordinary courts of the land as was the case in *Drybones*.[55]

In addition, Ritchie concurred with Pratte in arguing that Section 46 was valid because it was based on a 'relevant' distinction – in particular, on the pre-1971 assumption that 'women eight weeks before giving birth and for six weeks after, were, generally speaking, not capable of nor available for work.' He also reiterated the argument that if Section 46 treats unemployed pregnant women differently from others it is 'because they are pregnant and not because they are women'; he added further that 'any inequality between the sexes in this area is not created by legislation but by nature.'[56]

*Bliss* was significant because it indicated a considerable shift in the nature and terrain of struggles, not only with respect to the maternity question but more generally in terms of women's equality issues. Women and women's groups were making much more forcefully a rights-based argument for greater equality of treatment based on the view that women in the period around childbirth who were 'available and capable' had the right to welfare state benefits on the same basis as both men and women who were not pregnant. In doing so, they were also challenging the view that women did not belong in the public sphere in the period around childbirth. Furthermore, they were drawing more clearly the links between women's reproductive role and the conditions for gender equality.

On the other hand, despite some shift in thinking among some umpire judges, the section of the state represented by the upper-level courts (the Federal Court and the Supreme Court) continued to uphold the notion that pregnancy was a voluntary act and a private matter; the implication here was that women should bear responsibility for their actions instead of relying on state benefits, and that for reasons possibly of maternal 'protection' as well as what was considered 'seemly,' women did not belong in the labour force for the three or four months around childbirth. *Bliss* also raised the larger question of what constitutes equality or equal treatment and what constitutes discrimination. The argument being made was that while racial discrimination (as in *Drybones*) was unacceptable, differential treatment or discrimination in access to welfare state benefits could be accepted. The rulings suggested that benefits for pregnant women were not a right, based on participation in the labour force and contributions to a plan, so much as they were an act of charity. Moreover, the judges denied any link between inequality in income or access to income support and other forms of inequality. In addition, the judges were severing the association between the pregnant condition and that of being a woman; in doing so they were denying that the unfair treatment of pregnant women had ramifications for the larger group 'women,' while at the same time implicitly accepting it, in suggesting that there was a 'natural' sexual difference and inequality in this regard. Finally, the judges were putting forward the dangerous argument that if inequalities were based on 'nature' then they were acceptable, and that the legislation was simply a reflection of a 'natural' sexual division of labour. This obscured the extent to which women's biological role is socially constructed and that one's responses, and the social institutions and practices created to deal with pregnancy, are critical in determining the role women play, the extent to which they belong in the public sphere, and the extent to which they have access to welfare state entitlements. The judges were suggesting that one can distinguish in a judicially neutral way between a 'relevant' and an 'irrelevant' distinction, yet this too ignored that such distinctions are products of social relations and are institutionalized through public policies, which themselves reflect both the prevailing ideology and the strength of various forces at a particular period, which are subject to change.

Pal and Morton argue that though Bliss lost her case, her effort did much to increase pressure for changes both in the maternity legislation and in the equality clauses of the proposed new Charter of Rights and Freedoms.[57] I do not go so far as to say, as Pal and Morton do, that 'Bliss's 1978 legal defeat was completely neutralized through spectacular victories in the political arena by groups that took up her cause,'[58] but it was certainly true that the Supreme Court decision was out of step with the times. After *Bliss*, the government faced renewed pressure to change the relevant legislation and eventually women did achieve important victories, especially – as will be discussed later – with respect to maternity legislation.

## Challenges on Many Fronts

Sandra Burt has argued that during the 1970s the policy environment with respect to women's issues evolved from one that was 'state directed' to one of 'pressure pluralism,' characterized by a fragmentation both of agencies responsible for women's issues within the state and of women's groups attempting to influence state policy.[59] In keeping with this argument, by the late 1970s the leading forces challenging state policies on maternity had increasingly shifted from women within the state to a range of groups, especially women's and labour organizations. These groups not only opposed the discriminatory features of the UI program but also challenged traditional notions of pregnancy and maternity. The view was increasingly being promoted that child bearing and rearing was a social and not simply an individual or familial responsibility, that women should not pay a financial penalty for their maternal role, and that achieving equality for women was contingent on adequate maternity provisions. The increasing pressure from a range of sources, and the growing links between them, ultimately succeeded in bringing improvements and greater flexibility to maternity policy.

*Women's Organizations*

As the 1970s progressed, women's organizations outside the state became increasingly active in pushing for changes to UI maternity provisions. The CACSW, as noted earlier, continued to recommend changes to the maternity program. NAC also increasingly turned its attention to employment issues, including both UI and maternity. As Vickers and colleagues point out, the election of Marjorie Cohen, Laurell Ritchie, and Lynn Kaye to NAC's executive in 1977 meant that for the first time that organization had a strong left-wing voice.[60] Proposals from NAC's 1977 annual meeting included the following: that the 'magic 10' requirement be deleted, that benefits be extended to adoptive parents, and that either the mother or the father be eligible for benefits at the birth of a child.[61]

In March 1978 NAC presented a brief to the Canadian government in which, among other things, it objected to the disqualification of women from regular benefits in the period around childbirth and to the provisions that meant a pregnant woman's eligibility depended on her employment status at the date of conception. NAC further contended that the two-week waiting period was 'wholly inappropriate,' and objected to the requirement that women have 'firm and regular babysitting arrangements' in order to qualify for benefits. It noted that the latter was especially unreasonable for women earning minimal wages before being unemployed and that 'few women who are not working can maintain the luxury of unnecessary babysitting.'[62] Again, it was significant that at this time NAC was making proposals for a more comprehensive maternity leave program: 'The more basic problem, of course, is that maternity is not a form of unemployment. We need a proper system of maternity leave, as most European countries have. It would, desirably, include full pay for a period of maternity leave, and the possibility of longer leave without pay but with the option of returning to work without loss of seniority or the accumulation of pension credits and other fringe benefits.'[63]

While NAC seemed to concur with the judges and the UI Commission's assertions that maternity is not a form of unemployment, its arguments were very different. The judges in *Bliss* were using notions of women's condition during pregnancy to deny to women who *were* available and looking for work – that is, who *were* unemployed according to the standard definition – the right to draw unemployment benefits. In contrast, women's groups argued that women should have the right to equal treatment in access to regular UI benefits. NAC was pointing out that *also* needed was a specific program that would recognize women's particular needs with respect to maternity, and that their needs were different from the needs of those who were unemployed in the usual sense.

The following year, NAC reiterated a number of its recommendations and also expanded on them. Specifically, it was now also recommending that benefits not be restricted to the initial benefit period (with the note that this was 'particularly discriminatory in a period of high unemployment when many women have collected regular benefits previously as the result of layoff'), and that female employees be able to receive maternity benefits during labour disputes.[64] NAC also suggested a detailed alternative to maternity benefits. Ideally, it suggested, the government should establish a support system for paid maternity leave *outside* the UI system and increase the maximum period of benefits to twenty-two weeks. It also recommended a paternity leave at the time of birth and parental leave during the first two years after birth. In addition, NAC argued that three months of employment in the preceding twelve were all that should be required to qualify for maternity leave protections, and that these protections should include regulations prohibiting discrimination and refusal of promotion as a result of pregnancy.[65]

*Continued Legal Challenges*

In 1978 the Canadian Human Rights Commission was established. The CACSW and NAC had lobbied for this, and its creation provided an additional avenue for mounting challenges to the UI maternity provisions. In its first year of operation the CHRC received six complaints that Sections 30 and 46 of the UI Act discriminated on the basis of sex.[66] In November 1978 the same commission expressed concern about 'the economic penalties suffered by certain women' who were attempting to combine work and childbearing. It recommended repealing Section 46, the 'magic ten' requirement, and the requirement that maternity benefits be taken in the initial fifteen weeks of the benefit period.[67] Over the next five years the commission in its annual report repeatedly pointed to the discriminatory nature of these provisions. In 1979 the commission received complaints not only that regular or maternity benefits were being denied but also that female UI applicants were being subjected to searching personal questions about childcare and breastfeeding, were being demoted after becoming pregnant, and were being forced to cease work early in pregnancy.[68] In its 1980 report the CHRC highlighted maternity leave as an issue involving 'long-standing concerns.'[69] This report was significant not only because it pointed to discriminatory practices but also because it questioned whether maternity was solely an individual or familial responsibility and suggested that the 'economic and social costs related to child bearing and rearing' should not be borne solely by parents, but also by the state.[70] It noted that some working women 'are forced to pay a price for childbearing that is not required of people whose working life is interrupted for other reasons.'[71] It questioned whether maternity benefits should require a longer qualifying period than regular benefits, and it wondered why pregnant women not qualifying for maternity benefits were unable to claim regular benefits around childbirth. The commission also suggested that women be allowed to use sickness or disability benefits when they are medically unable to work because of pregnancy or childbirth. It also argued that the leave period that related to the child's need for care (rather than the medical situation of the mother) should be available to *either* the male or female parent, and to adoptive as well as natural parents. In 1981 the commission noted that 'the vital career building years (20s and 30s) overlap and conflict with a woman's ideal reproductive period.'[72] Furthermore, 'society cannot continue without children and must protect the health and wellbeing of the working woman and her child by guaranteeing the woman's right to obtain and keep employment. If women are to gain employment equality with men – they must not be penalized for child-bearing.'[73]

In its 1982 report the CHRC again raised concerns about the UI Act – in particular, that the 'legislation requires changes in relation to pregnant claimants, adoptive parents, fathers, and women who bear children during a strike.'[74] The commission was thus in the forefront in calling for a revised conception of responsibility for child bearing and rearing and linking these explicitly to women's equality.

Yet none of this was reflected in the cases that continued to be brought before the UI Umpire and the higher courts; both continued to support the position – put forward in *Bliss* – that discrimination based on pregnancy did not constitute sex discrimination. In June 1980 arguments were brought before the umpire that the maternity leave provisions contravened not only the Canadian Bill of Rights but also the new human rights legislation. This time, in a case brought by the Canadian Textile and Chemical Union, the focus was on the requirement of ten weeks' work at the time of conception. It was argued that this contravened the Bill of Rights because it required additional conditions not required for other special benefits (such as for sickness); that *Bliss* did not apply since it dealt only with Section 46; and that the CHRC considered that discrimination based on sex included discrimination because of pregnancy.[75] The umpire, however, argued that *Bliss* also applied to this situation, and dismissed the appeal.

Another case that reached the Federal Court of Appeal in 1982 involved a woman hospitalized for acute appendicitis, who was denied UI sickness benefits because she was pregnant and had fallen ill within the eight weeks prior to her date of confinement. She also was not eligible for maternity benefits – which she had not, in any event, applied for – because she only had seven instead of the necessary 'magic ten' weeks of employment. Here the umpire questioned whether women should be defined above all by their reproductive role and specifically whether the fact of pregnancy should determine a woman's eligibility for any benefits: 'It appears that the [UI] Commission policy is that if a married woman who is ill with any ailment becomes pregnant the commission will only consider a claim for pregnancy benefit. I have searched the *Act* for Regulations and can find no justification of any kind for such a policy.'[76] This decision was, however, overturned by the Federal Court of Appeal, which ruled that *Bliss* applied here as well. Again, it stated categorically that 'the only benefits to which a pregnant claimant is entitled during the relevant period are maternity benefits' and that 'she cannot claim the regular benefits to which she would otherwise be entitled because of her illness, if she were not pregnant.'[77]

Finally, the maternity issue arose in discussions about the proposed new Charter of Rights and Freedoms, which by the early 1980s was at the top of the federal government's agenda. In an attempt to prevent a ruling such as *Bliss* from occurring again, and to ensure stronger equality guarantees for women in the law, both NAC and the CACSW, as well as the National Association of Women and the Law (NAWL), focused considerable attention on the proposed wording of the new Charter.[78] For example, both the CACSW and NAC emphasized the inadequacy of the clause 'equality before the law,' arguing that what was needed was a stronger statement that the law *itself* must not be discriminatory.[79] NAC also argued that it needed to be spelled out clearly that discrimination on the basis of sex is proscribed whether the law discriminates against all women or only some of them.[80] It also urged that equality be seen as a positive objective – one that would allow, for example, the establishment of affirmative action programs,[81] and that might require consideration of differences in the life patterns of men and women.[82] The CACSW, pointing out that many differences are culturally imposed, also challenged the notion that differences between men and women are 'natural' and that it is 'reasonable' to have laws based on this distinction: 'The fact that there may be some biological differences between men and women should not make reasonable all distinctions imposed in the law or even most of them.'[83]

Women's groups ultimately succeeded in having the equality provisions of the Charter strengthened. At first, the wording had followed that in the Bill of Rights; however, after extensive lobbying it was revised to closely follow the CACSW's recommendations. This included renaming the revised Section 15 'equality rights' (rather than 'non-discrimination rights') and reinforcing the 'equality before the law' clause with two additional guarantees of 'equality under the law' and 'equal protection and benefit of the law.'[84] In addition, after the 'notwithstanding clause' was introduced into the Charter, feminists succeeded in having Section 28 added: 'notwithstanding anything in this Charter, the rights and freedoms referred to in it are guaranteed equally to male and female persons.' Even after the Charter, however, *Bliss* continued to be cited as a basis for ruling that discrimination on the basis of pregnancy did not constitute sex discrimination and that pregnant women could therefore be excluded from group disability benefits.[85] It was not until 1989 that the Supreme Court overturned *Bliss*, stating clearly that 'discrimination on the basis of pregnancy is discrimination on the basis of sex.'[86]

*Labour Organizations*

By the end of the 1970s the face of the labour movement had changed. More and more women were entering the labour force, becoming active union members, and beginning to articulate demands around women's issues. Paid maternity leave became a key issue in a number of unions in which women made up a large proportion of the workforce; it also became an important component in a series of public sector strikes. Indeed, in this period the trade union movement was in the forefront in challenging prevailing views of responsibility for social reproduction and in winning concrete gains relating to maternity and parental leave. In this respect a breakthrough was achieved in 1979 when Quebec public sector workers, organized as the Common Front, won an agreement that included twenty weeks of maternity leave at full pay, with the employer supplementing the fifteen weeks of UI and paying fully for the other five. The agreement also provided ten weeks' paid adoption leave for a father or mother, ten weeks' paid leave for pregnant women not eligible for UI but with twenty weeks of service, five days' paid paternity leave at the birth of a child, and two years' unpaid childcare leave for the father or mother. Accumulation of seniority and benefits during the leave, and the right of a pregnant woman whose work involved health risks to be transferred to a safe job (or, if that was not possible, to receive workers' compensation at 90 per cent of usual pay), were also part of the agreement.[87]

In 1980, paid maternity leave was also a key issue during a strike of federal government translators.[88] Although they did not win the strike, their effort provided momentum for the Canadian Union of Postal Workers' (CUPW) negotiations and strike the following year. A key demand in the CUPW strike was for paid maternity leave.[89] After a forty-two-day strike and considerable opposition from the employer, CUPW succeeded in achieving seventeen weeks' maternity leave at full pay (a top-up of UI benefits for fifteen weeks plus full payment for the two-week waiting period) as well as the inclusion of the maternity leave period in the calculation of benefits such as severance pay.[90] The provision of paid maternity leave soon spread throughout the public and para-public sectors.

The CUPW strike was important not only in terms of the concrete benefits that were won, but also in bringing the debate about maternity leave into the public arena and forcing a more general discussion of the issue. CUPW articulated – perhaps even more clearly than the women's organizations had done up to that point – the notion of maternity leave as a social right and a social responsibility. It argued that women should not have to suffer a financial penalty for bearing children, that equality for women was fundamentally tied to and contingent on adequate maternity-related provisions, and that maternity leave must be seen within 'the context of a broader struggle to achieve equality for women in all aspects of the work force.'[91] Furthermore, it argued that lack of adequate paternity leave 'serves to reinforce sex stereotyping and inequality by placing the major social and family responsibilities which accompany childbirth on the shoulders of the mothers.'[92] CUPW also pointed out how irrational it was to oppose maternity benefits when the cost involved was minimal, and suggested that the root of the opposition 'lies in a system – political, social and economic – that fosters sexist attitudes and exploitation of women for profit.'[93]

Jean-Claude Parrot, CUPW's president, argued that although collective bargaining had provided 'the impetus for putting paid maternity leave on the public agenda, it is not the whole answer,'[94] given the small proportion of working women who are covered by such agreements, and given that links needed to be made between workplace struggles and gains in the political arena:

> What is needed in this country to end the discrimination faced by pregnant working women is new legislation to provide a program of benefits which represents the workers' full wage while taking maternity leave. Spread among all employers in the country, the cost of providing this kind of universal maternity leave benefit is minimal. Once such a plan is in place, there would be no further excuse to discriminate against the hiring or promotion of female employees out of consideration for maternity leave costs.[95]

## Amendments to the UI Maternity Provisions

From the mid to late 1970s a series of amendments to the UI program initiated a process of retrenchment and restructuring in what ultimately was to be a neoliberal direction. It was in this context that demands were formulated to expand and reform the maternity leave program.

After the Supreme Court decision in *Bliss*, Bud Cullen, the Minister of Employment and Immigration, had announced there would be a review of maternity benefits; but little was done on the issue until the early 1980s.[96] Indeed, in the context of restructuring, maternity benefits, far from becoming more accessible, became less so. (For example, a 1979 amendment – discussed in chapter 6 – requiring at least twenty hours of work a week in order for that week to be considered insured employment made the 'magic 10' rule all the more difficult to satisfy.)[97] In July 1980 the Liberals, back in power after a brief interlude of Conservative rule, established a task force in the Department of Employment and Immigration to review the UI program. Among the issues it addressed were the terms and conditions of maternity benefits.[98] While the overall thrust of the task force's report was to develop policies 'consistent with a growing concern for government spending restraint,' it also acknowledged the increasing demands with respect to women's rights and recommended a number of changes, including in maternity provisions.[99]

The report noted that the initial rationale for maternity benefits was related to the mother's 'physical incapacity to work or look for work in the weeks surrounding the birth,'[100] but that since 1975 maternity benefits had been paid on a more flexible basis, and that more and more women were taking virtually all their benefits after the birth in order to take care of their child.[101] If maternity benefits were not related solely to physical incapacity, there was no longer a rationale for excluding adoptive parents from coverage or for disentitling women from regular benefits in the period around childbirth. The report therefore recommended extending benefits to adoptive parents and removing Section 46, but also requiring the claimant to prove either that she was capable and available for work (in order to receive regular benefits) or that she was incapable (in order to receive sickness benefits).[102]

The report also questioned the rationale for the 'magic 10' requirement, which had been introduced on the grounds that it established a work attachment or insurable interest at the time of conception. The report now noted that the rule probably did little to prevent program abuses, and pointed out that women with strong work records could be unfairly refused maternity benefits if they happened not to satisfy this requirement. Furthermore, extending maternity benefits to adoptive parents would make the 'magic ten' rule inappropriate. The report also recommended removing the rule that maternity benefits had to be taken in the first fifteen weeks of benefits. The report did not support waiving the two-week waiting period for maternity claimants, arguing that this would be inequitable to other claimants who *were* required to wait this period; also, it would create administrative difficulties, add to program costs, and 'create a precedent which would contribute pressure to waive it in other circumstances.'[103]

In June 1983, as part of Bill C-156, amendments were introduced to the UI maternity provisions, effective January 1984. These included the elimination of Section 46. Thus, even though the courts had rejected the claim that a denial of benefits in the period around childbirth constituted sex discrimination, some six years later, legislative changes removed the offending section. This, in effect, extended to women greater equality of treatment. The amendments also eliminated the 'magic ten' rule. They also allowed benefits to be paid at any time during a twenty-five-week period – in other words, they were no longer restricted to the first fifteen weeks of a claim. Finally, the amendments provided for benefits of up to fifteen weeks for adoptive parents, either the mother or father. The twenty-week entrance requirement and the two-week waiting period were kept in place. Lloyd Axworthy, Minister of Employment and Immigration, in introducing these changes, noted that they reflected women's changed workforce status: 'Women are no longer simply secondary workers ... but full-time workers, and therefore, must be recognized as such under the Unemployment Insurance Act.' He also noted that sections of the maternity provisions had been recognized as inequitable and that both the CHRC and women's organizations had made that clear.[104]

## Conclusion

We saw in chapter 3 that the combination of a growing influx of women into the labour force, pressures from individual women working out strategies for financial survival and making claims to UI adjudicators, the general expansionary climate, and growing mobilization for women's rights resulted in the 1971 implementation of maternity benefits for women. By the 1970s, then, both the state–family–market nexus and the wider ensemble of variables defining the regime had shifted considerably. This included the recognition that to some extent social reproduction and maternity needs had to be addressed by state programs in order to accommodate both the influx of women into the labour force and the new workplace structures.

During the 1970s women presented three major challenges to the maternity provisions as they had been instituted in 1971. First, women demanded greater flexibility in when they could take their leave; in doing so they were challenging the underlying rationale which suggested that the leave should be based on maternal protection and on the need for women to withdraw from the public sphere and the workplace for a certain period around childbirth. Second, they questioned the requirement of proving that they had worked for a certain period around the date of conception; here they were challenging the notion that women did not have a significant attachment to the labour force and were attempting to abuse the UI system by entering the workforce simply in order to obtain benefits. Third, they demanded that women who did not qualify for maternity benefits should not automatically be excluded from eligibility for regular benefits. This challenged the view that women should not be seen and were not capable of work during advanced stages of pregnancy; it also asserted the right to equal treatment in access to regular benefits. In presenting these challenges women were also calling into question prevailing notions of equality – in particular, that distinctions on the basis of pregnancy were justified and did not constitute sex discrimination.

Initially, it was women within the state who raised these issues; by the mid-1970s, however, women's organizations and labour groups were also becoming involved, challenging the old rules in the courts and in workplaces as well as at the legislative and bureaucratic levels. More and more, links were being forged between the women's movement and the labour movement; for example, women's organizations were supporting labour strikes on the issue,[105] and labour organizations were taking up women's issues. At the level of administrative tribunals and of the courts, groups were largely unsuccessful – at least in the short term – in asserting that women in the period around childbirth had the right to equal treatment within the UI program. At the legislative level, however, in part as a result of efforts around court cases such as *Bliss*, significant improvements were made to the maternity provisions. The 1983 amendments introduced greater flexibility, less restrictive conditions for entitlement, and, with the removal of Section 46, greater equality of treatment for pregnant women regarding access to regular benefits.

But in some respects the reforms remained limited. First, the child bearing and rearing aspects of social reproduction were only to a limited extent accepted as a social responsibility. For a brief period in the late 1970s both the CACSW and NAC presented demands for a more comprehensive maternity or parental plan separate from the UI program; but this was never discussed or developed in any detail and was never really on the state's agenda. Similarly, both CUPW and the CHRC made important statements about the importance for women's equality of accepting social or collective responsibility for children, but this was accepted only to a limited extent at an ideological level and in terms of concrete legislative changes. Second, related to this, legislative gains were made when the issue was one of equal treatment, but no new efforts were made to establish special programs that would do more to recognize women's differences with respect to childrearing. Third, this mobilization around women's rights occurred in the context of a growing concern with fiscal restraint and the beginning of a restructuring in a neoliberal direction. This meant that the gains women achieved – for example, in terms of greater flexibility – were counterbalanced by amendments that made it more difficult for those working part-time to receive not only regular but also maternity benefits, as well as by amendments that reduced the rate of benefits. The continued tying of maternity benefits to UI (see chapter 7) has meant that gains with respect to child bearing and rearing have generally been undermined by more general UI retrenchment.

Overall, what women did achieve in this period was a significant reevaluation of gender ideology, especially as reflected in notions of pregnancy and maternity. Women challenged effectively the notion that they should be defined above all by their reproductive functions and that they should retire to the private sphere when pregnant. They put forward the view that maternity benefits were a right and an entitlement, not a legislative measure instituted for maternal or child protection. Women asserted that they *did* have a major attachment to the labour force, that they were not simply there for a brief period before taking up their 'real' role as mothers and wives, and that they belonged in the public as well as the private sphere. These were important gains that not only won real improvements in maternity benefits for women, but further called into question prevailing views of both pregnancy and equal rights, and suggested that shifting definitions of equality formed a central component of the restructuring process itself.

# CHAPTER 6

# Gender, Economic Crisis, and Welfare State Restructuring in the 1970s

The events of the 1970s were pivotal in shaping the direction of welfare state and economic policy for the next quarter-century. The unprecedented mobilization for women's rights described earlier, which partly involved pressure to alter both maternity provisions and conceptions of pregnancy, took place within the context of a growing economic crisis and the beginning of overall welfare state retrenchment. Indeed, the movement for greater gender equality and the pressures to restructure the welfare state model had overlapping roots. The social and economic forces that were propelling women into the labour force – economic changes leading to greater financial pressures on families, a family and welfare state model that contained tensions and contradictions – were also manifested through the economic crisis and were creating pressures for welfare state restructuring. In this chapter I argue that gender dimensions were critical not only to the nature of the crisis, but also to the response by the state and by other actors.

The decade started out with the implementation of the most comprehensive UI plan to date. By the mid-1970s, however, amendments had been introduced to restrict both eligibility and benefit payments. Indeed, it can be argued that these UI amendments marked the beginning of a more general process of welfare state retrenchment that would be more fully accomplished in the 1990s. What caused this shift in orientation in such a short period of time? First, the traditional business community mounted swift, forceful, and relentless opposition to the new plan. It argued that the new UI structure greatly increased the difficulty of finding workers willing to work at minimal wages, and it demanded increases in the required qualifying times and in the penalties for voluntarily quitting work.[1] The campaign against the new program was taken up enthusiastically by the media, who were quick to point out the costs and alleged misuses of the program.[2] This was the kind of opposition that certain sectors of the business community – especially those dependent on low-wage labour – had traditionally mounted to changes that were likely to increase the bargaining power of labour.

Second, by the mid-1970s, opposition to the UI program had taken on a new dimension as unemployment rose, the symptoms of an economic crisis became more apparent, and the Keynesian model underpinning the welfare state programs of the postwar era was called into question. Increasingly, the view that UI payments were a stimulus to the economy was rejected in favour of a supply-side approach that focused not only on deficit reduction but also on individual behaviour and skill levels and on the nature of state programs themselves as explanations for the level of unemployment. To the traditional concerns of the business community, then, were now added the voices of 'think tanks' such as the Fraser Institute and of new business organizations such as the Business Council on National Issues (BCNI). The latter represented the most powerful sectors of the business community. Both the Fraser Institute and the BCNI became key proponents of supply-side policies, reducing inflation, decreasing government involvement in the economy, and restructuring and scaling down the welfare state.[3]

Especially significant for our purposes is the centrality of gender to the shift in macro-economic policy and to the welfare state restructuring that accompanied this shift. In response to growing female unemployment and increased UI costs, the notion – first put forward in the 1960s – was reiterated that women, especially married women, were in a position to 'choose' unemployment and thereby take unfair advantage of the UI program. It was suggested that women were contributing to rising UI costs and driving up the rate of unemployment. Initially, the state responded to rising UI expenditures by monitoring claimants more closely; here, women and 'women's occupations' were scrutinized with particular care. By the mid-1970s, however, it was judged that closer monitoring would not be enough; to reduce expenditures and to reorient the program so as to be more compatible with a supply-side approach, the UI program would have to be restructured and retrenched. This meant placing more emphasis on reducing any 'disincentives' to work that might be found in the program, encouraging workers to establish 'more stable employment patterns' to reduce their dependency on

UI, and creating a program that would encourage the 'proper functioning' of the labour market. The notion that women were 'secondary earners' who were playing a more important role in the labour market, but who wished to work only intermittently, became a key justification for this shift in orientation with respect to welfare state programs and for accepting higher levels of unemployment. It also became a justification for establishing a tiered benefit structure that would make it more difficult for those in temporary and part-time positions to qualify for UI.

Both labour groups and women opposed the shift to a supply-side focus, with its emphasis on welfare state retrenchment; yet at first they did not question the gendered assumptions at its base. The inability early in the decade of both labour and women's organizations to develop an analysis of emerging trends that took fully into account the changing position of women meant that as the crisis took hold, conservative forces were able to present a response that not only built on and reinforced gender inequalities but also undermined the importance of unemployment as an issue.

Only toward the end of the decade did women's organizations mount serious challenges to the view of women as 'secondary workers' and to the direction that UI reform was taking. Overall, women's organizations and women within the state enjoyed considerable success not only in challenging the divisions between the public and private spheres (see chapter 5), but also in having discriminatory provisions removed and in preventing the implementation of a UI plan based on family income. They were far less successful, however, in challenging the overall direction of economic and welfare state reform and in showing that women's structural position in the economy meant that provisions restricting benefits to those in certain categories, such as part-time work, disadvantaged women and were thus 'discriminatory in effect.'

The first section of this chapter describes women's changing labour force status and the initial reaction to women's increased unemployment. The second section examines the increasingly coercive measures that were established in the early 1970s in an effort to control UI expenditures. Discussed after this are the initial responses of the various forces to the emerging crisis of the mid-1970s – especially as reflected in the unemployment issue and in the UI restructuring of the 1975–8 period. The growing contention over the direction of UI reform in the late 1970s is also examined. The final section discusses the period when the Progressive Conservatives were in power, focusing in particular on the question of entitlement and family status.

## Women's Changing Labour Force Status:
## Gender and Unemployment

By the early 1970s the pattern of growing part-time work, feminization of the labour force, and increasing service sector jobs had become well established. Between 1961 and 1971 the proportion of women working part-time had increased from 19 to 25 per cent.[4] The Economic Council of Canada reported that between 1961 and 1974 nearly two-thirds of employment growth occurred in office, professional, and sales and service jobs, and also that wage gains in the service sector were substantially less than in sectors such as forestry and mining.[5] It found that of those Canadians who worked only part of the year in 1975, one-third were males and two-thirds were females, and furthermore, that discharges and quits tended to be significantly higher for females than for males.[6]

These trends continued throughout the 1970s. Between 1971 and 1975, women's labour force participation increased from 39.4 to 44.4 per cent.[7] More and more, women were in the labour force throughout their childrearing years, including when their children were very young. By 1975, 34 per cent of women with preschool children and a husband at home were in the labour force, as were 45 per cent of those with preschool children and no husband at home.[8]

Between 1975 and 1980 the trend toward increasing female labour force participation and part-time work continued apace. Again, particularly dramatic was the continued increase in working women with preschool children. The participation rate of women in this category with a husband at home increased from 34.1 per cent in 1975 to 51.5 per cent in 1983; that of women with no husband at home increased from 45.4 to 50.8 per cent in the same period.[9] Similarly, between 1975 and 1983 the percentage of women employed part-time (now defined as those working fewer than thirty hours a week) rose from 20.3 to 26.1 per cent, and women as a percentage of part-time workers increased from 69.5 to 71.3 per cent.[10]

Female unemployment rates were also growing. As noted in chapter 4, until 1969, women's registered rate of unemployment had consistently been less than that for men – a phenomenon explained by Ostry in terms of women's propensity to withdraw completely from the labour force once unemployed.[11] The gap between male and female rates of unemployment narrowed, however, through the 1960s until 1969, when women's unemployment rate was higher than men's (see Table 6.1).

Table 6.1    Unemployment Rate, Canada, 1967–80

|  | Men<br>15 years and over | Women<br>15 years and over | Total<br>15 years and over |
|---|---|---|---|
| 1967 | 3.9 | 3.7 | 3.8 |
| 1968 | 4.6 | 4.4 | 4.5 |
| 1969 | 4.3 | 4.7 | 4.4 |
| 1970 | 5.6 | 5.8 | 5.7 |
| 1971 | 6.0 | 6.6 | 6.2 |
| 1972 | 5.8 | 7.0 | 6.2 |
| 1973 | 4.9 | 6.7 | 5.5 |
| 1974 | 4.8 | 6.4 | 5.3 |
| 1975 | 6.2 | 8.1 | 6.9 |
| 1976 | 6.3 | 8.4 | 7.1 |
| 1977 | 7.3 | 9.4 | 8.1 |
| 1978 | 7.5 | 9.6 | 8.3 |
| 1979 | 6.6 | 8.8 | 7.4 |
| 1980 | 6.9 | 8.4 | 7.5 |

Source: Statistics Canada, cat. 71-201, *Historical Labour Force Statistics 1983* (Jan. 1984), pp. 181, 186, 191

The gap between the male and female unemployment rates widened in the early 1970s until by 1976 it was two full percentage points higher for women then for men (an unemployment rate of 8.4 per cent for women compared to 6.3 per cent for men – see Table 6.1).

These changes meant a significant shift in family work/life and in labour market patterns. More and more women, even women with young children, were in the labour force, yet they tended to occupy jobs that were unstable and had a high turnover. Despite these ongoing economic and structural shifts, state officials continued to view unemployed working women with suspicion as being especially likely to simply 'choose' unemployment. While overall unemployment rates were relatively low in the early 1970s, the costs of the UI program continued to rise, due largely to increased benefit levels and expanded coverage.[12] Much attention, however, focused on the growing female unemployment rate. It was argued that the act itself was contributing to these higher rates – in particular, that the new eight-week entrance requirement was inducing women to enter the labour force simply for the period needed to qualify for UI and then to register as unemployed. For example, a 1972 report for the UI Commission noted that in the months following the introduction of the new act, women made up 46 per cent of active UI claimants but only 23 per cent of the unemployed.

The report found this 'both puzzling and disconcerting,' and suggested that 'women more than men draw benefits when they are not, in fact, eligible for them.'[13]

Women's advisors within the state responded very tentatively to these allegations. This reflected both the difficulty of challenging the long-held view that women were likely to misuse the UI plan, and the largely middle-class bias of the women's movement, which was quite removed from concerns of working women and more preoccupied with issues such as juridical equalities than with structural factors that might be contributing, for example, to higher unemployment rates for women. It also reflected a concern, even among those dealing with women's equality issues, for demonstrating that women were or could act 'just like men.'

Some women within the state *did* address the issue of female unemployment and UI use. One official pointed out, for example, that female unemployment rates had begun increasing *before* the UI changes, and suggested that this could be because more and more young women were 'quite determined in their search for work, hence certain to be counted in the unemployment statistics,' and also because more men were competing for jobs in traditional women's occupations such as teaching.[14] Another official noted that there were two main points at issue:

> ... alleged misuse of the UIC, notably by females, and, closely related, a feeling that a great many women should not be counted as unemployed because their attachment to the labour force is peripheral – in some sense 'non-serious' ... If we look solely at the new claimant data emerging from the UIC since the act was changed, it is clear that women *are* making greater use of the UIC ... Lack of continuity in women's labour force attachment can mean different things, including undue propensity to quit work, at one end, and extreme hardship due to marginal employability at the other.'[15]

In general, however, the debate in this period was quite limited and reflected the difficulty in coming to terms with the large-scale changes in family structures, in work patterns, and even in what constituted unemployment in this period of flux. Unemployment rates for women *had* increased. But even the techniques for *measuring* unemployment rates for women were open to question. Morley Gunderson, for example, found that the 1971 Census – which asked quite directly, 'Did you look for work last week?' – recorded a female unemployment rate of 8.9 per cent, whereas the Labour Force Survey taken at the same time (May 1971) recorded a rate of 5.0 per cent. In the latter the question was, 'What did you do mostly last week?' and many women who had looked for work but responded 'kept house' were not counted as unemployed.[16] Similarly, when the Labour Force questionnaire was changed in 1975 to determine more precisely what efforts the respondents had made to find work, simply changing the question increased the female unemployment rate by 2 per cent and decreased the male rate by about 1 per cent.[17]

Unemployment rates were even higher for women with preschool children than for those without.[18] Women were indeed experiencing 'extreme hardship' because of the nature of the labour market; they tended to fill unstable, temporary, and contingent jobs, especially in the service sector, where they were more likely to be laid off or employed only for short periods. At the same time, women's role within the family – including responsibility for children, the elderly, and the sick, and the expectation that they would follow their husbands to another city – tended to force them to leave work more often than men and to accept part-time or contingent work. These were not competing explanations so much as two sides of the same coin. What both reveal is the difficulty that women – especially those with multiple responsibilities – were facing when entering the labour market.

## Emerging Pressures: Gender, UI Expenditures, and Increased State Controls

The state's response to increased UI expenditures and to the changing position of women in the labour force was to hold firmly to the notion that women were 'choosing' unemployment and driving up the costs of the UI program by claiming benefits when they did not really want to work. The 1971 UI program is generally seen as marking the most generous stage of the welfare state in Canada. The new legislation did provide for much greater accessibility and higher benefit levels, yet it was accompanied by a much closer monitoring of UI recipients and increased state coercion.

The costs of the UI program and alleged abuses received considerable media attention in the run-up to the 1972 election.[19] After the election, Robert Andras took over as Minister of Manpower and Immigration and considerably greater attention was paid to controlling expenditures and reducing abuses.[20] A special benefit control program was introduced in the summer of 1972 and went into full operation early in 1973. The staff for this program increased from 147 in 1972 to 424 in 1974;[21] it seems that many of the recruits were ex-policemen.[22] According to Regulation 145, passed in July 1972, UI claimants could be asked to prove that they were 'actively seeking work,' and it was no longer enough to have registered with the Canada Manpower Centre. A special computer program was put in place to identify claimants whose occupational skills were in demand in the area in which they lived, and these claimants were sent job search statement forms that required them to detail the efforts they had made to find work. In addition, home interviews were conducted by benefit control officers to determine whether the claimant had been actively seeking work and was genuinely available for work. In urban areas these investigations were part of an ongoing process; in smaller centres they involved 'blitzes,' with teams of benefit control interviewers moving in for short periods and each officer interviewing about six claimants a day.[23] In the first nine weeks of 1973, of the 62,879 claimants subjected to a special investigation, 40,846 or 65 per cent were disqualified.[24]

This crackdown on abuses had gender dimensions that revealed (again) continuing assumptions about women's domestic role, as well as the structural factors that were funneling women into occupations with a high labour turnover. A number of MPs reported that in their ridings, most of the people questioned were women – especially married women.[25] Other reports indicated that occupations drawing mainly on female labour were being targeted for special investigation. For example, in early 1973 the *Ottawa Citizen* reported that 'a special UIC investigation of stenographers, typists and waitresses drawing benefits in the Ottawa-Hull region has resulted in disqualification of as many as 85% of them.'[26] A similar investigation in Kingston resulted in the disqualification of more than 70 per cent of about two hundred secretaries, clerks, and general office workers who were receiving benefits.[27] An investigation of twenty-eight thousand UI recipients in the Toronto–Hamilton area resulted in a disqualification rate of 65 to 70 per cent.[28]

Figures on disqualifications confirmed a much higher rate for women than for men in this period. In 1973 the disqualification or disentitlement rate for 'non-availability, refusal of work and/or inadequate job search' for those who had previously worked eight to eleven weeks was 13.1 per cent for men and 23.5 per cent for women; for those with twelve or more weeks, the rate was 10.8 per cent for men and 29.4 per cent for women. In 1974 this pattern continued, with a rate of 13.9 per cent for men and 23.5 per cent for women with under twelve weeks and 11.7 per cent for men and 29.8 per cent for women with over twelve weeks.[29] Women were further disadvantaged in that they were disproportionately in unorganized workplaces. This made it more difficult for them to launch first-level appeals; not only that, but those in unorganized workplaces, unlike those with labour representation, were prohibited until the late 1970s from appealing a unanimous decision of the Board of Referees to the umpire.[30] In addition, unions with hiring halls were able to sign an 'umbrella agreement' with the UI Commission that exempted their members from any investigation of their job search efforts.[31]

Andras acknowledged that women were receiving particular attention when it came to controlling abuses, but he denied that this was in any way deliberate:

> In matching jobs to people who were unemployed certain occupations showed up in given areas as potential offenders. In certain areas there were a lot of secretarial jobs, waitress jobs, things like that ... Those were the jobs that were going begging and in many cases the people who were more likely to occupy them were women. But we did not start out with the presumption that women were going to be the guilty ones. It was done by a classification of occupations. It was not a witch hunt against women.[32]

Further reports, however, questioned both the tactics being used and whether jobs were available at all. For example, when a local UIC officer in the Toronto–Hamilton region was questioned about the special investigation in his area, he stated that his region did not have jobs for the twenty-eight thousand UI recipients being investigated: 'At any given point in time we're running roughly 2,500 jobs and we average 20,000 people looking for employment.'[33] Similarly, with respect to the Moncton area, MP Mr Thomas noted:

> The people who have been investigated certainly could not be identified by job classification because in most cases there were no jobs available at all, whether they were waitresses or sales clerks or whatever. The thing that always mystified me was that in a small town you would find maybe six people on benefits all at the same time, and maybe some over long periods of time. One would be investigated and told that he or she was not available for work and would be disentitled or disqualified and the

other five were overlooked. I am trying to get at the picture of how your investigators went out. How did they pick the houses? Was it just a matter of going to a house to investigate? Or was there some reason for their investigating one out of six in the same area?[34]

Similarly, William Knowles, representing the riding of Norfolk-Haldimand for the Progressive Conservatives, described the lack of jobs for people being investigated in his largely rural Ontario riding: 'In my area at the present time there is obviously no farm help required. There are very few small industries in the towns and villages in the area. As far as help is concerned, these plants are all filled to capacity. They do not want any more help. As a matter of fact, some are laying off employees. The benefit control officers are coming in and cutting these people off unemployment insurance, saying they are not looking for a job.'[35]

Figures from the federal Job Vacancy Survey also cast doubt on the types of jobs available. The Economic Council of Canada noted that although registered job vacancies reached all-time highs in 1973 and 1974, 54 per cent of the jobs were in the semi- and low-skilled categories, with pay rates 15 to 25 per cent below the going rates for those occupations.[36] They cited the example of sewing machine operators: 'The hiring rate of pay for sewing-machine operators, for example, was very low. Add to this the frequent layoffs, the fact that many small shops go bankrupt, the seasonal swings to which this occupation is susceptible, and the harsh working conditions in many establishments, and the large number of outstanding vacancies hardly seems surprising.'[37]

The tactics being used by benefit control officers were also questioned by William Knowles, who noted that he had received hundreds of complaints on the issue. Some of the complaints had to do with the treatment of seasonal workers in his riding, many of whom were new Canadians with limited English skills.[38] In addition, many of the questions, such as about childcare, seemed directed especially at women:

There is another trick which these officers play on these people being interviewed. When they enter a person's home and see small children, they ask whether that individual has a babysitter. Obviously, there is no babysitter because that person is home looking after the children. The honest answer is no. When the signed statement comes back, it states that the claimant has no child care arrangements and, therefore, is unable to accept work if suitable work were offered ... Another trick is with regard to transportation. The individual is asked whether he has a car. Perhaps the husband has a car but the wife has not. There is one car for the family. The officer does not say to the wife, if a job were offered in Simcoe, Delhi or on a nearby farm, could you get to work? The answer would be entirely different.[39]

Other MPs noted similar questionable tactics[40] and argued that claimants should be entitled to certain basic rights such as having a representative present when being interviewed, and being permitted to return signed statements instead of having to sign them in the presence of the interviewing officer.[41]

In response to numerous questions in the House of Commons, Andras announced a number of measures, including these: the UI Advisory Committee would undertake a study of the benefit control operations, instructions would be given to benefit control officers that 'the need for thoroughness in their work does not and must not justify an overzealous approach or underhanded methods,' and a pamphlet would be distributed to UI claimants outlining their rights and obligations.[42] The Liberals, however, continued to be concerned about limiting the UI program and controlling abuses. In 1973 they introduced Bill C-125, the intention which was to curb abuses by raising qualifying requirements and penalties for those who had quit voluntarily without just cause, who had lost employment because of misconduct, or who had failed to apply for or accept suitable employment.[43] But the NDP did not support the bill, and as a result the Liberals, who were in a minority position, withdrew it. Attention then focused on continuing administrative changes to curb abuses. In April 1974 a Special Job Finding and Placement Drive was instituted; this involved a mandatory Canada Manpower Centre (CMC) interview for claimants in occupations for which there was demand. In 1975 the special drive was expanded; overall in that year there were some 464,000 benefit control investigations, of which about 58 per cent resulted in disqualifications and disentitlements.[44]

Women, and unorganized workers in general, continued to receive special attention. Again, this was partly because they tended to be disproportionately in 'high demand' occupations. In addition, however, benefit control officers were directed to investigate certain categories of claimants who met particular descriptions 'for which the statistical incidence of irregular situations is particularly high.' This included married women between twenty-five and thirty-five, male non-union-ized workers between nineteen and thirty-five, and general labourers.[45] Women claiming regular benefits following maternity leave also continued to be singled out for special attention.[46] Finally, the UI Commission also made investigations based on third-party reports – in particular, it was receiving help from the business community in its efforts to curb abuses.[47] Here, too, unorganized workers and certain categories of women continued to receive special attention. For example, the president of the Niagara Falls Chamber of Commerce described his organization's efforts in the following way:

> As a result of recent discussions with UIC and CMC officials, the Chamber embarked upon a program to encourage businessmen to report potential employees, applicants for jobs as well as existing employees who, in the opinion of the employer are seeking the means to draw UIC benefits rather than be employed ... Of particular interest are the following: persons who refuse to accept job offers ... part-time workers who refuse to accept full time work when it is offered, persons who stop working due to pregnancy and refuse work after their child has been born.[48]

When questioned in April 1974 about control measures as they related to women, Andras again denied that discrimination was taking place:

> The Commission really does not have special control measures ... The Commission does look at the claim history of groups or occupations or other categories with a view to determining whether some emphasis should be given to assuring that the claimants involved are meeting the requirements of the act. This is all that really happens with respect to these female claimants. In view of the doubt that may exist with respect to their availability status following the birth of a child, they are being interviewed to establish they can meet this requirement under the act. Of particular interest ... is that many employers are committed to reinstate women in their jobs after confinement, indeed, many provincial governments insist upon this, by law.[49]

Referring both to control measures and to the requirement that women prove childcare arrangements, Andras noted: 'I can assure you that there is no discrimination involved, it is simply a reflection of the insurance principle as it relates to the administration of the programme.'[50]

## Economic Crisis, Fiscal Restraint, and Retrenchment in the UI Program

By 1974 a sea change was occurring in federal government macro-economic policy. Beginning with the November 1974 budget, but more clearly in 1975, a series of measures indicated a shift away from Keynesian demand management policies toward a focus on supply-side factors, monetarism, fiscal restraint, and putting inflation reduction ahead of unemployment. These measures included Finance Minister John Turner's June 1975 budget,[51] the announcement by the governor of the Bank of Canada of a new policy of controlling the growth of the money supply, and the introduction of the Anti-Inflation Program, which involved fiscal and monetary policies to reduce the rate of inflation, government expenditure restraint, and a policy of prices and incomes control.[52]

Again, the shift to monetarism and the adoption of fiscal restraint policies had important gender dimensions. The concept of unemployment was central to the ideological struggle that was to shape the direction of policy changes for the next twenty years. This was a profoundly gendered debate to which the question of female unemployment and UI use was critical, both in attempts to trivialize unemployment as an issue of importance and as a justification for beginning a process of retrenchment within the welfare state. As part of the shift in emphasis away from demand factors, such as job shortages, toward supply factors, including the attitudes and actions of workers in the labour market, considerable attention was paid to the changing nature of women's labour force participation and to the impact of programs such as UI on the rate of unemployment. To some extent these discussions reflected a recognition by analysts and policymakers that the economic changes that were occurring involved women in a fundamental way. They also, however, indicated the persistence of traditional values regarding women and the ability of conservative forces – which gained ascendency as the crisis deepened – to construct responses to the crisis in ways that reinforced women's unequal and dependent relationship.

Studies by Green and Cousineau, as well as the Economic Council of Canada report *People and Jobs*, point to the analytic shift that was occurring.[53] Evaluation of a family's income was no longer based on a 'family wage' from one male breadwinner, but rather on what was assumed to be the pooled income of a 'multi-earner' family – in which the husband nevertheless remained the primary figure. These works argued that the growth of 'secondary wage earners' (i.e., women and youth) contributing to family incomes, combined with more generous income security programs, meant that rising unemployment rates were not as serious as they might once have been; thus 'the aggregate unemployment rate is becoming less and less accurate as a measure of family income hardship.'[54] This was, they argued, because a larger and larger proportion of the unemployed were 'secondary workers' rather than heads of households, and because even if unemployment did occur, there was probably another source of family income.[55]

The same studies suggested that the growth in 'secondary workers' and multi-earner families was actually *contributing* to higher rates of unemployment because 'the typical unemployed person today can afford to be choosier than his counterpart of the 1930s, and for that matter the 1950s.'[56] The Economic Council of Canada again took up the argument that women's unemployment was 'different' from men's:

> Apart from overall demand factors, much of the unemployment of prime age men results from the discontinuity of jobs because of seasonal or related causes. For women who are not career-motivated, unemployment may be less the result of discontinuity and impermanence of jobs than of the voluntary turnover associated with a host of personal reasons and the relative unattractiveness of wages paid in the occupations customarily filled by females.[57]

These same studies further contended that the growth in secondary workers who could 'choose' whether to work meant that the UI program was more likely to influence labour market behaviour, both by attracting people into the labour market for the time required to collect benefits and by 'induc[ing] some job leavers who would otherwise have left the labour force to remain in it and claim UI.'[58] It was, they argued, women and students who were most likely to behave in this way.[59]

The Fraser Institute, founded in 1974, played an important role in advocating a turn toward fiscal restraint and reduced government intervention, and in suggesting that married women were contributing to higher rates of both unemployment and UI use. Herbert Grubel and Michael Walker, in a paper published by the institute, claimed that UI increases unemployment in part by creating incentives for certain groups – especially married women – to enter the labour market, work the minimum number of weeks to establish eligibility, and then have themselves laid off:[60] 'The existence of unemployment induced by unemployment insurance and other social welfare programs ... changes the meaning of the unemployment rate as first, an indicator of cyclical conditions in the economy and second, an indicator of human hardship and economic waste.'[61] As a consequence, they argued, the 'appropriate level of unemployment as a target for macroeconomic policies' needed to be re-examined. They suggested increasing the UI eligibility period, creating a type of workfare for young people, excluding seasonal workers, and establishing 'discriminatory rates of benefits for heads of households and secondary income earners in the same family. Induced unemployment effects appear to be especially strong in the case of wives and young people living in the same household, where unemployment constitutes an opportunity to do many of the chores existing in every household.'[62] Grubel and Walker did caution, however, that 'before such reforms can be undertaken it is necessary that the concept of unemployment induced by welfare programs be accepted more widely and that its effects be measured more carefully.'[63]

It would be almost twenty years before the reforms suggested by Grubel and Walker became politically feasible; nevertheless, such thinking began to change the direction of UI policy. The UI program became one of the first targets for restraint. It had already been under strong attack from both the business community and the media. In addition, given the new interest in supply-side approaches, the UI program, which centrally addressed questions of unemployment, labour markets, and income transfers, had become a prime target for reform.

A series of amendments between 1975 and 1978 marked the beginning of a period of retrenchment within the UI program – indeed, within the welfare state more generally. These amendments reflected a shift away from the view that unemployment could arise through market failures, toward a supply-side analysis focusing on individual behaviour and attitudes to work and the suggestion that income security programs were creating 'disincentives' to work. The first of the UI changes, announced in John Turner's June 1975 budget,[64] was incorporated into Bill C-69, which was introduced in October of that year (see Chart 6.1). The amendments reflected concerns about cost cutting and about the influence UI was having on labour market behaviour – in particular, the possibility that UI might be discouraging people from looking for jobs or making them less willing to keep their present jobs. Various measures were taken to address these concerns. The advance payment of three weeks of benefits for major attachment was eliminated; and the maximum period of benefit disqualification was doubled (from three to six weeks) for claimants who had left their job voluntarily without good cause, had refused suitable employment, or had been dismissed for misconduct. In addition, the special 75 per cent dependency rate was eliminated, and the age at which people would no longer pay premiums or be eligible for UI was reduced from seventy to sixty-five. The 4 per cent unemployment threshold used for determining the federal government's share of financing (and which suggested that the federal government had a responsibility for ensuring that unemployment remained below this level) was replaced by a new threshold 'adjusted automatically each year on the basis of a moving average of monthly unemployment rates over the preceding eight-year period.' This was designed to bring the UI financing formula 'into line with current economic reality.' For 1976 the unemployment trigger level was to be about 5.6 per cent.[65] So that the UI program could actively assist in the 'proper functioning of the labour market,' a pilot project was introduced in 1975 involving, for the first time, the use of UI funds for 'developmental' purposes – in this case, the payment of training allowances.[66] It was estimated that these changes would result in savings of $170 million for 1976 but that, given the change in the funding formula, the federal government share would be reduced by about $660 million.[67]

As justification for the UI program changes, arguments such as those being put forward by the Economic Council of Canada were reiterated: unemployment growth was concentrated among secondary earners, such as women, so growing unemployment rates were therefore not so significant; women were contributing to high levels of UI use; and the 'disincentive effect' was greatest among certain women, as well as young males, people over sixty-five, and people in clerical and service occupations.[68] Turner, in announcing the new unemployment level that would trigger federal government contributions, suggested that a higher acceptable rate of unemployment 'reflects broad social and demographic changes in the structure of the labour market, such as greater participation by married women, young people, students and other secondary wage earners.'[69]

The elimination of the dependency rate meant that for the first time since the UI Act was introduced, the notion of a family structure involving dependants was no longer part of the UI plan. This, however, did not reflect a significant shift away from the male-breadwinner ideal. Rather, the primary motive was to reduce expenditures (the change was expected to save $30 million).[70] The shift was justified on the grounds that family allowances had recently been increased and that this was 'a much more appropriate way to recognize the legitimate additional family need based on family size' than the essentially wage-related UI plan.[71]

The following year, unemployment reached 7.1 per cent. The federal government, increasingly influenced by supply-side arguments and preoccupied with fiscal restraint, placed further UI reform high on its agenda. A 'comprehensive review' of UI policy was initiated, and this resulted in the introduction of Bill C-27 in December 1976. The *Comprehensive Review* (tabled in Parliament shortly after the bill was introduced) reiterated many of the views expressed by the Economic Council of Canada and others that linked women and secondary workers in short-term occupations with increases in UI expenditures.[72]

To address these demographic and labour market changes and to control expenditures, the review suggested that eligibility be reduced for those with a minimal number (eight to eleven weeks) of employment. In addition, it recommended changing the five-phase benefit structure in ways that could both lower costs[73] and increase work incentives, by linking benefit entitlements more directly to the number of weeks worked and to regional (rather than a combination of national and regional) unemployment rates.[74] In February 1977, Bill C-27 was introduced for second reading. Its changes, based on the recommendations of the *Comprehensive Review*, included an increase from eight to twelve in the number of weeks required to qualify for UI and the replacement of the five-phase benefit structure with a three-phase structure that would link benefits more closely to the number of weeks worked and to the regional rate of unemployment. The bill also granted formal authority for the government to use UI funds 'in more directly productive or developmental ways,' including as income maintenance for claimants on special job-creation projects and training programs[75] (see Chart 6.1).

Bud Cullen, the new Minister of Employment and Immigration, in introducing the legislation, again suggested that it was the behaviour of women and young people that made the changes necessary. He stated that an examination of claimants with eight to eleven weeks of employment 'strongly suggests that an increase in the entrance requirement would constitute for many of them an incentive to work longer. In general eight to eleven weekers are younger than average, without dependants and many are secondary earners in families. Basically, they have what might best be described as an intermittent or unstable attachment to the active work force.'[76]

Chart 6.1   UI Legislative Amendments, 1975–1980

| | |
|---|---|
| 1975   Bill C-69 | • Benefit disqualification for claimants who quit voluntarily without just cause increased from 3 to 6 weeks<br>• 75% dependency rate eliminated<br>• 3-week advanced payment for major attachment claimants eliminated<br>• Age at which people would no longer pay premiums or be eligible for UI decreased from 70 to 65<br>• New formula for determining federal government share of UI financing |
| 1977   Bill C-27 | • Increase in weeks needed to qualify to a variable entrance requirement (VER) of 10–14 weeks, depending on the regional unemployment rate.<br>• 3-phase benefit structure introduced. Benefits more closely linked to weeks worked and regional unemployment rate.<br>• Authority granted to use UI benefits for 'developmental' purposes |
| 1978   Bill C-14 | • Benefit rate reduced from 66⅔% to 60% of earnings<br>• Higher entrance requirements for repeaters (those with a second claim in the same 52 weeks), dependent on regional unemployment rate.<br>• Entrance requirements for new entrants and re-entrants to the labour force increased to 20 weeks in the previous year<br>• Authority to make regulations to exclude those working fewer than 20 hours a week or receiving less than 30% of maximum insurable earnings<br>• High-income earners required to repay a portion of benefits<br>• Federal government share of financing reduced |

Opposition to the direction of change came at this point not so much from those considered 'secondary earners' but rather from high-unemployment regions with large seasonal workforces that would be strongly affected by the tougher requirements. Indeed, Liberal MPs from the Atlantic region threatened to vote against the bill and thereby bring the government down.[77] As a result, before the bill was passed, it was revised so that instead of increasing qualifying requirements across the board to twelve weeks, it provided for a 'variable entrance requirement' (VER) of ten to fourteen weeks depending on the regional rate of unemployment.

As the 1970s progressed, the Liberal government became more and more committed to a program of deficit reduction. On 1 August 1978, Prime Minister Trudeau, following an economic summit meeting in Bonn, announced that federal government expenditures would be reduced by \$2.5 billion.[78] Again, UI became a major area for cuts. With unemployment now above 8 per cent, Cullen announced on 1 September the government's intention to proceed with another series of amendments to the UI Act. In November 1978, Bill C-14 was introduced. While overall program expenditures were clearly a primary concern, Cullen again stated that the changes were designed to 'contribute in a positive way to strengthening the labour market,' to reduce 'disincentives to work,' and to 'encourage workers to establish more stable work patterns and develop longer attachments to the active work force, thereby reducing their dependency on unemployment insurance.'[79]

The Bill C-14 amendments were especially significant in that they went beyond the relatively small distinctions between 'major' and 'minor' labour force participants made in earlier legislation, and established more clearly a tiered system of eligibility that restricted the availability of UI for those who did not fit the full-time, full-year Fordist model of worker. The state's response to the growing numbers in short-term, intermittent employment and to those who may have been out of the labour force for some time (including many women) was to limit their access to state-provided income security. In particular, more stringent entrance requirements were established for 'repeat users' (people with a second claim in the same fifty-two weeks), and for 'new entrants' and 're-entrants' to the labour force (defined as those with fewer than fourteen weeks work in the fifty-two weeks before the start of the qualifying period).[80] It also became more difficult for part-time workers to qualify. The new legislation provided authority to make regulations excluding those who worked fewer than twenty hours a week or who received less than 30 per cent of maximum insurable earnings. In addition, a major reduction in the benefit rate, from 66⅔ to 60 per cent of earnings, was introduced. Furthermore, a clawback was introduced that required high-income claimants to repay a portion of their UI benefits, and the federal government's share of financing was further reduced.[81]

Business groups strongly endorsed the Bill C-14 changes;[82] however, labour groups opposed them just as strongly, and so did women's organizations as well as MPs and provincial governments representing high-unemployment areas. Again, the legislation was modified somewhat between the initial proposals and the version finally introduced, mainly as a result of opposition from Liberal MPs in the Atlantic provinces.[83] The tiered benefit structure remained in place, but the additional time that was to be required for repeat users, new entrants, and re-entrants was somewhat shortened.[84] Furthermore, this provision would not apply in any region where the unemployment rate was above 11.5 per cent.[85] Finally, in the original proposals the high-income clawback had been based on family income (over $22,000), but in the end the family basis for calculating the surtax was not implemented.[86] Cullen acknowledged that concerns had been raised about the implications of these changes for women and that, given the differences in work patterns between men and women, the latter might be more strongly affected by the new entrant, re-entrant, and part-time provisions.[87] Yet he also suggested that overall, women would not be disadvantaged,[88] and that they would be compensated for any hardships through continued efforts to improve their status in the labour force – for example, by monitoring the number of women in training programs and by setting targets for women in industrial training programs.[89] Bill C-14 was passed in December 1978, but only after the Liberals had introduced a motion of closure on debate and committed themselves to a further review of the program.

### Gender and UI Reform: Growing Contestation

In the mid-1970s, when macroeconomic and state income security policies were beginning to shift in response to the crisis, both women's organizations and labour were slow to respond to arguments concerning secondary workers and to attempts to limit working women's UI eligibility. As noted in chapter 5, women's groups and women within the state had concerns about issues such as restrictive maternity provisions, requirements with respect to childcare, and discriminatory practices. Yet they did not at first respond to the cutbacks in UI or to the suggestion that the rising numbers of 'secondary' earners made higher unemployment rates acceptable. Generally speaking, female unemployment and the gendered benefit control practices of the UI Commission[90] were not taken up as significant issues either by women's groups or by labour. Despite the significance of the elimination of the dependency rate for women – which for the first time implied a UI and welfare state model that did *not* have a family wage basis – there was little discussion of the cutback's implications for women. Indeed, what discussion there was revealed the persistence of assumptions about the financial needs and obligations of the male head of the household. Both the NDP and the CLC were against eliminating the dependency rate, on the grounds that it was a cost-cutting measure targeted at low-income Canadians,[91] and members of all three parties made clear their continued support for the family wage system.[92]

By 1977, however, women's organizations were beginning to monitor the implications of general economic and social policies for women and to draw the links between economic trends and women's equality issues. The National Action Committee on the Status of Women (NAC) also increasingly began to take up employment questions, including UI questions. The election of a more left-leaning NAC executive in 1977 was reflected, for example, in discussions of whether that organization should lobby against the Anti-Inflation Board's imposition of wage controls.[93] Also, NAC broadened its recommendations with respect to UI to include the general structure of the program rather than simply 'women's issues.' Specifically, NAC opposed the increase in UI eligibility requirements from eight to twelve weeks, urged the UIC to produce literature in a variety of languages where warranted, and called on it to 'inform all claimants that any statement made could be used to disentitle them.'[94]

The CACSW also broadened its analysis to include a more general assessment of women's economic position. In 1977 it published an extensive critique of the UI Commission's *Comprehensive Review*. This report, written by Elise Rosen, took issue with the comments about women's labour market behaviour, the description of women as 'secondary income earners with unstable employment patterns,' and inferences that women were abusing the UI system. Rosen pointed out that the statements made about women 'bear no relationship to the data presented.'[95] To the contrary, she argued that most women in the labour force work because of financial need, that high female unemployment rates could simply reflect women's greater difficulty in finding employment, and that high disqualification rates could indicate not so much that women were abusing UI but rather that they were being discriminated against by the plan.

The CACSW also voiced its objection to the unfair treatment that women seemed to be receiving in UI offices with respect to job search requirements – a continuation of the intensive monitoring earlier in the decade. In Toronto and Victoria and possibly other cities, it noted for example that 'women are reportedly being required by UIC officers to accept up to fifteen Canada Manpower referrals for job interviews per week while men are being required to accept only up to five before being cut off the UIC payroll. Some union officers in these cities are spending well over half their time having women who are eligible for UIC reinstated.'[96] These concerns were forwarded in May 1977 to Cullen, who again took the position that such practices did not constitute sex discrimination; rather, they reflected the types of positions that women tended to fill: 'The number of contacts that a claimant is requested to make in order to find a job is related to the opportunity of employment in claimant's living area ... type of occupation, specific conditions of employment and time of year which has direct bearing on job opportunities. The UI requirements are by no means based on sex.'[97]

In 1978 both NAC and the CACSW for the first time presented comprehensive briefs on the proposed legislative changes to the UI program. Differences emerged between the two organizations. The CACSW expressed support for budgetary restraint in general, as well as for many of the specific objectives of Bill C-14, which had been introduced in 1978. It argued that it was not against cutting costs – just against cutting costs in a way that would negatively affect women.[98] NAC was much more prepared to criticize the overall direction of government policy and to suggest alternatives. During 1978, for example, it put forward the idea that working toward 'full employment through an industrial strategy' was an important issue for women.[99] Both groups, however, began mounting a concerted challenge to the view that women were secondary earners who contributed to high unemployment rates and high UI costs; they also began to articulate alternative interpretations of female employment and unemployment patterns. During the Bill C-14 hearings, both organizations objected to the 'spurious conclusions' regarding women that had been put forward in the *Comprehensive Review* and to statements by Cullen which implied that those in short-term employment or with many spells of unemployment had chosen that form of work.[100] Both groups argued that the problem was not the attitude of workers but rather a lack of jobs,[101] and that the higher unemployment rates for women were due to factors such as unequal opportunity in the labour force and the concentration of women in low-paying job ghettoes and in sectors such as teaching and social services, which were being affected by the recession.[102]

Both NAC and the CACSW also objected to specific provisions in Bill C-14. They argued that the minimum insurability requirement of twenty hours a week would restrict the access of many part-time workers to UI,[103] and that the higher entrance requirements for new entrants and re-entrants to the labour force would be hard on young people and women re-entering the labour force after time away because of family responsibilities.[104] They also argued that the reduction in the benefit rate from 66⅔ to 60 per cent was especially hard on women, who tended to be disproportionately represented in low-income jobs.[105] The CACSW further objected to the higher entrance requirement for repeaters, arguing that this would discriminate against seasonal employees of industries such as processing and servicing, in which many women were working. In presenting these objections, both groups represented an important evolution, in that they were going beyond criticism of *overtly* discriminatory measures in order to draw attention to policies which, they argued, were discriminatory in their *effect*.

During the 1978 Bill C-14 hearings, labour also voiced strong opposition to the UI amendments. The CLC argued that the higher entrance requirements would especially affect those in primary industries and construction, and recommended that the bill 'be scrapped in its entirety.'[106] The CLC was obviously concerned about seasonal workers in traditional resource and construction industries; but now it was also taking up gender issues, criticizing the Bill C-14 amendments on the grounds that they discriminated against women and were based on the notion that women were secondary earners and therefore less entitled to benefits.[107] The CLC now argued that women's income was essential to maintain family living standards and to enable women to support themselves and their families.

The regional implications of the proposed changes were also a cause for concern. Social service ministers from New Brunswick, Newfoundland, and Ontario came to the Bill C-14 hearings to express, on behalf of nine out of ten provinces, concerns about the proposed changes.[108] The provincial ministers were particularly concerned that the new entrant, re-entrant, and repeater clauses would force many of those previously eligible for UI onto social assistance, at considerable extra expense to provincial governments. The minister from Newfoundland pointed to the large number of young people in the fishing industry, as well as in

seasonal industries such as construction, who would find it very difficult to qualify.[109] As an alternative, the ministers proposed a two-tiered
benefit structure whereby those *without* dependants would receive a
rate of 50 per cent and those *with* dependants would receive 66⅔ per
cent of earnings. They argued that the 'responsibilities and hence the
financial burden of the wage earner with dependents are greater than
the wage earner without dependents,'[110] and that with their plan there
would be both greater savings for the federal government and fewer
additional expenditures for the provincial governments.

Overall, in the reactions to the bill concerns had been expressed about
two major groups of workers, both of whom were outside the norm of
the Fordist industrial wage earner: women, who tended disproportionately to be in part-time, contingent work and whose work/life patterns
meant they often had to withdraw for periods from the labour force;
and workers in seasonal industries in the construction and resource
sectors who tended to be men and to be concentrated in particular
geographic areas. While representatives of both groups opposed amendments that would restrict UI for those in intermittent employment,
there appeared to be little communication between them. Indeed, the
alternatives presented – especially the two-tier proposal of the provinces – amounted to attempts to maintain the position of one at the
expense of the other. Women's groups were concerned about the provincial proposal and opposed what could be a return to a family wage
model. NAC, for example, expressed concern about proposals to take
family income into account – especially after the provincial ministers'
presented their alternative model. It argued that such a proposal 'con-
tradicts the fundamental insurance principle of the UI scheme' and that
relating benefits to need 'is misguided in light of the fact that salaries
paid to men and women are not related to need.' It further argued that
reducing benefit rates to 50 per cent for women without dependants
would place them in 'a desperate financial state,' given their already
low incomes, and that overall the effect would be to 'deny to Canadian
women the basic right to participate in the labour force on the same
terms and conditions as men.'[111]

While few substantive changes were made to Bill C-14, the federal
government seemed aware of the growing strength of the women's
movement and concerned about maintaining some kind of balance
between competing interests. It rejected the twofold proposals, citing
administrative difficulties; furthermore, a two-fold model would not
achieve the objective of establishing 'more stable work patterns' and

would be highly discriminatory toward women. (Figures from the *Comprehensive Review* had shown that if such a system were brought in, only 5 per cent of women would be likely to receive the higher rate, compared to 42 per cent of men.)[112] Clearly, the political implications of introducing a measure that would be seen as discriminating against women were becoming more of an issue for the Liberals. As Cullen stated: 'One of the criticisms of the changes that we are making is that there is a discrimination against women and yet the two-tier system ... massively discriminates against women. Is that the sort of thing that you if you were a minister, or I as a minister, want to face in the House or outside in the general public? I think not.'[113]

## The Progressive Conservatives in Power: Social Conservatives and Questions of Entitlement and Family Status

With the election of May 1979, the Progressive Conservatives came to power. They too were committed to a review and reform of the UI program. In the short period they were in office, conflicting views over the objectives and provisions of the UI program came to be sharply posed. To some extent this reflected the deepening contradictions between existing welfare state programs and a restructuring economy in which contingent work – and, increasingly, a female labour force – played a critical role. It also reflected a more polarized debate: on the one hand, women's groups and others were more clearly articulating their opposition to the direction that UI reform was taking; on the other, with the election of the Conservatives, social conservatives gained greater prominence within the government. These individuals were not only concerned with fiscal restraint, but also were influenced by traditional views of the family.

Responsibility under the Conservatives for overseeing the UI review process was assigned to Paul McCrossan, parliamentary secretary to the Minister of Employment and Immigration.[114] To initiate the review, in July 1979 Employment and Immigration Canada released a paper, *Unemployment Insurance in the 1980s: A Review of Its Appropriate Role and Design*. This review, among other things, was to address 'dramatically changing conditions in society, economy and the labour market,'[115] including the increasing labour force participation and rate of unemployment among women and youth and the increase in multiple-earner families.[116]

By this point, women's groups were becoming increasingly concerned about UI. There was ongoing opposition to the discriminatory features of the UI program, including the continuing requirement that women prove childcare arrangements.[117] The right of fisher women to UI had also become a significant issue. Regulations governing the determination of earnings in the case of fishers stated that 'where his [the fisherman's] wife shares as a member of the crew her share shall be added to his earnings.'[118] This meant that wives who fished with their husbands were not eligible for UI, even though they had contributed to the plan. In early 1979 a number of complaints were registered with the Canadian Human Rights Commission both about fisher's wives and about female squid jiggers not receiving UI benefits.[119] At the 1979 NAC annual general meeting a resolution was passed 'protesting the discriminatory treatment of women squid jiggers of Newfoundland and supporting their complaint before the Human Rights Commission.'[120] Other complaints received by the CHRC in 1979 related to maternity issues (see chapter 5) and, to the change in the UI Act with respect to part-time work, which was seen as discriminatory toward women.[121]

Within NAC, employment issues continued to grow in prominence. In 1978–9 the 'new generation of feminists representing a more radical grass roots' gained a majority on the executive; in 1979 NAC formed an Employment Committee, on which more radical women were active.[122] NAC continued to voice opposition to the recent Bill C-14 changes and to call for a 'national industrial strategy that puts full employment first.'[123] Meanwhile, the CACSW broadened its analysis to include how changing economic and state structures could be discriminatory in their effect. It now argued that there was a need for a different approach to income security if women were to be able to 'pursue employment objectives in combination with their family responsibilities' – specifically, women's different patterns of work and family life needed to be taken into account. It pointed out that women's reproductive role and their disproportionate share of family responsibilities, as well as the lack of adequate childcare services, limited the types of jobs available and meant that women were more likely to have their careers interrupted.[124] The CACSW also continued to criticize the Bill C-14 amendments, arguing that provisions with respect to benefit rates, new entrants, re-entrants, and part-time workers disproportionately affected women[125] and suggesting that UI program costs could be reduced through strategies to reduce unemployment or by increasing contribution levels 'rather than by using characteristics related to a narrow definition of attachment to the labour force (part-time, new entrants, repeaters, etc).'[126] Finally, feminist authors began to counter the argument that women were secondary earners. Pat Armstrong, for example, took on this notion, arguing that 'the jobs, not the workers are secondary':[127]

> The only way the distinction makes sense is if we talk about jobs. Jobs are not primary and secondary in terms of their importance to the employer or the employee but in terms of their pay, prestige, skill, responsibility, attractiveness, working conditions and future opportunities. And while there is not a precise coincidence between these jobs and the sex and age of the workers, it is clear that women and young people are disproportionately slotted into jobs that are secondary in these terms.[128]

Women's groups raised a number of concerns about proposals made under the Conservatives' UI review. Of particular concern was the proposal that benefits be based on family income or family status. Such a proposal had been put forward by the Conservatives and others earlier in the decade; proponents saw it partly as a means of reducing expenditures, but also as a means of strengthening the place of the traditional family.[129] During the Bill C-14 hearings, McCrossan had expressed the view that UI abuses were 'concentrated heavily in the secondary wage-earner area, not in the primary area.'[130] Essentially, he took up the proposal put forward by the provincial ministers for a two-tier system based on family status, that those with dependants be entitled to a benefit rate of two-thirds of previous earnings, and those without to a rate of 50 per cent. It was suggested that dependants could be identified by applying the definition in the Income Tax Act.[131] Another proposal was that benefit eligibility depend on total family income.

Women's groups strongly opposed the idea that benefits should be based on either dependants or family income. A background study on the two-tier proposal suggested that the husband – usually the higher income earner – would in most cases be the spouse to claim dependants, and that overall, benefit payments would be reduced for wives and children in multiple-earner households, as well as for independent single people and couples without children.[132] The CACSW argued that entitlement should be based on one's status as a worker, not marital status.[133] It argued that under a two-tier system, most married women would be likely to receive lower benefit levels since traditional attitudes and tax policies favoured the husband as the higher wage earner. It also argued that basing benefits on family income would mean that the husband's income, which was typically higher, would usually be the determining factor in establishing the married woman's eligibility for benefits, and that many women would be denied the right to benefits as a consequence.[134] The NAC executive also expressed opposition to the proposed reforms, especially the two-tier system. Pointing out that it is usually the higher income earner who claims dependants for income tax purposes, NAC estimated that if the Conservatives' proposal was implemented, 96 per cent of women would receive only the 50 per cent level of benefits.[135]

Margrit Eichler also contributed to the debate, presenting an important challenge to the idea of using 'family income' as the basis for UI reforms. She pointed out that income is not necessarily shared equally among all family members[136] and that measuring income based on the family as the economic unit 'systematically hides the greatest income disparity of all ... that between women and men' and thereby reduces its importance as a policy issue.[137] She pointed out that disentitling wives from public benefits creates major inequities because most married women find themselves alone at some point in their lives; 'while she has been disentitled as a *family member*, a woman will have to bear the consequences of repeated disentitlements as an *individual*.' Furthermore, she argued, when women are contributing through taxes or UI premiums to the general social welfare but are unable to receive benefits, a form of redistribution from 'poor women' to 'rich men' is taking place.[138]

Women within the bureaucracy, particularly Status of Women Canada, also raised concerns about the UI review process. They feared that a shift toward a strict insurance basis 'would penalize those workers who experience the greatest difficulty in finding work.' They also raised concerns about proposals to further increase the disqualification period for voluntary quits and argued that the definition of 'just cause' in such cases must include sexual harassment, mobility of spouse and inability to find suitable childcare arrangements. Women within the bureaucracy also called for a uniform entrance requirement for all types of benefits in all regions, and for UI to be available to part-time workers with a cut-off of perhaps seven hours a week.[139] In addition, they strongly objected to the perception that women were abusing the UI plan, pointing out that UI officers were often biased and that women in the labour force faced many barriers, including childcare responsibilities, lack of adequate training, and segregation into high-unemployment job ghettoes that made finding and keeping jobs more difficult.[140]

Women in Status of Women Canada echoed the concerns of women's groups that a two-tier or family-based structure could disadvantage women. They also pointed out that it was likely the man, as the higher income earner, who would claim dependants and receive a higher rate; this would mean hardship for low-income single women and establish a precedent in moving from UI eligibility based on the individual worker 'towards the principle that the individual's family situation should ... determine entitlement to benefits.'[141] Through David MacDonald, Minister Responsible for the Status of Women, concerns were raised with both Ron Atkey and Prime Minister Joe Clark. MacDonald was highly circumspect in his comments; he did, however, observe that a two-tier system could deny married women workers 'the right to participate in the labour force on the same terms and conditions as their male counterparts,'[142] and he cautioned that 'preliminary assessment indicates that while [the two-tier] system as written may not discriminate, the *operation* of the system will be different for the sexes ... I would like to point out that we may ultimately be faced with a conflict between rigid insurance principles and principles ensuring that government policies do not discriminate against women in form, or in operation.'[143] In early 1980, before it had introduced any changes to the UI program, the Conservative government was defeated.

## Conclusion

The 1970s was a decade of shifting labour market structures and changing family work/life patterns during which the direction of macroeconomic and welfare state policies was very much open to debate. Changes in the position of women – in particular, their continued entry into the labour force – were central to the underlying shifts in material conditions. Gender ideology was similarly critical to the way in which responses to those shifts were constructed. At the same time, women increased their political activity, and in the process contested that ideology and constructed new views of women's role in the workforce.

Early in the decade, the state responded to the changing labour force and to fiscal pressures mainly by increasing its monitoring of UI benefit recipients, with a focus on women. Existing gender ideologies that presented women as able to 'choose' unemployment and therefore as likely to abuse the UI system were drawn on as explanations for rising unemployment and for increased UI costs. Labour, women's groups, and women within the state initially did little to question the family wage assumptions on which attitudes to women's unemployment and to certain UI provisions were based. As the crisis emerged and government priorities shifted to focus on supply-side explanations and restraint issues, conservative forces were able to construct a response in ways that built on gender inequalities and that left both labour and women's groups in a weak position to respond.

In the mid-1970s, unemployment was rising and the symptoms of an economic crisis were becoming more apparent, and governments focused on reducing expenditures, with an emphasis on a supply-side solution. The UI program was one of the first welfare state programs to be targeted for both restraint and restructuring. Here again, gendered explanations – in particular the view that a 'secondary' labour force was causing high unemployment and UI use – were used as a rationale for restructuring. Benefit levels were reduced, eligibility was tightened, and the federal government reduced its share of financing. Especially significant, for the first time a two-tier benefit structure was clearly established, with more stringent entrance requirements for repeat users and for new entrants and re-entrants to the labour market.

Only toward the end of the 1970s did women's groups effectively challenge prevailing views of women's unemployment and mount opposition to specific amendments to the UI plan. These groups eventually succeeded in having the terms of the debate cast in more gender-neutral terms and in emphasizing the importance of ensuring that women were entitled to benefits on an individual rather than a family basis. They were considerably less successful, however, in stopping UI benefits from being restricted for those in part-time or intermittent work situations. This, to some extent, would have more directly challenged the overall direction of economic policy. In addition, policy shifts with respect to part-time work reflected the need to come to terms with a deeper contradiction between welfare state programs implemented in the Keynesian postwar era and a restructuring economy in which intermittent work was increasingly the norm. A concern both with fiscal restraint and with redesigning the UI program so as to address these structural and demographic changes was to shape the terms of the debate over the next decade.

# CHAPTER 7

# The Conservatives in Power: A Polarized Debate and the Shift to a Market-Based Approach

Throughout the 1980s and into the 1990s there was a sharp polarization over the questions of unemployment, income security, and how to respond to the emerging contradictions in the welfare state and the economy. The 1980s opened with the return of the Liberals to power. There was some attempt to restrain the power of business, as seen in Finance Minister Alan MacEachen's 1981 budget, but this was quickly abandoned in the face of business opposition. With the defeat of this budget, and despite record high levels of unemployment, the Liberals shifted ground, clearly accepting the priorities of deficit reduction, increased international competitiveness, and the development of a good climate for business. The Conservatives were elected in September 1984 on a platform of 'jobs, jobs, jobs.' While the new Conservative government recognized the importance of the employment issue to the electorate, it also accepted the deficit reduction agenda; indeed, it oversaw a shift to the right in the ideological debate.

This chapter examines the developments of the 1980s and early 1990s, from the Liberals' return to power through to the major UI reforms passed by the Conservatives in the early 1990s. During the Conservatives' first term in office the review of income security programs, including UI, built on and extended the discussions of the previous decade. UI review was treated at part of a broader, market-driven agenda. As Barbara McDougall, Minister of Employment and Immigration, expressed it in introducing the first major UI changes, 'privatization, deregulation, tax reform and free trade are all parts of the same agenda for revitalizing the Canadian economy to meet the requirements of increased globalization of markets and rapid technological change.'[1] Social and political divisions on the issue of UI reform were such, however, that the Conservatives were able to introduce substantive amendments only after their second electoral victory in 1988. With respect to UI, major revisions began with Bill C-21, which was introduced in June 1989 and passed after extensive hearings and considerable controversy in October 1990. Revisions continued with the passage of Bill C-113 in April 1993.

The 1980s prepared the ground for the new neoliberal paradigm. At an *ideological* level, statements by business organizations, by the state, and by government-initiated commissions – including the Royal Commission on the Economic Union and Development Prospects for Canada (the Macdonald Commission)[2] and the Forget Commission of Inquiry into UI[3] – were important in reinforcing a supply-side analysis, in helping construct new views of the role of the state in both the national and continental economies, and in detailing the ways in which social policy (including UI) was to adapt to a changing economic environment.

With respect to *gender issues*, the continued entry of women into the labour market combined with an active mobilization of women's organizations to ensure that women's demands were strongly voiced. The UI debate was increasingly put in gender-neutral terms, and it seemed that a range of gender issues including part-time work, employment equity, maternity/parental leave, and childcare was now on the state's agenda. The enactment of the Charter in 1982 and the coming into force of the equality provisions in 1985 further strengthened women's equality claims. These were important gains for women, despite the overall shift toward a neoliberal agenda.

At a *political* level, the relative strengths of various forces were reconfigured. While there was an unprecedented opposition by labour, women's organizations, and the 'popular sector' to the deficit-reduction, market-oriented agenda,[4] these groups as a whole did not succeed in changing the government's course. In terms of UI, the debate was increasingly put in gender-neutral terms, with fewer references to 'secondary workers,' yet at the same time, seasonal and short-term workers in general became subject to criticism, and deep overall cuts and extensive restructuring were recommended. While studies were conducted on a range of issues of concern to women, substantive reforms on issues such as childcare failed to materialize. Equity concerns, and social policy in general, were subsumed by an agenda that gave weight to market forces and a balanced budget. These priorities eventually deter-

Table 7.1   Unemployment Rate, Canada, 1981–1993

|      | Men 15 years and over | Women 15 years and over | Total 15 years and over |
|------|-----------------------|-------------------------|-------------------------|
| 1981 | 7.0  | 8.3  | 7.5  |
| 1982 | 11.1 | 10.9 | 11.0 |
| 1983 | 12.1 | 11.6 | 11.9 |
| 1984 | 11.2 | 11.3 | 11.3 |
| 1985 | 10.4 | 10.7 | 10.5 |
| 1986 | 9.4  | 9.8  | 9.6  |
| 1987 | 8.6  | 9.3  | 8.9  |
| 1988 | 7.4  | 8.3  | 7.8  |
| 1989 | 7.3  | 7.8  | 7.5  |
| 1990 | 8.1  | 8.1  | 8.1  |
| 1991 | 10.9 | 9.7  | 10.4 |
| 1992 | 12.1 | 10.4 | 11.3 |
| 1993 | 11.8 | 10.6 | 11.2 |

Source: Statistics Canada, cat. 71-201, *Historical Labour Force Statistics*, 1983; 1995

mined the direction of welfare state transformation and UI reform more specifically; they also came to define women's life conditions. These trends are described below.

## UI Review in the 1980s

In the early 1980s, Canada entered a major recession and unemployment rates reached their highest levels since the Depression of the 1930s. Between 1981 and 1983, unemployment increased from 7.5 to 12 per cent, and it would remain above 10 per cent until 1986 (see Table 7.1).[5] At the same time, demographic and family work/life patterns were undergoing profound changes. Women continued to enter the labour force in growing numbers, and again, these increases were especially dramatic for married women and women with children. Between 1981 and 1988 the participation rate of women with preschool children jumped from 47.7 to 61.2 per cent while the rate for those with children six to fifteen increased from 61.8 to 71.2 per cent.[6] Between 1981 and the end of the Conservatives' first term in 1988, women's overall participation rate increased from 51.7 to 57.4 per cent, while men's declined from 78.4 to 76.6 per cent. The result was a continued feminization of the workforce. Women's share of the labour force increased from 40.8 per cent in 1981 to 44.1 per cent in 1988.[7] Part-time work also continued to assume more importance: the proportion of women working part-time increased from 24.2 per cent in 1981 to 26.1 per cent in 1985, and remained at about 25 per cent for the rest of the decade. Throughout the 1980s, women were between 71 and 72 per cent of part-time workers.[8] These changes constituted an important shift in family/market relations. State policies both contributed to and responded to these profound economic and family/workplace changes.

Despite a continued emphasis on women's labour market behaviour, a comparison of the number of unemployed (as measured by the Labour Force Survey) and the number of 'regular' UI beneficiaries between 1977 and 1980 reveals that the ratio of UI beneficiaries to unemployed was consistently much smaller for women than for men, and further, that as women's groups had feared, women were especially affected by the UI changes of the late 1970s (see Table 7.2, columns 3 and 6).[9] In 1977 approximately 69 per cent of unemployed women received UI benefits, compared to 81 per cent of men. Between 1977 and 1980, as UI revisions were implemented, the proportion of unemployed men receiving UI dropped, from 81.4 to 73.6 per cent, but the proportion of unemployed women receiving UI dropped further, from 68.7 to 59 per cent. In 1977, women represented 44 per cent of the unemployed (see Table 7.2, column 10) but only 40 per cent of UI claimants (see Table 7.2, column 8). By 1980, women accounted for 44.6 per cent of the unemployed but only 39.2 per cent of UI claimants; again, this suggests that the legislative changes of the late 1970s were especially hard on women.

It was in the context of these shifting economic and labour market conditions, and of growing concern with fiscal restraint, that the UI review started in the previous decade was taken up anew. When the new Liberal government came to power in 1980, a task force on UI was established within the Department of Manpower and Immigration. Labour market policy was viewed as critical to new strategies for addressing the social and economic problems of the 1980s in ways 'consistent with a growing concern for government spending restraint.'[10] The task force's report, issued in July 1981, identified the increased labour force participation of women and young people as the major change in the labour market environment since the 1940s.[11] Echoing studies from the 1970s, it stated that the expansion in the number of 'multi-earner families' had changed the nature of unemployment and that unemployment no longer entailed financial hardship the way it used to.[12] It also suggested that women's increased labour force participation contributed to higher unemployment rates, in that job growth was not keeping pace with women's entry into the labour market and that the

Table 7.2  UI Beneficiaries (regular benefits)/numbers unemployed, Canada, 1977–97

| | Men | | | Women | | | (7) Total UI beneficiaries | (8) Women as % of UI beneficiaries | (9) Total unemployed | (10) Women as % of unemployed | (11) Women as % of lab. force |
|---|---|---|---|---|---|---|---|---|---|---|---|
| | (1) UI beneficiaries | (2) Number unemployed (ann. aver.) | % of unempl. receiving UI | (4) UI beneficiaries | (5) Number unemployed (ann. aver.) | % of Unempl. receiving UI | | | | | |
| 1977 | 402,010 | 494,000 | 81.4 | 266,530 | 388,000 | 68.7 | 668,540 | 39.9 | 882,000 | 44.0 | 38.0 |
| 1978 | 424,670 | 523,000 | 81.2 | 285,830 | 421,000 | 67.9 | 710,490 | 40.2 | 945,000 | 44.6 | 38.8 |
| 1979 | 361,100 | 471,000 | 76.7 | 254,120 | 399,000 | 63.9 | 615,220 | 41.3 | 870,000 | 45.9 | 39.3 |
| 1980 | 367,130 | 499,000 | 73.6 | 236,810 | 401,000 | 59.0 | 603,940 | 39.2 | 900,000 | 44.6 | 40.0 |
| 1981 | 370,100 | 519,000 | 71.3 | 250,080 | 415,000 | 60.3 | 620,180 | 40.3 | 934,000 | 44.4 | 40.6 |
| 1982 | 648,870 | 812,000 | 79.9 | 382,570 | 551,000 | 69.4 | 1,031,440 | 37.1 | 1,363,000 | 40.4 | 41.1 |
| 1983 | 691,970 | 899,000 | 77.0 | 427,040 | 605,000 | 70.6 | 1,119,010 | 38.2 | 1,504,000 | 40.2 | 41.6 |
| 1984 | 638,860 | 838,000 | 76.2 | 427,360 | 612,000 | 69.8 | 1,066,220 | 40.1 | 1,450,000 | 42.2 | 42.0 |
| 1985 | 594,300 | 787,000 | 75.5 | 424,700 | 594,000 | 71.5 | 1,019,000 | 41.7 | 1,381,000 | 43.0 | 42.5 |
| 1986 | 561,690 | 723,000 | 77.7 | 410,450 | 560,000 | 73.3 | 972,140 | 42.2 | 1,283,000 | 43.6 | 42.8 |
| 1987 | 510,920 | 662,000 | 77.2 | 398,120 | 546,000 | 72.9 | 909,040 | 43.8 | 1,208,000 | 45.2 | 43.2 |
| 1988 | 489,600 | 578,000 | 84.7 | 394,320 | 503,000 | 78.4 | 883,920 | 44.6 | 1,082,000 | 46.5 | 43.7 |
| 1989 | 490,750 | 578,000 | 84.9 | 397,870 | 487,000 | 81.7 | 888,620 | 44.8 | 1,065,000 | 45.7 | 43.9 |
| 1990 | 549,020 | 649,000 | 84.6 | 413,760 | 515,000 | 80.3 | 962,780 | 43.0 | 1,164,000 | 44.2 | 44.4 |
| 1991 | 691,180 | 866,000 | 79.8 | 464,830 | 626,000 | 74.3 | 1,156,010 | 40.2 | 1,492,000 | 42.0 | 44.7 |
| 1992 | 682,030 | 966,000 | 70.6 | 466,080 | 674,000 | 69.2 | 1,148,110 | 40.6 | 1,640,000 | 41.1 | 44.8 |
| 1993 | 634,420 | 952,000 | 66.6 | 440,760 | 697,000 | 63.2 | 1,075,180 | 41.0 | 1,649,000 | 42.3 | 44.9 |
| 1994 | 517,510 | 885,000 | 58.5 | 378,460 | 656,000 | 57.7 | 895,970 | 42.2 | 1,541,000 | 42.6 | 44.9 |
| 1995 | 428,890 | 801,000 | 53.5 | 307,690 | 621,000 | 49.5 | 736,580 | 41.8 | 1,422,000 | 43.7 | 45.1 |
| 1996 | 409,060 | 822,500 | 49.7 | 297,990 | 646,700 | 46.1 | 707,050 | 42.1 | 1,469,200 | 44.0 | 44.7 |
| 1997 | 340,810 | 779,100 | 43.7 | 247,860 | 634,300 | 39.1 | 588,670 | 42.1 | 1,413,400 | 44.9 | 45.6 |

Sources: UI beneficiaries – from Statistics Canada cat. 73-202S, *UI Statistics, 1995*; table 6, p. 24–6; 1996, 1997 – data supplied by Statistics Canada. Figures are 12-month averages. Labour Force figures – from Statistics Canada cat. 71-201, *Historical Labour Force Statistics, 1995*.

'behavioural aspects of youth and women have contributed to a relative increase in unemployment from factors other than cyclical business conditions.'[13]

The report's major emphasis was on ways to 'reduce or remove the barriers to labour market adjustments.'[14] It suggested that special provisions for new entrants, re-entrants, and repeaters should be removed (on equity and program simplicity grounds), but that there should also be a general increase in UI entrance requirements to something like a variable entrance of fifteen to twenty weeks.[15] It argued that increasing entrance requirements, reducing benefit duration, and increasing penalties for those who voluntarily quit without just cause would strengthen work attachments and job search incentives and 'reduce the seasonal cycle of dependency on UI.' It further recommended strengthening the developmental uses of UI 'to permit UI to contribute more positively to labour market objectives.'[16] While options such as basing UI on family income or dependency status were discussed, the report recommended *not* adopting measures like this. It argued that such an approach would introduce the criterion of need into the UI plan and would also seem to be attaching less value to the work of lower-income family members (usually women and young people) and could thus be considered discriminatory.[17] The government, faced with record high levels of unemployment for the postwar period, was not prepared to accept recommendations to tighten the program and distanced itself from the task force report.[18] Apart from introducing maternity amendments and lowering the minimum insurability requirements from twenty hours a week to fifteen, no major revisions to the UI program were undertaken by the Liberals in the early 1980s.

## The Conservatives' First Term

The Conservatives came to power in 1984. Despite continued high unemployment levels (unemployment remained as high as 11.3 per cent in 1984 – see Table 7.1), and election promises to give priority to job creation, in Finance Minister Michael Wilson's economic statement of November 1984 unemployment was to be dealt with only indirectly, through the creation of a good business climate.[19] With respect to social programs, the Conservatives indicated their intention to proceed with far-reaching reforms. They wished to end universality, to target programs to those most in need,[20] to contain costs, and to redesign programs such as UI in ways that would, again, 'facilitate labour market adjustments'[21] and 'foster adaptation, rather than inertia and fear of change.'[22] Wilson's statement expressed concern that UI was creating disincentives to work, discouraging mobility to other regions and industries, and imposing a tax burden on the private sector, especially small business.[23] Suggested directions for change included increasing the disqualification period for those who quit voluntarily, increasing entrance requirements, reducing benefits, and increasing the use of UI for labour market adjustment objectives such as training.[24] While Wilson identified UI as an area for further review, he also announced some immediate and significant 'administrative changes.' These included that severance pay and pension benefits would be treated as income in determining UI entitlement and that the claimant interview program would be intensified.[25] Of the $4.2 billion in expenditure reductions and 'revenue recovery measures' announced by Wilson for 1985–6, the biggest savings – $296 million – were to come from the UI program.[26] Wilson suggested that such reductions were not inappropriate at a time of high unemployment because many of the unemployed were not 'as rigorous as they might be in seeking employment.'[27]

The Conservatives indicated their commitment to equality both during the election campaign (which saw, for the first and effectively the last time, a leaders' debate on women's issues) and in their government's first Speech from the Throne. Finance Minister Michael Wilson's economic statement similarly seemed to give some consideration to equity concerns.[28] Gender equity concerns, however, were quickly subsumed by the larger agenda of reducing government intervention, cutting the deficit, fostering a positive climate for new enterprise, and increasing international competitiveness.[29]

The Conservatives' arguments for less government intervention, greater reliance on market forces, and the removal of obstacles to labour market adjustment were given further impetus by two major reports of the mid-1980s: the Macdonald Commission Report on the Economic Union and Development Prospects for Canada, and the Forget Commission of Inquiry into UI. The Macdonald Commission, established by the Liberals in 1982, was given a broad mandate to recommend goals and policies for the Canadian government. Most notably, it urged the negotiation of a Canada–United States free trade agreement, but it also recommended sweeping changes to the social security system. The commission argued that reforms were needed in order to make programs more compatible with the goals of economic efficiency, increased international competitiveness, and labour market adjustment.[30] Its report echoed the view that the UI program inhibited labour market adjustments and contributed to high unemployment rates, and that UI tended to subsidize industries with unstable employment patterns and to reinforce the concentration of short-term jobs in regions with high unemployment.[31]

The Macdonald Commission drew on unemployment studies from the 1970s to emphasize that demographic changes (the increased labour force participation of women and youth) and generous social programs (UI and minimum wages) were key contributors to the long-run rise in unemployment and to argue that unemployment no longer entailed the hardship that it once did.[32] It suggested, however, that the influence of these factors had peaked.[33] Overall, its analysis was cast in more-gender neutral terms – for example, references to those with 'unstable employment patterns' were directed as much to those in seasonal industries as to women.[34] However, the Macdonald Commission shared with the earlier studies an emphasis on supply-side factors, behavioural characteristics, and labour market 'rigidities' such as the UI program and minimum wage laws, contending that these factors did much to explain unemployment trends. It argued for changes in UI to reduce the unemployment rate.

Specific recommendations made by the commission for reforming the UI program included introducing experience rating (i.e., tying premiums to the risk of unemployment in particular industries), reducing the benefit rate (from 60 to 50 per cent of earnings), raising the entrance requirement to a variable requirement of fifteen to twenty weeks, tightening the link between benefits paid and time worked (e.g., by establishing a ratio of two or three weeks' work to qualify for one week of benefits), and, in order to encourage labour movement toward regions with higher levels of employment, eliminating the regional differentiation in program provisions. It also recommended that any savings generated by the UI changes be redirected to a transitional adjustment assistance package (TAAP) that would facilitate labour market adjustment through such measures as on-the-job training, wage subsidy programs, early retirement plans, and mobility grants.[35]

The Conservatives promised review of the UI program took the form of a Commission of Inquiry (the Forget Commission), established in July 1985.[36] Like the Macdonald Commission, the Forget Report emphasized supply-side factors, behavioural characteristics, unemployment as an individual problem and a matter of individual choice, the tendency for UI to create 'long-run dependencies,' and the need to improve work incentives.[37] Also like the Macdonald Commission, it cast its analysis of unemployment and its recommendations for changes to the UI program in mostly gender-neutral terms, with the emphasis, again, being on seasonal or short-term workers in general, rather than on women in particular. Indeed, the emphasis now seemed to be more on seasonal unemployment among construction workers and in regionally concentrated industries in fishing and forestry. Much concern was expressed about claimants who could repeatedly work for ten to fourteen weeks a year and collect UI for the remainder of the year.[38]

Yet in some respects the Forget recommendations seemed to address women's concerns. The report argued that different work patterns and needs arising, among other things, from women's increased participation, should be recognized. It suggested, for example, that UI be extended eventually to all part-time workers, and first to those working a minimum of eight hours a week.[39] Arguing that it was important to treat all types of work equally, the report also recommended a uniform entry requirement of 350 hours of work (equivalent to ten weeks at thirty-five hours a week), which would apply to all workers, including those applying for sickness and maternity benefits as well as new entrants, re-entrants, and repeaters. The report also recommended parental benefits to either parent (adoptive or natural), in addition to maternity benefits for the period surrounding childbirth.[40] Overall, however, the Forget recommendations would have made it much more difficult for many women to receive benefits – at least at anything like the rate then in place. The recommendations favoured maintaining benefits for those working full-time, full year, while restricting benefits for those with short-term or intermittent employment patterns. The report's most controversial recommendation was for an 'annualization' program, whereby benefits would be calculated on the basis of total earnings in the previous fifty-two weeks (and paid out in equal amounts for a maximum of fifty weeks.) Effectively, this would have greatly reduced the benefits for those with intermittent work and those who faced periods when no income was received.[41]

The report further recommended establishing a cumulative employment account so that long-term workers could build up credits to supplement benefits or to help adjust to employment changes.[42] However, access to the fund, available after approximately thirty years of employment, would require having worked full-time for twenty-six of the thirty years, and calculations would only start from the first full year of employment. Again, this was clearly targeted at those with a steady, long-term labour force attachment – more typically a male than a female work pattern – to the disadvantage of those working part-time in intermittent job situations, or who had spent time away from the labour force, for example, because of family responsibilities.[43] Furthermore, the Forget Commission suggested that a scheme based on family income and status, targeted at those most in need, and available to the 'working poor,' would be a more appropriate form of income supplementation than the UI program.

Both this supply-side orientation and the proposed new direction for social policy reform were strongly contested. The widespread consultations that were part of the Macdonald and Forget inquiries and the public's reaction after the reports were released revealed much polarization on the issue. Business was generally favourable to the new orientation. For example the Business Council on National Issues (BCNI) expressed strong support for the general orientation of the Macdonald and Forget reports. It favoured a shift from income replacement to skill development and 're-employment incentives,' as well as the idea that UI should primarily be for those who are seldom unemployed and restricted for those who are often unemployed. It further argued that UI benefits should be based on insurance considerations, not on such factors as regional unemployment; also, that eligibility periods should be increased and benefit duration reduced and that there would be higher penalties for voluntary job leavers.[44]

Labour, women's groups, and forces of the 'popular sector' strongly opposed the emphasis on supply-side factors and individual responsibility for unemployment, as well as specific recommendations that threatened to drastically reduce the amount of benefits available.[45] Labour's representatives on both commissions expressed their strong disagreement with the tenor and recommendations of the reports;[46] the labour representatives on the Forget Commission, Frances Soboda and Jack Munro, issued a ninety-page dissenting report. Labour representatives also argued that a number of the recommendations would disadvantage women; here they especially had in mind the proposed annualization program and special cumulative employment account.[47] They further emphasized the importance of retaining regional equalization through extended UI benefits, both as a recognition of the government's responsibility for unemployment, and because of the contribution that UI benefits made to local economies.[48] As an alternative, they proposed a more generous UI scheme with a uniform ten-week entrance requirement, increased benefits, greater coverage for part-time workers, and extended maternity and parental benefits.[49] Labour unions also pointed out that the emphasis on labour mobility could create hardship for women.[50]

Women's groups also strongly opposed both the supply-side orientation of the reform proposals and specific recommendations for UI reform. NAC argued that the problems of unemployment and high UI use were not the result of the UI system, women's increased labour force participation, or the attitude of Canadian workers; rather, they reflected a lack of jobs due to such factors as technological change and international capital mobility.[51] Both NAC and the CACSW argued that many of the proposed reforms would be especially hard on women and would reinforce their disadvantaged position. It was pointed out that a reduction in benefit levels would be very difficult for low-income earners, a large proportion of whom were women. It was noted that relocation requirements would pose difficulties for women, who were normally the lowest-paid workers in a family and could find it difficult to persuade their families to move. Both groups argued that the emphasis on long labour force attachment (through longer entrance requirements and the tying of benefits to weeks worked) would disadvantage women since they 'tend to be more heavily represented among part-time and temporary workers and they are more likely to be working in marginal industries which frequently lay off workers.'[52] Both the CACSW and NAC argued that Forget's proposals with respect to annualization, the cumulative account, and part-time work could have devastating consequences for women.[53] Both groups also opposed increased penalties for those quitting their jobs for 'just cause' and basing benefits on family income or status.[54]

The CACSW proposed that benefits be maintained at least at their current levels and urged that high rates of unemployment must be addressed 'by developing effective policies for full employment' that would 'incorporate a specific employment strategy based on the particular characteristics of women's employment and unemployment.'[55] As an alternative, NAC repeated its call for 'an industrial strategy and long term planning for Canada, with a full employment policy at its centre.'[56] Such a policy, it suggested, might involve revitalizing the manufacturing sector, reducing working time, offering more time away from work for parenting and for upgrading skills, and taking measures to discourage the flight of capital.[57]

The Conservative government distanced itself from the Forget recommendations and assigned the Standing Committee on Labour, Employment and Immigration to examine the issue further. This all-party committee held further hearings and issued its own report in March 1987.[58] This report, the Hawkes Report, strongly disagreed with Forget's concept of 'annualization.'[59] In contrast, it recommended a universally low entrance requirement (ten weeks), a relatively generous benefit duration (a maximum of fifty weeks), an increase in benefits to as high as $66^2/_3$ per cent, and greater provision for part-time workers. It further recommended that those leaving the labour force temporarily – for example, for schooling or childrearing – be able to 'bank' credits so that they could make a claim when returning to the labour force. The committee did, however, agree that UI should be 'a vehicle to help people realize better and more stable employment opportunities in the future,'[60] and recommended the increased use of UI for such 'active' labour market policies as training, work sharing, mobility assistance, self-employment projects, and job creation. In May 1987, Benoit Bouchard, Minister of Employment and Immigration, stated that the government had studied the various recommendations, that there were clearly 'sharp and irreconcilable differences' in approach, and therefore that no changes would be made at that time.[61]

In sum, despite early promises to review and reform the UI program, the Tories by the end of their first term had been confronted with deep divisions on the issue; faced with these, they made very few concrete changes. Even so, this period was important in laying the ideological foundations for a restructuring of the UI program; indeed, in many respects this was the time when the blueprint was developed for reforms that would finally be introduced in the 1990s. Labour, women's groups, and others made some effort to present alternatives, but these were not seriously considered. The business community, the major commissions and committees of inquiry, and the Conservative Party combined their voices to shift the terms of the debate. Their basic argument, which would resurface time and again over the next ten years, was that supply-side factors and behavioural characteristics caused high unemployment levels, that UI was creating dependencies, that the program should facilitate rather than hinder labour market adjustments, and that UI should be reserved for those with long-term, stable work attachments, while providing less income security to those in short-term, intermittent work situations. The language of the reports was increasingly gender neutral, but as women's groups warned, the proposals these reports advanced were likely to result in increased structural inequalities for women.

## Gender Equity in the 1980s

An equally important development that occurred at the same time as this rightward shift in economic and social policy issues was the unprecedented mobilization of women's organizations. Women's service and advocacy groups proliferated and the involvement of women within unions grew. This was a time when NAC was described as being 'very active, growing constantly in membership, high profile and effective in both public education and lobbying.'[62] In addition, the enactment of the Charter in 1982 and the coming into force of its equality provisions in 1985 provided an important framework for advancing women's equality claims. Women's groups such as NAC became an increasingly important voice not only with respect to 'women's issues' but also in opposing the direction of economic policy. For example, it became a highly visible presence in opposition to the Canada–United States free trade agreement. The growing participation of women in the labour force and the stronger representation of women's concerns by both women's organizations and trade unions generated a great deal of pressure to act on equity issues. The result was tension between gender equity concerns and the broader market-driven agenda being promoted by both the Liberals and the Conservatives. As described below, this was largely resolved by greater gender neutrality in government documents, by greater formal equality, and by some recognition of the need for programs such as maternity leave that would allow women greater continuity in the labour force. At the same time, however, policies were being introduced that were likely to deepen structural inequalities.

In the early 1980s, the Liberals appointed a number of task forces and commissions of inquiry to address issues of concern to women. These included the Commission of Inquiry into Part-Time Work (the Wallace Commission), established in 1982,[63] the Abella Commission, examining equality in employment, appointed in June 1983,[64] and the task force on childcare (the Cooke task force), appointed in 1984.[65] In addition, after the Conservatives came to power a parliamentary committee (the Boyer Committee) examined the coming into force of the Section 15 equality provisions of the Charter.[66]

These reports contributed to the debates over the need for maternity/parental provisions and over possible inequalities that might result from the regular UI program. For example, the Wallace Commission found that part-time workers were generally treated unfairly and made a number of recommendations to improve their position, including that the minimum number of hours per week needed for UI coverage be reduced from fifteen to eight.[67] In addition, the reports of this period were significant in that they pointed to the growing importance of gender equity issues and provided a forum for ongoing discussions of equality.[68] The reports of the Abella Commission and the Boyer Committee examined notions of equality and possible remedies for inequality and discrimination. Both made important contributions in arguing that equality does not necessarily mean 'sameness of treatment'; rather what was critical was 'equality of results.'[69] As the Abella Report expressed it: 'Sometimes equality means treating people the same, despite their differences, and sometimes it means treating them as equals by accommodating their differences.'[70] Both took the view that providing greater equality for women meant accommodating differences with respect to child bearing and rearing responsibilities.[71] In this regard the Boyer Committee devoted considerable space to a discussion of UI maternity benefits.[72] It recommended removing the special twenty-week entrance requirement, and also eliminating the fifteen-week aggregate limit on special benefits which meant that pregnant women who became ill and received sickness benefits had little left over for maternity purposes. In addition, the committee noted that the extension of benefits to either adoptive parent, effective January 1984, had created the anomalous situation that adoptive fathers were eligible for parental benefits whereas natural fathers were not. While asserting that UI maternity benefits payable to women involved 'no denial of equality to men,' the Boyer Committee contended that a shortcoming of the program was that natural fathers who wished to participate in early childcare were unable to claim benefits.

The Boyer Committee recommended a tiered system of maternity benefits: a first tier recognizing the physical needs of the mother in the period around childbirth and available to women only; and a second tier, corresponding to the period of adjustment and early childcare, which would be available to either parent (adoptive or natural), with the option for one parent to take it or for both parents to split it or take it concurrently. It argued that the existing fifteen weeks was not enough to accommodate both functions and that it risked 'tak[ing] away existing rights from one group (new mothers) in order to afford equality to another (fathers).'[73]

The Boyer Committee took what it described as a 'broad and generous' approach to the equality question,[74] and certainly took this approach to mean that different treatment for women and men on the maternity question was justified. Yet when it came to structural situations that might entail economic inequalities for women, the committee was more reluctant to recommend changes. It did follow the Wallace Commission and others in urging wider UI coverage for part-time workers,[75] but it also argued that the longer, twenty-week entrance requirement for new entrants and re-entrants did not raise a Section 15 issue.[76] In addition, it argued that the family represents an economic unit and that in some situations distinctions on the grounds of marital or family status (not explicitly enumerated in Section 15) could be 'demonstrably justified in the sense of section 1 of the Charter.'[77] Contrary to the arguments being made by women's groups, the committee thus suggested that a plan based on family rather than individual income was compatible with notions of equality.

The issue of maternity and parental benefits was also taken up by the Cooke Child Care Task Force. Task Force members pointed to a number of weaknesses in the UI maternity program, including its low take-up rate,[78] its two-week waiting period (which made no sense for maternity claimants), its qualifying requirements (which excluded many part-time workers, the self-employed, and those working fewer than twenty weeks a year), and the low benefit rate of 60 per cent of earnings.[79] The task force recommended that within five years maternity benefits increase to 75 per cent of earnings for a twenty-week period and that within ten years this be increased again to 95 per cent of earnings and a twenty-six-week benefit period.[80] It recommended that birth and adoption benefits be available to either parent and that an additional five days' paid leave for the father at the time of birth be available. In addition, it recommended that parental benefit coverage be extended to part-time employees who work at least eight hours per week and to claimants with ten weeks' employment.[81] However, the task force was unable to reach a consensus on the Boyer Committee's recommendation with respect to a two-tier parental benefit system: some task force members argued that a period of leave should be reserved for the mother's physical recuperation, while others argued that parents should be free to divide the benefit period between them as they wished.

Throughout this period, women's groups pushed for improved maternity and parental benefits and for the removal of inequalities in regular UI benefits. Both NAC and the CACSW continued to argue that special entrance requirements for new entrants and re-entrants should be removed[82] and that a higher proportion of part-time workers should receive UI coverage.[83] In addition, both groups supported the notion of an extended tiered system of parental benefits, with a number of weeks of maternity benefits available only to mothers, in recognition of the time needed for physical recuperation, and with additional weeks available to either parent.[84] In 1987 NAC called for increases in UI maternity and parental benefits to 95 per cent of insurable earnings and for up to ten days of benefits a year to care for family members.[85] The CACSW similarly urged that benefits not be reduced for natural mothers, that twenty-four weeks of childcare benefits be available to all new parents, and that the higher entrance requirement for special benefits be removed. Besides all this, both groups recommended that the two-week waiting period be eliminated and that the fifteen-week aggregate limit for sickness, maternity, and adoption benefits be removed.[86]

Finally, impetus for change on the issue of parental benefits came as a result of a Charter challenge. The case was brought by a father, Shalom Schachter, who wished to share the fifteen-week 'maternity' benefits available to his wife.[87] Pointing out that adoptive fathers now had that right, he argued that the denial of benefits to natural fathers contravened Section 15 of the Charter. Judge J. Strayer, writing the decision in June 1988, found that the denial of benefits to natural fathers constituted discrimination based on sex; that its roots were in the sexual stereotyping of the roles of father and mother; and that it was 'predicated on the belief that [the] natural mother is the natural and inevitable care-giver and that the father is the natural bread-winner.'[88] He found that the distinction created 'a disincentive for natural fathers to accept an equal role and responsibility with respect to the care of their newborn children' and an 'inequality of benefit' contrary to Section 15 of the Charter.[89] Following the arguments of the Women's Legal Education and Action Fund, which acted as an intervenor in the case,[90] and citing expert evidence that the physical demands on pregnant women and new mothers justified a period of at least fifteen weeks, the judge also stated that the fifteen weeks of benefits available to natural mothers should not be reduced.[91]

These developments suggested considerable evolution both in prevailing notions of equality and in the state's attitude toward working women. In the previous decade, policy was still being informed by two ideas: that pregnant women should withdraw to the private sphere for a certain period around childbirth; and that pregnancy and childrearing were individual responsibilities – 'the result of a voluntary act' – rather than societal ones. Many of the struggles in that period had centred on the right of women to receive the *same* treatment as men – especially the right of women who were available for and capable of work to receive regular benefits during the period around childbirth. Now, in contrast, the state was rejecting certain policies as discriminatory because they were based on the stereotype of the mother as caregiver and father as breadwinner. There was also a new recognition that equality for women sometimes meant the right to the same treatment as men, and other times the right to different treatment. This in turn signified that women could be entitled to special maternity benefits without it being considered a 'denial of equality to men.' Thus, state policies in this important era, during which a new market-oriented paradigm was being constructed, were no longer suggesting that women be relegated to the home; rather, they involved the assumption that women needed to be accommodated within the workforce.

## UI Reform: The Conservatives' Second Term in Power

Deep social and political divisions had effectively prevented the Conservatives from introducing reforms during their first term in power. After the 1988 election, however, they were in a much stronger position not only to proceed with Canada–United States free trade (the dominant electoral issue), but also to undertake sweeping social policy restructuring along the lines being suggested by the major business think tanks and by the federal government commissions of the mid-1980s.

UI reform began shortly after the election. The unemployment rate had dropped through much of the Conservatives' first term as the economy came out of the recession of the early 1980s; even so, the reforms were being introduced in the context of continuing relatively high unemployment levels (7.4 per cent for men; 8.3 per cent for women in 1988 – see Table 7.1). In addition, there was growing awareness of the changing structure of the labour market, as 'contingent,' 'non-standard,' service-sector work assumed a growing importance, as many plants shut down, especially in the months following the signing of the Free Trade Agreement, and as resource-based industries – particularly the fisheries – were faced with a depletion of both resources and jobs. Women's labour market participation continued to increase in the late 1980s, from 57.4 per cent in 1988 to 58.4 per cent in 1990.[92] Again, the increases were especially dramatic for women with preschool children (under six years), whose participation rate increased from 59.9 per cent in 1987 to 64.0 per cent in 1991. Overall, between 1981 and 1991 the participation rate for this group of women increased from 47.5 per cent to 64 per cent.[93] In the mid-1980s the proportion of unemployed receiving UI had been lower than in the previous decade (a low of 75.5 per cent for men in 1985 and of 70 per cent for women in 1984 – see Table 7.2),[94] but as the economy improved the proportion receiving income security started increasing again, reaching a new peak in 1989 of 85 per cent for men and 82 per cent for women (see Table 7.2). Thus, although the ratio of UI beneficiaries to unemployed remained smaller for women than for men, the gender gap in this period narrowed significantly.

During the 1988 election, little mention had been made of UI reform. As early as the April 1989 Speech from the Throne, however, the Conservatives were signalling their intent to proceed with major revisions. Proposals for UI reforms were contained in the policy paper *Success in the Works*, tabled by Barbara McDougall, Minister of Employment and Immigration, in the week following the Throne Speech.[95] More concretely, the May 1989 budget contained the provision that beginning in 1990 the federal government would withdraw from UI financing, leaving the UI account to be fully funded by employer and employee premiums.[96] Amendments to the UI Act were subsequently introduced in June 1989 in Bill C-21. After more than a decade of discussion and review, major revisions to the UI program were underway.

The changes outlined in *Success in the Works* followed the direction of the major reports of the decade and were consistent with the emphasis on fiscal restraint, a reduction of labour market rigidities, and the importance of supply-side factors in determining unemployment. Although it was not explicitly stated, there was much speculation that changes were being introduced in response to pressures associated with the free trade agreement – in particular, that the government was trying to create conditions that would allow Canadian businesses to compete on an equal basis with their American counterparts.[97] First, a number of measures were aimed at lowering costs and at reducing disincentives to work. The minimum qualifying period was to be increased from a variable entrance requirement (VER) of ten to fourteen weeks to a new VER of ten to twenty weeks, depending on the regional rate of unemployment. The cuts were larger than it first appeared. The previous minimum requirement of ten weeks had applied to regions where unemployment was above 9 per cent; now, a regional unemployment rate above 15 per cent was required for the minimum ten-week qualifying period to apply. In most areas the new requirement was six weeks longer.[98] Second, the maximum duration of benefits was to be reduced, except in those regions with the highest unemployment rates.[99] Third, the penalty for those who quit voluntarily without just cause, who refused a suitable job, or who were fired for misconduct was to be increased from a one- to six-week penalty to a penalty of seven to twelve weeks. In addition, the benefit rate for these workers would be reduced from 60 to 50 per cent of earnings.

The amendments were designed to emphasize active labour market measures such as training and skill development. These were seen as necessary both to maintain Canada's competitiveness and to deal with unemployment. The estimated $1.3 billion in savings[100] from the changes outlined above were largely to be redirected from 'passive income maintenance' toward a range of more active labour market programs. In keeping with the overall emphasis on the private sector as key to success,[101] this included programs to reinforce private sector training, which, it was argued, would further strengthen 'the competitiveness of Canadian industry.'[102] Other funding was to be provided for 'human resource planning,' for increasing employees' skill levels, for an expansion of training programs offered through the UI program,[103] for 'adjustment' for firms and employees facing major expansion or closure, and for 'rural communities whose economies have been affected by changing market conditions.'[104] Funding was also to be made available to help displaced older workers find jobs and to increase mobility assistance to UI recipients moving to low-unemployment areas. A few measures departed significantly from traditional uses of UI. Funds were to be used to expand federal/provincial joint initiatives to help social assistance recipients 'acquire the necessary skills and experience to become self-sufficient' and to encourage 'self-employment and entrepreneurship' by allowing UI claimants with viable business plans to use their benefits to help defray business start-up costs.[105]

Fifth, some $450 million of the savings was to go to improved parental, sickness, and other benefits. Proposed amendments included providing an additional ten weeks of parental benefits to natural or adoptive parents, either mother or father, while maintaining fifteen weeks of maternity benefits available to the mother for the period surrounding childbirth. In addition, the fifteen-week limit on combined maternity and sickness benefits was replaced by a thirty-week limit. Finally, in order, again, to ensure compliance with the Charter, UI coverage was to be extended to those over sixty-five who chose to remain in the labour market. While the Conservatives reiterated their concern to 'promote equality of opportunity in Canada's economic life,'[106] this was clearly secondary to other economic and labour market concerns. Increased parental benefits certainly represented a gain in terms of recognizing the need for a better balance of work and family responsibilities, but this amendment was essentially a response to the Charter ruling on *Schachter*, was to be paid for directly by cuts to overall UI benefits, and actually involved a reduction in benefits for adoptive parents. The tension between gender equity and other goals was resolved in that limited rights to equality were accorded; but overall, as a goal, gender equity had clearly been made secondary to other concerns.

Hearings on Bill C-21 took place in the fall of 1989. Business groups supported the proposals as a move in the right direction.[107] On the other hand, an outpouring of concern came from a range of groups, from the Catholic Bishops to unemployed help centres, from local women's groups to opposition parties, from national labour groups to women's organizations. These concerns touched on a number of issues. First, attention focused on the consequences of program cuts – in particular, the increased qualifying period and shortened duration of benefits. Government estimates suggested that the changes would create little hardship;[108] other studies suggested quite devastating consequences. For example, a study commissioned by the CLC estimated that an additional 128,000 claimants would have failed to qualify if Bill C-21 had been in place in 1988, compared to a government estimate of 30,000. In the Atlantic region, the government estimated that only 6,500 would fail to qualify as a result of the changes; CLC figures on UI claimants from 1988 showed that an additional 45,000 claimants would have been disqualified.[109] The CLC further estimated that 80 per cent of those who would become ineligible, or whose benefits would be reduced, had incomes below $25,000 per year.[110]

Testimony from different regions of the country echoed concern about the implications of the changes for poor regions of the country, for low-income workers, for seasonal and part-time workers, for immigrants, and for natives, as well as for women, many of whom were already having difficulty meeting the existing entrance requirement.[111] From the Atlantic region, it was noted:

> It is extremely difficult for fish plant workers to attain much more than ten or twelve weeks of work. It is not their fault ... That is the economic reality of living in an economically underprivileged and underdeveloped part of the country. Toughening entrance requirements, shortening benefit periods, and otherwise restricting and cutting back on the UI program will

only impose further hardship on people who can afford it the least. Coming at the same time as severe economic problems arising from failed federal management of the fishery, they constitute an economic double-whammy, with far-reaching effects.[112]

It was also pointed out that while Ontario – and Metro Toronto in particular – had low registered rates of unemployment, there had been many plant shutdowns, partly as a result of the free trade agreement; also that, some groups of workers (e.g., older workers, immigrants, and women) were experiencing a great deal of difficulty finding new employment, and that when they did find work it was often in the service sector, in non-unionized workplaces, and at lower rates of pay.[113]

Many expressed the fear that women would be especially hard hit. Employment and Immigration Canada itself estimated that women would be disproportionately affected by the UI cuts in the first year of operation.[114] NAC argued that 'women, even more than men,' would be hurt, given the large numbers working in part-time, short-term work situations and their higher rates of unemployment and given that 'they are still the last hired and the first fired and, in the present economic climate, the most vulnerable to layoffs due to technological change and the restructuring which will result from the Free Trade Agreement with the United States.'[115] It was predicted that women working in areas such as fish canning, clothing, and hotel and restaurant services, or as farmworkers, would be particularly affected by such changes.[116]

Testimony suggested that women across the country would likely experience UI changes in a different way then men. It was pointed out that in B.C.'s forestry sector, while much work for both women and men was seasonal, the season for women was often shorter than for men: 'In the north Okanagan both women and men are employed seasonally in the forest industry, but whereas men have a fairly long working season interrupted by spring break-up and the fire season, women employed as tree sorters and thinners have short working seasons of a few weeks, perhaps a couple of times a year, interrupted by a long session of being unemployed.'[117] Similarly, it was noted that on Prince Edward Island, the major industries – farming, fishing, and tourism – were all seasonal, but that where seasonally employed men were earning about $9,000, seasonally employed women were usually earning less than $6,000.[118] In single-industry towns, women faced particular challenges in finding long-term work. For example, representatives from Sudbury noted that 'Before the coming of the tax data centre there were not a lot of jobs for women, especially for single women ... With the advent of the new UI regulations, there will be a very severe impact on the largely female work force of the tax data centre. They employ ... between 1,000 to 1,500 contract employees, most of them, if not 99 per cent of them, female, and many of them work only ten weeks a year.'[119]

Others noted both the importance of women's work to family income – especially in recessionary times – and the general difficulties that women were facing finding employment in areas where there were few job possibilities. It was noted that in Saskatchewan, for example, continuing economic difficulties had meant an increase in off-farm labour, mostly undertaken by women: 'As the jobs they find are often part-time and insecure, the one-third of our farm families who are now relying on off-farm income also need the security of UI to help make ends meet. We cannot imagine what the past few years in this province would have been like if Bill C-21 had been in place.'[120] It was also pointed out that in the Atlantic provinces, women had few employment options:

> Just as in the rest of the country, women in the Atlantic region have been dramatically increasing their labour force participation. Here, however, a depressed economy provides them with fewer opportunities to pursue their aspirations through paid work. Their participation rate is still much lower than at the national level and they experience much more unemployment than men in the region and women nationally ... The labour force survey data on reasons for remaining in part-time jobs shows clearly that there are few options for people who want to improve their lot.[121]

Strong objections were also raised to the shift in orientation toward greater private responsibility for unemployment and toward more 'active' UI measures. The ending of federal contributions to UI financing was seen as an abdication of the federal government's responsibility for regional equalization, as well as for the costs of unemployment above certain levels. Many groups strongly objected to the use of UI funds for unrelated policy initiatives such as meeting Employment Equity Act objectives, training for social assistance recipients, and paying for entrepreneurship, mobility programs, and human resource planning.[122] Many pointed out that it was futile, and frustrating, to train workers for jobs that did not exist, and others pointed out that the sums now being proposed to add to training from the UI account were roughly equivalent to the amount that had been cut from employment and training programs between 1984 and 1989.[123]

Finally, concern was expressed about the increased penalties applied to those who had left their employment 'without just cause' or who had been fired for misconduct. Again, many groups emphasized that the implications for women were particularly serious. The CACSW noted that 'the federal government's own analysis suggests that women will be disproportionately affected by the increased penalties.'[124] Women's groups pointed out that women were often forced to leave jobs because of sexual harassment or the need to look after children or other family members, or because their hours of work had been changed or their spouse had been transferred. Groups also pointed out that considerable discretion was being left in the hands of insurance officers, who could make arbitrary decisions and in some cases be 'over-zealous.'[125] There was a right to appeal unfair decisions; however, the appeal process was long and the onus of proof was on the employee. Furthermore, many women were reluctant to go through the complaint process – especially given the costs and the length of time involved – because they lacked representation or (in the case of sexual harassment) because of the types of questions they might be asked. A number of groups argued that women, more often than men, found themselves in low-paying, dead-end, stressful, or exploitative work situations that could only be tolerated for relatively short periods of time.[126] This sentiment was expressed, for example, by the Ontario Nurses' Association:

> Working conditions in some health care institutions can be virtually intolerable: increased patient loads, rotating shift work, mandatory overtime, occupational health and safety hazards, unavailable day care, concerns for patient safety, sexual harassment and a pay scale too low to retain staff is not an exhaustive list of the problems of this female-dominated work force. The working life of nurses is extremely stressful, sometimes to the point that they must quit for their own reasons.[127]

It was argued that the new legislation would force people to stay in such exploitative work situations for longer, or to accept whatever other job – however poor the conditions might be – if they did decide to leave.[128] NAC urged that 'sexual harassment, dangerous working conditions and childcare problems associated with unreasonable hours or lengthy travelling times be listed as 'just cause' for quitting a job or for refusing a possible opening.'[129]

As an alternative to the Conservatives' proposals, both NAC and the CACSW again stressed that the problem was the high level of unemployment, not the UI system. They argued that UI benefits should be expanded and that inequalities – for example, with respect to part-time workers, new entrants, and re-entrants – needed to be addressed.[130] Both, again, urged the development of a full employment strategy, which (the CACSW argued) needed to incorporate an understanding of women's experience, including the need for affordable, quality childcare and comprehensive maternity and parental leave policies.[131]

The bill had a difficult passage through Parliament. The Conservative majority in the House of Commons ensured its passage there by early November 1989, but it was stalled by the Liberal-dominated Senate, which held more hearings and proposed a number of significant amendments.[132] The legislation finally passed the Senate, largely unchanged, in October 1990 after an additional eight Conservative senators were appointed.[133]

*UI Reform and the Recession of the Early 1990s*

The subsequent two years were ones of deep recession, with increased unemployment and more unstable working conditions. By 1990, unemployment was once again climbing, reaching a high of 11.3 per cent in 1992. Like the recession of the early 1980s, the downturn of the early 1990s affected the male-dominated industries more than the female-dominated. In 1992, unemployment for men was 12.1 per cent; for women it was 10.4 per cent (see Table 7.1). For the first time since the mid-1950s, women's labour force participation rate dropped, from 58.4 per cent in 1990 to 57.5 per cent in 1993. The male participation rate declined even more, from 75.9 per cent in 1990 to 73.3 per cent in 1993. In other words, there was continuing feminization of the labour force. By 1993, women accounted for 45.2 per cent of the labour force.[134]

'Contingent,' 'non-standard' work forms were also becoming more prevalent. The proportion of employed women working part-time began increasing again, from 24.4 per cent in 1990 to 26.4 per cent in 1993, while for men it increased from 8.1 to 9.7 per cent.[135] Overall, in 1993, 17 per cent of workers were part-time (working fewer than thirty hours a week), and 23 per cent of *jobs* were part-time (compared to 14 per cent in 1975).[136] Furthermore, part-time work was increasingly 'involuntary.' In 1993, 34.3 per cent of female and 38 per cent of male part-time workers were working part-time because that was the only work they

Chart 7.1   UI amendments, 1989–93

| 1989 Budget | • Federal government withdrawal from UI financing |
|---|---|
| 1990 Bill C-21 | • Increase in minimum qualifying period to a VER of 10 to 20 weeks<br>• Reduction in maximum duration of benefits<br>• Increased penalties for those who quit voluntarily, refuse a suitable job offer or are fired for misconduct<br>• Some UI funding re-directed to 'active' labour market programs, including the purchase of training courses<br>• Additional 10 weeks of parental leave made available |
| 1993 Bill C-113 | • Benefit rate reduced from 60% to 57%<br>• Complete disqualification for anyone who quits voluntarily, refuses a suitable job offer, or is fired for misconduct |

could find.[137] (Overall, involuntary part-time work increased from 12 per cent of part-time workers in 1976 to 23 per cent in 1990 and 36 per cent in 1994.)[138]

While part-time work represented the largest of the non-standard work forms, awareness of other forms was also growing. Concerns were expressed, for example, about the growing trend toward home-based work in industries ranging from the garment trades to pizza order-taking to data entry.[139] The Economic Council of Canada estimated that in 1989, 28 per cent of all workers were in non-standard employment, up from 25.4 per cent in 1980.[140] In that category were included part-time workers, short-term and temporary workers, 'own account' self-employed (i.e., self-employed who had not hired employees), and workers in the temporary help industry. The council reported that short-term and temporary employment experienced a 'modest increase' in the second half of the 1980s, with the highest rates being in construction, primary industry, and traditional services. It was estimated that of the jobs terminating in 1987, 11.1 per cent of men's jobs were temporary and 11.6 per cent of women's jobs.[141] 'Own account self-employment' accounted for 7.2 per cent of the labour force in 1989, was especially important in agriculture, and tended to draw disproportionately on a male workforce. (In 1989, 63.4 per cent were men, 36.5 per cent were women.)[142] Thus, while women constituted the majority of the non-standard work force, this was because of their predominance in part-time work, the largest of the non-standard categories.[143]

Subsequent studies found that the number of non-standard jobs had increased during the recession of the early 1990s. For example, Harvey Krahn found that non-standard employment increased from 28 per cent of the workforce in 1989 to 33 per cent in 1994.[144] Using a somewhat more restricted definition that included only part-time and temporary work (perhaps a more accurate measure, given the predominance of agriculture in the self-employed category), he found that non-standard work had increased from 19 per cent in 1989 to 21 per cent in 1994. Using this restricted definition, he found that 29 per cent of employed women were in non-standard work in both 1989 and 1994, compared to 11 per cent of men in 1989 and 14 per cent in 1994 (i.e., the male–female differences were reduced somewhat in this period.)[145]

Finally, there was also growing awareness of a polarization in hours worked and in income, and of a division of the labour market into 'good jobs' and 'bad jobs.' As early as the mid-1980s, studies were noting that the numbers working 'normal' hours (thirty to forty-nine per week) were dropping, while more were working both longer and fewer hours.[146] In a 1990 study, Picot, Myles, and Wannell found a polarization in wage rates, which tended to be compounded by changes in working time. In other words, changes in the bottom earnings levels were the result of both lower wages and fewer hours worked, whereas earners in the top levels had both higher relative wages and worked longer relative hours.[147] More recent studies have confirmed the polarization in hours worked – that both overtime and part-time work tend to grow,[148] that rising inequality in earnings is being 'driven by growing inequality in the distribution of working time,'[149] and, furthermore, that there is a significant gender dimension to the polarization of hours worked. Specifically, Sunter and Morrissette found that in 1993 almost one-third (31 per cent) of adult women worked fewer than thirty-five hours a week (up from 28 per cent in 1976), 61 per cent worked thirty-five to forty hours, and 8 per cent worked forty-one hours or more a week. In contrast, only 8 per cent of men worked fewer than thirty-five hours a week (up from 4 per cent in 1976), and 92 per cent worked more than thirty-five hours a week, with 22 per cent working more than forty hours a week.[150]

It was in this context of broad changes in the labour market, and with an unemployment rate of more than 11 per cent that Finance Minister Don Mazankowski, in December 1992, presented an economic statement outlining a number of measures 'to contain the deficit and to enhance economic recovery.' This included public sector cuts and wage freezes along with further changes to the UI program.[151] The latter were designed, again, to reduce both the debt and the disincentives for the unemployed to find work. Most significantly, UI benefit rates were to be reduced from 60 to 57 per cent and anyone who voluntarily quit a job without just cause or who had been fired for misconduct would be completely disqualified. In addition, exemptions from UI premiums were to be made for small businesses that were starting up or that were hiring more workers.

The ideological struggle was heightened in subsequent weeks as Employment and Immigration Minister Bernard Valcourt made a series of comments suggesting that the average unemployed person would be 'proud to help pay off Canada's debts' and would be glad to take a cut in benefits if he or she could be made to understand the seriousness of the debt situation;[152] that the government was simply 'responding to demands from Canadians to take freeloaders off the unemployment insurance rolls';[153] and that he wished to 'put an end to the cycle of dependency ... and make people more responsible.'[154] With respect to the voluntary quit provisions, he further stated that some 70 per cent of Canadians who quit or were fired from their jobs and collected UI were 'a second wage earner in the family unit ... This is a person who believes hard-working people will pay the tab for a few months while they do nothing.'

While business groups, again, supported the proposed changes,[155] strong opposition was immediately voiced by labour, by women's groups, and by opposition parties. It was pointed out that the complete disqualification for voluntary quits gave freer rein to employers and that those in low-paid, non-unionized workplaces would be most at risk. It was again noted that placing the onus on the unemployed to prove they had been fired unjustly or had left with good reason could be an onerous burden, given the time and expense involved in the appeal process and that it was the employer who filled out the form explaining why the employee has left.[156] Judy Rebick, President of NAC, pointed out: 'Obviously, if you are being sexually harassed in the workplace and the employer is not doing anything about it, he's not going to put down sexual harassment [on the form] ... So the woman's going to be denied her UI benefits and she's going to have to appeal it. Well, by the time it goes through the appeal, she's going to be a very long time without any benefits.'[157] While, as Valcourt's statements suggested, the Conservatives had expected support for the idea of cutting off 'UI cheaters,' the supply-side ideology with respect to unemployment and UI was far from being generally accepted. Indeed, the Conservatives had seriously misread the force of sentiment on the UI issue, particularly with respect to female workers and sexual harassment. To their apparent surprise, the voluntary quit issue quickly became a gender issue, with women's organizations, labour, and the opposition parties all pointing out the difficult position that women being sexually harassed in the workplace would now be in.[158] In addition, surveys showed that 'a significant majority of Canadians thought the [UI] changes would put too much power in the hands of employers,' that it would be 'very likely that women who were sexually harassed would be afraid to quit their jobs,' and that there was 'a clear class division in the reaction to the changes.'[159]

Especially strong opposition came from Quebec, where the unemployed began staging sit-ins at federal offices and demonstrations at Conservative constituency offices. The unemployment issue combined with the growing popularity of the Bloc Québécois to pose a serious threat to Conservative MPs, especially in high-unemployment areas. A group of Quebec Tory MPs publicly stated their opposition to the bill and threatened to vote against it.[160] Opposition to the UI cuts reached its peak with a demonstration of 50,000 in Montreal in February 1993.[161] In other parts of the country, too, opposition mounted. In Toronto, for example, it was reported that labour officials were threatening 'acts of civil disobedience, including plant occupations as [part of] a campaign to stop cuts to unemployment insurance.'[162]

Faced with this opposition, the Conservatives decided in mid-February to withdraw the bill and introduce a new one, Bill C-113. Despite the combined opposition of labour and women's groups, regional concerns backed by a growing separatist movement in Quebec, and opinion polls which showed that the majority opposed changes to the UI act,[163] only very minor changes were made to the bill.[164] For the most part, these amendments simply clarified what constituted just cause in the case of voluntary quits, and instituted administrative procedures to allow for greater sensitivity – for example, in sexual harassment cases. In 1990, as a result of concerns expressed about the increased penalties for voluntary quits, five items had been specified as constituting 'just cause': sexual or other harassment; obligation to accompany a spouse or dependant child to another residence; discrimination prohibited by the Canadian Human Rights Act; dangerous working conditions; and the obligation to care for a child.[165] (While obligation to care for a child was now considered a legitimate reason for leaving work, actually collecting UI still required proving childcare arrangements.) With Bill C-113, this was now expanded to fourteen 'just causes': the new ones included such things as a change in wages or working conditions, excessive overtime, and employer practices that were contrary to the law.[166] A number of further provisions addressed harassment and other 'sensitive' cases. Specially trained 'claimant service officers' would be provided to deal with 'delicate cases,' including harassment and discrimination. Claimants would be offered 'access to an agent of the same gender if they so desire,' and staff would be given extensive awareness training in dealing with 'sensitive and delicate situations.'[167] Also, *in camera* hearings at the Board of Referees would be allowed for sensitive cases.[168]

Critics continued to point out problems with the legislation, including the hardship that further rate cuts would impose and the inequity of cutting benefits for workers while providing, out of general government revenues, funds to pay for certain employers' premiums. The most strenuous objections still related to the voluntary quit issue; in particular, the burden of proof for UI eligibility still lay with the claimant and winning a case could be difficult.[169] It was estimated that because of the long appeal process, a claimant might have to wait twelve to fifteen weeks to receive a cheque if he or she won a favourable decision at the Board of Referees, and more than two years if it went to the UI Umpire.[170]

Max Yalden, Chief Commissioner of the CHRC, also expressed concern about the voluntary quit penalty:

> In the case of a claimant who alleges sexual harassment, for example, this could be tantamount to a miniature human rights investigation that is intrinsically unpleasant and could last for some time. This could face women with two almost equally difficult choices: to stay and fight the harassment in the workplace or to quit their job and have to fight it retroactively. The consequence could be to encourage victims to submit to a poisonous work environment rather than face that alternative. The effect could thus be, however indirectly or unintentional, to condone discriminatory behaviour.[171]

It was also pointed out that women occupying low-wage occupations rarely would have the savings or expertise necessary to go through an appeal process.[172] The National Association of Women and the Law pointed out that the just cause provision did not reflect the reality of women's lives:

> There are a variety of reasons why women leave the workplace, they can't be reduced to the cold, analytical reasons that the government has set forth in this bill. The power inequity, financial insecurity, lack of confidence, lack of self-esteem, lack of energy from being working women in the home and working women outside of the home – they can all contribute to an atmosphere of unhappiness and insecurity, based on women's societal disadvantage that is as compelling as any of the reasons in this bill for leaving one's job.[173]

Despite continued protests (some three thousand protested against the bill in Toronto in March 1993),[174] Bill C-113 was passed in April 1993 with just one Tory MP voting against it,[175] after just four hours of committee hearings and after limits were imposed on debate in the House of Commons.[176]

Thus, by the end of their second term, the Conservatives despite considerable opposition had begun fundamentally restructuring the UI plan. In many respects they were following the direction of change recommended by business groups and by the major inquiries into the UI program of the previous decade. The Conservatives had begun to incorporate more active measures into the program. There was a greater linking of benefits to length of time in the labour force. There was also a shift toward the notion that UI should be limited for seasonal and short-term workers. The concern with deficit-reduction priorities was evident in the benefit cuts, in the shift to financing training out of UI rather than general revenues, and in the withdrawal of federal financing from UI.

The consequence of the Conservatives' UI amendments, combined with labour market changes, was a dramatic drop in the proportion of unemployed receiving UI income security. In 1989, prior to the changes, the ratio of UI regular beneficiaries to the unemployed was 84.9 per cent for men and 81.7 per cent for women. By 1992, after the first round of cuts, and as the recession took hold, this had dropped to 70.6 per cent for men and 69.2 per cent for women (see Table 7.2). By 1993, as the second round of cuts was beginning to take effect, the ratio had dropped further, to 66.6 per cent for men and 63.2 per cent for women. Overall, in the 1989 to 1994 period, it can be seen that as UI benefits were levelled downwards, there was a closing of the gender gap for men and women, from a 3.2 percentage point spread to a 0.8 spread.[177] The narrowing of the gender gap is further reflected in figures showing that in 1989 women made up 45.7 per cent of the unemployed and 44.8 per cent of UI beneficiaries. By 1994 this difference had narrowed even further: women constituted 42.6 per cent of the unemployed and 42.2 per cent of UI beneficiaries (see Table 7.2).

The UI welfare state restructuring introduced by the Conservatives can be seen as having further tipped the balance of forces in a very significant way in favour of business. This can be seen not only in the far-reaching cuts in benefits to the unemployed, both women and men, but also in the introduction of such measures as the complete disqualification of those who voluntarily quit their jobs. These changes created much hardship for individuals attempting to survive on reduced incomes; they also gave employers far greater leeway to maintain exploitative working conditions, encouraged the growth of a low-wage 'secondary' labour market where such employers tend to be found, and promoted the notion that unemployment is the result of individual choices and actions.

## Conclusion

Looking at the period from the early 1980s until the end of the Conservatives' second term in power, it can be seen that advances were made with respect to some gender equity issues; for example, there was greater recognition within the UI program of parental childrearing responsibilities. As a result of continuous intervention by women's groups, the notion that achieving equality entailed accommodating differences in this regard became generally accepted. However, the 1980s, and the 1990s even more so, showed the limits of achieving equality and improvements in women's condition by either emphasizing formal equality (in the sense of treating men and women the same within programs such as UI) or emphasizing that differences have to be accommodated – important though both these notions of equality are. 'Equality of results' was to some extent accepted as the basis for evaluating discriminatory measures, but this did not extend to cover all structural economic inequalities. More fundamentally, commitment to improvements in women's condition was clearly becoming limited by the subordination of equity concerns to overall economic goals and policies. During the early 1980s, while there was some tension between gender equity issues and the economic restructuring agenda, the latter clearly predominated in policy decisions. This became ever more so as the decade proceeded and as social and economic reforms came to be seriously implemented during the Conservatives' second term. This occurred at the same time as funding was cut back for women's programs and groups, and as government ministers began refusing to attend the annual NAC lobby.[178] Women's life conditions – at home, in the labour market, and vis-à-vis the state – came increasingly to be defined by this larger agenda of deregulation, privatization, debt control, greater reliance on market forces, and greater emphasis on supply-side factors.

# CHAPTER 8

# Consolidating Neoliberal Reforms: Globalization, Multi-Earner Families, and the Erosion of State Support for the Unemployed

The reforms initiated by the Conservative government at the beginning of the 1990s were continued and deepened under the Liberals, elected in 1993. Indeed, it was under the Liberal government that the most far-reaching restructuring of the federal welfare state took place. By the end of the decade a new neoliberal welfare state had been consolidated and a new form of family–workplace–state arrangement had been established. Shortly after the Liberals came to power, an extensive review of federal social security programs took place under the direction of Human Resources Development Minister Lloyd Axworthy. By the mid-1990s, however, the review process had been put aside and the Minister of Finance had taken the lead in setting the parameters for social reform. The 1995 budget announced not only a major restructuring of federal–provincial transfers in the areas of health, education, and social services (the Canada Health and Social Transfer) but a UI funding reduction of 10 per cent. The amendments to the UI program, now renamed 'employment insurance' (EI), were announced in December 1995. Among the most significant changes was that eligibility would now be based on hours worked rather than weeks worked. This entailed greatly increased qualifying requirements, especially for those working part-time (fewer than thirty-five hours a week), and for new entrants and re-entrants to the labour force. Overall, the 1990s were marked by the severe fraying of the rights-based social safety net for most unemployed people and by the privatization or downloading of responsibility for unemployment to individuals and households. In 1989, 83.4 per cent of the unemployed received UI benefits, by 1997, only 41.6 per cent did.[1] For women, the proportion dropped from 81.7 to 39 per cent (see Table 7.2).

EI amendments involved more than a reduction in availability of benefits; they also involved a shift in the program's rationale and structure. The UI/EI restructuring had a number of interrelated characteristics. First, it was based on the idea – promoted by the Macdonald Commission and others since the mid-1980s – that unemployment is to some extent voluntary or a consequence of individual attributes or dependencies. The goals, captured in the change in name to 'employment' insurance, were to reduce disincentives to work and to shift from passive to active labour market programs, as well as to reduce the federal deficit. Second, and related to this, restructuring involved putting forward an 'employability' model of the welfare state based on the assumption of multi-earner families and on the notion that all adults, male and female, are or should be employed. One of the key characteristics of the new form of welfare state, then, is that there has been a clear move away from the male-breadwinner model on which the Keynesian welfare state was based toward a multi-earner family model. Third, there has been a shift from universality toward a two-tier program with limited benefits for those outside the full-time, full-year worker model. This has occurred precisely at a time when work is increasingly insecure, with part-time, temporary, home-based, and other 'non-standard' work forms continuing to grow. Finally, state income security policies have not merely responded to this type of low-wage, contingent work – they have encouraged it. They have done so by offering wage subsidies and income supplements to low-wage labour, by reducing opportunities for people to leave their employment, and by limiting the state's provisions for social reproduction in such a way that temporary or part-time work has become one of the few options for combining domestic and paid work. Thus, this welfare state model constitutes support for particular forms of production and social reproduction.

These reforms have certainly resulted in a reduction in federal expenditures. By the late 1990s, far from being an expense, the UI program, through premiums levied, had become a major source of revenue and was making a substantial contribution to eliminating the deficit. However, this restructuring has resulted in greatly increased insecurity and difficulties for the unemployed. Furthermore, given women's over-representation in part-time and other contingent work situations, and their continued domestic responsibilities within the home, this model has also led to increased polarization and gender inequalities.

A number of factors in the 1990s contributed to the consolidation of this model. As earlier chapters have argued, contradictions at the root of the postwar model were becoming exacerbated in the closing decades of the twentieth century. This included, most notably, a contradiction between, on the one hand, income security programs based on the notion of a full-time male breadwinner and, on the other hand, a labour force that was increasingly female and contingent. There was pressure to adapt state programs to new needs, and this contributed to growing fiscal pressure on the state. A market-driven corporate agenda was beginning to dominate internationally and domestically. At an ideological level, almost two decades of reports, commissions of inquiry, and papers put out by business think tanks had succeeded in eroding notions of state (or collective) responsibility for unemployment and in putting forward the idea that welfare state programs create dependencies. At an economic level, as noted in chapter 7, reforms already instituted helped tip the balance of power in favour of corporations, which were increasingly operating in a global arena. At a political and institutional level, the growing importance of international institutions such as the WTO and NAFTA both created and helped consolidate pressures for individual states to adopt neoliberal measures.[2] Shifts in the configuration of power have also been reflected domestically, within the state and its policymaking processes. As Keith Banting notes, there has been increased public consultation over the direction of social reform, giving the appearance of openness to 'citizen' participation; but at the same time, the Department of Finance – which is increasingly connected at an international level to the processes of globalization – has been assuming more and more importance in setting the social policy agenda.[3] These shifts have been accompanied, then, by a reduced role for a range of 'policy actors,' including women, labour, and other popular sector groups.

In this period, formal equality rights continued to be recognized, documents continued to be put in gender-neutral terms, and within documents there were attempts to show the implications of policies for women's equality goals. At the same time, however, the network of women's advisors within the state was dismantled, and funding for women's groups and women's equality projects was further reduced.[4] With the closing of the CACSW in 1995, women lost an important voice for equality. In addition, within the state, an approach incorporating special programs for women was replaced by a 'gender-based analysis' (GBA) or a 'gender lens' approach to policy[5] that involved simply assessing the possible gender impact of a policy prior to its implementation. As Burt and Hardman explain, this approach has been limited both because it does not take differences among women into account, and also because its application is limited in a policy context that includes economic restructuring, balanced budgets, and tax cuts.[6] Women's equality, then, like social policy more generally, has even more clearly than in the previous decade come to be subsumed by the economic goals of deficit reduction and international competitiveness.

## A Changing Labour Market: Feminization and the Continued Growth of Contingent Work

As noted in chapter 7, in the recessionary period of the early 1990s unemployment climbed to over 11 per cent. By later in the decade, however, the unemployment rate for both men and women had fallen substantially, so that by 1999 it was 7.3 per cent for women and 7.8 per cent for men.[7] To some extent, however, these unemployment figures mask the underlying shifts that were taking place in the labour market structure. As Picot and Heisz describe it, much of the 1990s was characterized by a weak economic recovery and by slow employment growth, especially for full-time jobs.[8] Job losses did occur, especially in the public sector and in consumer services.[9] In other sectors there was greater job stability, and employers were simply hiring less rather than increasing layoffs. The authors note that 'the biggest change [in the 1990s] was in the reduced likelihood of getting a job, not in the likelihood of losing it.'[10] Other reports in the late 1990s similarly indicated that the difficulty for many Canadians was to get a first job, or to regain employment after a long period without work.[11] Where job growth did occur, it tended not to be in full-time employment. Non-standard work – in particular, self-employment and part-time work – continued to increase. Between 1989 and 1997 the proportion of total employment accounted for by self-employment increased from 13.8 to 17.8 per cent, and part-time work increased from 16.6 to 19 per cent.[12]

Again, there were clear gender differences in labour market experiences. Women's labour force participation remained stable at about 58 per cent during the 1990s, while men's declined further, to 72.4 per cent.[13] The shifting nature of family/market relations was again reflected in the increased participation rate for women with preschool children (under five years). This rate increased from 61.2 per cent in 1988 to 66.8 per cent in 1998.[14] Women were, again, overrepresented in non-standard work categories. Statistics Canada reported that in 1999, 41 per cent of employed women, compared to 29 per cent of employed men, had non-standard employment (this included part-time work, temporary work, self-employed work, and multiple job holders).[15] About 29 per cent of women worked part-time, and women continued to make up about 70 per cent of part-time workers.[16]

## Consolidating a Two-Tier Model

The most recent period of UI restructuring started under the Conservative government in the previous decade; it has been since the election of the Liberals in the fall of 1993 that the most sweeping changes have taken place. In the budget of February 1994, the Liberals' priority was to reduce the deficit, mostly through cuts to the UI program. The announced $5.5 billion cut to UI over three years represented the most extensive reduction in UI program financing since the restructuring process began. (In contrast, when Bill C-21 was introduced in 1989, it was projected to save $1.29 billion.)[17] Changes included a reduction in the benefit rate to 55 per cent of earnings, an increase in the minimum qualifying requirement to eliminate the lower entrance requirement in regions of particularly high unemployment,[18] and a reduction in the possible duration of benefits. Arguing that it was necessary to 'improve the link between work history and UI benefits,'[19] the Liberals made cuts for those with 'short-term attachment' to the labour force that were much greater than for those with a longer work history.[20] In addition, for the first time since 1975, the government reintroduced dependants' allowances; providing a higher, 60 per cent rate for individual low-income claimants with dependants. This once again brought the criteria of need, based on family status, into the UI program. (See Chart 8.1 for a summary of the changes.)

In the fall of 1994 the Liberal government announced its new agenda for 'jobs and growth.'[21] This included a comprehensive review of federal social programs, to be conducted under the direction of Lloyd Axworthy, Minister of the newly created Human Resources Development Canada.[22] Also involved was a framework for economic and fiscal policy established by Finance Minister Paul Martin, which focused on 'creating a healthy fiscal climate' through deficit and debt reduction.[23] As part of Axworthy's review, the discussion paper *Improving Social Security in Canada* was released in October 1994.[24] This review covered a wide range of federal government social programs, including UI, child

Chart 8.1   UI changes announced in 1994 budget

---
- Benefits reduced to 55% of income
- Minimum qualifying requirement increased
- Duration of benefits reduced
- 60% rate for individual low income claimants with dependants
---

benefits, postsecondary education and social assistance. In the document it was argued that the social programs of the postwar era were no longer appropriate in a world characterized by technological change, globalization, and trade liberalization; as a consequence, a new social security model was needed. It also pointed out that the nature of work had changed fundamentally, that jobs were increasingly insecure, and that the entry of women into the labour market posed new challenges in terms of reconciling family and work responsibilities.

The solutions proposed by Axworthy's discussion paper involved two somewhat incompatible goals. First, the document emphasized increasing 'human capital' through training, skills development, and other 'active' labour market policies. It argued that such policies would not only help individuals 'retool themselves' for good jobs[25] but also help attract investment and promote economic growth. As the discussion paper put it, the 'next generation of social programs must not just share the wealth ... They must actively create opportunity for Canadians, and, in so doing, help drive economic growth.'[26] It recognized that there was a structural economic problem in that jobs were increasingly non-permanent; at the same time, it saw 'frequent use' of the UI program as an individual choice or a behavioural problem to be discouraged: 'Many are on a treadmill,' the paper argued, 'they need help getting off.'[27] Second, fiscal restraint was a central goal. This was clear both in Axworthy's discussion paper and in a statement by Paul Martin, also released that month. As the discussion paper stated: 'The reform of social security must take place within the fiscal parameters required to meet the government's target of reducing the deficit.'[28] This meant, at a minimum, that any additional funds for active measures would have to come from cuts in other social program areas (e.g., the funds for employment development services would have to come mainly from a reallocation of UI);[29] it also meant that the deficit reduction agenda as a whole would be driving social policy reform.[30]

With respect to UI, the discussion paper outlined two possible approaches. The first option was a new, tiered 'employment insurance' program. This would involve benefits similar to those already in place for the *occasionally* unemployed; *'frequent'* claimants would receive 'adjustment insurance': lower benefits combined with more 'active assistance' in finding a job. It was suggested that the adjustment insurance component could involve benefits based on individual or family income testing, or could be conditional on participation in an adjustment program or community service.[31] The second option was to adjust the existing program by increasing the number of weeks needed to qualify and/or by reducing the duration or level of benefits. The discussion paper noted that in either case, it would be important to consider improved coverage for non-standard employment, including part-time, temporary, self-employed, and multiple job holders.[32]

One of the most extensive public discussions on the direction for social security followed the release of Axworthy's discussion paper. Many viewed this process as a critical moment in social policy debate. There was widespread agreement that reform was needed, and the possibility still seemed open to influence the direction of change. The new Standing Committee on Human Resources Development, responsible for a cross-Canada consultation on the issue, received an overwhelming response.[33] In addition, a number of edited volumes provided critical commentaries on the social security review.[34] For the most part, the response to the discussion paper was critical. There was widespread criticism of the 'fiscal straitjacket'[35] that had been placed on the review process, given the priority that was placed on debt and deficit reduction and the assumption that this should occur primarily through a reduction in social expenditures. Many drew attention to the items left *off* the table – in particular, tax reform, macroeconomic policy (including high interest rates), and the growing use of 'tax expenditures,' which tend to disproportionately benefit the wealthy. Many argued that policies allowing persistently high unemployment, combined with a focus on individual responsibility for unemployment and a scaling down of social programs, would lead to much hardship.

Specific criticisms were also made of the two UI options. As the standing committee noted in its report: 'Few issues aroused as much concern and concentrated passion in our hearings as the questions surrounding the reform of unemployment insurance.'[36] A dichotomy of views emerged between those who argued that the current program contributed to high unemployment and should become smaller and more targeted, and those who emphasized the importance of UI not only to individuals, but also to the economy as a whole.[37] In the first group, for example, the Institute for Research on Public Policy (IRPP) argued that the social security system, including 'lenient' UI eligibility rules, had contributed to structural unemployment. The UI program, it was argued, must be returned to its initial purpose of insuring people against unexpected, involuntary unemployment.[38] Furthermore, it was suggested that 'reform must be aimed at encouraging the unemployed to adapt to the marketplace.'[39]

In the second category, a broad range of left-liberal and popular sector groups expressed concern about the subordination of social policy to economic objectives and about the hardships that were likely to result from the proposed reforms. Especially strong objections were raised to the proposal for a two-tier 'employment insurance' system. In particular, concern was expressed about the possible introduction of income testing, about mandatory community service or 'workfare,' about the targeting of frequent users, and about the overall reduction in benefits. Questions were also raised about the implications of the two proposals for women. NAC, the CACSW, and the NAWL all pointed to the lack of gender analysis in the social security review. The absence of an analysis of the systemic barriers facing women in the labour market was noted, and it was pointed out that equity was no longer part of the conceptual framework for analysing social policy reform.[40] Feminist groups again strongly opposed making UI contingent on family income. NAC further argued that both the targeting of frequent users and the lowering of benefit levels would disadvantage women.[41] (The federal government's own background documents showed that men were more likely than women to be frequent claimants. In 1991, 44 per cent of male UI claimants had three claims or more in a five-year period, compared to 31 per cent of female claimants.)[42]

Ultimately, Axworthy was unable to secure a consensus, either among the various social forces at a national level, or within the Liberal caucus, or among the provinces, on the direction of reform.[43] By the mid-1990s the Minister of Finance was more clearly taking the lead in setting the direction for social reform. The reform process effectively became more clearly subordinate to the deficit reduction agenda as defined by the Department of Finance.[44] As early as January 1995, Axworthy announced that the government would have to deal with its budgetary problems before it could 'get on with the reforms.'[45] Paul Martin's February 1995 budget, in particular, marked an important step in the 'fiscalization' of social policy.[46] The goal of the budget was to help 'redesign the role of the government in the economy.'[47] This involved providing 'a framework for the private sector to create jobs'; an 'aggressive trade strategy,' and ensuring that 'the nation's finances are healthy.'[48] The budget also announced the creation of a single transfer program to the provinces, the Canada Health and Social Transfer, which gave the provinces greater discretion in spending but at greatly reduced funding levels. In addition, it announced a federal government program review that would eliminate 45,000 public sector jobs,[49] and a UI program spending reduction of 10 per cent. Finally, it reiterated the need to move away from passive support toward active assistance and that 'a key job for unemployment insurance in the future must be to *help Canadians stay off unemployment insurance.*'[50] It was announced that with no increase in premium rates, the cumulative *surplus* in the UI account would be allowed to rise above $5 billion.[51]

In the months after the budget announcement, Axworthy's department continued to work on concrete reforms to the UI program. By the summer it was being reported that the two-tier plan had been dropped, but that there would be a 10 per cent cut in UI, with about half the savings being redirected to the 'human resouces investment fund' for employment-related measures such as job counselling.[52] The response to the possible changes was still highly critical. Strong opposition came from the Atlantic region, including from Atlantic Liberal MPs.[53] Business groups wanted the savings from UI changes to go toward a payroll tax cut rather than employment programs.[54] The CLC continued to voice its opposition to the cuts. Quebec politicians were concerned both with the implications of benefit reductions and with possible federal government involvement in areas such as training.[55] The announcement of the changes was delayed until after the Quebec referendum in the fall of 1995.

The amendments to the UI program were finally announced in December 1995. They constituted the most significant reformulation of federal income security benefits since the early 1970s. Symbolically, the shift was captured in the change in program name from 'unemployment insurance' to 'employment insurance.' Consistent with the statements of the previous year, the goal was to move away from passive income support toward an active labour market program[56] – one that would reduce the disincentive to work, reinforce 'the value of work,' and offer 'unemployed Canadians the tools to lift themselves up and find new opportunities.'[57] Benefit costs were to be reduced by about $2

Chart 8.2    EI amendments, 1996

---

- *Eligibility*: Based on hours worked, not weeks worked

- *Benefit rate*: Basic rate set at 55% of earnings, but this could be altered by the following:

  - *The divisor*: Past earnings calculations to be averaged over a period two weeks longer than the minimum required to qualify, thereby reducing the rate for those only able to work the minimum
  - *Intensity rule*: Frequent users would have their benefit rate reduced to a possible floor of 50%
  - *Clawback*: Increased for high-income earners
  - *Family Income Supplement*: Provided a higher rate to those with children and a total family income of less than $26,000

- *Duration of benefits*: Determined by the amount of hours worked, as well as by the regional rate of unemployment
- Overall, the maximum duration of benefits reduced from 50 to 45 weeks

- *Maternity benefits:* Work time required to qualify increased to 700 hours (the equivalent of 35 hours a week for 20 weeks)

- *Employment benefits*: Introduced, including wage subsidies and earnings supplements

---

billion a year, of which $800 million would be reinvested in EI employment benefits.[58] Extensive changes to income benefits were also announced (these are summarized in Chart 8.2).

*Eligibility based on hours, rather than weeks worked*
Among the most significant of the reforms was a change in the basis of eligibility from weeks worked to hours worked.[59] Under the previous system a person could qualify having worked for twelve to twenty weeks (depending on the regional unemployment rate) and having worked at least fifteen hours (or earned $163) each week with a single employer. Under the new system, a minimum of twelve to twenty weeks was still required, but based on a *thirty-five hour* week (see Table 8.1). Overall, there was more than a doubling of the minimum number of hours required. Previously, in high-unemployment areas a minimum of 180 hours had been needed;[60] this was now increased to 420.[61] In low-unemployment regions, the equivalent of 300 hours had been required;

Table 8.1   Eligibility requirements: UI/EI

| Regional rate of unemployment | UI Required number of weeks of insurable employment | EI Required number of hours of insurable employment |
|---|---|---|
| Less than 6% | 20 | 700 (20 weeks x 35 hours) |
| 6–7% | 19 | 665 |
| 7–8% | 18 | 630 |
| 8–9% | 17 | 595 |
| 9–10% | 16 | 560 |
| 10–11% | 15 | 525 |
| 11–12% | 14 | 490 |
| 12–13% | 13 | 455 |
| More than 13% | 12 | 420 |

Source: Canada, *Unemployment Insurance Act*, Aug. 1994, table 1, p. 104; Canada, *Employment Insurance Act*, 1996, p. 10

now 700 were. New entrants and re-entrants to the labour force faced some of the largest increases. (A new entrant or re-entrant was defined as someone with fewer than 490 hours of work in the year before the fifty weeks counting toward the benefit claim.)[62] There was an increase not only in the number of hours per week, but also in the number of weeks expected, from a previous minimum of 300 hours (twenty weeks at fifteen hours) to 910 hours (twenty-six weeks at thirty-five hours each).[63] In other words, before being able to access EI, an individual now could require proof of work over a two-year period: the equivalent of about twelve weeks the first year and twenty-six weeks the second. The rationale for this was that people might 'become reliant on UI early in their working lives' and then 'quickly begin to factor it into their annual work pattern.' In order to break the cycle of UI dependency and the 'incentive to mix spells of work with UI,' the EI amendments made it much more difficult for new entrants and re-entrants to qualify.[64]

### Benefit Rates
While the basic benefit rate remained set at 55 per cent, four new provisions created a complex benefit rate structure that effectively lowered the rate for many claimants.

*The Divisor* A new formula was implemented to calculate the past *earnings* on which the benefit rate would be based. To encourage people to work longer, the new legislation specified that earnings were to be

Table 8.2   The divisor

| Unemployment rate | Minimum entrance requirement expressed in weeks of 35 hours | Minimum divisor |
|---|---|---|
| 6% and under | 20 | 22 |
| Over 6–7% | 19 | 21 |
| Over 7–8% | 19 | 20 |
| Over 8–9% | 17 | 19 |
| Over 9–10% | 16 | 18 |
| Over 10–11% | 15 | 17 |
| Over 11–12% | 14 | 16 |
| Over 12–13% | 13 | 15 |
| Over 13% | 12 | 14 |

Source: Canada, Human Resources Development Canada, *Employment Insurance: A Guide to Employment Insurance* (Ottawa, July 1996), p. 7.

averaged over a fixed period. To obtain the full 55 per cent level, it was now necessary to work at least two weeks longer than the regional minimum entrance requirement. For example, in high-unemployment areas, the equivalent of twelve weeks at thirty-five hours per week were needed to *qualify*, but the calculation of *earnings* was based on the previous fourteen weeks (see Table 8.2). In effect, this lowered the rate considerably for those only able to find work for the minimum period before being laid off.[65]

*Intensity Rule* 'Frequent users' would have their benefit rates gradually reduced to a possible floor of 50 per cent.[66] (A frequent user was defined as someone with more than twenty weeks of benefits in the past five years.) Again, this change was seen as an incentive 'aimed at encouraging people to reduce the length of time on claim.'[67] This provision had implications for many claimants. Government background documents noted that in 1982, 15 per cent of UI claimants had collected benefits three or more times in the last five years, but by 1994 this had risen to almost 40 per cent.[68]

*Increased clawback* A greatly strengthened clawback provision effectively lowered the benefit rate for higher-income earners. The new provision required claimants with incomes over $39,000 and who had received more than twenty weeks of benefits in the past five years to pay back from 50 to 100 per cent of their benefits, depending on the number of weeks of benefits received.[69] For claimants with fewer than twenty weeks of benefits in the past five years, the existing 30 per cent clawback remained in place. However, the clawback now started at incomes above $48,750, compared to the previous level of $63,570. It was estimated that the clawback provision would affect 7.5 per cent of EI claimants, compared to 1 per cent previously under UI.[70]

*Family Income Supplement*  The 1994 reform had allowed a higher benefit rate of 60 per cent for *individual* low-income earners with dependants. This was replaced by a new Family Income Supplement providing a higher rate for those with children and a yearly *family* income of less than $26,000. This supplement was tied to the Child Tax Benefit. For those who qualified, the supplement on their EI cheque was equal to the weekly amount of their Child Tax Benefit. Like the latter, the benefit would increase with the number of children. The supplement was to be phased in, providing a benefit rate of up to 65 per cent of earnings in January 1997 and up to 80 per cent by January 2000.

*Length of Time on Benefits*
The possible length of time on benefit was now also to be determined by hours worked, as well as by the regional rate of unemployment. This meant that the duration of benefits for part-time workers was reduced, while those working overtime and longer hours within a week were now eligible to receive benefits for a longer period of time. Overall, the maximum length of time a person could receive benefits was reduced from fifty to forty-five weeks.[71] In low-unemployment regions (6 per cent and under), the seven hundred hours required to qualify for EI would entitle a claimant to only fourteen weeks of benefits.

*Premium Reductions*
The basic premium rate was reduced somewhat for both workers and employers. In addition, it was announced that a 'rainy day reserve' would be built up in the EI account, to be drawn on in the event of any future economic slowdowns.[72]

*Maternity Benefits*
The new hours-based legislation also applied to maternity and parental benefits. Previously, it had been necessary to have worked for a minimum of fifteen hours a week for twenty weeks (three hundred hours) in order to qualify for maternity benefits. With the EI changes, seven

hundred hours, or the equivalent of thirty-five hours a week for twenty weeks, were required.

*Employment Benefits*  The EI legislation provided for a range of 'employment' benefits.[73] This included wage subsidies and earnings supplements aimed at encouraging work – for example, by providing incentives for employers to hire workers or provide on-the-job experience. In addition, self-employment assistance was to be offered in order to help unemployed people start businesses. Furthermore, job creation partnerships were to be established involving groups of EI claimants working with the provinces, the private sector, and/or community organizations. In addition, loans and/or grants were to be made available to 'attend provincial or other accredited institutions to develop needed job skills.' The amount of money to be provided for these 'active' reemployment measures was actually relatively small. Of the $2 billion projected savings from UI benefit changes, $800 million was to be reinvested in these 'active re-employment benefits,' and a large part of it was simply a supplement to low-wage incomes.

Axworthy was claiming that the two-tier option had been dropped, yet these reforms clearly constituted a two-tier arrangement. Benefits were left relatively unchanged for full-time, full-year workers. For three groups of workers, however, obtaining benefits became much more difficult. Part-time workers were faced both with much longer qualifying periods and with a reduced possible length of time on benefits. Those seeking a first job or re-entering the labour market would have to find work for a much longer period of time before becoming eligible for income security benefits. Seasonal workers and others relying on EI on a regular basis faced reduced benefit rates. Thus, there was one tier for workers with relatively stable jobs *and* access to UI/EI income security, and a second tier for those with more irregular or contingent work, or who were trying to establish or re-establish themselves in the labour force. These latter had little in the way of a safety net.

Following the enactment of the EI legislation, opposition remained strong, especially from Quebec and Atlantic Canada, where the high proportion of seasonal workers meant that the EI changes would have a far-reaching impact. Indeed, the loss of Liberal seats in Atlantic Canada in the 1997 federal election was largely attributed to hostility over the EI legislation. Further amendments to the program were announced in September 2000, just prior to the next federal election, which was held in November of that year. (The legislation, which did not pass before

Chart 8.3   EI amendments, Bill C-2, 2001

- Intensity rule eliminated
- Clawback provision amended
- Higher re-entrant requirement (910 hours) no longer applied to parents of young children

the election, was reintroduced as Bill C-2 in February 2001.) While the basic framework was left untouched, some modifications were made to the program. It was announced that the intensity rule, which had reduced the benefit rate for frequent claimants, would be eliminated. In addition, the clawback provision was amended[74] and the higher re-entrant rate (910 hours) was no longer to apply to parents of young children returning to the labour market[75] (see Chart 8.3). In addition, the October 1999 Speech from the Throne announced the extension of combined maternity/parental benefits from twenty-five weeks to a full year. This formed part of the larger federal 'agenda for children' and represented an important extension of benefits for those able to meet the qualifying requirements, which nevertheless remained at the higher level of seven hundred hours of work.

## EI Reform and Its Implications for Women

Both assessments by the Liberal government prior to the introduction of the legislation and the HRDC gender impact analysis (now required for all new policies) had presented an optimistic view of the likely impact of the new EI legislation on women. The government documents that accompanied the new legislation argued that the change to an hours-based system would be 'fairer and more flexible,' would allow many new part-time workers to be insured for the first time (including those with fewer than fifteen hours a week), and would be 'particularly more equitable for women.'[76] HRDC's gender impact analysis presented a more balanced picture, but on the whole it also portrayed the changes as being positive for women. While noting that the changes could disproportionately affect women's ability to qualify, and also lower their weeks of possible benefits, this analysis nevertheless argued that the new legislation would benefit part-time women workers.[77] It estimated that overall, by 2001–2, total insurance benefits would be reduced by 9 per cent for women compared to 13 per cent for men,[78] but at the same time, it noted that this estimate was based not on the number of claims, but rather on funds paid out, and that given women's lower average earnings, 'a strict comparison of percentages may understate the relative impact for women.'[79] The Family Income Supplement was also presented as beneficial: it was estimated that two-thirds of those receiving the supplement would be women. Finally, the gender impact analysis claimed that a number of the new employment benefits, as well as childcare assistance, were designed to support the participation of women in the labour force.

Some aspects of the EI legislation came into effect in July 1996 and others in January 1997. Within a few years it was clear that the combination of EI changes and continued economic restructuring was having a devastating impact on the availability of income security for the unemployed. The most significant consequence of a decade of UI reform was the removal of a rights-based social security net for the majority of the unemployed, both men and women. The proportion of unemployed receiving UI had already dropped significantly by the mid-1990s, a result both of the UI restructuring earlier in the decade and of the shifting labour market structure.[80] In 1989 there had been virtually universal coverage, with 83 per cent of the unemployed receiving UI benefits; by 1995 this proportion had dropped to 51.8 per cent (derived from Table 7.2). Dramatic reductions in income security for the unemployed also occurred *after* the new EI legislation was introduced, with the proportion of the unemployed receiving UI dropping further to 41.6 per cent by 1997.

Despite the optimistic tone of government publications, evidence quickly indicated that women in particular were being severely affected by the restructuring. Between 1996 and 1997 the proportion of unemployed men receiving regular UI/EI dropped from 49.7 per cent to 43.7 per cent; for women it dropped from 46.1 to 39.1 per cent (see Table 7.2). That women were particularly affected was further confirmed by reports from the CLC[81] and by the EI Monitoring report submitted to HRDC. The latter, for example, reported that in the first year of operation, new claims for regular benefits fell by 20 per cent for women compared to 16 per cent for men.[82] While the proportion receiving UI/EI is now very low for both men and women, the proportion of unemployed women receiving such benefits has been consistently smaller than the proportion of men. The CLC estimated that in 1999, 42 per cent of unemployed men and 32 per cent of unemployed women received EI.[83]

Women and men are affected in different ways by EI program and labour market changes. Men have been overrepresented in seasonal industries, in resource-based sectors, and in construction. A higher proportion of 'frequent' users are men, and they were thus more affected by the 'intensity' rule that lowered the benefit rate for this category of claimant.[84] Because men tend also to be higher-income earners, about 87 per cent of the claimants affected by the clawback were men.[85] Women, on the other hand, are disproportionately found in the part-time labour force and in certain parts of the service sector. Women thus tend to have significantly fewer hours of paid labour in a week then men. One study found that in 1998, 50 per cent of women but only 28 per cent of men worked fewer than thirty-five hours per week.[86] Clearly, then, women are much more likely to be affected by provisions that make it more difficult for those working fewer than thirty-five hours a week to qualify.

Men and women also experience unemployment in different ways. Men tend to be overrepresented among those laid off; women are disproportionately among the unemployed who are new entrants or re-entrants to the labour force. Statistics Canada reported that in 1999, 53 per cent of unemployed men compared to 41 per cent of unemployed women had either lost or been laid off from their last job. On the other hand, 26 per cent of unemployed women were labour force re-entrants 'who had not worked for pay or profit in the last year,'[87] and 13 per cent were new job entrants.[88] It is possible, then, that there are gender differences in the explanation for the drop in the ratio of UI beneficiaries to unemployed; it could be that for men it reflects the length of unemployment and the exhaustion of unemployment benefits,[89] whereas for women, other factors may be at work, including the part-time, intermittent nature of their work and other difficulties in getting the weeks needed to qualify, such as higher qualifying requirements for new entrants or re-entrants to the labour market.[90]

In addition, the changes that are taking place do not simply affect workers as wage labourers; they also have implications for gender relations within families. Consistent with both the supply-side emphasis and the trend toward privatization, there has been a downloading of responsibility for unemployment from the state to both individuals and households, which are having to bear more and more the costs and responsibility. Income security reductions have implications for women's domestic workloads (as they try harder and harder to make ends meet); these reductions also contribute to women's marginalization in the labour market as the juggling of jobs, daycare, and other responsibilities becomes more difficult. This is all the more so as UI cuts are accompanied by the scaling down of other social programs in such areas as health and education, and by the abandonment of equity objectives within some programs.

The inclusion of maternity benefits in the new hours-based system and the requirement of seven hundred hours' work has made it much more difficult for many women – especially those working part-time – to qualify. This too has implications for gender relations within families. The extension of maternity/parental benefits to a year is certainly helpful to some, but it does not address the problems of those many who do not initially qualify. In addition, like regular UI, the rate for maternity benefits has been reduced from 66⅔ per cent in the 1970s to 55 per cent in the 1990s, even though providing an incentive to work is a questionable rationale for making changes to a maternity program. These trends have increased the disparities between groups of women in access to maternity benefits. Three groups in particular can be identified: those in the public sector or in certain (more likely) large or unionized workplaces, who have access not only to UI/EI but also to an employer-provided top-up to bring income close to regular wage levels; those who rely solely on UI/EI; and those with access to neither.

The introduction of family-based income testing through the Family Supplement also has implications for women's access to an independent source of income and for relations within families. As noted in earlier chapters, women's groups and individual feminist authors have long been opposed to basing social program eligibility on family income. It has been pointed out that married women often lose their entitlements, that it should not be assumed that income will be shared equally among family members, and that an independent source of income is an important means for maintaining a more equal balance of power within the household. Government documents note that two-thirds of claimants receiving the new Family Supplement are women, and cite this as evidence that women have made 'significant gains' through the new system.[91] A more detailed assessment by Phipps and colleagues, however, indicates a much more mixed impact. These authors conclude that while the Family Supplement provides increased targeting to low-income households, many married women lost the entitlement they had under the previous (1994) dependency rate (which was based on individual income). They found that whereas 29 per cent of women collecting UI benefits received the 1994 dependency rate, only 13.8 per cent of women collected Family Supplements under EI. The largest decline was for married mothers (from 29.8 to 6.5 per cent), whereas there was an increase for single mothers (25.9 to 38.3 per cent). Under UI, 79.4 per cent of the dependency rate recipients were women, compared to 62.6 per cent under EI.[92] Beyond that, focus groups revealed considerable concern and anger among women that household income was being used as the criterion for determining eligibility; women reiterated the view that they also have financial responsibilities, that they cannot always rely on husbands and partners, and that having one's own income is important for independence and dignity.

Thus, a number of the EI changes, including the decreased availability of regular benefits in categories where women predominate, the increased difficulty of obtaining maternity benefits, and the trend toward basing benefits on family income, have operated to reduce women's independent source of income and to reinforce dependencies. As Vosko and Pulkingham note, though women are no longer formally excluded, there has been a *de facto* exclusion, as 'irregular' workers have difficulty qualifying.[93] Certainly, these changes have moved the welfare state even farther from a model that Ann Orloff, for example, identifies as being critical for women – one that enables them to support and maintain an autonomous household.[94]

As the 1990s progressed, 'popular sector' actors came to play a reduced role in the policy arena. Funding cuts for women's groups and the dismantling of the CACSW made it increasingly difficult for women to raise concerns. The growing role of the Department of Finance in setting policy direction through the budget further limited the possibilities for intervention. Tripartite bodies (made up of representatives of labour, business, and government) had once played a critical role in setting UI policy; by the 1970s their role had been much diminished.[95] The most effective opposition has been at the regional level, especially in the Atlantic provinces and Quebec; in part, this is because regional concerns can be expressed through the parliamentary system. One consequence is that more effective pressure has been mounted to change those provisions (such as the intensity rule for frequent users) which affect regionally based seasonal workers than to amend provisions with respect to the female-dominated part-time workforce, which is spread throughout the country.

## Conclusion

Overall, a decade of reform to the UI/EI program resulted in far-reaching restructuring not just of income security for the unemployed, but of the welfare state as a whole. While the roots of pressures for change and of proposed solutions were found in earlier decades, a number of factors came together in the 1990s to consolidate a neoliberal welfare state model. These included growing pressure from economic globalization, the continued growth of a contingent, female workforce for whom the postwar welfare state was ill designed, and pressure to address the deficit and debt. Also critical was a shift with respect to the relative power of various social actors.

A very different type of safety net is now in place, and very different pattern of family–market–state relations has been established. First, there has been a shift to an 'employability' model that emphasizes self-reliance and individual responsibility for unemployment. UI restructuring has entailed attempts to remove 'disincentives' to work and to reduce 'dependency' on state-provided income security. These goals have been achieved by lengthening UI qualifying times, by providing full benefit rates only for those who work beyond the minimum number of weeks, by disqualifying those who quit work voluntarily, and so on. As Scott, Pulkingham, and others have pointed out, in current welfare state models, women are increasingly being defined as 'employable' or as 'workers' rather primarily as mothers or housewives.[96]

Second, benefits have been restricted for the growing class of workers who are outside the full-year, full-time worker model. There has been an erosion of universality: previously, almost all paid occupations were insured against the risk of unemployment; now a minority are. Increased clawback provisions and the Family Income Supplement, which amount to targeting on the basis of individual and family income levels, also constitute a move away from universality.

This approach has addressed immediate fiscal pressures, has created a climate that is more conducive to business operations, and is compatible with an economic growth strategy based on the maintenance of a low-wage, contingent work sector and on a 'competitive austerity'[97] that is viewed as necessary to compete in the global economy. It is also, however, an approach that has entailed increased polarization and growing gender inequalities, and that bases income security programs on, and further reinforces, existing labour-market-based inequalities. It has also entailed increasing difficulty for many women: their needs as mothers are not being adequately met, nor are their needs as workers,[98] and the juggling of work and family responsibilities has as a result become more difficult.

# Conclusion

This book has presented a number of interrelated arguments. First, at a theoretical level it has emphasized the centrality of gender to an understanding of the political economy of the welfare state. Second, more concretely, it has pointed to the ways that gender has been implicated in the formation and restructuring of welfare state regimes. Gender constituted a vital element in the construction of the postwar welfare state, in the tensions and pressures for change within that regime, and in the neoliberal form eventually taken by welfare state restructuring. Third, this book has examined the concrete implications of UI restructuring for women. It argues that overall, women have achieved greater formal equality and some recognition of their needs – for example, with respect to maternity – but that at the same time, restructuring has resulted in polarization, persistent gender inequalities, and considerable difficulty for many women. Finally, the book is concerned with the processes of transformation from the Keynesian welfare state of the postwar era to the current neoliberal state – in particular, the role of and constraints faced by various political actors in those processes. These aspects are discussed below.

## Gender and the Political Economy of the Welfare State

At a theoretical level, this book is situated within a feminist political economy approach. It puts forward a model in which a complex ensemble of variables – including gender ideology, juridical norms, political struggles, production and consumption patterns, family structures, and race and ethnicity – are seen as shaping the direction of welfare state regimes. It argues that the relationship between production and social reproduction is of central importance within this ensemble. While the particular institutions that ensure social reproduction have varied historically, of particular importance since the Second World War has been the relationship between families, the market, and the state. An analysis of the welfare state involves, then, considering the contradictions, tensions, and limitations in the way that relationship has been defined and how the various social, political, and economic forces that are part of the broader ensemble have interacted to change it.

More concretely, this book has pointed to the gendered basis both of the postwar welfare state regime and of the restructuring that has taken place. Gender is understood in a dynamic sense to include shifts in the social relations between men and women, in ideology, in women's paid and unpaid work, in women's material resources, and in the ways women have organized and represented themselves in the political arena. The welfare state of the postwar era drew on Keynesian notions about the state's role in the economy; it also entailed a particular gender order and a particular relationship between families, the market, and the state. This regime was constructed on the basis of a male-breadwinner family, and it both assumed and reinforced a position of dependency for women. State income security policies were intended essentially as a supplement to the temporary unemployment of the male breadwinner. Within the UI program, this gender order was reinforced by administrative practices and by juridical norms. Formal inequalities with respect to married women formed a part of this gender order. Even within rights-based programs such as UI there was inequality of treatment, and women were often denied an independent source of income security. The postwar regime, then, was constructed on the basis of gender inequalities in the labour market and in the administration of a key welfare state program, as well as by formal inequalities.

Gender dimensions were also critical to the tensions, contradictions, and pressures for change within the postwar welfare state regime. This regime, in place from 1945 to the early 1970s, was characterized not so much by stability as by extensive change, including – quite centrally – change with respect to gender. Postwar employment policies had encouraged women to return to the home; however, the economy could not be sustained with that type of family/workplace arrangement. This arrangement did not provide sufficient income either to buy the new consumer goods that were central to postwar economic growth or to maintain standards of living. Family incomes had to be supplemented both by state income support programs and by the increased employment of women, including married women. In addition, many women did not accept the nuclear-family, male-breadwinner model. Thus, their attempts to achieve greater financial security, to break out of the confines of this family structure, and to participate on more equal terms in the public sphere became a powerful force for change. One of the most significant changes of the postwar period, then, was the massive entry of women into the labour market. This change was driven both by financial need and by women's desire to enter the public world of work.

In part as a consequence of these widespread changes in women's activities, gender was also central to the economic crisis, restructuring, and political debate between the early 1970s and the late 1990s. Key aspects of the neoliberal solution included an emphasis on restraining expenditures and controlling inflation, and a shift to a supply-side analysis. The latter focused on individual behaviour and skill levels as explanations for rising unemployment. Central to these interpretations was the construction of women (and youth) as 'secondary' workers able to 'choose' unemployment, who were driving up the rate of unemployment and contributing to rising welfare state costs by drawing on unemployment insurance even though they were not seriously 'attached' to the labour force. This became a justification for marginalizing unemployment as an issue, for allowing unemployment levels to rise far beyond what had been acceptable in the 1960s, and for beginning a process of restraint in the UI program. Gender was central, then, to the ideological and political interpretation of and response to the economic crisis that was taking place. As a consequence, restructuring built on and took shape around gendered divisions and inequalities.

The neoliberal welfare state, consolidated in the 1990s, has involved a new gender order. It has built on a particular construction of notions of unemployment and has emerged out of and addressed gender tensions evident in the postwar regime. It has also responded to and been influenced by the mobilization for women's rights and the demand for greater equality, although in ways that clearly indicate that equity concerns are subordinate to the larger economic agenda of greater reliance on market forces and international competitiveness. Gender ideology, changes in family structure and women's work patterns, and shifts in women's state entitlements and in notions of equality have all shaped the new economy and state.

*Shifting Family-Market-State Relations*

One of the arguments made in this book is that the shift in the welfare state regime has involved not only a changed relationship between the state and the economy, but also a shift in the relationship between families, the state, and the market. The postwar regime was built on a particular type of family–market–state relationship in which the male was the breadwinner, women's dependency within the home was assumed and reinforced, and state income security was meant as a supplement to the male wage. By the early 1970s a very different relationship had developed. Women were spending more and more of time in the paid workforce, the state was playing a much greater role in providing income support to both individuals and families, and labour market structures were taking new forms, particularly with the growth of both service industries and part-time work. There was greater juridical equality. There were fewer discriminatory practices. There was some recognition that women had a role as both workers and mothers. By the 1990s, further shifts had occurred. The male-breadwinner family had essentially been eroded, both as a reality and as an ideological underpinning to the welfare state. The welfare state regime consolidated in the 1990s was based on multi-earner families.[1] Women were increasingly in the labour force throughout the childbearing and early childrearing years, and it was assumed that women, like men, were employable in the marketplace.

*UI Restructuring and Its Implications for Women*

The UI restructuring that began in the mid-1970s and was more fully implemented in the 1990s has involved a number of interrelated elements. First, it has involved a shift toward a model that emphasizes individual rather than state responsibility for unemployment. The notion that unemployment is largely a consequence of individual attributes or dependencies has provided the rationale for a wide range of program changes, including attempts to remove 'disincentives' to work by lengthening the work time required to qualify, by reducing the duration and rate of benefit, and by disqualifying those who quit their work voluntarily. Second, restructuring has involved adopting an 'employability' model which assumes that all individuals, male and female, are or should be employed. This has involved not only attempts to remove 'disincentives' to work, but also a shift from 'passive' income support to 'active' measures encouraging re-employment. For the most part, these measures have taken the form of wage subsidies and income supplements for low-wage employment. Third, consistent with other welfare state restructuring, the reforms of the 1990s have involved a shift from a universal to a more targeted provision of benefits.[2] There has been a move to a more specific allocation of benefits according to such criteria as stability of employment history, frequency of program use, and individual and family income levels. Finally, a major impetus behind UI restructuring has been the perceived need to reduce expenditures and state deficit and debt levels. By the late 1990s the UI program had become, through premiums levied, a source of revenue, and was contributing in important ways to reducing the deficit and adding to state surpluses.

What have the implications of this UI restructuring been for women? In the introduction, a number of questions were posed. Are women more or less able to provide for themselves and their families? Has restructuring led to more or less gender equality? How have conflicting tensions between working in the paid labour force and in the home, and between women's role as mother and as worker been addressed? Overall, restructuring has made it more difficult for women to gain access to a rights-based, state-provided income security program, thus increasing the difficulty that women, or at least some women, face in providing for themselves and their families. One of the key characteristics of the new EI model is that it has established a two-tier system of benefits, with income security primarily provided for those who are employed full-time and full-year but who are subject to periodic layoffs; for those with more intermittent employment, benefits are limited. Benefit eligibility has been restricted in particular for repeat users, for new entrants and re-entrants to the labour force, and for part-time workers. Since women are overrepresented in the latter type of employment it has been especially difficult for them to qualify or to receive benefits for an extended period. As a result, now only somewhat more than one-third of unemployed women receive UI/EI.

The most recent EI changes also have direct implications for women's position in the domestic sphere. Given women's role within the family and their continued domestic responsibilities, cuts in state income security benefits have affected them in many ways. For example, cuts have increased their domestic labour, and also marginalized them within the labour market as ways to acquire income while meeting the needs of social reproduction become more difficult to find. This has been compounded by the reduction in the availability of maternity benefits and by the trend to family-based income testing; both these things reduce women's autonomy and independence within the household.

Has restructuring led, then, to more or less gender equality? Overall inequalities persist, but they have taken new forms. The postwar period is sometimes presented as the golden age of the welfare state, yet as this book has attempted to demonstrate, it was also a period that involved extensive inequalities. Because of the contradictions and inequalities at the base of the postwar welfare state, it is neither feasible nor desirable to return to such a model. The restructuring since that time has meant some gains, but it has also meant new forms of inequality for women. Partly as a result of the Charter, by the late 1980s there were stronger guarantees of formal equality. Furthermore, women gained greater acceptance in the public sphere of work and the right to be considered as 'employable' as men. And there was some recognition that equality for women entailed not only at times the right to the same treatment as men, but also, at other times, the right to different treatment.

Yet for many women the overall withdrawal of state support for the unemployed, the targeting of part-time workers as subject to more stringent entrance requirements, and the growth of part-time work have all led to increased polarization, persistent gender inequalities, and an overall deterioration in the quality of life. A complex restructuring of family–market–state relations has left women with major responsibilities both for addressing the needs of social reproduction in the home and for obtaining an income in the marketplace. Women's activities have shifted increasingly away from the *family* toward the market; at the same time, there has been a major restructuring of the relationship between the *state* and the market, including a major decrease in state responsibility for the unemployed. In other words, just as women have entered the labour market, the rights and entitlements that once went with labour force participation have been ended. Moreover, the downloading of responsibilities for unemployment from the state to individuals and households has entailed increased stresses and costs. Finally, the increasing tendency for social policy directions to be set by an agenda of global economic competitiveness has made it more difficult for equity concerns to be heard and accommodated. All these changes, then, have increased substantive inequalities. In addition, they have moved the welfare state even further off a model that Ann Orloff, for example, identifies as critical for women – being able to support and maintain an autonomous household.

*The Shift to Neoliberalism: Policy Actors and Political Economic Forces*

One of the concerns of this book has been to come to a better understanding of the *processes* by which changes in state policy come about. I have argued that to understand the nature of the shift from a Keynesian to a neoliberal welfare state and why restructuring has taken the particular shape that it has we must consider how various forces and factors have come together in ways that create tensions and pressures, and in cumulative patterns that can bring about or forestall more substantive changes.

I have noted that between 1945 and the early 1970s a particular complex of forces shaped welfare state development and helped set the context in which the relationship between families, the market, and the state, and between production and social reproduction, was being reformed. The welfare state regime as it was constructed in the immediate postwar period assumed that women would be primarily at home; yet at the same time economic considerations and the desire for something beyond the nuclear family structure drew a great many women into the labour force. As women entered the paid labour force, a series of tensions and contradictions in the welfare state regime became apparent. First, as early as the 1950s a contradiction was developing between women's status as individuals entering into contract in the labour force and a welfare state structure that was often explicitly discriminatory and that assumed women belonged in the home. Attempts to change the juridical norms on which the welfare state was based, and to achieve equal treatment within programs such as UI, became a powerful force for change. Second, as women entered the public sphere, the need to reconcile domestic responsibilities – particularly with respect to childrearing and childcare – with responsibilities in the workplace created by the mid-1960s pressure not only for equality of treatment but also for special programs such as maternity leave, that would recognize women's differences. Finally, a major structural contradiction developed between a welfare state based on the assumption of a full-time, full-year male worker, and the reality that the labour force was increasingly female and contingent. This was apparent as early as the 1960s, and became much more obvious in later decades, and created further pressure for a restructuring of welfare state programs.

By the early 1970s these pressures, unfolding in the context of economic growth and increased militancy of labour and women's groups, had resulted in some changes, including (as noted earlier) an expanded welfare state, greater juridical equalities, and a maternity plan within the UI program. Some of the tensions in the postwar model had been at least partially resolved; others became more apparent. Between 1970 and the end of the 1990s a different complex of forces and a new series of tensions came to shape welfare state development. In the 1970s and 1980s policy was increasingly being formulated in the context of the emerging economic crisis, growing fiscal pressure on the state, and the growing impact of global economic restructuring. New contradictions between women's role in the labour force and the legal/juridical structures emerged, in particular with respect to definitions of equality and what might be considered 'discriminatory in effect.' The limits of the UI-based maternity plan became apparent, and so did new pressures with respect to women's ability to adequately maintain workforce continuity and address the needs of social reproduction. The continued growth of the service sector and of a part-time, contingent workforce further increased pressures on state programs that had been built around a full-time, full-year labour force. Finally, a reconfiguration of political forces meant a shifting context for policy development. This new ensemble, then, constituted by continued shifts in the organization of production, in employment patterns, in legal/juridical structures, in family–work–life patterns, and in the relative strength of political forces, led to a restructuring of the welfare state and a new family–market–state arrangement. With respect to UI, this meant the replacement of 'unemployment insurance' by a more market-oriented 'employment insurance' program.

One of the underlying concerns of this book has been to better understand the conditions under which particular political actors have influenced the state agenda. Women's groups (as well as labour and other popular sector organizations) have had varying success in influencing the direction of state policies, depending in part on the ways in which particular political strategies and agendas interact with the larger complex of forces. Women's groups, both on their own and in conjunction with other groups and actors, achieved particular visibility and presence between 1960 and the late 1980s. These were both the key years of the second wave of the women's movement and the transition period from one welfare state regime to another. In the immediate postwar period the initial major impetus for change was women 'voting with their feet' as individual women left the confines of the nuclear family, entered the labour force, attempted to work out strategies for financial survival, and came to challenge the norms and conventions that formed a part of the male-breadwinner ideology. Initially working women were not well represented either by trade unions or by women's organizations, but eventually both sets of organizations, as well as parts of the state itself, began to take up the question of equality for women. The biggest concerns at this point were equality of treatment and the elimination of discriminatory provisions, but within a framework that did not fundamentally challenge the family-wage norm. By the mid-1960s, new, rights-based women's organizations were challenging to a much greater extent the male-breadwinner ideology and the gender division of labour on which it was based. They came to demand not only equality of treatment but also the right to special programs (such as maternity leave), as a precondition for equality. The growing presence of women in the labour force, a period of almost full employment, the growth of new women's and labour organizations, and an expansionary state laid the basis by the early 1970s not only for a new family–market–state relationship but also for a more significant presence for women in the political arena.

In the 1970s and early 1980s a network of women's advisors within the state, and an increasingly sophisticated and politically active group of women's organizations outside the state, combined to exert considerable pressure on the state for policy changes. Women, however, gained that increased presence just as the expansionary state was being questioned and just as the shift to a neoliberal framework was taking place. Overall, women's representatives inside and outside the state had considerable success in raising the importance of gender issues, in changing the terms of the debate (e.g., with respect to pregnancy and maternity issues), and in eliminating overtly discriminatory practices. These were important gains; they were also responses to demands at the root of the second wave of the women's movement. This phase of the women's movement was successful in having discriminatory provisions removed, in a sense, because such changes were consistent with and perhaps necessary for a restructuring economy that was increasingly dependent on women's work in the labour force. Women were far less successful in challenging provisions and policies (such as those limiting UI benefits for part-time workers) that, while not explicitly discriminatory, were 'discriminatory in effect,' given women's structural location within the economy. To a much greater extent, these demands were incompatible with the direction of economic change, and they could not be accommodated without accentuating the underlying contradictions and increasing fiscal pressures on the state.

The limits on the ability of women's groups to make demands that run counter to the direction of economic change became much more evident by the late 1980s. Funding for women's organizations began to be cut under the Mulroney Conservatives in the late 1980s, and the Liberals continued these cuts in the 1990s. The network of women's advisors within the state was also scaled back, most notably with the closing of the CACSW in 1995. Furthermore, within state programs there has been a shift from special programs for women to conducting analyses to identify the possible gender impact. To some extent, this decline in women's visibility and presence is part of a broader reconfiguration of power involving reduced power for a range of popular sector organizations, and the growing strength of a global corporate agenda. One of the challenges for women's groups and for others is to find new ways of organizing and of having their voices heard in this changed political-economic context.

Neoliberal restructuring absorbed within it many of the demands of the second wave of the women's movement; it also resolved some of the contradictions of the earlier postwar model. One of the major contradictions of the postwar regime was between a welfare state based on the assumption of a full-time, full-year male worker and the reality of an economy based on part-time, intermittent work and an increasingly feminized labour force. The restructuring of the 1990s resolved this particular contradiction by allowing greater formal equality but also restricting benefits for those working on a part-time, intermittent basis. This solution addressed demands for formal equality, created a climate conducive to certain types of business operations, and addressed immediate fiscal pressures, but it did not at all address a series of other demands and concerns raised by women and others and indeed, it can be argued, has generated new contradictions and tensions.

This form of welfare state restructuring has resulted in a growing polarization between those who have access to relatively stable jobs *and* UI/EI income security, and those who are only able to find short-term, intermittent work and who have little access to other forms of social security. The accentuation of these forms of inequality and the growing polarization between different groups in society is likely to generate new tensions in the larger complex of forces and is not likely to lead to lasting social stability. In addition, a new series of contradictions is being generated between an economy increasingly reliant on women's paid labour and a welfare state reliant on women in the home.[3] While women's formal equality demands, and demands for the right to enter the public sphere of work, have largely been met, substantive inequalities remain and in some cases may have deepened. Furthermore, the solutions provided have left the issue of social reproduction largely as a private, individual or household matter. This solution has meant an overemphasis on market competitiveness, a delinking of production and social reproduction, and a neglect of social reproduction issues. Such a model places excessive pressure on families, and given women's role within the home, on women in particular, in terms of being able to both meet financial needs and look after domestic concerns.

The limits and new contradictions generated by this new welfare state model mean that there are likely to be ongoing challenges, although these will no doubt be organized in different ways than in the second half of the twentieth century. Certainly, the new approaches to organizing and to questioning the welfare state model will have to address the limitations and contradictions noted above. The consideration of alternative ways of organizing the relationship between households, work, and the state and alternative ways of having voices from all sectors heard remains one of the central challenges of the twenty-first century.

# Notes

## Introduction

1 Canada, *A 21st Century Employment System for Canada: Guide to the Employment Insurance Legislation* (Ottawa: December, 1995), 1.

2 Joan Wallach Scott, 'Some Reflections on Gender and Politics,' in Myra Marx Ferree, Judith Lorber, and Beth B. Hess, eds., *Revisioning Gender* (Walnut Creek, CA: AltaMira Press, 2000).

3 A useful discussion is found in Myra Marx Ferree, Judith Lorber, and Beth B. Hess, eds., *Revisioning Gender*. See, for example, the article in this volume by Evelyn Nakano Glenn, 'The Social Construction and Institutionalization of Gender and Race: An Integrative Framework.'

4 UI statistics and materials gathered from archival and other sources commonly made distinctions based on sex or marital status (the latter of more relevance, it seemed, for women than for men), but rarely, or less overtly, on the basis of race or ethnicity. The major focus of this study is on the former distinctions.

5 Canada, House of Commons, Report of the Standing Committee on Human Resources Development, *Security, Opportunity and Fairness: Canadians Renewing their Social Programs* (Ottawa: 1995), 88.

6 See, for example, Barbara Nelson, 'The Origins of the Two-Channel Welfare State: Workmen's Compensation and Mother's Aid,' in Linda Gordon, ed., *Women, the State and Welfare* (Wisconsin: University of Wisconsin Press, 1990); Nancy Fraser and Linda Gordon, 'Contract versus Charity: Why is There No Social Citizenship in the United States?,' *Socialist Review* 22, no. 3 (1992); Carole Pateman, 'The Patriarchal Welfare State,' in Amy

Gutmann, ed., *Democracy and the Welfare State* (Princeton: Princeton University Press, 1988).

7 Recently more attention been been paid to how women have fared in rights-based programs. On UI/EI, see Leah Vosko, 'Irregular Workers, New Involuntary Social Exiles: Women and UI Reform,' in J. Pulkingham and G. Ternowetsky, eds., *Remaking Canadian Social Policy: Social Security in the Late 1990s* (Halifax: Fernwood Publishing, 1996); Jane Pulkingham, 'Remaking the Social Divisions of Welfare: Gender, "Dependency" and UI Reform,' *Studies in Political Economy* 56 (Summer 1998); Martha MacDonald, 'Restructuring, Gender and Social Security Reform in Canada,' *Journal of Canadian Studies* 34, no. 2 (Summer 1999); and Patricia M. Evans, 'Divided Citizenship? Gender, Income Security, and the Welfare State,' in Patricia M. Evans and Gerda R. Wekerle, *Women and the Canadian Welfare State: Challenges and Change* (Toronto: University of Toronto Press, 1997).

8 The political economy literature on welfare state restructuring is large. Examples include Gary Teeple, *Globalization and the Decline of Social Reform* (Toronto: Garamond Press, 1995); Jamie Peck, *Workfare States* (New York: Guildford Press, 2001); Richard Clayton and Jonas Pontusson, 'Welfare State Retrenchment Revisited: Entitlement Cuts, Public Sector Restructuring, and Inegalitarian Trends in Advanced Capitalist Societies,' *World Politics* 51 (October 1998); Bob Jessop, 'Towards a Schumpeterian Workfare State? Preliminary Remarks on Post-Fordist Political Economy,' *Studies in Political Economy* (Spring 1993); John Myles, 'Decline or Impasse? The Current State of the Welfare State,' *Studies in Political Economy* 26 (1988); Dexter Whitfield, *Public Services or Corporate Welfare: Rethinking the Nation State in the Global Economy* (London: Pluto Press, 2001); and Colin Leys, *Market-Driven Politics: Neoliberal Democracy and the Public Interest* (London: Verso, 2001). The UI program has been the subject of a lively debate about the relative importance of class and the state, but these works did not look at gender. See Carl Cuneo, 'State, Class and Reserve Labour: The Case of the 1941 Canadian Unemployment Insurance Act,' *Canadian Review of Sociology and Anthropology* 16, no. 2 (1979); Carl Cuneo, 'Restoring Class to State Unemployment Insurance,' *Canadian Journal of Political Science* XIX (1986); and Leslie A. Pal, *State, Class and Bureaucracy: Canadian Unemployment Insurance and Public Policy* (Montreal and Kingston: McGill-Queen's University Press, 1988).

In some recent work gender or the family does figure more prominently in analyses of welfare state development. See Gosta Esping-Andersen, *Social Foundations of Postindustrial Economies* (Oxford: Oxford University Press, 1999), John Myles and Jill Quadagno, 'Political Theories of the Welfare State,' *Social Service Review* (March 2002); Walter Korpi, 'Faces of

Inequality: Gender, Class, and Patterns of Inequality in Different Types of Welfare States,' *Social Politics* (Summer 2000).

9  Gosta Esping-Andersen, 'After the Golden Age? State Dilemmas in a Global Economy,' in Gosta Esping-Andersen, ed., *Welfare States in Transition: National Adaptations in Global Economics* (London: Sage, 1996); Walter Korpi: 'Faces of Inequality: Gender, Class, and Patterns of Inequality in Different Types of Welfare States,' *Social Politics* (2000).

## 1: Gender and the Political Economy of the Welfare State

1  Rianne Mahon uses this expression in referring to Bob Jessop, *State Theory: Putting the Capitalist State in Its Place* (London: Polity Press, 1990) (Mahon, 'From "Bringing" to "Putting": The State in Late Twentieth-Century Social Theory,' *Canadian Journal of Sociology* 16, no. 2 [1991], 138). Maroney and Luxton have argued that most feminist political economy now recognizes 'a complex interplay of capital accumulation, labour markets, state policies ... reproduction of labour power in daily and generational cycles, family household demographics, forms of organization and divisions of labour, and workplace trade-union and political organizing by workers' (Heather Jon Maroney and Meg Luxton, 'Gender at Work: Canadian Feminist Political Economy since 1988,' in Wallace Clement, ed., *Understanding Canada: Building on the New Canadian Political Economy* [Montreal and Kingston: McGill-Queen's University Press, 1997], 92).

2  See, for example, the collection of articles in Bonnie Fox, ed., *Hidden in the Household: Women's Domestic Labour Under Capitalism* (Toronto: The Women's Press, 1980).

3  Heidi Hartmann, 'The Unhappy Marriage of Marxism and Feminism: Towards a More Progressive Union,' in *Women and Revolution* (Boston: South End Press, 1981), reprinted in Linda Nicholson, ed., *The Second Wave: A Reader in Feminist Theory* (New York: Routledge, 1997).

4  See, for example, Mary McIntosh, 'The State and the Oppression of Women,' in Annette Kuhn and Ann Marie Wolpe, eds., *Feminism and Materialism* (London: Routledge and Kegan Paul, 1978); Elizabeth Wilson, *Women and the Welfare State* (London: Tavistock Publications, 1977); and Michele Barrett, *Women's Oppression Today* (London: Verso, First Edition, 1980).

5  McIntosh, 'The State and the Oppression of Women.'

6  Zillah Eisenstein, *Feminism and Sexual Equality* (New York: Monthly Review Press, 1984), especially chapter 4, 'The Relative Autonomy of the Capitalist Patriarchal State'; Jane Ursel, 'The State and the Maintenance of Patriarchy: A Case Study of Family, Labour and Welfare Legislation in Canada,' in James Dickinson and Bob Russell, eds., *Family, Economy and the*

*State: The Social Reproduction Process under Capitalism* (Toronto: Garamond Press, 1986); and Jane Ursel, *Private Lives, Public Policy: 100 Years of State Intervention in the Family* (Toronto: Women's Press, 1992).

7 Dorothy Smith, 'Women's Inequality and the Family,' in Allan Moscovitch and Glen Drover, *Inequality: Essays on the Political Economy of Social Welfare* (Toronto: University of Toronto Press, 1981); and Wally Seccombe, *A Millenium of Family Change* (London: Verso, 1992), and *Weathering the Storm: Working Class Families from the Industrial Revolution to the Fertility Decline* (London: Verso, 1993).

8 Smith, 'Women's Inequality and the Family.'

9 On the latter point, see Pat Armstrong and Hugh Armstrong, 'Beyond Sexless Class and Classless Sex: Towards Feminist Marxism,' *Studies in Political Economy* 10 (Winter 1983), 7, 8.

10 See, for example, McIntosh, 'The State and the Oppression of Women'; and Ursel, 'The State and the Maintenance of Patriarchy.' In Ursel's work the stages of patriarchy seem to be ultimately determined by stages in economic development. Ursel argues that patriarchy's 'fundamental function' in class societies is to ensure 'the continued organization of repoduction in the interests of production.' Ursel, *Private Lives*, 54.

11 See, for example, Ursel, *Private Lives*; Smith, 'Women's Inequality and the Family'; and McIntosh, 'The State and the Oppression of Women.'

12 See, for example, Pat Armstrong and Hugh Armstrong, *The Double Ghetto* (Toronto: McClelland & Stewart, 1978); Armstrong and Armstrong, 'Beyond Sexless Class and Classless Sex: Towards Feminist Marxism,' *Studies in Political Economy* 10 (Winter 1983); Martha MacDonald and Patricia Connelly, 'Class and Gender in Fishing Communities in Nova Scotia,' *Studies in Political Economy* 30 (Autumn 1989); Meg Luxton, *More Than a Labour of Love: Three Generations of Women's Work in the Home* (Toronto: The Women's Press, 1980); and Heather Jon Maroney and Meg Luxton, 'From Feminism and Political Economy to Feminist Political Economy,' in Maroney and Luxton, eds., *Feminism and Political Economy: Women's Work, Women's Struggles* (Toronto: Methuen, 1987).

13 Joan Wallach Scott, 'Gender: A Useful Category of Historical Analysis,' in Scott, *Gender and the Politics of History* (New York: Columbia University Press, 1988), 29.

14 See, for example, Caroline Andrew, 'Women and the Welfare State,' *Canadian Journal of Political Science* 27, no. 4 (Dec. 1984); Jane Jenson, 'Gender and Reproduction, or Babies and the State,' *Studies in Political Economy* 20 (1986); Linda Gordon, 'The Welfare State: Towards a Socialist-Feminist Perspective,' in Ralph Miliband and Leo Panitch, eds., *Socialist Register,*

*1994* (London: Merlin Press, 1994). For more recent work, see Margaret Little, *'No Car, No Radio, No Liquor Permit': The Moral Regulation of Single Mothers in Ontario, 1920–1997* (Toronto: Oxford, 1998); Barbara Hobson and Marilka Lindholm 'Collective Identities, Women's Power Resources, and the Making of Welfare States,' *Theory and Society* 26 (1997); Wendy McKeen, 'The Shaping of Political Agency: Feminism and the National Social Policy Debate, the 1970s and Early 1980s,' *Studies in Political Economy* 66 (2001).

15  Jane Jenson, 'Gender and Reproduction, or Babies and the State,' *Studies in Political Economy* 20 (1986); Anne Showstack Sassoon, 'Introduction,' and 'Women's New Social Role: Contradictions of the Welfare State,' in *Women and the State* (London: Unwin Hyman, 1987).

16  For an early discussion of these issues see, for example, Kum-Kum Bhavnani and Margaret Coulson, 'Transforming Socialist-Feminism: The Challenge of Racism,' *Feminist Review* 23 (June 1986); and Michele Barrett and Mary McIntosh, 'Ethnocentrism and Socialist Feminist Theory,' *Feminist Review* 20 (1985), 23–47.

17  See, for example, Michele Barrett, *Women's Oppression Today* introduction to the revised 1988 edition; and Joan Scott, 'Gender: A Useful Category of Historical Analysis.'

18  Pat Armstrong and M. Patricia Connelly, 'Feminism and Political Economy: An Introduction,' *Studies in Political Economy* 30 (1989), 5.

19  Wally Seccombe and D.W. Livingstone, '"Down to Earth People": Revising a Materialist Understanding of Group Consciousness,' in D.W. Livingstone and J. Marshall Mangan, eds., *Recast Dreams: Class and Gender Consciousness in Steeltown* (Toronto: Garamond Press, 1996), 133.

20  Joan Acker, 'Class, Gender and the Relations of Distribution,' *Signs* 13 (1988).

21  Joan Acker, 'Rewriting Class, Race and Gender: Problems in Feminist Rethinking,' in Myra Marx Ferree, Judith Lorber, and Beth B. Hess, eds., *Revisioning Gender* (Walnut Creek, CA: AltaMira Press, 2000), 53.

22  Evelyn Nakano Glenn, 'The Social Construction and Institutionalization of Gender and Race,' in Myra Marx Ferree, Judith Lorber, and Beth B. Hess, eds., *Revisioning Gender* (Walnut Creek, CA: AltaMira Press, 2000), 9.

23  See, for example, Wally Seccombe, *A Millennium of Family Change: Feudalism to Capitalism in Northwestern Europe* (London: Verso, 1992), Marilyn Waring, *Counting for Nothing: What Men Value and What Women Are Worth* (Toronto: University of Toronto Press, 1999); Nancy Folbre, *The Invisible Heart: Economic and Family Values* (New York: The New Press, 2001); and Diane Elson, 'The Economic, the Political and the Domestic: Businesses,

States and Households in the Organisation of Production,' *New Political Economy* 3, no. 2 (1998).

24  See, for example, Chandra Talpade Mohanty, 'Women Workers and Capitalist Scripts: Ideologies of Domination, Common Interests, and the Politics of Solidarity,' in M. Jacqui Alexander and Chandra Talpade Mohanty, *Feminist Genealogies, Colonial Legacies, Democratic Futures* (New York: Routledge, 1997); Karen Hassfeld, '"Their Logic Against Them": Contradictions in Sex, Race and Class in Silicon Valley,' in Katheryn Ward, ed., *Women Workers and Global Restructuring* (Ithaca: IRL Press, 1990); S. Rowbotham and S. Mitter, eds., *Dignity and Daily Bread* (London and New York: Routledge, 1994); M. Patricia Fernandez-Kelly and S. Sassen, 'Recasting Women in the Global Economy: Internationalization and Changing Definitions of Gender,' in C. Bose and E. Acost-Belen, eds., *Women in the Latin American Development Process* (Philadelphia: Temple University Press, 1995).

25  See Patricia Hill Collins, *Black Feminist Thought: Knowledge, Consciousness and the Politics of Empowerment* second edition, (New York: Routledge, 2000); Kimberle Williams Crenshaw, 'Mapping the Margins: Intersectionality, Identity Politics and Violence Against Women of Color,' *Stanford Law Review* 43, no. 6 (1991); and Johanna Brenner, 'Intersections, Locations and Capitalist Class Relations: Intersectionality from a Marxist Perspective,' in Johanna Brenner, *Women and the Politics of Class* (New York: Monthly Review Press, 2000).

26  Johanna Brenner, 'Intersections, Locations, and Capitalist Class Relations: Intersectionality from a Marxist Perspective,' in Johanna Brenner, *Women and the Politics of Class.*

27  Carole Pateman, 'The Patriarchal Welfare State,' in Amy Gutmann, ed., *Democracy and the Welfare State* (Princeton: Princeton University Press, 1988). See also Pateman, 'The Fraternal Social Contract,' in John Keane, ed., *Civil Society and the State* (London: Verso, 1988); and 'Feminism and Democracy,' in Pateman, *The Disorder of Women* (Cambridge: Polity Press, 1989).

28  Gillian Pascall, *Social Policy: A Feminist Analysis* (London: Routledge, 1991); Hilary Land, 'Who Still Cares for the Family? Recent Developments in Income Maintenance, Taxation and Family Law,' in Jane Lewis, ed., *Women's Welfare, Women's Rights* (London: Croom Helm, 1983); Anne Showstack-Sassoon, 'Women's New Social Role: Contradictions of the Welfare State,' in Anne Showstack Sassoon, ed., *Women and the State* (London: Unwin Hyman, 1987); Jane Lewis, 'Gender and the Development of Welfare Regimes,' in Julia S. O'Connor and Gregg M. Olsen, eds., *Power*

*Resources Theory and the Welfare State* (Toronto: University of Toronto Press, 1998).

29 See, for example, Barbara Nelson, 'The Origins of the Two-Channel Welfare State: Workmen's Compensation and Mother's Aid,' in Linda Gordon, ed., *Women, the State and Welfare* (Wisconsin: University of Wisconsin Press, 1990); Diana Pearce, 'Welfare is not *for* Women: Why the War on Poverty Cannot Conquer the Feminization of Poverty,' in Linda Gordon, ed., *Women, the State and Welfare*; Nancy Fraser and Linda Gordon, 'Contract versus Charity: Why Is There No Social Citizenship in the United States?' *Socialist Review* 22, no. 3 (1992); Carole Pateman, 'The Patriarchal Welfare State,' in Amy Gutmann, ed., *Democracy and the Welfare State* (Princeton: Princeton University Press, 1988). For a discussion in the Canadian context see Patricia M. Evans, 'Divided Citizenship? Gender, Income Security and the Welfare State,' in Patricia M. Evans and Gerda Wekerle, eds., *Women and the Canadian Welfare State: Challenges and Change* (Toronto: University of Toronto Press, 1997).

30 See, for example, Anette Borchorst and Birte Siim, 'Women and the Advanced Welfare State – A New Kind of Patriarchal Power?' in Anne Showstack Sassoon, ed., *Women and the State* (London: Unwin Hyman, 1987). On Denmark see Birte Siim, 'Towards a Feminist Rethinking of the Welfare State,' in Kathleen B. Jones and Anna G. Jonasdottir, *The Political Interests of Gender* (London: Sage, 1988). On Sweden see Jane Lewis and Gertrude Astrom, 'Equality, Difference and State Welfare: Labor Market and Family Policies in Sweden,' *Feminist Studies* 18, no. 1 (1992).

31 Lewis and Astrom, 'Equality, Difference and State Welfare,' 67, 74.

32 Borschorst and Siim, 'Women and the Advanced Welfare State.'

33 Siim, 'Towards a Feminist Rethinking of the Welfare State,' 179.

34 Lewis, 'Gender and the Development of Welfare Regimes.'

35 Diane Sainsbury, 'Women's and Men's Social Rights: Gendering Dimensions of Welfare States,' in D. Sainsbury, ed., *Gendering Welfare States* (London and Thousand Oaks: Sage, 1994), 155.

36 Patricia Evans, 'Single Mothers and Ontario's Welfare Policy: Restructuring the Debate,' in Janine Brodie, ed., *Women and Canadian Public Policy* (Toronto: Harcourt Brace, 1996).

37 Katherine Scott, 'The Dilemma of Liberal Citizenship: Women and Social Assistance Reform in the 1990s,' *Studies in Political Economy* 50 (Summer 1996).

38 Leah Vosko, 'Irregular Workers, New Involuntary Social Exiles: Women and UI Reform,' in J. Pulkingham and G. Ternowetsky, eds., *Remaking Canadian Social Policy: Social Security in the Late 1990s* (Halifax: Fernwood

Publishing, 1996); and Jane Pulkingham, 'Remaking the Social Divisions of Welfare: Gender, "Dependency" and UI Reform,' *Studies in Political Economy* 56 (Summer 1998).

39 Janine Brodie, 'Restructuring and the Politics of Marginalization,' in Manon Tremblay and Caroline Andrew, eds., *Women and Political Representation in Canada* (Ottawa: University of Ottawa Press, 1998); and Janine Brodie, *Politics on the Margins: Restructuring and the Canadian Women's Movement* (Halifax: Fernwood, 1995), 56–62.

40 Gosta Esping-Andersen, *The Three Worlds of Welfare Capitalism* (Cambridge: Polity Press, 1990).

41 Ann Shola Orloff, 'Gender and the Social Rights of Citizenship: State Policies and Gender Relations in Comparative Perspective,' *American Sociological Review* 58 (1993); Julia O'Connor, 'Gender, Class and Citizenship in the Comparative Analysis of Welfare State Regimes: Theoretical and Methodological Issues,' 1993, *British Journal of Sociology* 44, no. 3 (1993); and Jane Lewis, 'Gender and the Development of Welfare Regimes.' See also Diane Sainsbury, ed., *Gendering Welfare States*; D. Sainsbury, *Gender, Equality and Welfare States* (Cambridge: Cambridge University Press, 1996); and Julia S. O'Connor, Ann Shola Orloff, and Sheila Shaver, *States, Markets, Families: Gender, Liberalism and Social Policy in Australia, Canada, Great Britain and the United States* (Cambridge: Cambridge University Press, 1999).

42 Orloff, 'Gender and the Social Rights of Citizenship'; O'Connor, 'Gender, Class and Citizenship in the Comparative Analysis of Welfare State Regimes.'

43 O'Connor, 'Gender, Class and Citizenship.'

44 Orloff, 'Gender and the Social Rights of Citizenship,' 320.

45 See, for example, Rianne Mahon, 'Child Care in Canada and Sweden: Policy and Politics,' *Social Politics* (Fall 1997); and Barbara Hobson and Marika Lindholm, 'Collective Identities, Women's Power Resources, and the Making of Welfare States,' *Theory and Society* 26 (1997).

46 Fiona Williams, 'Race/Ethnicity, Gender and Class in Welfare States: A Framework for Comparative Analysis,' *Social Politics* (Summer 1995).

47 See, for example, Gary Teeple, *Globalization and the Decline of Social Reform* (Toronto: Garamond Press, 1995); Jamie Peck, *Workfare States* (New York: Guildford Press, 2001); Richard Clayton and Jonas Pontusson, 'Welfare State Retrenchment Revisited: Entitlement Cuts, Public Sector Restructuring and Inegalitarian Trends in Advanced Capitalist Societies,' *World Politics* 51 (October 1998); Gosta Esping-Andersen, *Social Foundations of Postindustrial Economies* (Oxford: Oxford University Press, 1999); Dexter

Whitfield, *Public Services or Corporate Welfare: Rethinking the Nation State in the Global Economy* (London: Pluto Press, 2001); Colin Leys, *Market-driven Politics: Neoliberal Democracy and the Public Interest* (London: Verso, 2001); Paul Hirst and Grahame Thompson, *Globalization in Question: The International Economy and the Possibilities of Governance* second edition (Cambridge: Polity Press, 1999), ch. 6; and Paul Pierson, ed., *The New Politics of the Welfare State* (Oxford: Oxford University Press, 2001).

48 John Myles, 'Decline or Impasse? The Current State of the Welfare State,' *Studies in Political Economy* 26 (1988); Bob Jessop, 'Towards a Schumpeterian Workfare State?' *Studies in Political Economy* 40 (1993).

49 Bob Jessop, 'Towards a Schumpeterian Workfare State?' *Studies in Political Economy* 40 (1993).

50 Ibid., 22–3.

51 Myles, 'Decline or Impasse?'

52 Linda McDowell, 'Life without Father and Ford: The New Gender Order of Post-Fordism,' *Transactions of the Institute of British Geographers* 16 (1991). On this point see also Nancy Fraser, 'After the Family Wage: Gender Equity and the Welfare State,' *Political Theory* (Nov. 1994). Fraser refers to the transition to a 'post-industrial' rather than a 'post-Fordist' phase of capitalism.

53 See, for example, Sylvia Walby, 'Flexibility and the Changing Sexual Division of Labour,' in Stephen Wood, ed., *The Transformation of Work? Skill, Flexibility and the Labour Process* (London: Unwin Hyman, 1989); Martha MacDonald, 'Post-Fordism and the Flexibility Debate,' *Studies in Political Economy* 36 (Autumn 1991); Isabella Bakker, ed., *The Strategic Silence: Gender and Economic Policy* (London: Zed Books 1988); Isabella Bakker, ed., *Rethinking Restructuring: Gender and Change in Canada* (Toronto: University of Toronto Press, 1996); M. Mies, *Patriarchy and Accumulation on a World Scale*; Lourdes Beneria, 'Globalization, Gender and the Davos Man,' *Feminist Economics* 5, no. 3 (1999); and Shirin M. Rai, *Gender and the Political Economy of Development* (Cambridge: Polity Press, 2002).

54 See, for example, Janine Brodie, *Politics on the Margins: Restructuring and the Canadian Women's Movement* (Halifax: Fernwood, 1995); Pat Armstrong et al., *Exposing Privatization: Women and Health Care Reform in Canada* (Aurora: Garamond Press, 2002); Jane Aronson and Sheila Neysmith, 'The Retreat of the State and Long-Term Provisions: Implications for Frail Elderly People, Unpaid Family Carers and Paid Home Care Workers,' *Studies in Political Economy* 53 (Summer 1997).

55 Michel Aglietta, *A Theory of Capitalist Regulation* (London: New Left Books, 1979).

56  See, for example, Robert Brenner and Mark Glick, 'The Regulation Approach: Theory and History,' *New Left Review* 188 (July/August 1991), 52.
57  Aglietta, *A Theory of Capitalist Regulation*, ch. 3.
58  See, for example, Pat Armstrong and Hugh Armstrong, *The Double Ghetto: Canadian Women and Their Segregated Work*, third edition (Toronto: McClelland & Stewart, 1994), ch. 3; Meg Luxton, *More Than a Labour of Love*; Veronica Strong-Boag, 'Keeping House in God's Country: Canadian Women at Work in the Home,' in Craig Heron and Robert Storey, eds., *On the Job: Confronting the Labour Process in Canada* (McGill-Queen's, 1986); Bettina Bradbury, *Working Families: Age, Gender and Daily Survival in Industrializing Montreal* (Toronto: McClelland & Stewart, 1993); Bettina Bradbury, ed., *Canadian Family History* (Mississauga: Copp Clark Pitman, 1992); and Denyse Baillargeon, 'La crise ordinaire: Les ménagères montréalaises et la crise des années trente,' *Labour/Le Travail* 30 (1992).
59  See, for example, Bradbury, *Working Families*, and Marjorie Griffin Cohen, *Women's Work, Markets and Economic Development in Nineteenth Century Ontario* (Toronto: University of Toronto Press, 1988).
60  Wendy McKeen and Ann Porter, 'Politics and Transformation: Welfare State Restructuring in Canada,' in Wallace Clement and Leah F. Vosko, eds., *Changing Canada: Political Economy as Transformation* (Montreal and Kingston: McGill-Queen's University Press, 2003).
61  Monica Boyd and Edward T. Pryor, 'The Cluttered Nest: The Living Arrangements of Young Canadian Adults,' *Canadian Journal of Sociology and Anthropology* 14, no. 4 (1989).
62  The question of the political forces behind recent welfare state restructuring has been addressed to a greater extent in more recent work by Myles, as well as others. This later work, however, provides less sense of the changing nature of political-economic structures. See, for example, Paul Pierson, 'The New Politics of the Welfare State,' *World Politics* 48 (January 1996); John Myles and Paul Pierson, 'Friedman's Revenge: The Reform of "Liberal" Welfare States in Canada and the United States,' *Politics and Society* 25, no. 4 (December 1997).
63  McDowell, 'Life without Father and Ford,' 412, 403.

**Part I: Contradictions and Transformations in Families, Markets, and the Welfare State, 1940–1971**

1  See, for example, Linda Carty, 'African Canadian Women and the State: "Labour only, please,"' in Peggy Bristow et al., *'We're Rooted Here and They Can't Pull Us Up: Essays in African Canadian Women's History* (Toronto: University of Toronto Press, 1994), 208.

## 2: Gender and the Construction of the Postwar Welfare State

1 Linda McDowell, 'Life Without Father and Ford: The New Gender Order of Post-Fordism,' *Transactions of the Institute of British Geographers* (1991).

2 See, for example, Canada, Advisory Committee on Reconstruction, *Post-War Problems of Women: Final Report of the Subcommittee* (Ottawa, 1944), 22–3; 32–3.

3 Labour Canada, Women's Bureau, *Women in the Labour Force: Facts and Figures (1973 edition)* (Ottawa, 1974), 227. The proportion of the female labour force in manufacturing increased from 27 per cent in 1939 to 37 per cent in 1943, while that in domestic service dropped from 18.6 per cent to 9.3 per cent (Canada, Department of Labour, *Canadian Labour Market* [June 1946], 20).

4 For a discussion of the recruitment of women into the labour force during the war, see Ruth Roach Pierson, *'They're Still Women After All': The Second World War and Canadian Womanhood* (Toronto: McClelland & Stewart, 1986), ch. 1.

5 Canada, Department of Labour, *Canadian Labour Market* (December 1946), 16. In the prewar period the highest weekly wage paid to women was an average of $15.83 in the fur goods industry. In contrast, during the war, in aircraft manufacturing, and shipbuilding and repairs, women received an unprecedented average of $31.81 per week. See June 1946, 20–1.

6 See, for example, Leonard Marsh, *Report on Social Security for Canada, 1943* (reprinted Toronto: University of Toronto Press, 1975), especially the chapter devoted to 'women's needs,' 209–14.

7 Ibid.

8 Ibid., 58.

9 Ibid.

10 Ibid., 210.

11 Ibid., 244.

12 Ibid.

13 Canada, Advisory Committee on Reconstruction, *Post-War Problems of Women: Final Report of the Subcommittee* (Ottawa, 1944). On the subcommittee, see Gail Cuthbert Brandt, '"Pigeon-Holed and Forgotten": The Work of the Subcommittee on the Post-war Problems of Women, 1943," *Histoire sociale/Social History* xv, 29 (May 1982); and Annalee Golz, 'Family Matters: The Canadian Family and the State in the Postwar Period,' *Left History* 1, no. 2 (Fall 1993).

14 Canada, Advisory Committee on Reconstruction, *Post-war Problems of Women*, 7.

15 Ibid., 9.

16  Ibid., 22–3; 32–3. They also recommended extending UI coverage to the female-dominated occupations of nursing, teaching, and social work.
17  Ibid., 10.
18  Ibid., 28.
19  Ibid.
20  Brandt, '"Pigeon-Holed and Forgotten,"' 239–40.
21  Marsh, *Report*, 212; Canada, Department of Reconstruction, *Employment and Income with Special Reference to the Initial Period of Reconstruction* (Ottawa, 1945), 3.
22  Canada, Advisory Committee on Reconstruction, *Post-War Problems*, 15–16.
23  Pierson, *'They're Still Women,'* 55–60.
24  Ibid., 82.
25  Ibid., 49.
26  Ibid., 83–8.
27  Dionne Brand, '"We Weren't Allowed to Go into Factory Work until Hitler Started the War,"' in Peggy Bristow et al., *We're Rooted Here*, 175.
28  Ibid., 187.
29  Dionne Brand, 'Black Women and Work: The Impact of Racially Con-structed Gender Roles on the Sexual Division of Labour,' in Enakshi Dua and Angela Robertson, *Scratching the Surface: Canadian Anti-Racist, Feminist Thought* (Toronto: Women's Press, 1999), 90.
30  Brand, 'Black Women and Work,' 89.
31  Gillian Creese, *Contracting Masculinity: Gender, Class and Race in a White-Collar Union, 1944–1994* (Don Mills: Oxford University Press, 1999), 59. On racialized and gendered divisions in the automobile industry, see Pamela Sugiman, 'Privilege and Oppression: The Configuration of Race, Gender and Class in Southern Ontario Auto Plants, 1939 to 1949,' *Labour/Le Travail* 47 (Spring 2001).
32  Canada, Department of Reconstruction, *Employment and Income*, 1.
33  Canada, Department of Labour, *Canadian Labour Market* (June 1946), 23.
34  Labour Canada, Women's Bureau, *Women in the Labour Force (1973 edition)*, 227.
35  For an overview of the provisions of the 1940 UI Act, see Gary Dingledine, *A Chronology of Response: The Evolution of Unemployment Insurance from 1940 to 1980*, prepared for Employment and Immigration Canada (Ottawa 1981); Leslie Pal, *State, Class and Bureaucracy*; and Ray Brown, 'Unemploy-ment Insurance and the National Employment Service,' *Labour Gazette* (September 1950).
36  Canada, *Unemployment Insurance Act 1940*, s. 28.
37  Canada, *Unemployment Insurance Act 1940*, Third Schedule, 36.

38 Canada, *Report of the Committee of Inquiry into the Unemployment Insurance Act* (Gill Committee Report) (Ottawa: Queen's Printer, 1962), 125.
39 Dingledine, *A Chronology of Response*, 9–11.
40 The initial name was the 'Court of Referees.' It was changed to the 'Board of Referees,' in the 1950s. I have used 'Board of Referees' throughout.
41 Dingledine, *A Chronology of Response*, 13.
42 Ruth Roach Pierson, 'Gender and the Unemployment Insurance Debates in Canada, 1934–1940,' *Labour/Le Travail* 25 (1990), 102.
43 Ibid., 81, 84.
44 Pierson notes that the CCF and the Communist Party of Canada, as well as women's groups such as the Canadian Federation of Business and Professional Women's Clubs and the Ottawa Women's Liberal Club, expressed opposition to discrimination on the basis of sex in the UI proposals of the 1930s. See 'Gender and the Unemployment Insurance Debates in Canada,' 83–4.
45 Ibid., 84.
46 Ibid., 93–5.
47 Canada, *UI Act, 1940*, Third Schedule, 36, s. 1. In 1955 the definition of a dependant was revised somewhat. Section (iii) was revised to read 'a person who maintains wholly or mainly one or more children under the age of 16'; and there was the addition of (iv) 'a person who maintains a self-contained domestic establishment and supports therein, wholly or mainly, a person connected with him by blood relationship, marriage or adoption.' Canada, *UI Act 1955*, s. 3(a), 21. This definition remained unchanged in the 1971 UI Act.
48 National Archives of Canada (NAC), Unemployment Insurance Commission (UIC) Records, RG50, vol. 53, 16th meeting UIAC, 'Special Tabulation of Unemployment Insurance Benefit Statistics Prepared for the Meetings of the Unemployment Insurance Advisory Committee,' Dominion Bureau of Statistics, 18 July 1949.
49 NAC, RG50, vol. 58, UIAC Report and Minutes, 1961, 'Special Tabulation of the 1960 Benefit Statistics,' table 4, 16–17.
50 Canada, Unemployment Insurance Commission, *Decisions of the Umpire, 1943–1948* (Ottawa: n.d.), CUB-168, 29 November 1946, 196.
51 Ibid., CUB-122, 6 September 1946, 158.
52 Ibid., CUB-317, 5 February 1948, 327.
53 Canada, House of Commons, *Debates*, 14 July 1947, 5637.
54 Ibid., 5638.
55 Ibid.
56 A government document noted that in 1946 demand for women was

concentrated in the lower-paying occupations such as service work, textile work, and unskilled positions. Canada, Department of Labour, *Canadian Labour Market* (June 1946), 21–2.

57  Canada, *Report of the Committee of Inquiry into the Unemployment Insurance Act* (Gill Committee), 31.

58  Pierson, 'Gender and the Unemployment Insurance Debates,' 95.

59  Ibid.

60  National Archives of Canada (NAC), Unemployment Insurance Commission (UIC) Records, RG50, vol. 53, 18th meeting UIAC, July 1950, UI Commission to UIAC, 27 June 1950.

61  NAC, UIC Records, RG50, vol. 60, UIAC Reports 1941–1947, 'Raiding Jobless Insurance Fund,' *Edmonton Journal and Edmonton Bulletin*, 20 (December 1946).

62  NAC, UIC Records, RG50, vol. 53, 16th meeting UIAC, July 1949, submission from Canadian Manufacturers Association to UIAC, 13 July 1949; submission from Canadian Construction Association to UIAC, 16 July 1949.

63  See, for example, NAC, UIC Records, RG 50, vol. 59, file 1, UIAC Correspondence 1946–1947, J.G. Bisson, Chief Commissioner to Hon. Humphrey Mitchell, Minister of Labour, 30 August 1947; vol. 53, 16th meeting UIAC, July 1949; C.A.L. Murchison, Commissioner UIC to UIAC, 11 July 1949.

64  Canada, Unemployment Insurance Commission, *Annual Report* (1951), 37.

65  NAC, UIC Records, RG50, vol. 53, 16th meeting UIAC, July 1949, C.A.L. Murchison to UIAC, 11 July 1949; 'Minutes of the Meeting,' 9.

66  NAC, UIC Records, RG50, vol. 53, 17th meeting UIAC, January 1950, 'Actuarial Report for the UIAC,' 23 December 1949, 24, 28.

67  Ibid.

68  NAC, Department of Labour Records, RG 27, vol. 3458, file 4-11, pt 5, ' M.M. Maclean, Director, Industrial Relations Branch to A. MacNamara, 3 October 1950.

69  During the war Fraudena Eaton was the head of the Women's Division of the National Selective Service agency, which had been created to oversee the recruitment and allocation of labour. See Alison Prentice et al., *Canadian Women: A History* (Toronto: Harcourt Brace Jovanovich, 1988), 297. In the 1956 she became president of the National Council of Women. Rosa L. Shaw, *Proud Heritage: A History of the National Council of Women of Canada* (Toronto: Ryerson Press, 1957).

70  NAC, Department of Labour Records, RG 27, vol. 3458, file 4-11, pt 5, MacNamara to Mrs Eaton, 1 April 1950. For another exchange of letters in

a similar vein see ibid., Claude Dubuc to MacNamara, 28 October 1950; MacNamara to Bengough, 30 October 1950.

71 NAC, UIC Records, RG50, vol. 53, 16th meeting UIAC, July 1949, 'Minutes of the Meeting.' The three labour representatives were George Burt (Canadian Congress of Labour), Percy Bengough (President of the Trades and Labour Congress), and Romeo Vallee (Canadian and Catholic Confederation of Labour).

72 NAC, UIC Records, RG50, vol. 53, 18th meeting UIAC, July 1950, 'Minutes of the Meeting.'

73 NAC, Department of Labour Records, RG27, vol. 3458, file 4-11, pt 5. G.M. Ingersoll to A. MacNamara, 23 November 1949; NAC, UIC Records, RG50, vol. 53, 17th meeting UIAC, January 1950, 'Minutes of the Meeting,' 8; NAC, Canadian Labour Congress (CLC) Files, MG28 I103, vol. 25, file 2 United Automobile, Aircraft and Agricultural Implement Workers of America, George Burt, 1947–50, Burt to A.R. Mosher, President, CCL, 9 August 1949.

74 NAC, UIC Records, RG50, vol. 53, 17th meeting UIAC, January 1950, 'Minutes of the Meeting'; submission, Dominion Joint Legislative Committee, Railway Transportation Brotherhoods.

75 Canadian Congress of Labour, *Proceedings of the Ninth Annual Convention* (October 1949), 96, 98; CCL, *Proceedings of the 10th Annual Convention* (1950), 76–7.

76 See, for example, NAC, CLC Files, MG28 I103, vol. 25, file 2, Andy Andras to Pat Conroy, Secretary Treasurer CCL, 7 March 1950; ibid., vol. 238, file 238-16, Sam Wolstein to Pat Conroy, 4 March 1950.

77 *Canadian Unionist* (April 1950), 80.

78 See, for example, *Canadian Unionist* (April 1950), 80. See also NAC, CLC files, MG28 I103, vol. 25, file 2, Andras to Conroy, 7 March 1950; CCL, *Proceedings of the 10th Annual Convention* (1950), 76.

79 Trades and Labor Congress of Canada, *Report of the Proceedings of the Annual Convention* (September 1950), 444.

80 NAC, Department of Labour Records, RG27, vol. 3458, file 4-11, pt 5, Bengough to MacNamara, 24 October 1950.

81 Ibid. MacNamara to Norman Robertson, Clerk of the Privy Council and Secretary to the Cabinet, 26 October 1950.

82 NAC, UIC Records, RG50, vol. 59, Ingersoll to A.H. Brown, 30 April 1947. This was Miss Estelle Hewson, from the Border Branch of the Canadian Red Cross Society, Windsor.

83 It is not clearly specified why this change took place. At this time the number of employer and employee representatives was increased from

two to three each and it was argued that this did not leave room for a
women's representative. It appears that the change may have been to
ensure regional representation and to allow the addition of a representative from the Quebec labour movement. Ibid, MacNamara to V.R. Smith,
23 June 1947; Mackintosh to Stangroom, 20 August 1946; Ingersoll to
Brown, 30 April 1947.

84 Canada, House of Commons, *Debates*, 10 June 1955, 4625. See also Canada, House of Commons, Standing Committee on Industrial Relations,
*Minutes of Proceedings and Evidence*, 26 May 1955, 187–8.

85 The regulations were amended somewhat in subsequent years. For instance, the ninety-day requirement was reduced to sixty days, first for
those required to work after the first separation after marriage (1951), and
later in all cases (1952). The exemptions were also expanded somewhat,
for instance, to include women who had left employment voluntarily
because of just cause for reasons solely and directly connected with their
employment, such as a dangerous work situation (1951).

86 Canada, House of Commons, *Debates*, 19 February 1951, 453.

87 Canada, House of Commons, Standing Committee on Industrial Relations,
*Minutes of Proceedings and Evidence*, 6 June 1955, 475.

88 Canada, Unemployment Insurance Commission, *Digest of the Decisions of
the Umpire* (Ottawa 1960), CUB 848, 21 August 1952.

89 Canada, House of Commons, Standing Committee on Industrial Relations,
*Minutes of Proceedings and Evidence*, 26 May 1955, 262, letter from locals
521 and 514, United Electrical, Radio and Machine Workers of America
(UE).

90 NAC, Stanley Knowles Papers, MG32 C59, file 19-A, UIC cases, correspondence 1942–1952, Mrs Dora Doersam to Stanley Knowles, 10 May 1951;
Milton F. Gregg, Minister of Labour, to Stanley Knowles, 11 June 1951.

91 NAC, Stanley Knowles Papers, MG32 C59, file 19-A, UIC cases, correspondence, 1942–1952, Mrs Dora Doersam to Stanley Knowles, 10 May 1951.

92 See NAC, UIC Records, RG 50, vol. 53, 16th meeting UIAC, July 1949,
C.A.L. Murchison, Commissioner, UIC to UIAC 11 July 1949. See also
NAC, Department of Labour Records, RG 27, vol. 3458, file 4-11, pt 7, J.G.
Bisson, Chief Commissioner, UIC, to Minister of Labour, 3 September
1954, and Canada, Unemployment Insurance Commission, *Digest*, CUB
1101, 8 December 1954. In the latter case an employer laid off a pregnant
woman six months before her due date and she was disqualified for two
years from receiving UI. See also Canada, House of Commons, *Debates*,
13 June 1952, 3197–8.

93 Canada, Unemployment Insurance Commission, *Digest*, CUBs 772 and 773, 6 December 1951. Other people who voluntarily left their employment without just cause were generally disqualified for up to six weeks. Gary Dingledine, *A Chronology of Response*, 13. Regulation 5A also went much further than the general provision of the act in recognizing as just cause for leaving employment only those reasons solely and directly connected with employment.

94 See for instance, Canada, Unemployment Insurance Commission, *Digest*, CUB 1457, 7 February 1958.

95 Canada, Unemployment Insurance Commission, *Annual Report* (1951), 25.

96 Ibid. (1952), 14. See also ibid. (1951), 25.

97 Ibid. (1954), 14.

98 Quoted by Ellen Fairclough. Canada, House of Commons, *Debates*, 18 June 1952, 3396–7.

99 Canada, House of Commons, *Debates*, 18 May 1951, 3203.

100 This was pointed out by Svanhuit Josie. NAC, Gill Commission Records, RG33/48 vol. 10, Submission to the Committee of Inquiry into Unemployment Insurance, 31.

101 This was later pointed out by the CLC at the 1961 hearings of the Committee of Inquiry into the UI Act. See NAC, Gill Commission Records, RG33/48 vol. 10, Submission to the Committee of Inquiry into the Unemployment Insurance Act by the Canadian Labour Congress, 58.

102 In addition to the resolutions passed at the 1949 and 1950 conventions (see notes 65, 68), resolutions on the subject were passed in 1951–4. See CCL, *Proceedings of the Annual Convention* (1951), 98; (1952), 71; (1953), 87; (1954), 94. For the annual briefs, see *Canadian Unionist*, April 1950, April 1951, April 1952, March 1953, November 1954, and December, 1955. On the CCL submissions to the UIAC, see NAC, UIC Records, RG50, vol. 53, 19th meeting UIAC, July 1951; 21st meeting UIAC, July 1952; 23rd meeting UIAC July 1953; RG50 vol. 54, 24th meeting UIAC, July 1954. On the submission to the UI Commission see NAC, CLC Files, MG28 I103, vol. 238, file 238-19; UIC, 'Minutes of the Meeting with Representatives of Labour Organizations, May 10, 1951.'

103 NAC, CLC Files, MG28 I103 vol. 284, file UI pt 5, 1951–1952, J. Marchand, CCCL to A. Andras, CCL, 7 March 1951; A. Andras to Conroy 16 March 1951; vol. 238, file 238-20, 'Joint Submission to the Umpire Re Appeals Against Disqualification Under Benefit Regulation 5A,' 1–6.

104 *Labour Gazette* (May 1951), 647; (April 1952), 411; (April 1953), 542; (December 1954), 1705; (January 1956), 50; (January 1957), 154.

105 Quoted in *Labour Gazette* (May 1951), 647.
106 Trades and Labor Congress of Canada, *Report of the Proceedings of the Annual Convention* (1951), 196, 276–7; (1952), 173–4; (1954), 475; (1955), 377.
107 TLC, *Report of the Proceedings of the Annual Convention*, 1949–55.
108 *Trades and Labor Congress Journal* (April 1952), 14.
109 Ibid. (November 1954), 8; (January 1956), 9–10.
110 See, for example, NAC UIC files, RG50, vol. 53, 19th meeting UIAC, July 1951, TLC submission to the UIAC.
111 NAC, UIC Records, RG 50, vol. 54, 32nd meeting UIAC, July 1957, CLC Submission to the UIAC, 3.
112 The United Electrical, Radio and Machine Workers of America (UE) was especially active in this regard. For example, they appeared, along with the CCL, before the umpire to urge that Regulation 5A be rescinded. See CUB 655, 22 March 1951, reprinted in full in *Labour Gazette* (May 1951), 711–13. Two locals of UE also appeared before the 1955 hearings on the amendments to the UI Act to protest the case of two married women denied benefits and to urge the elimination of the regulations. Canada, House of Commons, Standing Committee on Industrial Relations, *Minutes of Proceedings and Evidence*, 26 May 1955, 262.
113 For example, that they were not initially notified of the 1955 hearings on amendments to the UI Act. The issue was raised by Ellen Fairclough, Canada, House of Commons, Standing Committee on Industrial Relations, *Minutes of Proceedings and Evidence*, 17 May 1955, 61.
114 For an analysis of the National Council of Women in an earlier period, see Veronica Strong-Boag, *The Parliament of Women: The National Council of Women of Canada, 1893–1929*, History Division Paper no. 18 (Ottawa: National Museums of Canada, 1976). See also Shaw, *Proud Heritage*.
115 See, for example, NAC, National Council of Women (NCW) Papers, MG28 I25, vol. 97, file 7, Brief to Prime Minister St Laurent, December 1953; vol. 93, file 9, Milton F. Gregg to Mrs R.J. Marshall, 5 September 1951; vol. 97, file 11, Resolutions, 1953–4.
116 NAC, NCW Papers, MG28 I25, vol. 97, file 12, Annual Report, Economics and Taxation Committee, 1953–4.
117 NAC, NCW Papers, MG28 I25, vol. 96, file 1: Annual Meeting, 1954, 'Minutes, 61st Annual Meeting June 25–July 1, 1954,' 4.
118 Ibid.
119 See NAC, NCW Papers, MG28 I25, vol 100, file 1: Annual Meeting, 'NCW, Resolutions for Annual Meeting, 1956'; vol. 103, file 7: P.M. and Cabinet Correspondence 1956–7, Milton F. Gregg to Mrs F.F. Worthington, 30 October 1956.

120  NAC, NCW Papers, MG28 I25, vol. 103, file 7, PM and Cabinet: Correspondence, 1956–7, Milton F. Gregg to Mrs F.F. Worthington, 30 October 1956; *Labour Gazette* (March 1957), 267.

121  See, for example, NAC, Papers of the Canadian Federation of Business and Professional Women's Clubs (BPW Papers) MG28 I55, vol. 44, 'Minutes of the 13th biennial convention, July, 1952.'

122  See, for example, NAC, BPW Papers, MG28 I55, vol. 44, 'Minutes of the 10th Convention, July, 1946,' 3; vol. 65, Resolutions: 15 June 1948; vol. 45, 'Minutes of the Meeting of the Board of Directors 4 June 1955,' 6.

123  NAC, BPW Papers, MG28 I55, vol. 12, 'Report of Chairman of Standing Committee on Legislation, 1950–52.'

124  NAC, BPW Papers, MG28 I55, vol. 44, Minutes of the Biennial Convention, July 1954, 38; Minutes of the Biennial Convention July 1956, 19; vol. 45, Reports 1954–6.

125  See NAC, BPW Papers, MG28 I55, vol. 34, 1955 Correspondence, BPW of Ontario, Ontario Provincial Conference, Sept. 30–Oct. 2, 1955, Report of the Provincial President. Canada, Standing Committee on Industrial Relations, *Minutes of Proceedings and Evidence*, 6 June 1955, 472–3. On the meetings with Prime Ministers St Laurent and Diefenbaker, see NAC, BPW Papers, MG28 I55, vol. 81, *The Business and Professional Woman*, xxv (May–June 1957), 6; xxv, (Jan.–Feb. 1958), 16.

126  See for example, Canada, House of Commons, *Debates*, 18 June 1952, 3397. Canada, House of Commons, Standing Committee on Industrial Relations, *Minutes of Proceedings and Evidence*, 26 May 1955, 183–7.

127  Knowles, Canada, House of Commons, *Debates*, 4 June 1952, 2913.

128  The role of these groups is frequently cited in assessments of why the regulation was eventually revoked. See, for example, Canada, *Report of the Committee of Inquiry into Unemployment Insurance* (Gill Committee), 38. NAC, Gill Commission Records, RG33/48, vol. 10, Svanhuit Josie, Submission to the Committee of Inquiry into Unemployment Insurance, 1961, 32; NAC, CLC files, MG28 I103, vol. 285, UI Misc. Inquiries 1959–60, part 2, Andras to O'Sullivan, 9 February 1960.

129  On Ellen Fairclough's role, see NAC, NCW Papers, MG28 I25, vol. 125, file 2: Correspondence 1957–8, Mrs Rex Eaton to the Honourable Ellen Fairclough, 19 December 1957.

130  Canada, House of Commons, *Debates*, 15 November 1957, 1171–2.

131  NAC, Department of Labour Records, RG 27, vol. 3458, file 4-11, pt 8, Submission to the Standing Committee on Industrial Relations of the House of Commons on Bill C-43, An Act to Amend the Unemployment Insurance Act by the Canadian Manufacturers' Association, 21 May 1959,

16. Same, pt 8, J.C. Whitelaw, General Manager, Canadian Manufacturers' Association to Michael Starr, Minister of Labour, 20 December 1960.
132 NAC, UIC Records, RG50 vol. 56, 38th meeting UIAC, April 1960; UI Commission to UIAC, 12 July 1960, 'Impact of Benefit Regulations to Married Women,' 3.
133 NAC, UIC Records, RG50, vol. 56, 40th meeting UIAC, October 1960, 'Special Report of the UIAC resulting from Meeting October 27, 1960.'
134 See, in particular, submissions by Dr Warren James and Dr Sylvia Ostry, Canada, Senate, *Proceedings of the Special Committee of the Senate on Manpower and Employment*, 1960, 207–57, 355–72.
135 Canada, Senate, *Report of the Special Committee of the Senate on Manpower and Employment* (Ottawa 1961), 66.
136 This included the Canadian Manufacturers' Association, the Canadian Construction Association, the Canadian Retail Federation, the Canadian Chamber of Commerce, the Canadian Life Insurance Officers' Association, the Canadian Metal Mining Association, the Canadian Lumberman's Association, and the Canadian Pulp and Paper Association. NAC, Gill Commission Records, RG 33/48 vol. 10, for all briefs.
137 NAC, Gill Commission Records, RG 33/48, vol. 10, Submission from the National Council of Women.
138 NAC, Gill Commission Records, RG 33/48, vol. 10, Submission from the Canadian Federation of Business and Professional Women's Clubs.
139 NAC, Gill Commission Records, RG 33/48, vol. 10, Submission from the National Legislative Committee, International Railway Brotherhood; Submission from Svanhuit Josie, 11.
140 Canada, *Report of the Committee of Inquiry into the Unemployment Insurance Act* (Gill Committee Report) (Ottawa, 1962), 12.
141 Figures on the number of women in unions are not available for the 1950s. In 1963 women accounted for 16.3 per cent of trade union membership. Canada, Ministry of Trade and Commerce and Dominion Bureau of Statistics, *Annual Report under the Corporations and Labour Unions Return Act, Part II: Labour Unions, 1963* (Ottawa, 1966), 37, table 15A. In 1959 a special course on the role of women in trade unions was held for the first time at the CLC Ontario summer school. It was noted that each year the number of women enrolled in various courses had increased. *Labour Gazette* (September 1950), 910. In 1960 a women's committee was also established in the Ontario Federation of Labour. *Labour Gazette* (December 1960), 1290. In 1959 the CLC established a committee to coordinate white-collar organizing. *Labour Gazette* (August 1959), 797.
142 By 1961 equal pay laws had been enacted by eight provinces and by the federal government. *Labour Gazette* (June 1965), 518.

143 Dennis Guest, *The Emergence of Social Security in Canada*, second edition (Vancouver: University of British Columbia Press, 1985), 129, 130. On the role of family allowances, see also Dominique Jean, 'Family Allowances and Family Autonomy: Quebec Families Encounter the Welfare State, 1945–1955,' in Bettina Bradbury, ed., *Canadian Family History* (Mississauga: Copp Clark Pitman, 1992).

144 Sylvia Ostry, *The Female Worker in Canada* (Ottawa: Dominion Bureau of Statistics, 1968), 4.

## 3: From Exclusion to Entitlement

1 On this point, see also Joan Sangster, 'Doing Two Jobs: The Wage-Earning Mother, 1945–70,' in Joy Parr, ed., *A Diversity of Women: Ontario, 1945–1980* (Toronto: University of Toronto Press, 1995), 109–11.

2 See, for example, Patricia Huckle, 'The Womb Factor: Pregnancy Policies and Employment of Women,' in Ellen Boneparth, ed., *Women, Power and Policy* (New York: Pergamon Press, 1982); Beth Symes, 'Equality Theories and Maternity Benefits,' in Sheilah L. Martin and Kathleen E. Mahoney, eds., *Equality and Judicial Neutrality* (Toronto: Carswell, 1987); and Carole Pateman, 'Equality, Difference, Subordination: The Politics of Motherhood and Women's Citizenship,' in Gisela Bock and Susan James, eds., *Beyond Equality and Difference* (London: Routledge, 1992).

3 Pateman, 'Equality, Difference, Subordination,' 17.

4 In this sense, Joan Scott's caution against 'writing the history of feminism as a story of oscillations between demands for equality and affirmations of difference' is well taken. See Joan Wallach Scott, 'The Sears Case,' in Scott, *Gender and the Politics of History* (New York: Columbia University Press, 1988), 176.

5 Dennis Guest, *The Emergence of Social Security in Canada*, second edition, (Vancouver: University of British Columbia Press, 1985), ch. 5. See also Margaret Little, 'The Blurring of Boundaries: Private and Public Welfare for Single Mothers in Ontario,' *Studies in Political Economy* 47 (Summer 1995); and Margaret Little, *No Car, No Radio*.

6 Guest, *Social Security*, 128–33; Jane Ursel, *Private Lives, Public Policy: 100 Years of State Intervention in the Family* (Toronto: Women's Press, 1992), 190–8; and Dominique Jean, 'Family Allowances and Family Autonomy: Quebec Families Encounter the Welfare State, 1945–1955,' in Bettina Bradbury, ed., *Canadian Family History* (Toronto: Copp Clark Pitman, 1992).

7 By the 1960s, only four provinces had maternity-related legislation of any sort. In Alberta and Ontario, legislation authorized regulations for pregnant working women, but no regulations had been made under them.

British Columbia and New Brunswick provided for a leave of absence of six weeks prior to delivery and *prohibited* employment for six weeks following delivery. Sheila Woodsworth, *Maternity Protection for Women Workers in Canada* (Ottawa: Canada Department of Labour, Women's Bureau, 1967), 11–12.

8 On the ideology of the 1950s portraying working women as 'middle class wives and mothers freely choosing to enter the labour force,' see Veronica Strong-Boag, 'Canada's Wage-Earning Wives and the Construction of the Middle-Class, 1945–60,' *Journal of Canadian Studies* 29, no. 3 (Autumn 1994), 6.

9 Sangster, 'Doing Two Jobs,' 109–10.

10 See Canada, UIC, *Decisions of the Umpire*, CUB (1924, 1961).

11 Ibid., CUB 926, April 1953.

12 NAC, UIC Records, RG50, vol. 53, 16th meeting UIAC, July 1949, C.A.L. Murchison, Commissioner, UIC to UIAC, 11 July 1949.

13 Canada, Unemployment Insurance Commission, *Decisions of the Umpire*, CUB 184.

14 See, for example, Canada, UIC, *Decisions of the Umpire*, CUB-766, CUB-1093, CUB-1094, CUB-1141, CUB-1505, CUB-1644, CUB-2200.

15 Ibid., CUB 1093, October 1954.

16 Ibid., CUB 926, April 1953.

17 Ibid., CUB 819, 1952.

18 Ibid.

19 Ibid., CUB 932, May 1953.

20 Ibid., CUB 932, May 1953.

21 Ibid., CUB 1193, Dec. 1955.

22 Ibid., CUB 1205, Dec. 1955; see also *Labour Gazette* (March 1956), 310.

23 Ibid., CUB 530, Dec. 1949.

24 Ibid., CUB 530, Dec. 1949.

25 Ibid., CUB 620, Sept. 1950.

26 See, for example, CUB 1513, May 1958, involving a woman who left her job as a fitter, said she would accept lighter work, and later did work as a charwoman.

27 Ibid., CUB 734, August 1951.

28 Ibid., CUB 930, Feb. 1953.

29 Ibid., CUB 1023, March 1954.

30 Ibid., CUB 1111, Jan. 1955.

31 Ibid., CUB 1166, June 1955.

32 Ibid., CUB 1220, March 1956.

33 Ibid., CUB 1308, Nov. 1956; CUB 1441 and 1441A, Dec. 1957/Feb. 1958;

CUB 1502, April 1958. A number of other cases in the 1950s also reaffirmed that a woman voluntarily leaving employment on account of pregnancy was presumed not to be available for work and was therefore ineligible for benefits. See, for example, CUB 790, Feb. 1952; CUB 1243, May 1956; CUB 1254, June 1956; CUB 1329, Jan. 1957; CUB 1614, Feb. 1959; CUB 1635, May 1959.

34  Ibid., CUB 1166, June 1955.
35  Ibid., CUB 1502, April 1958.
36  See, for example, ibid., CUB 1340, Feb. 1957; CUB 1505, April 1958; CUB 1539, Aug. 1958.
37  Ibid., CUB 1539, Aug. 1958.
38  Canada, UIC, *Decisions of the Umpire*, CUB 1483/1484 (March 1958).
39  Ibid., CUB 1738 (May 1960).
40  It was reiterated, for example, in Canada, Unemployment Insurance Commission, *Digest of Benefit Entitlement Principles*, 1968, I-282.
41  Canada, UIC, *Decisions of the Umpire*, CUB 1720 (February 1960).
42  Ibid.
43  Ibid., CUB-1738, May 1960.
44  Ibid., CUB 2024, July 1962.
45  Ibid., CUB 2055, October 1962.
46  Ibid., CUB 1792, November 1960.
47  Ibid., CUB 1924, 1961.
48  Ibid., CUB 2147, April 1963.
49  Ibid.
50  Canada, *Report of the Committee of Inquiry into the Unemployment Insurance Act* (Gill Committee) (Ottawa: Queen's Printer, 1962), 134.
51  Ibid., 12, recommendation 16.
52  Ibid., 13, recommendation 17.
53  See ibid., 135.
54  Ibid., 135.
55  NAC RG27, vol. 3390, file 8-4-18, pt 4, Report of the Interdepartmental Committee on the Gill Committee Report, 23 October 1963, 14; NAC RG27 vol. 3390, file 8-4-18, pt 5, Interdepartmental Committee on Gill Committee recommendations, minutes of meeting, 20 August 1963, 3.
56  Trades and Labor Congress of Canada, *Report of the Proceedings of the Annual Convention*, 1954, 399.
57  Ibid., Delegate L. Rosen, Toronto.
58  Ibid., Delegate D. Swailes, Winnipeg.
59  Ibid., Delegate H. Henderson, Windsor.
60  Ibid., Delegate G. Redwood, Toronto.

61 Ibid., Delegate A. Gardiner, Calgary.
62 See, for example, ibid., Delegate E. Ross, Edmonton.
63 TLC, *Report of the Proceedings*, 1955, text of memorandum presented to the federal government, 9 November 1954.
64 TLC, *Report of the Proceedings of the Annual Convention*, 1953, 25; 1951, 29–30; 1952, 44–5; 1955, 34; 1956, 32.
65 CCL, *Proceedings of the Annual Convention*, 1954, 95.
66 Ibid.
67 See, e.g., CCL, *Proceedings of the Annual Convention*, 1950, 31.
68 See, for example, TLC, *Report of the Proceedings*, 1953, 38; 1954, 352; 1956, 29; CCL, *Proceedings of the Annual Convention*, 1953, 88–9; 1954, 93; CLC, *Report of the Proceedings*, 1956, 59; 1960, 10; 1964, 49.
69 CLC, *Report of Proceedings*, 1956, 103–4. In 1958 the CLC specified that a national social security plan should provide for 'needy mothers and widows' (ibid., 1958, 16).
70 NAC, RG27, vol. 3390, file 8-4-18, pt 5, C. Jodoin et al. to Allan MacEachen, Minister of Labour, 22 November 1963, 13.
71 See, for example, CLC legislative submission, 2 February 1961, in *Canadian Labour* 6(2) (February 1961); CLC memorandum to the federal government 10 March 1965, in *Canadian Labour* 10(4) (April 1965), 42.
72 The issue does not, for example, appear to have been much discussed at a 1965 CLC conference on social security. See *Canadian Labour*, September 1965. Nor was it part of resolutions on social security or statements about labour's social objectives in the latter part of the 1960s. See, for example, reports on CLC conventions in *Canadian Labour*, May 1966, May 1968, June 1970; and 'Labour's Social Objectives,' *Canadian Labour*, September 1969.
73 NAC, MG28 I25, vol. 134, 'Dept. of Labour, 1963–64,' Hayes to Royce, 22 August 1963.
74 Ibid.
75 See NAC, MG28 I25, vol. 133, Trades and Professions Committee, 1962–63, Clara McAuley to Chairmen of Provincial and Local Committees on Trades and Professions, September 1962, Study Outlines 1962–63, Circular Letter #1. In 1963, 1964, and 1967 briefs to the prime minister, the NCW requested income tax deductions for household assistants. MG28 I25, vol. 143, file 48: Parliamentary Committee 1966–67, Brief to Pearson by NCW, 30 January 1967.
76 NAC MG28 I25, vol. 134, 'Dept. of Labour 1963–64,' Hayes to Royce 22 August 1963.
77 NAC, MG28, I25, vol. 135, 'Trades and Professions Committee 1963–64,' C.

McAuley, National Chairman of the Committee on the Trades and Professions of Women, May 1964, responses to questionnaire no. 2, International
Council of Women.
78 Ibid., McAuley to Chairmen of Trades and Professions Committees, 11 May
1964.
79 Ibid.
80 NAC, MG28 I55, acc 76/127, vol. 81, *The Business and Professional Woman*,
May–June 1964, 35; MG28 I25, vol. 133, 'Trades and Professions Committee, 1962–63,' BPW, Memorandum to P.M. Pearson, 11 July 1963, 5.
81 NAC, MG28 I55, acc/76/127, *The Business and Professional Woman*, July–
August 1964, 8.
82 NAC, MG28 I55, acc. 68/311, vol. 70, 'Reports 1963,' memorandum to PM
Diefenbaker, 21 November 1962, reaffirmation of resolution 10/1958; acc/
65/103, vol. 7, 'Employment Conditions Committee, 1964–66,' N. Dane
to IFBPW Employment Conditions Committee; acc. 76/127, vol. 82, 'Resolutions, Regulations and By-Laws, 1960–67,' Resolutions for the 1966
CFBPWC Convention, no. 11/66.
83 NAC, MG28 I55, acc. 65/153, vol. 7, 'Employment Conditions Committee
1962–63,' E.G. MacGill, President to M. Royce, Women's Bureau, 31 August 1963.
84 Canada, UIC, *Report of the Study for Updating the Unemployment Insurance
Programme* (Ottawa, 1968), ch. 2, 30. On this view being expressed by UI
officials, see also NAC RG27, vol. 4159, file 722-4-2, pt 3, Gelber to file, 5
August 1970.
85 NAC, RG27, vol. 3392, file 8-9-185, wallet, 'Report to the Minister of
Labour by the Interdepartmental Committee on Changes to the Unemployment Insurance Programme,' 25 March 1966, 47–8; 51–2.
86 Ibid., 51–2.
87 Sandra Burt, 'Organized Women's Groups and the State,' in William D.
Coleman and Grace Skogstad, eds., *Policy Communities and Public Policy in
Canada: A Structural Approach* (Mississauga: Copp Clark Pitman, 1990), 202.
88 In 1963 it published a bulletin on the subject, and in response to an ILO
report, distributed a questionnaire on the employment of women with
family responsibilities. This in turn prompted both the NCW and the BPW
to give some consideration to the issue. In 1965 it sponsored a one-day
consultation. See NAC, MG28 I55, acc. 65/153, vol. 7, 'Employment Conditions Committee, 1962–63,' E.G. MacGill to M. Royce, 31 August 1963;
MG28 I25, vol. 134, 'Dept. of Labour 1963–64,' Hayes to Royce, 22 August
1963. See NAC, MG28 I55, acc. 65/153, vol. 7, 'Employment Conditions

Committee, 1962–63,' Royce to N. Dane, 15 January 1965; MG28, I 25, vol. 141, file 9: mailings 1964–65, NCW, *Newsletter* 12, no. 6 (Feb. 1965). Woodsworth, *Maternity Protection for Women Workers in Canada*.

89  NAC, RG27, vol. 3391, file 8-9-185-1, pt 1, Royce to Burton, 21 April 1966.

90  NAC, RG27, vol. 1904, file 38-11-6-3, 'Notes on Maternity Protection Legislation in the Federal Jurisdiction,' Women's Bureau, November 1966, item VII, 42; Royce to Findlay, Despres, 19 January 1967.

91  NAC RG27, vol. 1904, file 38-11-6-3, 'Notes on Maternity Protection Legislation in the Federal Jurisdiction,' Women's Bureau, November 1966, item VII. See also RG27, vol. 3391, file 8-9-185-1, pt 1, Royce to Burton, 21 April 1966, re: the report on changes to UI.

92  NAC RG 27, vol. 1908, file 38-9-9, Royce to MacInnis, 2 June 1966.

93  On contact with the BPW, CFUW, see NAC, RG27, vol. 1908, file 38-9-23. See RG27, vol. 4160, file 722-4-3, Gelber to Despres, 23 October 1968.

94  NAC RG27, vol. 1905, file 38-6-2-7-2, NEC, 'Report of the Subcommittee on the Problems of Women in Relation to Employment.' See also RG27, vol. 1904, file 38-11-6-3, Marchand to Nicholson, 28 February 1967.

95  Canada, House of Commons, *Debates*, September 20, 1968, 262; March 4, 1968. 7199–7200, 3 November 1970, 841–2.

96  NAC RG27, vol. 1908, file 38-9-9, MacInnis to Royce, 9 June 1966.

97  Canada, House of Commons, *Debates*, 3 November 1970, 841–2; See also ibid., 4 March 1968, 7199–200.

98  See, for example, comments on the difficulty of attracting members. NAC, MG28 I 25, vol. 135, Annual Meeting, 1965, Address of the President, Pearl Steen.

99  See, for example, NAC MG28 I25, vol. 144, file 8: Trades and Professions, 1969–70, Mrs M. Colpits, Chairman to Standing Study Committee on Trades and Professions, Circular Letter #1, 1969–70, August 1969.

100  NAC, MG28 I25, vol. 143, file 89: Status of Women, 1967–68, Brief to Royal Commission on the Status of Women, 15 February 1968 (draft).

101  NAC, MG28 I55, acc.76/127, vol. 81, *The Business and Professional Woman*, September–October 1968, 1. These requests were incorporated in briefs to the PM and Cabinet in February 1970 and June 1971. Ibid., March 1970, 6; NAC RG27, vol. 1904, file 38-11-3-4, Love to Crowe, 21 June 1971.

102  Cerise Morris, '"Determination and Thoroughness": The Movement for a Royal Commission on the Status of Women in Canada,' *Atlantis* 5, no. 2 (1981), 19; NAC RG27, vol. 4159, file 722-4-2, vol. 1, Despres to Waisglass, 30 July 1968.

103  Cerise Morris, '"Determination and Thoroughness"'; Monique Begin, 'The Royal Commission on the Status of Women in Canada: Twenty Years

Later,' in Constance Backhouse and David H. Flaherty, eds., *Challenging Times: The Women's Movement in Canada and the United States* (Montreal and Kingston: McGill-Queen's University Press, 1992).

104 Morris, 'With Determination and Thoroughness.'

105 Begin, 'The Royal Commission on the Status of Women,' 26.

106 Canada, *Report of the Royal Commission on the Status of Women* (Ottawa: Information Canada, 1970), vii.

107 Ibid., 84–5.

108 Ibid., 84–5.

109 Ibid., xii.

110 Ibid., 87–8.

111 See, for example, Thelma Cartwright, '20th Century Trying Time for Women,' *Canadian Labour* (Feb. 1967), 26.

112 See, for example, *Canadian Labour* (July–August 1966), 48; 'OFL Conference Wants More Day-Care Centres,' *Canadian Labour* (July–August 1967), 45.

113 See, 'OFL Proposes Tax Allowances for Working Mothers,' *Canadian Labour* (June 1968), 59; 'Women Suffer Job Discrimination,' *Canadian Labour* (October 1968).

114 At this time CLC demands focused on the question of a guaranteed annual income. See 'A Social Policy for Canada,' *Canadian Labour* (January 1970); 'Guaranteed Income the Major Gap in Social Policy,' *Canadian Labour* (February 1970); 'Social Policy Is Incomplete,' *Canadian Labour* (April 1970); 'Guaranteed Annual Income', *Canadian Labour* (April 1970).

115 NAC MG28, I55, acc. 76/127, *The Business and Professional Woman* (May–June 1968), 27.

116 NAC RG27 vol. 4159, file 722-4-2, vol. 1, Minutes, Working Party Committee to Study Maternity Leave (WPC), 12 July 1968; ibid., memo from Waisglass, 1 October 1968.

117 NAC RG27, vol. 4159, file 722-4-2, vol. 1, Mainwaring to Sufrin.

118 The convention also called for free medical care for mothers, benefits to be provided either out of public funds or by means of a system of insurance, some employment protection for women during pregnancy and maternity leave, and the provision of nursing breaks for mothers during working hours. Sheila Woodsworth, *Maternity Protection for Women Workers in Canada*, 5–6.

119 NAC RG27, vol. 4159, file 722-4-2, 7/68-12/73; Sufrin to Mainwaring, 14 January 1969.

120 NAC RG 27, vol. 4159, file 722-4-2 (7/68-12/73), J.K. Wanczycki, International Labour Affairs Branch to Mainwaring, 21 January 1969.

121  Ibid. Sufrin to Mainwaring, 14 January 1969.
122  Harry J. Waisglass. NAC RG27, vol. 4159, file 722-4-2, pt 1, Working Party
     Committee on Maternity Leave, Minutes, 21 February 1969, 4. Eileen
     Sufrin expressed a similar concern. See RG 27, vol. 4159, file 722-4-2 (7/
     68-12/73), Sufrin to Mainwaring, 14 January 1969; Sufrin to Mainwaring,
     24 January 1969; RG 27, vol. 4159, file 722-4-2, pt 2, Minutes of Meeting,
     WPC on Maternity Leave, 13 March 1969.
123  See NAC RG 27, vol. 4159, file 722-4-2, pt 1, WPC on Maternity Leave,
     Minutes of Meeting, 29 November 1968, 3; Minutes of Meeting, 21 Febru-
     ary 1969; Sufrin to Lennox, 20 February 1969; ibid., part 2, Minutes of
     Meeting, 13 March 1969; Sufrin to Harkins, 24 March 1969. See also RG27,
     vol. 4159, file 722-4-2 (7/68-12/73), Sufrin to Mainwaring, 14 January
     1969; Sufrin to Mainwaring, 24 January 1969.
124  NAC RG27, vol. 4159, file 722-4-2, pt 2, Mitchell to Peart, 2 May 1969.
125  These included, for example, that an employee could not be dismissed
     after having requested leave; that the employee be placed in her former
     or an equivalent position on return to work; and that continuity of ser-
     vice for purposes of earning benefits be resumed when the woman
     returned to work. NAC RG27, vol. 4159, file 722-4-2, pt 1, Report of the
     Working Party on Maternity Leave, 21 May 1969.
126  See, for example, NAC, RG27, vol. 4159, file 722-4-2, vol. 1, WPC on Mat.
     Leave, Minutes of Meeting, 31 October 1968, 3. Ibid., Gelber to Despres,
     5 November 1968; WPC on Mat. Leave, Minutes of Meeting, 29 Novem-
     ber 1968.
127  NAC RG27, vol. 4159, file 722-4-2, pt 1, Report of the Working Party on
     Maternity Leave, 8–9.
128  NAC RG27, vol. 4159, file 722-4-2, vol. 1, Gelber to Despres, 5 November
     1968.
129  NAC RG 27, vol. 4159, file 722-4-2, pt 3, Gelber to J.P. Despres, 17 Febru-
     ary 1970; 'Maternity Leave,' memo from Gelber, February 1970.
130  NAC RG27, vol 4159, file 722-4-2, pt 3, Gelber to Despres, 17 February
     1970.
131  NAC RG 27, vol. 4159, file 722-4-2, pt 3, 'Maternity Leave,' memo from
     Gelber, February 1970.
132  NAC RG27, vol. 4159, file 722-4-2, pt 3, Gelber to Despres, 17 February
     1970.
133  Waisglass was the former Canadian research director of the Steelworkers
     and was appointed Director General of Research and Development for
     the Department of Labour in 1967. See *Canadian Labour*, December 1967,
     26. Sufrin had been active in the attempt to organize Eaton's in the early

1950s. In the 1960s she was working in the research section of the Department of Labour.

134 NAC RG27, vol. 4159, file 722-4-2, pt 3, Waisglass to J.D. Love and J.P. Despres, 13 February 1970.

135 NAC RG27, vol. 4159, file 722-4-2, pt 3, Despres, ADM to Love, DM, 4 November 1970.

136 NAC RG27, vol. 4159, file 722-4-2, pt 3, Despres to Love, 4 November 1970.

137 NAC RG27, vol. 4159, file 722-4-2, pt 3, Mitchell to Love, Despres, Hardie, Bennett; Canada, House of Commons, *Debates*, 26 April 1971, 5237.

138 Canada, UIC, *Report of the Study for Updating the Unemployment Insurance Programme* (Ottawa, 1968), ch. 2, 30.

139 See, for example, Canada, UIC, *Report of the Study for Updating the Unemployment Insurance Programme* (Ottawa, 1968), ch. 3, 28; ch. 2, 30; ch. 7, 13.

140 Canada, Department of Labour, *Unemployment Insurance in the 70s* (Ottawa: Queen's Printer, 1970), presented by the Hon. Bryce Mackasey, Minister of Labour.

141 Canada, Department of Labour, *Unemployment Insurance in the 70s*, 10.

142 Canada, House of Commons, Standing Committee on Labour, Manpower and Immigration, *Minutes of Proceedings and Evidence*, 15 September 1970, 10: 12.

143 This was stated, for example, by Mr Steele, UIC. See RG 27, vol. 4159, file 722-4-2, pt 3, Gelber to file, 5 August 1970.

144 Canada, House of Commons, *Debates*, 19 April 1971, 5040.

145 Gary Dingledine, *A Chronology of Response: The Evolution of Unemployment Insurance from 1940 to 1980*, prepared for Employment and Immigration Canada (Ottawa: Minister of Supply and Services, 1981), 61–3.

146 NAC RG27, vol. 4159, file 722-4-2, pt 3, Waisglass to J.D. Love and J.P. Despres, 13 February 1970.

147 NAC RG27, vol. 4159, file 722-4-2, pt 3, 'Maternity Leave,' memo from S. Gelber, February 1970. Ibid., Waisglass to J.D. Love and J.P. Despres, 13 February 1970.

148 Ibid., 67. 'Disentitlement' resulted in a postponement of benefits, but not necessarily a loss of benefit weeks.

## 4: Women in the Labour Force, UI Review, and Expansion

1 Other welfare state measures introduced in the 1960s included the Canada Pension Plan (1965) and the Guaranteed Income Supplement (1966), providing greater income security to those in retirement, and the Medical

Care Act (1966), and the Canada Assistance Plan (1966), allowing for greater federal involvement in medical care and social assistance.

2 Canada, Department of Labour, *Women at Work in Canada* (Ottawa, 1964), Table 2, 11; Canada, Department of Labour, Women's Bureau, *Women in the Labour Force, 1970: Facts and Figures* (Ottawa: Information Canada, 1971), Table 9, 19.

3 Canada, Department of Labour, *Women at Work in Canada*, 1964, Table 1, 10; Canada, Department of Labour, *Women in the Labour Force, 1970, Facts and Figures*, Table 9.

4 Canada, Department of Labour, *Women in the Labour Force, 1970: Facts and Figures*, Table 9, 19.

5 Canada, Department of Labour, *Married Women Working for Pay in Eight Canadian Cities* (Ottawa, 1958); Canada, Department of Labour, *Occupational Histories of Married Women Working for Pay in Eight Canadian Cities* (Ottawa, 1959), 11.

6 Sylvia Ostry, *The Female Worker in Canada*, 1961 Census monograph program (Ottawa: Dominion Bureau of Statistics, 1968), 36–7. See also Ostry, *Unemployment in Canada* (Ottawa: Dominion Bureau of Statistics, 1968) 64–5.

7 Hugh Armstrong and Pat Armstrong, 'The Segregated Participation of Women in the Canadian Labour Force, 1941–71,' *Canadian Review of Sociology and Anthropology* 12, no. 4 Part I (1975), 381–2.

8 Ostry, *The Female Worker in Canada*, 3–8.

9 Ostry, *The Female Worker in Canada*, 3–9. See also Sylvia Ostry, 'The Female Worker: Labour Force and Occupational Trends,' in Canada, Department of Labour, Women's Bureau, *Changing Patterns in Women's Employment*, Report of a Consultation (Ottawa, 1966).

10 See Sylvia Ostry, 'The Female Worker,' Table 2, 8; Canada, Department of Labour, Women's Bureau, *Women in the Labour Force, 1970: Facts and Figures*, Table 11, 23.

11 Ostry, *Unemployment in Canada*, 33.

12 Canada, Department of Labour, Women's Bureau, *Women in the Labour Force 1970: Facts and Figures*, Table 7, 15.

13 Canada, Department of Labour, Women's Bureau, *Women in the Labour Force 1970: Facts and Figures*, Table 7, 15.

14 Part-time work had been increasing at least since 1953. See 'Women as Part-Time and Part-Year Workers,' *Labour Gazette* (29 July 1960), Table 1, 670. See also Ann Duffy and Norene Pupo, *Part-Time Paradox: Connecting Gender, Work and Family*, (Toronto: McClelland & Stewart, 1992), 43–4.

15 Women as Part-Time and Part-Year Workers,' *Labour Gazette* (29 July 1960), 669. See also Ostry, 'The Female Worker,' 13.

16 Ostry, *Unemployment in Canada*, 33; Table 17, 34.
17 The Report of the Royal Commission on the Status of Women notes that a 1964 survey of some 3,500 women by the Women's Bureau of the Ontario Department of Labour found that only 26 per cent were interested in full-time employment, while 74 per cent were interested in part-time employment. Canada, *Report of the Royal Commission on the Status of Women in Canada*, (Ottawa: Information Canada, 1970), 102.
18 'Women as Part-Time and Part-Year Workers,' *Labour Gazette* (29 July 1960), 669.
19 Comments made by Marion Royce. 'OFL conference on women workers,' *Canadian Labour* (July–August 1966).
20 A resolution in this regard was passed in 1963. NAC MG28, I25, vol. 134, Dept of Labour 1963–64, Mrs Saul Hayes, to M. Royce, Women's Bureau, 26 September 1963.
21 NAC MG28, I25, vol. 134, Dept. of Labour 1963–64, Hayes to Royce, 22 August 1963.
22. See, for example, Canada, Unemployment Insurance Commission, *Annual Report*, 1961, 17; 1963, 15; 1964, 17; 1965), 19.
23 Canada, Unemployment Insurance Commission, *Annual Report*, 1960, 19.
24 Ibid. See also Canada, UIC, *Annual Report*, 1965, 18.
25 Canada, UIC, *Annual Report*, 1962, 14. See also Canada, UIC, *Annual Report*, 1963, 15.
26 Between 20 and 28 per cent of placements in the 1960–6 period were in this category. Canada, UIC, *Annual Reports*, 1960–66.
27 NAC MG 28 I55, acc. 76.127, vol. 81, *The Business and Professional Woman* 27, no. 6 (May–June 1961), 5.
28 NAC MG28, I25, vol. 133, letters to Cabinet, Mrs S. Hayes to MacEachen, 11 July 1963; MG28, I25, vol. 133, 'annual meeting 1964.'
29 NAC MG28, I25, vol. 141, file 9, mailings 1964–65, R. Struthers, NEC representative to Presidents of Federated Societies and Chairmen of Trades and Professions Committees, March 1965.
30 Ostry, *Unemployment in Canada*, 5–7. See also Canada, Department of Labour, *Women at Work in Canada*, 6–7.
31 Ostry, *Unemployment in Canada*, 6–7.
32 Ibid., 39.
33 Ostry, *The Female Worker in Canada*, 1.
34 Canada, Unemployment Insurance Commission, *Report of the Study for Updating the Unemployment Insurance Programme*, vol. 3, ch. 12, 11–12 and Tables 12–4, 12–4a, 18–19.
35 Canada, Department of Labour, *Women at Work in Canada*, Table 3, 12.
36 NAC, RG50, vol. 58, UIAC, Minutes of Meeting, 1964, 'Unemployment

Insurance Statistics, 1963,' Table 3, 21. The special tabulation of UI statistics for the UIAC was not broken down by sex after 1964.

37 The four-person committee included two insurance company presidents and no labour representatives. The commissioners were Gill, President of the Canada Life Assurance Co., Etienne Crevier, President, La Prevoyance Compagnie d'Assurances; Dr John Deutch, Queen's University, and Dr J. Richards Petrie, 'consulting economist.' Canada, *Report of the Committee of Inquiry into the Unemployment Insurance Act* (Gill Committee Report) (Ottawa: Queen's Printer, 1962), Appendix I, 183–4.

38 Ibid., 5.

39 Ibid., 6.

40 Ibid., 13, recommendation 17.

41 Ibid., 133–4.

42 Ibid, 12, recommendation 15.

43 Ibid., 135.

44 Ibid., 159.

45 NAC RG27, vol. 3390, file 8-4-18, pt 5, Fortier, UIC to Interdepartmental Committee Studying the Report of the Gill Committee, 9 January 1963, 5.

46 NAC, RG27, vol. 3390, file 8-4-18, pt 4, Report of the Interdepartmental Committee on the Gill Committee Report, 23 October 1963, 5, 11.

47 Ibid.

48 The committee also indicated support for the recommended eligibility restrictions for pregnant women and women with young children. Ibid., 14.

49 NAC, RG27, vol. 3390, file 8-4-18, pt 5, Haythorne, DM of Labour to M. Starr, Minister of Labour, 14 January 1963, 10–11. Concerns were also raised by the Women's Bureau of the Department of Labour. Ibid., Francis to Haythorne, 10 January 1963, 5.

50 NAC, RG27, vol. 3390, file 8-4-18, pt 3, Hayes; Struthers (NCW) to Colonel Laval Fortier, Chief Commissioner, UIC, 6 March 1963.

51 NAC MG28, I55, acc. 76/127, vol. 81, *The Business and Professional Woman* 27, no. 6 (May–June 1961).

52 See 1963 brief to Prime Minister Lester Pearson. NAC, MG28, I55, acc. 76/127, vol. 81, *The Business and Professional Woman* (May–June 1964), 35. The 1964 BPW convention, however, defeated a resolution requesting, in part, 'that classes of women be not singled out as targets for arbitrary and discriminatory action and in particular that no discriminatory regulations relating to Unemployment Insurance benefits be enacted against: (a) married women as such; (b) women with children under their care, as such.' Ibid., July–August 1964, 8.

53  NAC, RG27, vol. 3390, file 8-4-18, pt 5, C. Jodoin et al. to Allan MacEachen, Minister of Labour, 22 November 1963, 9–10.
54  Ibid., 13.
55  See, for example, NAC, RG27, vol. 3390, file 8-4-18, pt 3, Minutes of Inter-departmental Committee, 11 Jan. 1963, 2.
56  See, for example, NAC RG27, vol. 3390, file 8-4-18, pt 4, Gray to Nutkins, 29 Oct. 1963. The Liberal government did, however, suggest in its first Throne Speech that it would proceed with amendments based on the Gill Committee Report. See John Saywell, ed., *Canadian Annual Review, 1963* (Toronto: University of Toronto Press, 1964), 189.
57  Leslie A. Pal, *State, Class and Bureaucracy: Canadian Unemployment Insurance and Public Policy* (Kingston and Montreal: McGill-Queen's University Press, 1988), 41; 74–5.
58  The NCW, for example, decided to not take 'any further action' on the UI question until Interdepartmental Committee had finished studying the Gill Committee Report. See MG28 I25, vol. 135, UI Act, Committee of Inquiry, 1964, Ruth Struthers to Mrs Askwith, 22 Feb. 1964; MG28, I25, vol. 135, Trades and Professions Committee 1963–64, Corresponding Secretary to McAuley, June 1964.
59  *Labour Gazette*, June 1962, 616. See also annual brief to cabinet, reproduced in *Labour Gazette*, Jan. 1964, 16; report of 1966 convention, *Labour Gazette*, June 1966, 286; convention resolutions, *Canadian Labour*, June 1970, 63.
60  See, for example, NAC RG50, vol. 58, UIAC, Minutes of meetings, 1961–7.
61  See, for example, RG27, vol. 3391, file 8-4-18, pt 6, Haythorne to MacEachen, 10 February 1964.
62  NAC, RG27, vol. 3458, file 4-11, pt 9, Dymond, ADM, Dept of Labour, to Haythorne, DM, Dept. of Labour, 8 January 1964; RG 27, vol. 3391, file 8-4-18, pt 6, Haythorne to MacEachen, 10 February 1964.
63  See NAC, RG27, vol. 3391, file 8-4-18, pt 6, *Income Maintenance and Employment Adjustment Program*, 28 February 1964.
64  Ibid., 20, 2.
65  Ibid., 2.
66  Ibid., 3.
67  Ibid., 4, 15.
68  Ibid., 2; NAC RG27, vol. 3391, file 8-4-18, pt 6, Haythorne to MacEachen, 10 February 1964.
69  See Robert Malcolm Campbell, 'The Full-Employment Objective in Canada in the Postwar Period,' in Surendra Gera, ed. *Canadian Unemployment: Lessons from the 80s and Challenges for the 90s* (Ottawa: Minister of Supply and Services Canada, 1991), 25.

70 The Department of Labour rejected the idea of special restrictions on female workers and, following Gill, argued that if there was a problem, it could be addressed by 'more vigorous placement efforts for married women.'

71 NAC, RG27, vol. 3391, file 8-4-18, pt 6, 'Income Maintenance and Employment Adjustment Program,' 28 February 1964, 11.

72 Ibid., 6, 11. The report recommended that the number of weeks of regular benefits be one-quarter the number of contribution weeks in the previous two years. (Gill had recommended benefits of one-half the number of contribution weeks in the last year, although this could be followed by a period of extended benefits.) Both Gill and the Department of Labour also recommended that extended benefits be one-and-a-half times the maximum duration of regular benefits, thus reinforcing the tendency for those with longer work records to have longer benefit claims available. Ibid., see Table 1, 9.

73 Ibid., 6.

74 Ibid., 6. While this could perhaps be taken to mean that they should be incorporated in overall plans for manpower training, this was not addressed directly.

75 Ibid., 6.

76 NAC, RG27, vol. 3392, file 8-9-185, wallet, *Report to the Minister of Labour by the Interdepartmental Committee on Changes to the UI Programme*, 25 March 1966; ibid., letter, Minister of Labour to the Chief Commissioner of the UIC 21 July 1965.

77 The UI Commission, for example, reported that in 1962–3 women made up 25 per cent of the total number of unemployed who were directed or referred to vocational training courses (slightly less than the proportion of women in the labour force), but in 1966 women made up 39.8 per cent of students enrolled in training courses sponsored by the federal and provincial governments. See Canada, Unemployment Insurance Commission, *Annual Report*, 1963, 15; *Annual Report*, 1964, 17; *Annual Report*, 1966, 108. The majority were enrolled in courses in female-dominated sectors, including for 'stenographers, typists, salesclerks, hairdressers, cooks, waitresses, power sewing machine operators or nursing assistants.' Canada, UIC, *Annual Report*, 1963, 15.

78 The NCW passed a resolution on employment counselling for girls and women and studied the need for basic training and retraining for mature women returning to the labour market. NAC MG28, I25, vol. 141, file 10: mailings 1965–6, action taken on resolutions at annual meeting, June 1966; NAC MG28 I25, vol. 142, file 42: committees and associations, 1966–7,

Devereux to Committees on Trades and Professions, Circular letter #1, 1966–7. In 1968 the BPW brief to Cabinet also stressed the need for vocational and counselling services for women. NAC MG28, I55, acc. 76/127, vol. 81, *The Business and Professional Woman* 31, no. 11 (March–April 1968). On the Women's Bureau, see Marion V. Royce, 'The Women's Bureau,' *Canadian Labour* (June 1965), 5–6.

79 NAC RG27, vol. 3392, file 8-9-185, wallet, 'Report to the Minister of Labour by the Interdepartmental Committee on Changes to the U.I. Programme,' 25 March 1966, 19–20. Specifically, they recommended that fifteen weeks employment in the last year be required to qualify for UI and that a benefit duration be established of one week of benefits for each contribution week in the previous year.

80 In the United States a similar tendency to make a distinction between 'primary' and 'secondary' wage earners and 'to provide more restrictive eligibility conditions or shorter duration of benefits for the latter' had already been noted. See Eveline Burns, 'New Problems in Social Security,' *Canadian Labour* (September 1965), 19.

81 NAC, RG27, vol. 3392, file 8-9-185, wallet, Report to the Minister of Labour by the Interdepartmental Committee on Changes to the UI Programme, 25 March 1966, 21.

82 NAC, RG27, vol. 3392, file 8-9-185, wallet, Report to the Minister of Labour by the Interdepartmental Committee on Changes to the UI Programme, 25 March 1966, 26.

83 Both the 1963 and 1966 throne speeches promised amendments to the UI Act. *Canadian Annual Review*, 1963, 189; *Canadian Annual Review*, 1966, 271.

84 On the latter point, see NAC RG27, vol. 3391, file 8-4-18, pt 6, Ian Campbell to W.R. Dymond, 20 March 1964; ibid., Burton to Dymond, 15 May 1964.

85 *Canadian Annual Review*, 1966, 271.

86 NAC, RG27, vol. 3392, file 8-9-185, memo to Cabinet from J.L. Nicholson, 12 May 1967, 1.

87 See NAC RG27, vol. 3392, file 8-9-185, Portigal to Schonning, 23 May 1967.

88 NAC RG27, vol. 3392, file 8-9-185, memo to Cabinet from J.L. Nicholson, UIC, 12 May 1967, 3–4.

89 NAC, RG27, vol. 3392, file 8-9-185, Portigal to Schonning, 23 May 1967; RG 27, vol. 3391, file 8-9-185-1, pt 1, Portigal to Haythorne and Schonning, 31 May 1967; ibid., Haythorne to Nicholson, 26 May 1967. The Department of Labour, for example, had suggested a higher rate for those with a number of dependants and that a minimum of $20 per week was needed to constitute a contribution week.

90 See NAC RG 27, vol. 3392, file 8-9-185, memo to Cabinet from John R. Nicholson (UIC), 6 October 1967; RG27, vol. 3392, file 8-9-185/2, pt 3, Schonning to Haythorne, 2 June 1967.
91 NAC RG27, vol. 3392, file 8-9-185, Meeting of Interdepartmental Committee of Officials on UI, 7 June 1967.
92 See, for example, NAC, RG 27, vol. 3392, file 8-9-185, wallet, Interdepartmental Committee of Officials on UI, Minutes of Meeting, 7 June 1967; 15 June 1967.
93 Ibid., Interdepartmental committee of officials on UI, Minutes of Meeting, 15 June 1967, 4.
94 NAC RG27, vol. 3392, file 8-9-185, wallet, Memo from John L. Nicholson, UIC to Cabinet, 6 October 1967.
95 See Gary Dingledine, *A Chronology of Response: The Evolution of Unemployment Insurance from 1940 to 1980* (Ottawa: Employment and Immigration Canada, 1981), 47.
96 This was decided following a two-day conference in March 1968 attended by the executive of the UI Commission and various experts. Canada, Unemployment Insurance Commission, *Report of the Study for Updating the Unemployment Insurance Programme* (Ottawa, 1968), 1.
97 Canada, Unemployment Insurance Commission, *Report of the Study for Updating the Unemployment Insurance Programme* (Ottawa, 1968).
98 See *Canadian Annual Review*, 1967, 298–9; *Canadian Annual Review*, 1968, 301.
99 See, for example, Campbell, 'Full Employment Objective,' 26–7; Robert M. Campbell, *Grand Illusions: The Politics of the Keynesian Experience in Canada, 1945–1975* (Peterborough: Broadview Press, 1987), 157–68.
100 NAC, RG27, vol. 3391, file 8-9-185-1, pt 1, Schonning to Haythorne, 21 June 1967.
101 Ibid.
102 On the latter point see Andrew F. Johnson, 'A Minister As An Agent of Policy Change: The Case of Unemployment Insurance in the Seventies,' *Canadian Public Administration* 24, no. 4 (Winter 1981).
103 Canada, *Report of the Royal Commission on the Status of Women.*
104 See 'OFL Proposes Tax Allowances for Working Mothers,' *Canadian Labour*, June 1968, 59; 'Women Suffer Job Discrimination,' *Canadian Labour*, October 1968.
105 Canada, Unemployment Insurance Commission, *Report of the Study for Updating the Unemployment Insurance Programme* 4, ch. xvii, 10; vol. 5, Exhibit D, 86.

106  Ibid., vol. 1, ch. I, 1.
107  Ibid.
108  Ibid., vol. 2, ch. vii, 45.
109  See vol. 1, ch. iv, for example, 12, 22.
110  Ibid., vol. 2, ch. v, 22. The rationale for the increase in rate for those with dependants at the last stage was the belief that benefits should meet the cost of non-deferrable expenditures, which tend to rise with time.
111  Ibid., ch. xx, 17–19.
112  Ibid., ch. xx, 22–5.
113  Ibid., see vol. 5, ch. xx, 16–17.
114  Ibid., see vol. 2, ch. vii, 40; ch. viii, 45–7.
115  Ibid., ch. 3, 32.
116  Ibid., vol. 2, ch. 6, 22.
117  Ibid., vol. 2, ch. v, 17–18.
118  Canada, Department of Labour, *Unemployment Insurance in the 70s* (Ottawa: Queen's Printer, 1970), 5.
119  Specifically, the White Paper proposed a phase 1, for those with a labour force attachment of twenty weeks or more in the past fifty-two, consisting of a three-week lump sum payment following a two-week waiting period. Those with eight weeks of work could enter the program at phase 2, where it was possible to collect eight to twelve weeks of benefits, depending on the number of weeks spent in the labour force. Benefits in phase 3 were to be related to the national unemployment rate, with the rationale that a higher rate usually means a longer search for employment. (Claimants would receive ten weeks of benefits if the rate was 4 per cent or less, four additional weeks if the rate was between 4 and 5 per cent, and eight additional weeks if the rate was over 5 per cent.) Phase 4 was again related to the length of time spent in the labour force. If an individual's labour force attachment was twenty weeks or more, he or she would be eligible for up to eighteen weeks of benefit payments. Phase 5 benefits were to reflect regional differences in unemployment and were to apply when the regional unemployment rate was above 4 per cent and exceeded the national level by more than 1 per cent. Claimants could draw up to eighteen weeks of benefits depending on the regional rate.
120  Canada, UIC, *Report of the Study for Updating the Unemployment Insurance Programme*, ch. xx, 7.
121  See Gary Dingledine, *A Chronology of Response: The Evolution of Unemployment Insurance from 1940 to 1980* (Ottawa: Employment and Immigration Canada, 1981), 63–5.

122 For example, those who had worked for twenty weeks were entitled to an additional two weeks of benefits; those who had worked fifty-two weeks were entitled to an additional eighteen weeks.

123 Phase 4 provided four weeks of benefits if the national unemployment rate was between 4 and 5 per cent and eight weeks if it was over 5 per cent. Phase 5 provided up to eighteen weeks of benefits when the regional rate of unemployment exceeded the national rate by more than 1 per cent.

124 They could receive more if the national unemployment rate was above 4 per cent or if the regional unemployment rate exceeded the national rate by more than 1 per cent. Dingledine, *A Chronology of Response*, 63–5.

125 With the 1971 act, the UI Fund was replaced by a new account called the Unemployment Insurance Account. Premiums, repayments, and so on were paid into the Consolidated Revenue Fund (CRF) and credited to the UI account. UI benefits and other costs were paid out of the CRF and charged to the UI account. The government cost of paying UI benefits was paid out of the CRF. See Dingledine, *A Chronology of Response*, 68.

126 Canada, Department of Labour, *Unemployment Insurance in the 70s*, 18; Dingledine, *Chronology of Response*, 60. Under the new act, the minimum earnings required in a week for UI coverage was one-fifth of the maximum insurable earnings or twenty times the applicable provincial minimum wage.

127 See Canada, House of Commons, Standing Committee on Labour, Manpower and Immigration, *Minutes of Proceedings and Evidence* 3/12/1970, 9: 24.

128 Regulations under the new 1971 act stated that 'where a person's income from all sources, including unemployment insurance benefits, exceeds 25 per cent of the maximum weekly insurable earnings ... that person shall not be regarded as being maintained wholly or mainly by the claimant or as being a dependent on the claimant.' The definition of a 'person with a dependent' remained as: '(a) a man whose wife is being maintained wholly or mainly by him; (b) a wife whose husband is dependent on her; (c) a person who maintains wholly or mainly one or more children under the age of 16 years; and (d) a person who maintains a self-contained domestic establishment and supports therein wholly or mainly a person connected with him by blood relationship, marriage or adoption.' Canada, House of Commons, *Debates*, 2 April 1973, 2828–9; Dingledine, *A Chronology of Response*, Appendix D, 149.

129 See Bryce Mackasey, Canada, Standing Committee on Labour, Manpower and Immigration, *Minutes of Proceedings and Evidence*, 15 September 1970, 10: 9. See also Canada, House of Commons, *Debates*, 27 October, 8568, 8581; Standing Committee, 3/12/70, 9:22–9:24.

130 Canada, House of Commons, Standing Committee on Labour, Manpower and Immigration, *Minutes of Proceedings and Evidence*, 29/10/70, 7:41–7:42.

131 See comments by Desroches, ibid., 7: 42.

132 See, for example, Mackasey's comments, Canada, House of Commons, Standing Committee on Labour, Manpower, and Immigration, *Proceedings*, 15 September 1970, 10: 11.

133 As noted earlier, it was suggested that women would move from being net contributors to net beneficiaries of the plan.

134 See, for example, 'Employment Security: New Manpower Concepts,' *Labour Gazette*, October 1967, 631; 'Work-Opportunity Programs, *Labour Gazette*, October 1965, 897; Campbell, 'The Full Employment Objective'; Campbell, *Grand Illusions*.

135 Canada, Unemployment Insurance Commission, *Report of the Study for Updating the Unemployment Insurance Programme*, vol. 3, ch. xii, 11–13, Tables 12–14, 1–4a, 18–19.

136 Ibid., vol. 1, ch. iv, 22, 25.

137 Ibid., vol. 3, ch. xii, 7–8. It was estimated, for example, that in the Maritimes the number of contributors would rise, while the amount of benefit payments would fall. This would partly be due to changes in seasonal regulations. Calculations were also based on a simulation model that assumed a 4 per cent national unemployment rate, a local unemployment rate of 5 per cent seasonally adjusted, and a regional unemployment rate of 4 per cent seasonally adjusted.

**Part II: On the Path to Neoliberalism**

1 David Langille, 'The Business Council on National Issues and the Canadian State,' *Studies in Political Economy* 24 (Autumn 1987).

2 Andre Drainville, 'Monetarism in Canada and the World Economy,' *Studies in Political Economy* 46 (Spring 1995); Ricardo Grinspun and Robert Kreklewich, 'Consolidating Neoliberal Reforms: "Free Trade" as a Conditioning Framework,' *Studies in Political Economy* 43 (Spring 1994).

3 See Jill Vickers, Pauline Rankin, and Christine Appelle, *Politics as if Women Mattered: A Political Analysis of the National Action Committee on the Status of Women* (Toronto: University of Toronto Press, 1993), 4; ch. 1.

4 In 1972 a Coordinator of the Status of Women was appointed by the Privy Council Office, a Cabinet position of Minister Responsible for the Status of Women was created, and the Women's Program of the Secretary of State was established with the goal of funding 'service-oriented, community-based projects.' In 1976 the Office of the Coordinator of the Status of Women was removed from the PCO and Status of Women Canada was

formed. For a description of this network see Sue Findlay, 'Facing the State: The Politics of the Women's Movement Reconsidered,' in Heather Jon Maroney and Meg Luxton, eds., *Feminism and Political Economy* (Toronto: Methuen, 1987) 36–8; Vickers et al., *Politics as if Women Mattered*, 78; Sandra Burt, 'Women's Issues and the Women's Movement in Canada Since 1970,' in Alan Cairns and Cynthia Williams, eds., *The Politics of Gender, Ethnicity and Language in Canada* (Toronto: University of Toronto Press, 1986), 154–5; and Sandra Burt, 'Organized Women's Groups and the State,' in William D. Coleman and Grace Skogstad, eds., *Policy Communities and Public Policy in Canada* (Mississauga: Copp Clark Pitman, 1990), 198–200.

5  Canada, Advisory Council on the Status of Women, *Annual Report*, 1973–74.

6  Sandra Burt and Sonya Lynn Hardman, 'The Case of Disappearing Targets: The Liberals and Gender Equality,' in Leslie A. Pal, ed., *How Ottawa Spends, 2001–2002* (Don Mills: Oxford University Press, 2001).

## 5: Social Reproduction in a Transition Period

1  Canada, House of Commons, Standing Committee on Labour, Manpower and Immigration, *Minutes of Proceedings and Evidence*, 11 May 1971, 20:16–20:17, 20:20–20:24.

2  Ibid., 20:17. Statements made by Mr DesRoches, Chief Commissioner, UIC.

3  See, for example, National Archives of Canada (NAC), Grace MacInnis's files, MG32 C12, vol. 17, file 'UI 1973-77,' Lorna Stinson to MacInnis, 10 December 1973; Department of Labour Files, RG27, vol. 4151, file 720-2E-14, vol. 1, Kathleen Ruff, Director, Human Rights Act, Department of Labour, B.C. to R. Andras, Minister of Manpower and Immigration, 5 September 1974.

4  This point was made, for example, by Kathleen Ruff, Director, B.C. Human Rights Act. See NAC, RG27 vol. 4151, file 720-2E-14, vol. 1, Ruff to Andras, 5 September 1974. See also ibid., Leslie Shaw Peterson to Andras, 20 October 1974.

5  See, for example, Canada, House of Commons, Standing Committee on Labour, Manpower and Immigration, *Minutes of Proceedings and Evidence*, 11 May 1971, 20:13. For the case of a B.C. woman whose baby was born prematurely and who was left with only six weeks to care for her child, see NAC, RG27, vol. 4151, file 720-2E-14, vol. 1, Leslie Shaw Peterson to the Hon. Robert Andras, Minister of Manpower and Immigration, 20 October 1974.

6  See, for example, Canada, Unemployment Insurance Canada, *Decisions of the Umpire*, CUB 3255, 8 February 1973; CUB 3454, 5 February 1974; CUB 4796, 13 October 1977; CUB 7375; CUB 7855, 18 October 1982; CUB 3743, 27 November 1974.

7  See, for example, Canada, *Decisions of the Umpire*, CUB 7268, 21 May 1982. Also cites CUB 6598; CUB 6603; CUB 6635.

8  Ibid., see, for exmple, CUB 7299, June 1982.

9  Ibid., see, for example, CUB 3812, 11 February 1975.

10  Ibid. See, for example, CUB 3377, 13 September 1973; CUB 3703, 23 October 1974; CUB 6879, 28 August 1981; CUB 7617, August 1982.

11  Ibid. See, for example, CUB 3259, 21 February 1973; CUB 3818, 13 February 1975; CUB 4150, CUB 4235, 18 November 1976.

12  Vickers et al., *Politics as if Women Mattered*, 94.

13  These themes dominated the 1976 AGM workshops. Ibid., 83.

14  Findlay, 'Facing the State,' 33.

15  See, for example, NAC RG27 vol. 4151, file 720-2E-14, vol. 1, Leslie Shaw Peterson to Robert Andras, Minister of Manpower and Immigration; Kathleen Ruff Director, Human Rights Act, Department of Labour, B.C., to R. Andras, 5 September 1974. See also Grace MacInnis files, MG32, C12, vol. 17, file 'UI 1973–74,' Lorna Stinson to MacInnis, 10 December 1973.

16  NAC MG32, C12, vol. 17, file 'UI 1972,' NDP Press Release, 21 March 1972.

17  Canada, Advisory Council on the Status of Women, *What's Been Done?* March 1974, 4. This report assessed the federal government's progress in implementing the recommendations of the Royal Commission on the Status of Women.

18  Canada, House of Commons, *Debates*, 29 May 1975, 6238. This was part of Bill C-16, an omnibus bill on the Status of Women.

19  Canada, House of Commons, *Debates*, 29 May 1975, 6241.

20  NAC, RG27 vol. 4151, file 720-2E-14, vol. 1, Gelber to Beatty, UIC, 28 August 1973; Gelber to Beatty, 14 September 1973; Gelber to Hynna, 14 September 1973.

21  Ibid. Beatty to Gelber, 5 September 1973; Beatty to Gelber, 21 September 1973.

22  Ibid. Hynna to Gelber, 25 September 1973; Hynna to Trottier, PCO, 13 November 1973; Trottier to Cousineau, 27 November 1973.

23  Ibid. Hynna to Michel Trottier, Secretaire adjoint au Cabinet, PCO, 27 September 1973; Hynna to Trottier, 13 November 1973.

24  Ibid. Hynna to Trottier, 13 November 1973.

25  NAC, Status of Women Canada File, RG 106, vol. 97, file 1230-UI, pt 4, UI Canada: Bulletin ED/DA-19, 22 April 1975, Re: Childcare arrangements.

26  NAC, RG106, vol. 97, file 1230-UI, pt 4, UI Canada; Bulletin ED/DA-19, 22 April 1975 to all DGs, RCCBs, DMs CCOs, Boards of Referees, Re: Childcare arrangements.
27  NAC, RG106, vol. 97, file 1230-UI, pt 4, L.E. St Laurent, UI Canada to Directors General, All Regions, 3 March 1977.
28  Canadian Advisory Council on the Status of Women, *Recommendations of the Canadian Advisory Council on the Status of Women by Subject* (Ottawa: January 1981), 60.
29  NAC, RG106, vol. 87, file 1115-UI, Rousseau to Lalonde, 3 May 1977.
30  Elsie Robindaine-Saumure, *Maternity Leave and Benefits* (Ottawa: The Council, 1976). CACSW, *The Price of Maternity* (Ottawa: The Council, 1976).
31  CACSW, *Recommendations of the Canadian Advisory Council on the Status of Women by Subject* (Ottawa: The Council, 1981), 60–1.
32  Ibid., 58.
33  Robindaine-Saumure, *Maternity Leave and Benefits*, 35–6.
34  Canada, UIC, *Decisions of the Umpire*, CUB 3977, 6 August 1975.
35  Ibid.
36  Ibid., CUB 4510, 10 February 1977, 6–7.
37  See Leslie A. Pal and F.L. Morton, '*Bliss v. Attorney General of Canada*: From Legal Defeat to Political Victory,' *Osgoode Hall Law Journal* 24, no. 1 (1986), 144.
38  Canada, Unemployment Insurance Commission, *Decisions of the Umpire*, CUB 4510, 10 February 1977, 11.
39  Ibid., 12, 17–18.
40  Ibid., 17.
41  *Re Attorney-General of Canada and Bliss* (1977), 77 DLR (3d), 613.
42  See Patricia Huckle, 'The Womb Factor: Pregnancy Policies and Employment of Women,' in Ellen Boneparth, ed., *Women, Power and Policy* (New York: Pergamon Press, 1982), 148–9. The two cases were *Gedulding v. Aiello* (1974) and *Gilbert v. General Electric* (1976).
43  *Re Attorney-General of Canada and Bliss* (1977) 77 DLR (3d), 613.
44  Ibid., 614.
45  Ibid. Pratte argued that 'the distinction is relevant when there is a logical connection between the basis for the distinction and the consequences that flow from it; the distinction is irrelevant when that logical connection is missing.'
46  Ibid., 615.
47  Ibid., 615–16.
48  Mary Eberts, 'Women and Constitutional Renewal,' in Audrey Doerr and Micheline Carrier, eds., *Women and the Constitution in Canada* (Ottawa: Canadian Advisory Council on the Status of Women, 1981), 11.

49  Beverley Baines, 'Women, Human Rights and the Constitution,' in Doerr and Carrier, eds., *Women and the Constitution in Canada*, 55.

50  Pal and Morton, '*Bliss v. Attorney General of Canada.*'

51  CACSW, *Recommendations by Subject* (1981), 87.

52  NAC, 1977, *Status of Women News* 3, no. 4 (May 1977), 10. See also NAC, *Index of Abridged Resolutions of NAC, 1972 to 1989*, 10.

53  *Bliss v. Attorney-General of Canada* (1979), 92 DLR (3d), 417–25.

54  Ibid., 419.

55  Ibid., 423.

56  Ibid., 422.

57  Pal and Morton, '*Bliss v. Attorney General of Canada.*'

58  Ibid., 142.

59  Sandra Burt, 'Organized Women's Groups and the State.'

60  Vickers et al., *Politics as if Women Mattered*, 85–6.

61  NAC, *Status of Women News* 3, no. 4 (May 1977), 10. See also NAC, *Index of Abridged Resolutions of NAC, 1972 to 1989*, 10–11.

62  WMA, 'NAC Briefs,' NAC presentation to the Government of Canada, March 1978, 3–4.

63  Ibid., 4.

64  NAC, Presentation to the PM and Members of Cabinet, 22 February 1979, 7.

65  Ibid. NAC also recommended that a parent be able to use workplace sick leave for health care of a child, that the start date of an employee's maternity leave not be advanced to encompass a period of illness, and that an employee has the right to regular sick leave during the nine months prior to delivery.

66  Gary Dingledine, *A Chronology of Response: The Evolution of Unemployment Insurance from 1940 to 1980* (Ottawa: Employment and Immigration Canada, 1981), 95.

67  Canada, House of Commons, Standing Committee on Labour, Manpower and Immigration, *Minutes of Proceedings and Evidence*, 27 November 1978, Appendix LMI–2, 8A:1, R.G.L. Fairweather, Chief Commissioner, Canadian Human Rights Commission, to Bud Cullen, Minister of Employment and Immigration.

68  CHRC, *Annual Report 1979*, 30.

69  CHRC, *Annual Report 1980*, 43–4.

70  Ibid., 43.

71  Ibid., 43–4.

72  CHRC, 1981, *Newsletter* 4, no. 2 (March 1981).

73  Ibid. See also CHRC *Annual Report, 1981*.

74  CHRC, *Annual Report 1982*, 9–10.

75  Canada, UIC, *Decisions of the Umpire*, CUB 5933, June 1980, 6–8.

76  Ibid., CUB 6792; Federal Court of Appeal A-507-81, June 1982.
77  Ibid.
78  See, for example, Audrey Doerr and Micheline Carrier, eds., *Women and the Constitution in Canada* (Ottawa: Canadian Advisory Council on the Status of Women, 1981), especially articles by Mary Eberts, 'Women and Constitutional Renewal,' and Beverley Baines, 'Women, Human Rights and the Constitution'; Canada, Parliament, Special Joint Committee of the Senate and House of Commons on the Constitution of Canada, *Minutes of Proceedings and Evidence*, 20 November 1980, presentations by NAC, CACSW.
79  Canada, Special Joint Committee of the Senate and House of Commons on the Constitution of Canada, *Minutes of Proceedings and Evidence*, 20 November 1980; CACSW, NAC briefs.
80  Ibid., NAC brief, 9:59, 9:72.
81  Ibid., NAC brief, 9:59, 9:65.
82  Ibid., 9:57.
83  Ibid., CACSW brief, 9:126.
84  See Pal and Morton, *'Bliss v. Attorney General of Canada,'* 154–6.
85  See, for example, Sheilah L. Martin, 'Persisting Equality Implications of the "Bliss" Case,' and Beth Symes, 'Equality Theories and Maternity Bene-fits,' both in Sheilah L. Martin and Kathleen E. Mahoney, eds., *Equality and Judicial Neutrality* (Toronto: Carswell, 1987). This was the case, for example, in the May 1986 ruling of the Manitoba Court of Appeal in *Brooks v. Canada Safeway* (subsequently overturned), which found that exclusion of pregnant women from disability benefits did not violate the Manitoba Human Rights Act (see Symes, 'Equality Theories and Maternity Benefits,' 212).
86  *Brooks v. Canada Safeway Ltd*, [1989] 1 S.C.R., 1221.
87  Madeleine Parent, 'Women In Unions: Past, Present and Future,' in *Strong Women, Strong Unions: Speeches by Union Women* (Canada Employment and Immigration Union/Participatory Research Group, 1985), 29. See also Laurell Ritchie, 'Maternity and Parental Leave,' *Status of Women News* 7, no. 2 (Winter 1981/2), 10.
88  See Julie White, *Mail and Female: Women and the Canadian Union of Postal Workers* (Toronto: Thompson Educational Publishing, 1990), 159.
89  See 'Jean-Claude Parrot: An Interview,' *Studies in Political Economy* 11 (1983), 57; White, *Mail and Female*, ch. 9.
90  Ibid., 156.
91  Jean-Claude Parrot, 'Paid Maternity Leave,' *Status of Women News* 7, no. 2 (Winter 1981/2), 8.
92  Canadian Union of Postal Workers, 'Parental Rights,' Negotiations

Backgrounder No. 3, Ottawa, March 1981, 10, quoted in White, *Mail and Female*, 152.

93  Parrot, 'Paid Maternity Leave,' 7.

94. Ibid., 8.

95  Ibid., 8.

96  Canada, House of Commons, *Debates*, 9 November 1978, 985.

97  See Canada, *Decisions of the Umpire*, CUB 6548, April 1981, FC judgment no. A-235-81; CUB 6896, August 1981; CUB 7060, November 1981; CUB 7390, June 1982; CUB 7596, August 1982.

98  Employment and Immigration Canada, *Unemployment Insurance in the 1980s* (Ottawa: Minister of Supply and Services, 1981). See Appendix I, Terms of Reference.

99  Ibid., 1.

100  Ibid., 70.

101  Ibid., 67; 69–70.

102  Ibid., 69.

103  Ibid., 69.

104  Canada, House of Commons, *Debates*, 2 June 1983, 25959.

105  'Jean-Claude Parrot: An Interview,' 56; White, *Mail and Female*, 152–3.

## 6: Gender, Economic Crisis, and Welfare State Restructuring in the 1970s

1  Many complaints came from the low-wage, male-dominated sectors, such as logging, farming, trucking, and so on – sectors that had long expressed concerns about UI on the grounds that it adversely affected their labour supply. There were now also complaints from companies drawing more on a female labour force, such as those employing secretaries and typists. For examples of complaints, see NAC, RG 50, vol. 38, file 528-2, pt 20, Howard Hurt, President, Canadian Pulp and Paper Association to Hon. Robert Andras, 18 December 1972; R. Andras to Mr R. Armitage, Robson-Lang Leathers, Oshawa, 1 February 1974; Judy Loberg, President, Chamber of Commerce, Niagara Falls, to R. Andras, 19 September 1974; Gerard A. Taylor, Beaver Asphalt Paving Co., Montreal, to F. Pelletier, UI Office, Montreal, 6 November 1974; Dan McKenzie, MP, Winnipeg South Centre, to Andras, 29 October 1974; G. Wilson, Dot Personnel, to Michael J. Webb, Vice-President, Liberal Party, 23 October 1974.

2  The Globe and Mail, for example, referred to the 1971 Act as 'immoral and stupid' (6 September 1971). See Saywell, *Canadian Annual Review*, 1971, 358.

3 On the BCNI, see David Langille, 'The Business Council on National Issues and the Canadian State,' *Studies in Political Economy* 24 (Autumn 1987).

4 Labour Canada, Women's Bureau, *Women in the Labour Force: Facts and Figures*, 1971, Table 7. Until 1975, part-time was considered less than thirty-five hours a week.

5 Economic Council of Canada, *People and Jobs: A Study of the Canadian Labour Market* (Ottawa, 1976), 7; 11.

6 Discharges and quits as a proportion of average annual payroll. Economic Council of Canada, *People and Jobs*, 9–10.

7 Statistics Canada, *Women in Canada* (1985), Table 1, 47.

8 Ibid., Table 3, 49.

9 Ibid., Table 3, 49.

10 Statistics Canada, *Women in the Workplace* (1993), Table 1.8, 21.

11 Ostry, *Unemployment in Canada*, 5.

12 Benefit payments more than doubled from $891 million in 1971 to $1,868 million in 1972 and increased further to $2 billion in 1973 and $2.1 billion in 1974. In its annual reports, the UI Commission attributed this to higher wages forcing up benefit payments, benefits being extended to cover sickness and maternity, a longer claim period being allowed, and the extension of UI to cover more workers. See UI Commission, *Annual Report*, 1973–5.

13 NAC RG 106, vol. 97, file 1230-UI, pt 1, Nancy Y.M. Chinfen and Ellen Richardson, *Canadian Unemployment Insurance as a Measure of Social Security for Women*, UIC, November 1972.

14 NAC, RG 106, vol. 96, file 1230-UI, pt 1, F. Paltiel, Monitoring Note – Re: Women and Unemployment in Canada, 16 October 1972, 2.

15 NAC RG 106 vol. 97, file 1230-UI, pt 1, Helen Buckley to F. Paltiel, 6 November 1972.

16 Morley Gunderson, 'Work Patterns,' in Gail C.A. Cook, ed., *Opportunity for Choice: A Goal for Women in Canada* (Ottawa: Statistics Canada in association with the C.D. Howe Research Institute, 1976), 103–4.

17 Lorna Marsden, 'Unemployment Among Canadian Women: Some Sociological Problems Raised By Its Increase,' in Patricia Marchak, ed., *The Working Sexes* (Vancouver: Institute of Industrial Relations, UBC, 1977), 37–40. See also Beverly Tangri, 'Women and Unemployment,' *Atlantis* 3, no. 2, part II (Spring 1978).

18 In 1975, for women with a husband at home, those with preschool children had an unemployment rate of 11.7 per cent and those without chil-

dren under sixteen years, an unemployment rate of 6.5 per cent. For those
with no husband at home, those with preschool children had an unemployment rate of 13.6 per cent, and those without children under sixteen
years, 4.2 per cent. See Statistics Canada, *Women in Canada: A Statistical
Report* (Ottawa, 1985), Table 16, 59.

19  See Andrew F. Johnson, 'Political Leadership and the Process of Policy-
Making: The Case of Unemployment Insurance in the 1970s,' PhD diss.
McGill University, 1983, 108, 113.

20  Ibid., 111–12.

21  NAC RG50, vol. 39, file 528-4, pt 3, Lucien Bradet, Chief Enquiries and
Analysis Division to J.W. Dobson, Manpower and Immigration, 13 August
1974.

22  NAC RG 106, vol. 97, file 1230-UI, pt 1, 'UIC "Purge" Brings Call for Probe
in Commons,' *Hamilton Spectator* (5 March 1973). See also Canada, House
of Commons, *Debates*, 16 February 1973. In 1977 a report prepared for the
Law Reform Commission also noted that a high proportion of control
officers were former policemen, private detectives and investigators for
commercial collection agencies. Pierre Issalys and Gaylord Watkins, *Unemployment Insurance Benefits: A Study of Administrative Procedure in the
Unemployment Insurance Commission*, Prepared for the Law Reform Commission of Canada (1977), 75.

23  Canada, House of Commons, *Debates*, statement by Robert K. Andras,
Minister of Manpower and Immigration, 13 March 1973, 2152–4.

24  Ibid., 2153–4.

25  See, for example, statements by Mr Thomas (Moncton) and Mr Rodriguez
(Nickel Belt), Canada, House of Commons, Standing Committee on Lab-
our, Manpower and Immigration, *Minutes of Proceedings and Evidence*,
March 22 1973, 10:11–12; 10:15.

26  NAC, RG106, vol. 97, file 1230-UI, pt 1, Patrick Best, 'Many cut from UIC
roll after probe,' *Ottawa Citizen* (22 January 1973).

27  'UIC "purge."'

28  Ibid. In this case the investigation was targeted to a broader range of
seventeen or eighteen groups.

29  Canada, Unemployment Insurance Canada, *Comprehensive Review* (1977),
C-13.

30  Dingledine, *Chronology of Response*, 90–1.

31  Issalys and Watkins, *Unemployment Insurance Benefits*, 78–9.

32  Canada, House of Commons, Standing Committee on Labour, Manpower
and Immigration, *Minutes of Proceedings and Evidence*, 22/5/73, 10:11.

33 'UIC "purge."'
34 Canada, House of Commons, Standing Committee on Labour, Manpower and Immigration, *Minutes of Proceedings and Evidence*, 22/5/73, 10:11–10:12.
35 Canada, House of Commons, *Debates*, 12 March 1973, 2127–8.
36 Economic Council of Canada, *People and Jobs*, 12, 102–3.
37 Ibid., 103.
38 Canada, House of Commons, *Debates*, 12 March 1973, 2127–8.
39 Ibid.
40 See, for example, Rodriguez, Nickel Belt. Canada, House of Commons, *Debates*, 13 March 1973, 2156. See also Paddy Neale, 12 March 1973, 2119–20.
41 Paddy Neale, Vancouver East, Canada, House of Commons, *Debates*, 12 March 1973, 2119–20.
42 Canada, House of Commons, *Debates*, 13 March 1973, 2152–3.
43 See Dingledine, *Chronology of Response*, 72.
44 Canada, Unemployment Insurance Commission, *35th Annual Report* (June 1976), 2.
45 Issalys and Watkins, *Unemployment Insurance Benefits*, 74–5; 78.
46 See NAC, RG 106, vol. 97, file 1230-UI, pt 2, Munro to Andras, 22 February 1974.
47 The Canadian Manufacturers' Association, for example, referred to 'several localized efforts involving close cooperation between the Manpower Department and the UIC ... which produced very encouraging results in terms of placements and attitudinal changes' and which, it felt, if extended, would 'reflect favourably in the next year's total unemployment insurance costs.' NAC, RG 50, vol. 38, file 528-2, pt 19, W.H. Wightman, Canadian Manufacturers' Association to John Turner, Minister of Finance, 25 November 1974.
48 NAC RG50, vol. 38, file 528-2, pt 20, G.W. Dalby, President, Chamber of Commerce, Niagara Falls, Canada to Hon. Robert Andras, Minister of Manpower and Immigration, 4 March 1975.
49 NAC RG 106, vol. 97, file 1230-UI, pt 2, Andras to Munro, 18 April 1974.
50 Ibid.
51 Canada, House of Commons, *Debates*, 23 June 1975, 7027.
52 See David Wolfe, 'The Rise and Demise of the Keynesian Era in Canada: Economic Policy, 1930–1982,' in Michael S. Cross and Gregory S. Kealey, *Modern Canada, 1930–1980s* (Toronto: McClelland & Stewart, 1984), 71–2.
53 See, for example, Christopher Green and Jean-Michel Cousineau, *Unemployment in Canada: The Impact of Unemployment Insurance* (Economic Council of Canada, 1976); Economic Council of Canada, *People and Jobs* (Ottawa, 1976).

54  Economic Council of Canada, *People and Jobs*, 25, 210–12.
55  Green and Cousineau, *Unemployment in Canada*, 27–8, 115.
56  Ibid., 116. See also Economic Council of Canada, *People and Jobs*, 151–8.
57  Economic Council of Canada, *People and Jobs*, 144–7.
58  Green and Cousineau, *Unemployment in Canada*, 115, 10; Economic Council of Canada, *People and Jobs*, 19.
59  Economic Council of Canada, *People and Jobs*, 156–8.
60  Herbert G. Grubel and Michael A. Walker, 'Moral Hazard, Unemployment Insurance and the Rate of Unemployment,' in *Unemployment Insurance: Global Evidence of its Effects on Unemployment* (The Fraser Institute, 1978), 17–18.
61  Ibid., 31–2.
62  Ibid., 35.
63  Ibid.
64  Canada, House of Commons, *Debates*, 23 June 1975, 7027.
65  The changed funding formula was applicable only to the costs of initial regular benefits; the cost of extended benefits was to continue to be financed entirely from the federal government's consolidated revenue fund.
66  Dingledine, *Chronology of Response*, 75, 77.
67  Ibid., 80.
68  Canada, Unemployment Insurance Commission, *Unemployment Insurance Program Proposed Legislative Changes in Bill C-69*, tabled 12 November 1975. Quoted in Dingledine, *Chronology of Response*, 80–1.
69  Canada, House of Commons, *Debates*, 23 June 1975.
70  Andras, Canada, House of Commons, *Debates*, 5 November 1975, 8899.
71  Canada, House of Commons, *Debates*, 27 October 1975, 8568.
72  Canada, Unemployment Insurance Canada, *Comprehensive Review of the Unemployment Insurance Program in Canada* (Ottawa: 1977). See, for example, B-7, E-5, C-57, C-58.
73  Ibid., K-30.
74  Ibid., K-3–K-18.
75  The possibility of work-sharing arrangements was also introduced. Ibid., 2592.
76  Canada, House of Commons, *Debates*, 1 February 1977, 2591.
77  Saywell, *Canadian Annual Review*, 1977, 11–12.
78  Saywell, *Canadian Annual Review*, 1978, 8.
79  Canada, House of Commons, *Debates*, 9 November 1978, 983.
80  Dingledine, *Chronology of Response*, 98.
81  The bill provided for the tripartite financing of benefits in the labour force

extended phase, instead of having them financed by the federal government alone. Canada, House of Commons, *Debates*, 983.

82 Canada, House of Commons, Standing Committee on Labour, Manpower and Immigration, *Minutes of Proceedings and Evidence*, Canadian Manufacturers' Association presentation, 23 November 1978, 6:73–6:75.

83 Canada, House of Commons, *Debates*, 9 November 1978, 983.

84 Originally, forty weeks of insured employment within two years was proposed for new entrants and reentrants; this was later changed to a requirement for twenty weeks of insured employment in the previous year.

85 According to the original proposals, repeat users would have been required to work at least as long as the period for which they drew benefits before being eligible again. For example, if they had received benefits for twenty-six weeks, they would have to work another 26 weeks before becoming eligible for a new claim. This was changed to a requirement for an additional six weeks beyond the VER of ten to fourteen weeks.

86 Saywell, *Canadian Annual Review*, 1978, 10–11.

87 Canada, House of Commons, *Debates*, 9 November 1978, 984; Standing Committee on Labour, Manpower and Immigration, *Minutes*, 16 November 1978, 2:58.

88 Canada, House of Commons, Standing Committee on Labour, Manpower and Immigration, *Minutes*, 16 November 1978, 2:58.

89 Canada, House of Commons, *Debates*, 9 November 1978, 985.

90 Hynna noted in 1973 that new efforts to tighten the UI administration by subjecting certain groups of women to special interviews 'is discriminatory.' On the whole, however, prior to 1975, there seems to have been little response on the part of women's representatives to the benefit control operations. NAC RG 27, vol. 4151, file 720-2E-14, vol. 1, Hynna to Trottier, 13 November 1973. See also RG 106, vol. 97, file 1230-UI, pt 1.

91 See, for example, Canada, House of Commons, *Debates*, speeches by Orlikow, 29 October 1975, 8677; Knowles, 5 November 1975, 8894; Cyril Symes, 4 November 1975, 8850; Broadbent, 20 December 1975, 10238. Canada, House of Commons, Standing Committee on Labour, Manpower and Immigration, *Minutes of Proceedings and Evidence*, 20 November 1975, 23:6–23:7.

92 Andras, Liberal Party, Canada, House of Commons, *Debates*, 27 October 1975, 8568, Stuart Leggatt, NDP, Canada, House of Commons, *Debates*, 5 November 1975, 8885. Speech by Lincoln Alexander, Conservative Party. Canada, House of Commons, *Debates*, 27 October 1975, 8576.

93 Vickers et al., *Politics as if Women Mattered*, 85–6.

94 Women's Movement Archives (WMA), University of Ottawa, file 'NAC AGM 1977,' Proposals arising from the workshops; see also NAC, *Index of Abridged Resolutions of NAC, 1972 to 1989*, 10–11.

95 Elise Rosen, *A Report on the Comprehensive Review of the Unemployment Insurance Program in Canada* (Ottawa: The Advisory Council on the Status of Women, October 1977).

96 NAC, RG106, vol. 87, file 1115-UI, Y. Rousseau, President, CACSW, to M. Lalonde, Minister Responsible for the Status of Women, 3 May 1977.

97 NAC, RG106, vol. 97, file 1230-UI, pt 1, Cullen to Lalonde, 11 July 1977.

98 Canada, House of Commons, Standing Committee on Labour, Manpower and Immigration, *Minutes*, 21 November 1978, 4:86, 4:92.

99 At NAC's annual meeting in March 1978, a resolution was passed condemning the high levels of unemployment, urging the 'development of a long term industrial strategy,' and affirming 'the right of every woman to employment.' see WMA, file 'NAC AGM, 1978, 'Conference Report and Minutes of Annual Meeting,' March 1978, 5. Similar arguments were presented in the NAC's response to Cabinet's requests for comments on the *Economic Outlook for Canada* that year. See WMA, 'NAC Presentation to the Cabinet of the Government of Canada,' March 1978, *The Economic Outlook*.

100 Canada, House of Commons, Standing Committee on Labour, Manpower and Immigration, *Minutes*, CACSW brief, 21 November 1978, 4:90–4:91; NAC brief, 27 November 1978, 8:6–8:8, 8:10.

101 Ibid., NAC, 8:16, 8:21; CACSW, 4:86–4:88.

102 Ibid., NAC, 8:10, 8:20.

103 Ibid., NAC brief, 27 November 1978, 8:13, 8:34; CACSW brief, 21 November 1978, 4:87.

104 Ibid., CACSW, 4:87; NAC, 8:13–8:14.

105 Ibid., NAC, 27 November 1978, 8:14; CACSW, 21 November 1978, 4:88.

106 Ibid., 4:5–4:11.

107 Canada, House of Commons, Standing Committee on Labour, Manpower and Immigration, *Minutes*, CLC presentation, 27 November 1978, 4:7.

108 Canada, House of Commons, Standing Committee on Labour, Manpower and Immigration, *Minutes*, 30 November 1978, 11:5–11:56.

109 Ibid., 11:11.

110 Ibid., 11:9.

111 WMA, NAC AGM misc. (M. Cohen papers), NAC Memo, December 1978. See also NAC brief, Canada, House of Commons, Standing Committee on Labour, Manpower and Immigration, *Minutes*, 27 November 1978, 8:14. The CACSW had also expressed its approval of the decision to

determine benefit repayment for those with high income on an individual rather than a family basis. Ibid., 21 November 1978, 4:88.

112 Canada, House of Commons, Standing Committee of Labour, Manpower
and Immigration, *Minutes*, 1 December 1978, 12:7–12:9.

113 Ibid., 1 December 1978, 12:12–12:13.

114 McCrossan, an actuary with Canada Life Assurance Company before
entering politics, was concerned with applying insurance principles to
UI. See NAC RG106, vol. 66, file 1230-UI, pt 6; Anderson, 'Justice not
Thrift.'

115 NAC, RG 106, vol. 66, file 1230-UI, pt 6, Employment and Immigration
Canada, *Unemployment Insurance in the 1980s: A Review of Its Appropriate
Role and Design*, July 1979, 1.

116 Ibid., 4–7.

117 Both CACSW and NAC brought up this issue during the Bill C-14 hearings. See Canada House of Commons, Standing Committee on Labour,
Manpower and Immigration, *Minutes*, 21 November 1978, 4:91; 27 November 1978, 8:19. The NAC also raised it during its 1978 presentation to
Cabinet. See WMA, 'NAC Presentation to the Cabinet of the Government
of Canada,' March 1978, *The Economic Outlook*, 3.

118 See Dingledine, *Chronology of Response*, 155.

119 Canadian Human Rights Commission, *Annual Report*, 1979, 30, 33.

120 WMA, 'NAC AGM 1979,' recommendations from workshops.

121 Canadian Human Rights Commission, *Annual Report*, 1979.

122 Vickers et al., *Politics as if Women Mattered*, 91, 100, 110.

123 NAC, Presentation to the PM and Members of Cabinet, 22 February 1979.

124 NAC RG 106, vol. 66, file 1230-UI, pt 6, *The Unemployment Insurance Program Review: Implications for the Status of Women*, Initial Recommendations
of the Canadian Advisory Council on the Status of Women, September
1979, 3. These recommendations had not yet been endorsed by the entire
council.

125 Ibid., 7–8; 11.

126 Ibid., 11.

127 Pat Armstrong, 'Women and Unemployment,' *Atlantis*, 6, no. 1 (Fall
1980), 5.

128 Ibid., 3.

129 See, for example, 1975 discussion of dependency provision. Mr Darling,
Conservative Party, Canada, House of Commons, *Debates*, 3 November
1975, 8797.

130 Canada, House of Commons, Standing Committee on Labour, Manpower

and Immigration, *Minutes of Proceedings and Evidence*, 23 November 1978, 6:65.

131 See NAC, RG 106, vol. 66, file 1230-UI, pt 6, *Possible Amendments to the UI Act, 1980*, 15 October 1979.

132 NAC RG 106, vol. 66, file 1230-UI, pt 6, UI Relative Cost Ratios in Relation to the Two-Tier Benefit Structure, Strategic Policy and Planning, 10 October 1979.

133 NAC RG 106, vol. 66, file 1230-UI, pt 6, *The UI Program Review: Implications for the Status of Women*, 4.

134 Ibid., 5. See also Canadian Advisory Council on the Status of Women, *Recommendations of the Canadian Advisory Council on the Status of Women by Subject*, January 1981, 87–8.

135 NAC, *Status of Women News* 6, no. 1 (Winter 1979–80), 19.

136 Margrit Eichler, '"Family Income" – A Critical Look at the Concept,' *Status of Women News* 6, no. 2 (Spring 1980).

137 Ibid., 21.

138 Ibid., 24.

139 RG 106, vol. 66, file 1230-UI, pt 6, Status of Women Canada, 'Comments on Possible Amendments to the UI Act, 1980,' November 1979.

140 RG 106, vol. 67, file 1230-UI, pt 8, M. O'Neil, Status of Women Canada to Minister, 12 December 1979.

141 NAC, RG 106, vol. 66, file 1230-UI, pt 6, Swan to O'Neil, 4 September 1979; 17 September 1979.

142 RG 106, vol. 66, file 1230-UI, pt 6, MacDonald to Atkey, 20 September 1979.

143 RG 106, vol. 66, file 1230-UI, pt 6, MacDonald to Clark, 20 September 1979.

## 7: The Conservatives in Power

1 Canada, House of Commons, *Debates*, 6 June 1989, 2675.

2 Canada, Royal Commission on the Economic Union and Development Prospects for Canada (Macdonald Commission), *Report* (Ottawa, 1985).

3 Canada, Commission of Inquiry on Unemployment Insurance (Forget Commission), *Report* (Ottawa: Ministry of Supply and Services Canada, 1986).

4 On popular mobilization against a market-oriented agenda, see Jeffrey M. Ayres, *Defying Conventional Wisdom: Political Movements and Popular Contention against North American Free Trade* (Toronto: University of Toronto

Press, 1998); Peter Bleyer, 'Coalitions of Social Movements as Agencies for Social Change: The Action Canada Network,' in William K. Carroll, ed., *Organizing Dissent: Contemporary Social Movements in Theory and Practice*, 2nd ed., (Toronto: Garamond, 1997); Daniel Drache and Duncan Cameron, eds., *The Other Macdonald Report* (Toronto: James Lorimer and Co., 1985).

5 In 1982 and 1983 the unemployment rate for women was slightly less than for men, largely because the recession hit the male-dominated resource, manufacturing, and construction industries with particular severity.

6 Labour Canada, *Women in the Labour Force, 1990–91*, Table 8, 22.

7 Ibid., Table 2, 11.

8 Statistics Canada, *Women in the Workplace, 1993*, Table 1.8, 21.

9 'Regular beneficiaries' exclude those receiving UI benefits for sickness, maternity, retirement, fishing, training, work sharing, job creation or self-employment. It has been pointed out that comparisons of the number of unemployed as measured by the Labour Force Survey and the number of UI recipients have to be treated with caution. Both sets of figures represent twelve-month averages rather than the actual number of unemployed receiving UI at any point in time. The two sets of data are measuring different things that are not always comparable. For example, some UI recipients may work part-time to supplement their benefits, and would therefore not be included in the LFS unemployment figures. At the same time, some seasonal workers in high unemployment regions have not at times been required to do an active job search and would therefore not always be counted in the LFS, but could have been UI beneficiaries. On the differences between the Labour Force Survey and UI figures, see, for example, Statistics Canada Catalogue 73-001, January 1976, *Statistical Report on the Operation of the Unemployment Insurance Act*, Appendix II, 'Comparing Unemployment Statistics with Data from the Unemployment Insurance Commission,' 32–5; Jean-Marc Levesque, 'Unemployment and Unemployment Insurance: A Tale of Two Sources,' in Statistics Canada, *Perspectives on Labour and Income*, Winter 1989; F. Roy, 'Unemployment and Unemployment Insurance: An Update,' in *Canadian Economic Observer* (January 1994); Canada, Human Resources Development Canada, 'An Analysis of Employment Insurance Benefit Coverage,' Applied Research Branch, Strategic Policy, HRDC, October 1998. A comparison of the two sets of figures over time do, however, clearly show broad trends.

10 Canada, *Unemployment Insurance in the 1980s* (Ottawa: Employment and Immigration Canada), 1.

11 Ibid., 9–11.

12 Ibid., 11–13.

13 Ibid., 11, 13.

14 Ibid., 43.

15 Ibid., 55.

16 Ibid., 43.

17 Ibid., 57–60. In this respect the task force seems to have been influenced by the views of women's representatives, who continued to voice their opposition to such policies. See NAC RG 106 vol. 67, file 1230-UI, pt 8, Swan to O'Neil, 16 September 1980. Swan notes that Sid Gershberg, who directed the task force, had indicated that it was considering changing UI to take account of multiple-earner families, but that if Status of Women Canada opposed such a scheme it would not be pursued further. Both the NAC and the CACSW had also reiterated their position that UI should be based on individual attachment to the labour force rather than on family status. See NAC, 'Resolutions Accepted at the Annual Meeting, March 1980,' *Status of Women News* 6, no. 3 (Summer 1980), CACSW, *Recommendations of the CACSW by Subject*, January 1981 (recommendations passed January 1980, 87).

18 See Employment and Immigration Minister Axworthy's comments, Canada, House of Commons, Standing Committee on Labour, Manpower and Immigration, 20 April 1982, 24:13; 19 May 1983, 42:17, 42:19; Canada, House of Commons, *Debates*, 2 June 1983, 25956.

19 Canada, Department of Finance, *A New Direction for Canada: An Agenda for Economic Renewal*, presented by the Honourable Michael H. Wilson, Minister of Finance, 8 November 1984.

20 Ibid., 71–7.

21 Ibid., 46.

22 Ibid., 51.

23 Ibid., 46, 77–8.

24 Other suggestions included separating the program into two distinct components, one based on insurance objectives and the other on 'social and redistribution considerations,' as well as possibly changing the financing basis of maternity benefits, job creation, and work sharing (for example, possibly funding maternity benefits out of general revenues). Ibid., 78.

25 Ibid., 78.

26 See Thomas Walkom, 'PCs to Cut Spending by $4.2 Billion,' *The Globe and Mail* (9 November 1984); Charlotte Montgomery, 'Social Spending to Be Slashed; Programs Face Reassessment,' *The Globe and Mail* (9 November 1984).

27 In Walkom, 'PCs to Cut Spending.'

28 Department of Finance, *A New Direction for Canada*, 8 November 1984.

29  Ibid. See also Canada, House of Commons, *Debates*, 8 November 1984, 96–103.
30  Canada, Royal Commission on the Economic Union and Development Prospects for Canada (Macdonald Commission), *Report* (Ottawa, 1985), 554, 576–7.
31  Ibid., vol. 2, 610–13.
32  See, for example, ibid., vol. 2, 15–17, 282, 285, 594–5.
33  Ibid., vol. 2, 595.
34  Ibid., vol. 2, 604–6.
35  Ibid., vol. 2, 616. In addition, the commission recommended eliminating a range of federal income security programs, including the Guaranteed Income Supplement for the elderly, Family Allowances, Child Tax Credits, federal social housing programs, and federal contributions to the Canada Assistance Plan, and their replacement by a Universal Income Security Program providing a basic income supplement and very low level of guaranteed minimum income for all.
36  Canada, Commission of Inquiry on Unemployment Insurance (Forget Commission), *Report* (Ottawa: Ministry of Supply and Services Canada, 1986).
37  Ibid., 50.
38  Ibid., 52, 57–9.
39  Ibid., chapter 6, see, for example, 154.
40  It also recommended the removal of the fifteen-week limit for combined maternity and sickness benefits and that the payment of such benefits not be confined to the 'initial benefit phase' – that is, the first twenty-five weeks of unemployment. Ibid., 122–4.
41  Ibid., 183–4.
42  Ibid., 187–91.
43  The report also recommended eliminating regionally extended benefits, which it argued created an unfair advantage for those in high-unemployment regions and had become a form of income supplement for short-term and seasonal workers. The report recommended replacing these benefits with a range of 'human resource development programs,' including economic and community development initiatives, education, literacy, and basic training programs, and policies and other programs to facilitate greater flexibility in the labour market. Ibid., see ch. 4.
44  See comments by Sydney Jackson, BCNI, Canada, House of Commons, Standing Committee on Labour, Employment and Immigration, *Minutes of Proceedings and Evidence* (hearings of Hawkes Committee examining UI) 4 February 1987, 23:11–23:14.

45 See Drache and Cameron, *The Other Macdonald Report*, for briefs and contributions to the Macdonald Commission from the 'popular sector.'

46 Gerard Docquier, the representative on the Macdonald Commission, criticized the general market orientation of the report, and the lack of importance attributed to unemployment, and disagreed with particular recommendations, including the proposed cuts to UI. See Drache and Cameron, *The Other Macdonald Report*, 10. The concern about the neglect of the unemployment issue echoed that expressed during the commission hearings both by individual trade unions and by many groups in the broader 'popular sector.' See briefs collected in Drache and Cameron.

47 Canada, Commission of Inquiry on Unemployment Insurance (Forget Commission), *Report*, 'Supplementary Statement,' commissioners F.J. Soboda and J.J. Munro. They estimated, for example, that under the annualization plan more than 23 per cent of women whose UI claims terminated in 1984 would have received less than $50 per week, compared to 13 per cent of men (455–7).

48 Ibid., 439–44.

49 Ibid., 429, 475–6.

50 See, for example, CUPE, *The Facts* 8, no. 2 (March–April 1986), Special Issue, 'Rebutting the Macdonald Report'; Monica Townson, 'Income Security,' in ibid., 29.

51 NAC, *The Problem is Jobs ... Not Unemployment Insurance*. Brief to the Commission of Inquiry on Unemployment Insurance, January 1986, 2; Marjorie Cohen, NAC Vice-President, *The Macdonald Report and Its Implications for Women* (NAC, November 1985), 8–9.

52 Cohen, *The Macdonald Report and Its Implications*, 8–9.

53 CACSW, *Integration and Participation: Women's Work in the Home and in the Labour Force* (Ottawa: The Council, 1987), 54–62; NAC, *Feminist Action*, January 1987, 3. See also 1987 resolution that 'NAC oppose the majority report of the Forget Commission on unemployment insurance, and condemn the failure of the review committee to hear NAC's response to the Forget Report,' NAC, *Index of Resolutions*, 11.

54 Both these proposals had been contained in the Forget Commission Participation Guide. See CACSW, *Brief* (1986), 20–1; *Recommendations*, B1.7; NAC, *The Problem Is Jobs*.

55 See CACSW, *Brief* (1986), 28–9; *Recommendations*, B1.6 (October 1985); *Integration and Participation*, 65–7.

56 NAC, *The Problem Is Jobs*, 44.

57 Ibid., 44–9.

58 Canada, House of Commons, Standing Committee on Labour, Employ-

ment and Immigration, *Minutes of Proceedings and Evidence*, 17 March 1987, 28:3–28:20.

59  Ibid., 28:4.
60  Ibid., 28:3.
61  Statement by Benoit Bouchard, Canada, House of Commons, *Debates*, 15 May 1987, 6145–7.
62  Vickers, et al., *Politics as if Women Mattered*, 141.
63  Canada, Labour Canada, *Part-time Work in Canada: Report of the Commission of Inquiry into Part-Time Work* (Wallace Commission) (Ottawa, 1983).
64  Canada, *Report of the Commission on Equality in Employment* (Abella Commission) (Ottawa, 1984).
65  Status of Women Canada, *Report of the Task Force on Childcare* (Katie Cooke Task Force) (Ottawa, 1986).
66  Canada, Parliament, House of Commons Sub-Committee on Equality Rights, *Equality for All: Report of the Parliamentary Committee on Equality Rights* (Boyer Committee) (Ottawa, 1985).
67  Labour Canada, *Part-time Work in Canada*, 24.
68  For a discussion of employment equality and childcare, see Annis May Timpson, *Driven Apart: Women's Employment Equality and Child Care in Canadian Public Policy* (Vancouver: UBC Press, 2001).
69  Canada, *Report of the Commission on Equality in Employment*, 3; *Equality for All*, 5.
70  Canada, *Report of the Commission of Equality in Employment*, 3.
71  Ibid., 4; *Equality for All*, 5.
72  *Equality for All*, ch. 2.
73  Ibid., 12. This had been a concern expressed by several women's groups.
74  Ibid., 5.
75  It recommended reducing the minimum required to not less than eight hours per week. Ibid., 95–101.
76  Ibid., 13–14.
77  Ibid., 34.
78  The Cooke task force reported that Employment and Immigration Canada estimated that in 1982, prior to the liberalization of maternity benefits, only 45 per cent of potentially eligible claimants received benefits, and that even after the changes were introduced in 1984, it was expected that only 55 per cent of women workers who gave birth or adopted a child would claim maternity benefits. Status of Women Canada, *Report of the Task Force on Child Care*, 25.
79  Ibid., 27–9.
80  Ibid., 313–19.
81  Ibid., 317.

82 NAC, *Index of Abridged Resolutions of NAC, 1972 to 1989*, 11, resolution passed in 1980; NAC, *The Problem Is Jobs*, CACSW, *Recommendations (1973–1988)*, B1.6 (January 1980 recommendation); CACSW, *Brief Presented to the Commission of Inquiry on Unemployment Insurance*, prepared by Monica Townson (Ottawa: January 1986).

83 NAC, *The Problem Is Jobs*, 15–16; CACSW, *Brief* (1986), 17. The NAC recommended a minimum of eight hours a week, not necessarily with the same employer.

84 The NAC specified that seventeen weeks of benefits should be available to the mother and at least another twenty-four weeks be available for parental benefits. NAC, *The Problem Is Jobs*, 19–22; *Index of Resolutions*, 11, resolution passed in 1986.

85 NAC, *Index of Resolutions*, 11.

86 NAC, *The Problem Is Jobs*, 23; CACSW, *Brief* (1986), 25–7; CACSW, *Recommendations*, B1.8–B1.9.

87 See *Schachter v. Canada*, 52 DLR (4th) 525–53 [1988].

88 Ibid., 539.

89 Ibid., 542.

90 See Sherene Razack, *Canadian Feminism and the Law* (Toronto: Second Story Press, 1991), 89–94.

91 *Schachter v. Canada*, 545–6.

92 Statistics Canada, *Women in the Labour Force 1994*, cat. 75–507E, Table 1.1, 10.

93 Ibid., Table 6.3, 52.

94 This perhaps reflects that toward the end of the recession the long-term unemployed no longer qualified for benefits.

95 Canada, Employment and Immigration Canada, *Success in the Works: A Policy Paper* (Ottawa, 1989).

96 Canada, House of Commons, *Debates*, 15 May 1989, 1747.

97 See, for example, comments by the NDP's Dave Barrett, Canada, House of Commons, *Debates*, 1 May 1989, 1153, the Liberals' Warren Allmand, Canada, House of Commons, *Debates*, 6 June 1989, 2678–9; Msgr Gilles Ouellet, Canadian Conference of Catholic Bishops, Canada, House of Commons, Legislative Committee on Bill C-21, *Minutes*, 25 September 1989, 15:8; NAC, *The Problem Is Still Jobs*, 13–14.

98 Canada, *Success in the Works: A Policy Paper*, 11 and Appendix 2. For a description of the 1986 requirements, see Commissioners F.J. Soboda and J.J. Munro, 'Supplementary Statement,' Forget Commission, *Report*, 507.

99 For example, in regions where the unemployment rate was 11 per cent, claimants with thirty weeks' work who previously were entitled to fifty weeks of benefits, would now only be entitled to forty-two weeks. Canada, *Success in the Works*, 12; Appendix 3.

100  Ibid., Appendix 1.
101  Speech by Barbara McDougall, Canada, House of Commons, *Debates*, 6 June 1989, 2675.
102  Canada, *Success in the Works*, 5.
103  This would include paying not only for income maintenance for UI recipients taking training, but also for the purchasing of courses. This had previously been paid for through the Canadian Job Strategy out of general revenues. McDougall, House of Commons, *Debates*, 6 June 1989, 2676.
104  Canada, *Success in the Works*, 6–7.
105  Ibid., 8–9.
106  Throne Speech, Canada, House of Commons, *Debates*, 3 April 1989, 3–4.
107  See Canada, House of Commons, Legislative Committee on Bill C-21, *Minutes of Proceedings and Evidence*, statements by Timothy Reid, Canadian Chamber of Commerce, 26 September 1989, 16:121–123. John Howatson, Canadian Manufacturers Association, 6 September 1989, 3:7–3:13; Barrie Sprawson, Board of Trade of Metro Toronto, 6 September 1989, 3:44–3:46.
108  See, for example, comments by McDougall, Canada, House of Commons, Legislative Committee on Bill C-21, *Minutes*, 3 October 1989, 19:8; Ibid., McCreath, 28 September 1989, 18:32–33.
109  Presentation by CLC, Canada, House of Commons, Legislative Committee on Bill C-21, *Minutes*, 28 September 1989, 18:26–27. The CLC commissioned a study by Global Economics. The United Steelworkers of America hired Tristat Resources to make an independent assessment of the changes. Its analysis also led to the conclusion that the government data massively understated the impact of cuts on UI benefits, and that the impact on Quebec and Atlantic Canada had been understated while that on Ontario had been overstated. Also, low-income Canadians would be the most severely hit. See Gerard Docquier, Hugh Mackenzie and Richard Shillington, *Victimizing the Unemployed: How UI Cuts Will Promote Poverty in Canada* (Ottawa: Canadian Centre for Policy Alternatives, December 1989).
110  OFL Submission, Canada, House of Commons, Legislative Committee on Bill C-21, *Minutes*, 6 September 1989, 3:36.
111  Ibid.
112  Ibid., Earl McCurdy, Fishermen, Food and Allied Workers' Union, 18 September 1989, 11:7–11:9.
113  Ibid. See, for example, comments by Linda Torney, Labour Council of Metro Toronto, 6 September 1989, 3:73–3:82; Bob Sutton, Hamilton and

District Labour Council, 6 September 1989, p 3:26–3:28; Rosalyn Water, Etobicoke Anti-Poverty Coalition, 6 August 1989, 3:18–3:19; Brenda Wall, Metro Labour Education and Skills Training Centre, 6 September 1989, 3:62–3:66.

114 Canada, Employment and Immigration Canada, *Success in the Works, a Labour Force Development Strategy for Canada: Analysis of Structural Changes to the UI Program* (Ottawa, 1989) 25, 39. Cited in CACSW, *Submission to the Legislative Committee on Bill C-21, An Act to Amend the Unemployment Insurance Act* (Ottawa: The Council, 1989), 7.

115 NAC, *The Problem Is Still Jobs* (1989), 2, 4; NAC, *A Critical Time for Canada's Unemployment Insurance Programme: A Brief to the Special Committee of the Senate on Bill C-21* (January 1990); Laurell Ritchie, 'Bad Signs for Working Women: Overhaul of Unemployment Insurance Program May Hit Them Hard,' *The Globe and Mail* (27 April 1989).

116 CACSW, *Submission to the Legislative Committee on Bill C-21*, 7; NAC, *A Critical Time* (1990) 7.

117 Robin A. LeDrew, B.C. and Yukon Association of Women's Centres, Canada, House of Commons, Legislative Committee on Bill C-21, *Minutes*, 11 September 1989, 6:76.

118 Ibid., PEI Advisory Council on the Status of Women, 20 September 1989, 13:18.

119 19. Ibid., Mrs Marleau, Sudbury, 5 September 1989, 2:22. The problems women face finding work in single-industry towns was also pointed to by the Saskatchewan Action Committee on the Status of Women, 14 September 1989, 9:28.

120 Ibid., Trish Elliott, Saskatchewan Action Committee on the Status of Women, 14 September 1989, 9:25–9:26.

121 Ibid. the Rev. Leslie Jay, Church and Society Committee of the Maritime Conference of the United Church of Canada, appearing with the Atlantic Region Coalition for Fair Unemployment Insurance, 20 September 1989, 13:91–13:92.

122 Ibid. See, for example, comments by Community Unemployed Help Centre, Manitoba, 15 September 1989; Saskatchewan Action Committee on the Status of Women, 14 September 1989, 9:27; NAC, *The Problem Is Still Jobs*, 16; CACSW, *Submission* (1989); comments by Warren Allmand, Canada, House of Commons, *Debates*, 11 April 1989, 318–19.

123 Liberal UI critic Warren Allmand argued that between 1984 and 1989 employment and training programs were cut by 30 per cent, a reduction of $700 million. The Conservatives were now proposing to put $800 million back into training programs, but rather than paying for them out

of general revenues, they were now to be paid for from the UI Fund. Canada, House of Commons, *Debates*, 11 April 1989, 318–19.

124 CACSW, *Submission* (1989), 9. Cites Employment and Immigration Canada, *Success in the Works: A Labour Force Development Strategy for Canada: Analysis of Structural Changes in the UI Program* (Ottawa, 1989).

125 See, for example, comments by Community Unemployed Help Centre, Manitoba, Canada, House of Commons, Legislative Committee on Bill C-21, *Minutes*, 15 September 1989, 10:7; Dawn Black, NDP MP, Canada, House of Commons, *Debates*, 12 April 1989, 391; 25 April 1989, 958.

126 This point was made, for example, by the B.C. and Yukon Association of Women's Centres. Canada, House of Commons, Legislative Committee on Bill C-21, *Minutes*, 11 September 1989, 6:79.

127 Ibid., 6 September 1989, 3:91–3:92.

128 On pressure to accept any job, see, for example, ibid., Gilles Ouellet, Canadian Conference of Catholic Bishops, 25 September 1989, 15:5; NAC, *The Problem Is Still Jobs*.

129 NAC, *The Problem Is Still Jobs*, 18.

130 NAC, *The Problem Is Still Jobs*; CACSW, *Submission* (1989), 14.

131 CACSW, *Submission* (1989), 8, 20.

132 See William Walker, 'Vicki's Baby Won't Wait for Parliament,' *Toronto Star* (12 May 1990).

133 See William Walker, 'Tory Senators Pass UI Bill as Liberals Cry "Shame,"' *Toronto Star* (23 October 1990).

134 Statistics Canada, *Women in the Labour Force 1994*, cat. 75-507E, Table 1.1., 10.

135 Ibid., Table 2.4, 18.

136 See Henry Pold, 'Jobs! Jobs! Jobs!' Statistics Canada, *Perspectives*, (cat. 75-001E), Autumn 1994. He also notes that between 1975 and 1993 almost half (46 per cent) of the job increase came from part-time jobs.

137 Statistics Canada, *Women in the Labour Force*, 1994, cat. 75-507E, Table 2.6, 19.

138 Harvey Krahn, 'Non-standard work on the rise,' Statistics Canada, *Perspectives* (Catalogue 75-001E), Winter 1995, 36.

139 See *From the Double Day to the Endless Day: Proceedings from the Conference on Homeworking, November 1992* (Canadian Centre for Policy Alternatives, April 1994).

140 Economic Council of Canada, *Employment in the Service Economy* (Ottawa: The Council, 1991), 81. Harvey Krahn similarly estimated that in 1989 almost one in three Canadians had a non-standard job. See Harvey Krahn, 'Non-Standard Work Arrangements,' Statistics Canada, *Perspectives on Labour and Income*, Winter 1991.

141 Ibid., 77–8.
142 Ibid., 80.
143 Ibid., 82.
144 Harvey Krahn, 'Non-Standard Work on the Rise,' Estimates are based on Statistics Canada General Social Survey. He examined part-time work, temporary or contract work, own-account self-employment, and multiple job holding.
145 Ibid., 40.
146 D. Van Cleef, 'Persons Working Long Hours,' *The Labour Force*, Statistics Canada cat. 71-001, May 1985; D. Gower, 'Characteristics of Persons with Long Work Weeks,' *The Labour Force*, Statistics Canada cat. 71-001, September 1986. Both quoted in Garnett Picot, John Mylesm and Ted Wannell, *Good Jobs, Bad Jobs and the Declining Middle: 1967–1986* (Statistics Canada 1990).
147 Picot et al., *Good Jobs, Bad Jobs*, 29–30.
148 Deborah Sunter and Rene Morissette, 'The Hours People Work,' Statistics Canada, *Perspectives on Labour and Income*, Autumn 1994.
149 Rene Morissette, John Myles, and Garnett Picot, 'Earnings Polarization in Canada, 1969–1991,' in Keith Banting and Charles Beach, eds., *Labour Market Polarization and Social Policy Reform* (Kingston: Queen's University School of Policy Studies, 1995), 24.
150 Deborah Sunter and Rene Morissette, 'The Hours People Work.'
151 See speech by Don Mazankowski, Deputy Prime Minister and Minister of Finance, Canada, House of Commons, *Debates*, 2 December 1992, 14417–27.
152 Patrick Doyle, 'Be Proud to Take Cut in Payments, Valcourt Tells Jobless,' *Toronto Star* (4 December 1992).
153 Edison Stewart, 'Opposition Says Tory Moves Put Women at Risk,' *Toronto Star* (4 December 1992).
154 Rosemary Speirs, 'Tories Chided for Calling UI Protesters Separatists,' *Toronto Star* (10 February 1993).
155 See Canada, House of Commons, Legislative Committee on Bill C-113, *Minutes of Proceedings and Evidence*, comments by John Howatson, Canadian Manufacturers' Association, 10 March 1993, 4:22–4:25; Michael Walker, Fraser Institute, 11 March 1993, 6:4–6:9; comments by Timothy Reid, David McLean, Canadian Chamber of Commerce, quoted in McInnes, *The Globe and Mail* (4 December 1992); Shawn McCarthy, 'UI changes Necessary, Business Group Says,' *Toronto Star* (9 February 1993).
156 Comments by Linda Torney, Metro Toronto Labour Council, Judy Rebick, NAC, quoted in Craig McInnes, 'Changes to UI Harm Workers, Critics Charge,' *Globe and Mail* (4 December 1992); comments by Liberal MP

Mary Clancy, quoted in Rosemary Speirs, '"Scandalous" UI Plan Neglects Women Victims MP Complains,' *Toronto Star* (9 December 1992).

157 Quoted in Craig McInnes, 'Changes to UI Harm Workers.'

158 Hugh Winsor, 'The High and Bumpy Road,' *The Globe and Mail* (4 December 1992).

159 The study had been conducted for the Department of Employment and Immigration by Frank Graves for Ekos Research Associates shortly after Mazankowski's announcement. See Graham Fraser, 'Widening Split Along Class Lines Revealed by Proposed UI Changes,' *The Globe and Mail* (2 March 1993).

160 Ross Howard, 'Tories Stall Quebec Revolt over UI Change,' *The Globe and Mail* (1 February 1993); Shawn McCarthy, '8 Quebec MPs Rebel over UI Bill,' *Toronto Star* (27 January 1993); Lysiane Gagnon, 'The UI Outcry Was Just the Issue the Bloc Needed,' *The Globe and Mail* (20 February 1993).

161 Graham Fraser, 'Ottawa Proposes, Quebec Disposes,' *The Globe and Mail* (10 February 1993).

162 Leslie Papp, 'Labor Vows to Step Up Battle Against UI Cuts,' *Toronto Star* (5 February 1993).

163 A Gallup poll taken in mid-February showed that 54 per cent opposed changes that would severely limit benefits and eligibility, while only 33 per cent favoured such a move. For a description of the surveys, see Nicolaas van Rijn, 'Majority Oppose UI Changes, Poll Shows,' *Toronto Star* (20 February 1993).

164 For description of Bill C-113 changes, see Mazankowski speeches, Canada, House of Commons, *Debates*, 18 February 1993, 16103–11; Canada, House of Commons, Legislative Committee on Bill C-113, *Minutes*, 8 March 1993, 1:56–1:65; Government of Canada, *News Release*, 17 February 1993.

165 Prior to 1990, just cause was not defined in the legislation. The guidelines used arose from jurisprudence.

166 Government of Canada, *News release*, 17 February 1993, Backgrounder #3. The fourteen reasons now enumerated as being 'just cause' for leaving employment were (a) sexual or other harassment; (b) obligation to accompany a spouse or dependent child to another residence; (c) discrimination on a prohibited ground of discrimination within the meaning of the Canadian Human Rights Act; (d) working conditions that constitute a danger to health or safety; (e) obligation to care for a child or an immediate family member; (f) reasonable assurance of another employment in the immediate future; (g) significant modification of terms and conditions respecting wages or salary; (h) excessive overtime work or refusal to pay

for overtime work; (i) significant changes in work duties; (j) antagonistic relations between an employee and a supervisor for which the employee is not primarily responsible; (k) employer's practices that are contrary to the law; (l) discrimination with regard to employment because of membership in an employee organization; (m) undue pressure by an employer on employees to leave their employment; and (n) such other circumstances as are prescribed. (Item 'n' would allow Employment and Immigration Canada to make further regulations on 'just cause'.)

167 Canada, House of Commons, Legislative Committee on Bill C-113, *Minutes*, 8 March 1993, 1:57–1:61.

168 Ibid., 1:57.

169 It was reported, for example, that referees criticized people for not approaching the CACSW, or for not going to see their union. Claimants were supposed to exhaust all other means open to them before leaving their jobs. See comments by Mouvement Action-chomage, Canada, House of Commons, Legislative Committee on Bill C-113, *Minutes*, 9 March 1993, 2:38.

170 Ibid. See comments by William DeMerchant, Mouvement Action Chomage, 9 March 1993, 2:25–2:40; CLC, 11 March 1993, 5A:40–55; NAC, 15 March 1993, 7:5–7:26; National Association of Women and the Law, 15 March 1993, 7:27–7:33.

171 Ibid., 15 March 1993, 8:5–8:6.

172 Ibid., National Association of Women and the Law, 15 March 1993, 7:30; NAC, 15 March 1993.

173 Ibid., 15 March 1993, 7:28.

174 Nicholas Ionides, 'Planned UI Cuts Cudgel for Bosses, Groups Charge,' *The The Globe and Mail* (15 March 1993).

175 Jean-Pierre Blackburn voted against it. Another Quebec Conservative who opposed the bill Guy St-Julien, was absent. Shawn McCarthy, 'Tory MPs Ram through Vote on UI,' *Toronto Star* (25 March 1993).

176 'Tougher UI Rules Passed into Law,' *Toronto Star* (3 April 1993); Shawn McCarthy, 'Tory MPs Ram Through Vote on UI.'

177 This is consistent with Pat Armstrong's findings that in terms of participation rates, employment patterns, and conditions of work there was a downward harmonization for women and men. Pat Armstrong, 'The Feminization of the Labour Force: Harmonizing Down in a Global Economy,' in Isabella Bakker, ed., *Rethinking Restructuring: Gender and Change in Canada* (Toronto: University of Toronto Press, 1996).

178 See comments by Mary Clancy, Canada, House of Commons, *Debates*, 29 May 1989.

## 8: Consolidating Neoliberal Reforms

1 Figures derived from Table 7.2.

2 See, for example, Ricardo Grinspun and Robert Kreklewich, 'Consolidating Neoliberal Reforms: "Free Trade" as a Conditioning Framework,' *Studies in Political Economy* 43 (Spring 1994).

3 Keith Banting, 'Social Policy,' in Bruce Doern, et al., eds., *Border Crossings: The Internationalization of Canadian Public Policy* (Toronto: University of Toronto Press, 1996).

4 See C. Bergqvist and S. Findlay, 'Representing Women's Interests in the Policy Process: Women's Organizing and State Initiatives in Sweden and Canada, 1960s–1990s,' in L. Briskin and M. Eliasson, *Women's Organizing, Public Policy and Social Change in Sweden and Canada* (Montreal & Kingston: McGill-Queen's University Press, 1999); Sandra Burt and Sonya Lynn Hardman, 'The Case of Disappearing Targets: The Liberals and Gender Equality,' in Leslie A. Pal, ed., *How Ottawa Spends, 2001–2002* (Don Mills: Oxford University Press, 2001); Sylvia Bashevkin, *Women on the Defensive: Living Through Conservative Times* (Toronto: University of Toronto Press, 1998), 224–5.

5 Burt and Hardman, 'The Case of Disappearing Targets.'

6 Ibid., 210.

7 Canada, Statistics Canada, *Women in Canada 2000*, cat. 89-513XPE, 108.

8 G. Picot and A. Heisz, 'The Labour Market in the 1990s,' *Canadian Economic Observer* (January 2000).

9 Ibid., 3.9–4.0.

10 Ibid., 3.8.

11 Canada, Human Resources Development Canada, Applied Research Branch, 'An Analysis of Employment Insurance Benefit Coverage,' W-98-35E, October 1998, 45; Canada, Statistics Canada, *Women in Canada 2000* (Ottawa, 2000) 109.

12 Canada, HRDC, 'An Analysis of Employment Insurance Benefit Coverage,' 15–16; Picot and Hiesz, 'The Labour Market in the 1990s,' 3.3.

13 Richard Chaykowski and Lisa M. Powell, 'Women and the Labour Market: Recent Trends and Policy Issues,' *Canadian Public Policy* XXV Supplement, 1 (1999), S4.

14 Canada, Labour Canada, *Women in the Labour Force, 1990–91*, Table 8, 22; Chaykowski and Powell, 'Women and the Labour Market.'

15 Canada, Statistics Canada, *Women in Canada 2000*, 103.

16 Ibid., Table 5.9, 123.

17 Canada, Employment and Immigration Canada, *Success in the Works: A Policy Paper* (Ottawa, 1989), 11.
18 See Canada, Human Resources Development Canada, *Proposed Changes to the Unemployment Insurance Program: Backgrounder* (Ottawa, February, 1994), 18. Previously the minimum requirement was ten weeks' work, available if unemployment was 15 per cent or higher. The minimum was increased to twelve weeks, available at a 13 per cent or higher unemployment rate.
19 Ibid., 3.
20 According to the new formula, those with less than forty weeks worked would receive one week of benefits for every two weeks of work. For anything worked beyond that, there would be one week of benefits for each week worked, to a maximum of 12 weeks of benefits. Those living in areas of high unemployment would receive additional weeks of benefit. For example, someone with thirty-five weeks of work (in an area with an unemployment rate between 10 and 11 per cent) would see their maximum claim reduced from forty-five weeks to thirty-one weeks – a decrease of about 31 per cent. For those working fifty-two weeks the maximum duration of benefits would be reduced from fifty weeks to forty-six weeks – a decrease of about 8 per cent. See benefit schedules, *Unemployment Insurance Act* (Office Consolidation 27 May 1991), Table 2, 100 and Human Resources Development Canada, *Proposed Changes*, Annex I, 16.
21 In September 1994 Prime Minister Chrétien announced a 'jobs and growth' agenda consisting of four key components: reforming social security; ensuring a healthy fiscal climate; reviewing government priorities and programs, and strengthening the Canadian economy. See Canada, *Improving Social Security in Canada: A Discussion Paper* (Ottawa: Human Resources Development Canada, 1994), 5.
22 In the summer of 1993, a new 'superministry' combining elements from five departments, including Health and Welfare, Labour and Employment and Immigration, had been created. This was just before the Conservatives left power. See Herman Bakvis, 'Shrinking the House of "AHRIF"': Program Review and the Department of Human Resouces Development,' Gene Swimmer, ed., *How Ottawa Spends 1996–97* (Ottawa: Carleton University Press, 1996).
23 The discussion paper released by Axworthy was Canada, *Improving Social Security in Canada: A Discussion Paper* (Ottawa: Human Resources Development Canada, 1994). Those released by Martin were Canada, *A New Framework for Economic Policy* (Ottawa: Department of Finance, 1994) and

Canada, *Creating a Healthy Fiscal Climate* (Ottawa: Department of Finance, 1994).
24  Canada, *Improving Social Security.*
25  Ibid., 8.
26  Ibid., 9.
27  Ibid., 21.
28  Ibid., 23.
29  Ibid., 52.
30  See Ken Battle and Sherri Tjorman, 'How Finance Re-Formed Social Policy,' in Daniel Drache and Andrew Ranachan, eds., *Warm Heart, Cold Country: Fiscal and Social Policy Reform in Canada* (Ottawa: The Caledon Institute of Social Policy, 1995), 419.
31  Canada, *Improving Social Security*, 47.
32  A more detailed discussion of these two options was provided in Canada, *From Unemployment Insurance to Employment Insurance: A Supplementary Paper* (Ottawa: Minster of Human Resources Development, 1994).
33  The committee received over 1,200 submissions and 25,000 workbooks with responses to the proposed changes and delivered its own report to the House of Commons in January 1995. Canada, House of Commons, Report of the Standing Committee on Human Resources Development, *Security, Opportunity and Fairness: Canadians Renewing their Social Programs* (Ottawa, 1995), Introduction.
34  In addition to reports from hearings, see Keith Banting and Ken Battle, eds., *A New Vision for Canada? Perspectives on the Federal Discussion Paper on Social Security Reform* (Queen's School of Policy Studies, Caledon Institute: 1994); Caledon Institute, *Critical Commentaries on the Social Security Review* (Ottawa: The Caledon Institute of Social Policy, 1995); Daniel Drache and Andrew Ranachan, eds., *Warm Heart, Cold Country*; Institute for Research on Public Policy, 'The IRPP Position: Axworthy Proposals: Too Timid, Reforms Should Go Further,' *Choices*, 1, no. 1; Institute for Research on Public Policy, 'Commentaries on the Axworthy Green Paper,' *Choices* 1, no. 2; Jane Pulkingham and Gordon Ternowetsky, eds., *Remaking Canadian Social Policy: Social Security in the Late 1990s* (Halifax: Fernwood, 1996).
35. See, for example, Battle and Torjman, 'Green Light, Red Flag: Caledon Statement on the Social Security Review,' in *Critical Commentaries on the Social Security Review*, 222.
36  Canada, House of Commons, *Security, Opportunity and Fairness*, 88.
37  Canada, House of Commons, *Security, Opportunity and Fairness*, 43–4. On the latter point, see also CLC statement, Canada, House of Commons, Committee on Human Resources Development, *Minutes of Proceedings and*

*Evidence*, 3 November 1994; 32:26–32:28; Ken Battle, 'Foreword,' in Caledon Institute, *Critical Commentaries*, 2–3.

38  IRPP, 'The IRPP Position: Axworthy Proposals too Timid.'
39  Ibid., 5.
40  See NAC presentation, Canada, House of Commons, Committee on Human Resources Development, *Minutes of Proceedings and Evidence*, 8 November 1994, 35:67–35:73; NAWL 8 November 1994, 35:109–35:114; CACSW, *Submission to the Ministerial Task Force on Social Security Reform* (Ottawa: The Council, March 1994). The CACSW also commissioned four authors to evaluate the gender impact of various aspects of the social security review. On UI, see Monica Townson, 'Research Notes: The Social Security Review and Its Implications for Women: #4 Unemployment Insurance' (Ottawa: The Council, 1994).
41  Leah Vosko pointed out that while overall men in the early 1990s made more repeat claims than women, the latter made up a *growing* proportion of frequent claimants. Leah Vosko, 'Recreating Dependency: Women, Unemployment and Federal Proposals for UI Reform,' in Drache and Ranachan, *Warm Heart, Cold Country*, 220–1. Cites Employment and Immigration Canada, 'The Unemployment Insurance Program and the Canadian Labour Market (Additional Information),' unpublished brief, 1993.
42  Canada, *From Unemployment Insurance to Employment Insurance: A Supplementary Paper* (Ottawa: Human Resources Development Canada, 1994), Table 4.1, 33.
43  See Keith G. Banting, 'The Social Policy Review: Policy Making in a Semi-Sovereign Society,' *Canadian Public Administration* 38, no. 2 (Summer 1995); James J. Rice, 'Redesigning Welfare: The Abandonment of a National Commitment,' in Susan Phillips, ed., *How Ottawa Spends, 1995–96* (Ottawa. Carleton University Press, 1995); Herman Bakvis, 'Shrinking the House of "HRIF."' On widespread opposition, see Derek Ferguson, 'Acrimony Rises on All Sides over Social Reforms,' *Toronto Star* (17 December 1994).
44  On the increasing influence of the Department of Finance over social policy, see Battle and Tjorman, 'How Finance Reformed Social Policy,' 418.
45  Edward Greenspon, 'Social Reforms Take Back Seat: Deficit, Unity Problems More Rressing, Axworthy Acknowledges,' *The Globe and Mail* (31 January 1995); Edward Greenspon, 'Why a Left-Winger Skated Off Side,' *The Globe and Mail* (15 February 1995).
46  James J. Rice and Michael J. Prince, *Changing Politics of Canadian Social Policy* (Toronto: University of Toronto Press, 2000), 143. Rice and Prince define the 'fiscalization' of social policy as a 'period when financial con-

cerns, especially considerations of expenditure restraint and deficit reduction, dominate deliberations on setting public priorities.'
47 Canada, Department of Finance, *Budget Speech*, The Honourable Paul
Martin, Minister of Finance, 27 February 1995, 7.
48 Ibid., 8.
49 Canada, Department of Finance, *Budget in Brief*, February 1995; Canada,
Department of Finance, Paul Martin, Minister of Finance, *Budget Speech*,
February 1995.
50 Canada, Department of Finance, *Budget Speech*, 16, italics in original.
51 Canada, Department of Finance, *Budget in Brief*, 11–12.
52 See, for example, Edward Greenspon, 'Axworthy Drops Two-Tier UI Plan,'
*The Globe and Mail* (16 May 1995); 'Axworthy Grilled on UI Proposals,' *The
Globe and Mail* (13 June 1995); 'Liberals Lay Groundwork for UI Overhaul,'
*The Globe and Mail* (10 August 1995).
53 Edward Greenspon, 'Atlantic Politicians Lean on Axworthy,' *The Globe and
Mail* (20 October 1995).
54 Edward Greenspon, 'Empoyers Target Ottawa over UI Savings,' *The Globe
and Mail* (17 August 1995).
55 Edward Greenspon, 'Unity Issue Delays Axworthy Reforms,' *The Globe
and Mail* (28 November 1995); Bob White, President, CLC, *The Globe and
Mail* (17 August 1995).
56 Canada, *A 21st Century Employment System for Canada: Guide to the Employment Insurance Legislation* (Ottawa, December 1995), 19.
57 Ibid., 1.
58 Canada, Human Resources Development Canada, *Employment Insurance: A
Guide to Employment Insurance* (July 1996), 1.
59 See Canada, *A 21st Century Employment System for Canada: Guide to the
Employment Insurance Legislation*, December 1995, 5–6.
60. Twelve weeks at fifteen hours a week.
61 Twelve weeks at thirty-five hours.
62 Canada, *Employment Insurance Act*, July 1996, section 6(4).
63 Canada, *A 21st Century Employment System*, 18.
64 Ibid.
65 'Benefit levels are based on total earnings during all weeks of work within
the 26 week period immediately preceding the establishment of a claim.
These earnings are then averaged by dividing by the minimum divisor
(ie 14 to 22, as determined by the unemployment rate in the region) or the
actual weeks of work, whichever is higher.' Canada, Employment Insurance Commission, *1997 Employment Insurance Monitoring and Assessment
Report*, 3; see also Canada, Human Resources Development Canada,

*Employment Insurance: A Guide to Employment Insurance* (Ottawa, July 1996),
6–8. Previously benefits were 55 per cent of earnings during the last
twelve to twenty weeks of work (depending on the regional rate of unemployment). For a analysis of the implications of these changes in Atlantic
Canada, see Martha MacDonald, 'Restructuring, Gender and Social Security Reform in Canada,' *Journal of Canadian Studies* 34, no. 2 (Summer
1999).

66 Specifically, claimants lose one percentage point for every additional
twenty weeks of benefits received in the previous five-year period, to a
floor of 50 per cent.

67 Canada, *A 21st Century Employment System*, 12.

68 Ibid., 12.

69 Human Resources Development Canada, *A Guide to Employment Insurance*
(July 1996). Claimants with annual incomes 'well above average' and who
had received more than 120 weeks of benefits in the last five years (over
twenty-four weeks each year) were now required to pay back 100 per cent
of their benefits.

70 Ibid., 11.

71 Canada, *A 21st Century Employment System*, 7–8. For example, previously
someone working for forty-five hours a week and another for twenty
hours a week would both have been eligible for the same number of
weeks of benefits. Under the new system, those working forty-five hours
are entitled to thirty-two weeks of benefits (in an 11.5 per cent unemployment region), while those working twenty would only be entitled to
twenty-three weeks.

72 Canada, *A 21st Century Employment System*, 16.

73 Ibid., 21–4.

74 The amendment meant that the clawback would not apply to first-time
claimants or to those collecting sickness, maternity, or parental benefits.
In addition, for frequent claimants, the net income above which benefits
must be paid back was increased from $39,000 to $48,750, and the maximum repayment above this threshold limited to 30 per cent.

75 See Canada, House of Commons, *Debates*, 5 February 2001, statement by
Raymonde Folco (Parliamentary Secretary to Minister of Human Resouces
Development).

76 Human Resources Development Canada, *Employment Insurance: A Guide to
Employment Insurance*, July 1996, 2.

77 Canada, Human Resources Development Canada, 'Employment Insurance: Gender Impact Analysis,' submitted to the House of Commons,
Standing Committee on Human Resources Development, 24 January 1996.

78  Ibid., ii. In the June 1996 revised impact analysis following amendments made to the legislation, it was estimated that total benefits would be reduced by 7 per cent for women and 10 per cent for men. Canada, Human Resources Development Canada, 'Update of Gender Impact Analysis,' June 1996.
79  Canada, Human Resources Development Canada, 'Employment Insurance: Gender Impact Analysis,' Submitted to the House of Commons Standing Committee on Human Resources Development, 24 January 1996, 5.
80  Canada, Human Resources Development Canada, 'Analysis of Employment Insurance Benefit Coverage,' October 1998. This study estimated that less than 50 per cent of the decline between 1990 and 1997 could be attributed to changes to the EI program and that over 50 per cent was a result of other factors, such as changes in the composition of the workforce and unemployment (e.g., more long-term unemployed).
81  CLC figures showed that the proportion of unemployed women receiving UI dropped from 37 per cent in 1996 to 31 per cent in 1997 while the proportion of unemployed men receiving dropped from 44 to 39 per cent. Canadian Labour Congress, *Left out in the Cold: The End of UI for Canadian Workers* (1999), 3. The proportion for both is lower because these figures exclude UI recipients who are receiving some earnings.
82  Canada, Human Resources Development Canada, *1998 Employment Insurance Monitoring and Assessment Report*, submitted to the Minister of Human Resources Development Canada by the Canada Employment Insurance Commission, 18 December 1998, ii. The EI legislation specified that a report measuring the impact of the EI changes had to be undertaken in each of the first five years of operation.
83  CLC, *Unemployment Insurance Bulletin* 4, no. 1 (February 2002).
84  In 1999–2000 men filed about two-thirds of frequent claims and more than two-thirds of all claimants affected by the intensity rule were men. Canada Employment Insurance Commission, *Employment Insurance 2000 Monitoring and Assessment Report*, 8, 10.
85  Ibid., 11.
86  In contrast, 43 per cent of men compared to 39 per cent of women worked between thirty-five and forty hours and 15 per cent of men compared to 7 per cent of women worked between forty-one and forty-nine hours per week. Karen Hall, 'Hours Polarization at the End of the 1990s,' *Perspectives* (Summer 1999), 30.
87  Note well that this is a different definition of re-entrant than used in the *Employment Insurance Act*.
88  Statistics Canada, *Women in Canada 2000*, 109.
89  Statistics Canada, *Women in Canada: A Statistical Report*, 1995, Table 3.7, 28.

The average length of time unemployed has increased substantially for both men and women since the early 1980s. In 1980, 15 per cent of both male and female unemployed had been unemployed more than six months. This increased to 21 per cent of unemployed men and 19 per cent of unemployed women in 1989. See Gary Cohen, 'Then and Now: The Changing Face of Unemployment,' *Perspectives on Labour and Income* (Spring 1991). In 1993 almost one-third of unemployed men (32.8 per cent) had been unemployed more than six months (twenty-six weeks), with 15.6 per cent unemployed for more than a year. For women, the figures were 28 and 11.2 per cent.

90  Further research is needed to verify the exact factors behind the drop in this ratio.

91  Canada, Human Resources Development Canada, *1998 Employment Insurance Monitoring and Assessment Report*, ii; in 1999–2000, 55 per cent of these payments were to women. Canada, Human Resources Development Canada, *2000 Employment Insurance Monitoring and Assessment Report*, 17.

92  Shelley Phipps et al., 'Gender Equity within Families versus Better Targeting: An Assessment of the Family Income Supplement to Employment Insurance Benefits,' *Canadian Public Policy* 27, no. 4 (2001), 429–30.

93  Vosko, 'Irregular Workers, New Involuntary Social Exiles'; Pulkingham, 'Remaking the Social Divisions of Welfare.'

94  Ann Shola Orloff, 'Gender and the Social Rights of Citizenship: State Policies and Gender Relations in Comparative Perspective,' *American Sociological Review* 58, no. 3 (1993).

95  Indicative of this shift, the most recent EI bill ended the role that the EI Commission had in providing advice on the level of premiums, and that decision is now made by the federal Cabinet alone. *The Globe and Mail*, 6 February 2001.

96  Katherine Scott, 'The Dilemma of Liberal Citizenship: Women and Social Assistance Reform in the 1990s,' *Studies in Political Economy* 50 (Summer 1996); Pulkingham, 'Remaking the Social Divisions of Welfare.'

97  Gregory Albo, '"Competitive Austerity" and the Impasse of Capitalist Employment Policy,' in Ralph Miliband and Leo Panitch, eds., *Socialist Register 1994* (London: Merlin Press, 1994).

98  Pulkingham, 'Remaking the Social Divisions of Welfare'; MacDonald, 'Restructuring, Gender and Social Security Reform in Canada.'

## Conclusion

1  Between 1967 and 1989 the number of dual-earner families increased from one-third to 62 per cent of all husband-wife families. See Raj K. Chawla,

'The Changing Profile of Dual-Earner Families,' *Perspectives on Labour and Income* (Summer 1992).

2 See John Myles and Paul Pierson, 'Friedman's Revenge: The Reform of "Liberal" Welfare States in Canada and the United States,' *Politics and Society* 25, no. 4 (1997).

3 Anne Showstack Sassoon, 'Women's New Social Role: Contradictions of the Welfare State,' in Anne Showstack Sassoon, ed., *Women and the State* (London: Unwin Hyman, 1987); Linda McDowell; 'Life without Father and Ford: the New Gender Order of Post-Fordism,' *Transactions of the Institute of British Geographers* 16 (1991).

# Bibliography

## Archival Sources

*National Archives of Canada* (NAC)

Canadian Federation of Business and Professional Women's Clubs Papers MG28
Canadian Labour Congress Files MG28
Department of Labour Records RG27
Gill Commission Records RG 33/48
Grace MacInnis Files MG32
National Council of Women Papers MG28
Stanley Knowles Papers MG32
Status of Women Canada Files RG106
Unemployment Insurance Commission Records RG50

*Canadian Women's Movement Archives* (WMA), Morissette Library, University of Ottawa

National Action Committee on the Status of Women Files

## Labour Sources

Canadian Congress of Labour. *Proceedings of the Annual Convention.* 1949–55.
Trades and Labor Congress of Canada. *Report of the Proceedings of the Annual Convention.* 1949–55.

Canadian Labour Congress. *Left Out in the Cold: The End of UI for Canadian Workers* (1999).
Canadian Labour Congress. *Report of the Proceedings*. 1956–70.
Canadian Labour Congress. *Unemployment Insurance Bulletin* 4, no. 1 (February 2002).
*Canadian Unionist*. 1949–55.
*Trades and Labor Congress Journal*.
*Canadian Labour*. 1956–70.

## Women's Organizations: Sources and Publications

*Canadian Advisory Council on the Status of Women*

*Annual Reports*
*What's Been Done?* March 1974.
*Recommendations of the Canadian Advisory Council on the Status of Women by Subject*. January 1981.
*Recommendations*. 1973–88.
*Brief Presented to the Commission of Inquiry on Unemployment Insurance*. January 1986.
*Integration and Participation: Women's Work in the Home and in the Labour Force*. 1987.
*Submission to the Legislative Committee on Bill C-21, An Act to Amend the Unemployment Insurance Act*. 1989.

*National Action Committee on the Status of Women*

*Status of Women News*.
*Feminist Action*.
*Index of Abridged Resolutions of NAC, 1972 to 1989*.
*Presentation to the PM and Members of Cabinet*. 22 February 1979.
*The Problem Is Jobs ... Not Unemployment Insurance*. Brief to the Commission of Inquiry on Unemployment Insurance. January 1986.
*The Problem Is Still Jobs ... Not Unemployment Insurance, A Brief to the Legislative Committee on Bill C-21*. August 1989.
*A Critical Time for Canada's Unemployment Insurance Programme, a Brief to the Special Committee of the Senate on Bill C-21*. January 1990.

## Government Documents

Canada. *A 21st Century Employment System for Canada: Guide to the Employment Insurance Legislation*. Ottawa, December 1995.

Canada, Advisory Committee on Reconstruction. *Post-War Problems of Women: Final Report of the Subcommittee.* Ottawa, 1944.

Canada, Commission of Inquiry on Unemployment Insurance (Forget Commission). *Report.* Ottawa, 1986.

Canada, Department of Finance. *A New Direction for Canada: An Agenda for Economic Renewal.* Presented by the Minister of Finance, 8 November 1984.

Canada, Department of Finance. *A New Framework for Economic Policy.* Ottawa, 1994.

Canada, Department of Finance. *Budget in Brief.* February 1995.

Canada, Department of Finance, Paul Martin, Minister of Finance. *Budget Speech.* February 1995.

Canada, Department of Finance. *Creating a Healthy Fiscal Climate.* Ottawa, 1994.

Canada, Department of Labour. *Annual Reports.*

Canada, Department of Labour. *Canadian Labour Market.* 1946, various issues.

Canada, Department of Labour. *Changing Patterns in Women's Employment.* Report of a Consultation. Ottawa, 1966.

Canada, Department of Labour. *Labour Gazette.*

Canada, Department of Labour. *Labour Organization in Canada.*

Canada, Department of Labour. *Married Women Working for Pay in Eight Canadian Cities.* Ottawa, 1958.

Canada, Department of Labour. *Occupational Histories of Married Women Working for Pay in Eight Canadian Cities.* Ottawa, 1959.

Canada, Department of Labour. *Unemployment Insurance in the 70s.* Ottawa, 1970.

Canada, Department of Labour. *Women at Work in Canada.* Ottawa, 1964.

Canada, Department of Labour. *Women in the Labour Force, 1970: Facts and Figures.* Ottawa, 1971.

Canada, Department of Reconstruction. *Employment and Income with Special Reference to the Initial Period of Reconstruction.* Ottawa, 1945.

Canada, Dominion Bureau of Statistics. *Annual Report on Current Benefit Years under the Unemployment Insurance Act.* Ottawa, 1945.

Canada, *Employment Insurance Act and Other Related Legislation.* August 1996.

Canada, Employment Insurance Commission. *Employment Insurance Monitoring and Assessment Reports.* Annual. Ottawa, Human Resources Development Canada, 1997–2000.

Canada, House of Commons, Legislative Committee on Bill C-21. *Minutes of the Proceedings and Evidence.* 1989.

Canada, House of Commons, Legislative Committee on Bill C-113. *Minutes of the Proceedings and Evidence.* 1993.

Canada, House of Commons, Report of the Standing Committee on Human

Resources Development. *Security, Opportunity and Fairness: Canadians Renewing their Social Programs.* 1995.

Canada, House of Commons, Standing Committee on Labour, Manpower and Immigration. *Minutes of Proceedings and Evidence.* Various years.

Canada, House of Commons, Standing Committee on Industrial Relations. *Minutes of Proceedings and Evidence.* 1955.

Canada, House of Commons. *Debates.* 1946–94.

Canada, Ministry of Trade and Commerce and Dominion Bureau of Statistics. *Annual Report under the Corporations and Labour Unions Return Act, Part II: Labour Unions, 1963.* Ottawa, 1966.

Canada, Parliament, House of Commons, Sub-Committee on Equality Rights, *Equality for All: Report of the Parliamentary Committee on Equality Rights* (Boyer Committee). Ottawa, 1986.

Canada, Parliament, Special Joint Committee of the Senate and House of Commons on the Constitution of Canada. *Minutes of Proceedings and Evidence.* 1980.

Canada. *Report of the Commission on Equality in Employment.* (Abella Commission). Ottawa, 1984.

Canada. *Report of the Committee of Inquiry into the Unemployment Insurance Act* (Gill Committee Report). Ottawa, 1962.

Canada. *Report of the Royal Commission on the Economic Union and Development Prospects for Canada* (Macdonald Commission). Ottawa, 1985.

Canada. *Report of the Royal Commission on the Status of Women in Canada.* Ottawa, 1968.

Canada, Senate. *Proceedings of the Special Committee of the Senate on Manpower and Employment.* 1960.

Canada, Senate. *Report of the Special Committee of the Senate on Manpower and Employment.* Ottawa, 1961.

Canada, Unemployment Insurance Commission. *Digest of the Decisions of the Umpire.* Ottawa, 1960.

Canada, Unemployment Insurance Canada. *Comprehensive Review of the Unemployment Insurance Program in Canada.* Ottawa, 1977.

Canada, Unemployment Insurance Commission. *Annual Reports.*

Canada, Unemployment Insurance Commission. *Decisions of the Umpire.*

Canada, Unemployment Insurance Commission. *Digest of Benefit Entitlement Principles.* Ottawa, 1968.

Canada, Unemployment Insurance Commission. *Report of the Study for Updating the Unemployment Insurance Programme.* Ottawa, 1968.

Canadian Human Rights Commission. *Annual Reports.*

Canadian Human Rights Commission. *Newsletter.* Various issues.

Economic Council of Canada. *People and Jobs: A Study of the Canadian Labour Market*. Ottawa, 1976.

Employment and Immigration Canada. *Success in the Works: A Policy Paper*. Ottawa, 1989.

Employment and Immigration Canada. *Unemployment Insurance in the 1980s*. Ottawa, 1981.

Human Resources Development Canada. 'An Analysis of Employment Insurance Benefit Coverage.' Applied Research Branch, Strategic Policy, HRDC, October 1998.

Human Resources Development Canada. *Employment Insurance: A Guide to Employment Insurance*. Ottawa, July 1996.

Human Resources Development Canada. 'Employment Insurance: Gender Impact Analysis,' submitted to the House of Commons Standing Committee on Human Resources Development, 24 January 1996.

Human Resources Development Canada. *From Unemployment Insurance to Employment Insurance: A Supplementary Paper*. Ottawa, 1994.

Human Resources Development Canada. *Improving Social Security in Canada: A Discussion Paper*. Ottawa, 1994.

Human Resources Development Canada. *Proposed Changes to the Unemployment Insurance Program: Backgrounder*. Ottawa, 1994.

Human Resources Development Canada. 'Update of Gender Impact Analysis to reflect amendments made to Bill C-12 (Employment Insurance) at report stage in the House of Commons.' June 1996.

Human Resources Development Canada, Applied Research Branch. 'An Analysis of Employment Insurance Benefit Coverage,' W-98-35E. October 1998.

Labour Canada. *Part-Time Work in Canada: Report of the Commission of Inquiry into Part-Time Work*. (Wallace Commission). Ottawa, 1983.

Labour Canada. *Women in the Labour Force, 1990–1991*.

Labour Canada, Women's Bureau. *Women in the Labour Force: Facts and Figures (1973 edition)*. Ottawa, 1974.

Labour Canada, Women's Bureau. *Women in the Labour Force: Facts and Figures*. 1971.

Statistics Canada. *Women in Canada: A Statistical Report*. Ottawa, 1985.

Statistics Canada. *Women in the Labour Force, 1994*.

Statistics Canada. *Women in Canada 2000*. Ottawa, 2000.

Status of Women Canada. *Report of the Task Force on Childcare* (Katie Cooke Task Force). Ottawa, 1986.

Status of Women Canada. *Towards Equality for Women: A Progress Report, 1979–82*. Ottawa, Ministry of Supply and Services, 1984.

## Secondary Sources

Acker, Joan. 'Class, Gender and the Relations of Distribution.' *Signs* 13, no. 3 (1988).
– 'Rewriting Class, Race and Gender: Problems in Feminist Rethinking.' In *Revisioning Gender*, ed. Myra Marx Ferree, Judith Lorber, and Beth B. Hess. Walnut Creek, CA: AltaMira Press, 2000.
Aglietta, Michel. *A Theory of Capitalist Regulation*. London: New Left Books, 1979.
Akyeampong, Ernest B., 'Discouraged Workers – Where Have They Gone?' *Perspectives on Labour and Income*. Statistics Canada, Autumn, 1992.
Albo, Gregory. '"Competitive Austerity" and the Impasse of Capitalist Employment Policy.' In *Socialist Register 1994*, ed. Ralph Miliband and Leo Panitch. London: Merlin Press, 1994.
– 'The Impasse of Capitalist Employment Policy? Canada's Unemployment Experience, 1956–1974.' PhD thesis, Carleton University, 1994.
Andrew, Caroline, 'Women and the Welfare State.' *Canadian Journal of Political Science* 27, no. 4 (December 1984).
Andrew, Caroline, and Sanda Rodgers, eds. *Women and the Canadian State*. Montreal and Kingston: McGill-Queen's University Press, 1997.
Armstrong, Pat, 'Women and Unemployment,' *Atlantis* 6, no. 1 (Fall 1980).
– *Labour Pains: Women's Work in Crisis*. Toronto: The Women's Press, 1984.
– 'The Feminization of the Labour Force: Harmonizing Down in a Global Economy.' In *Rethinking Restructuring: Gender and Change in Canada*, ed. Isabella Bakker. Toronto: University of Toronto Press, 1996.
Armstrong, Pat, et al. *Exposing Privatization: Women and Health Care Reform in Canada*. Aurora: Garamond Press, 2002.
Armstrong, Pat, and Hugh Armstrong. 'The Segregated Participation of Women in the Canadian Labour Force, 1941–71.' *Canadian Review of Sociology and Anthropology* 12, no. 4, Part I (1975).
– 'Job Creation and Unemployment for Canadian Women.' In *Women and the World of Work*, ed. Anne Hoiberg. New York: Plenum Press, 1982.
– 'Beyond Sexless Class and Classless Sex: Towards Feminist Marxism.' *Studies in Political Economy* 10 (Winter 1983).
– *Theorizing Women's Work*. Toronto: Garamond Press, 1990.
– *The Double Ghetto: Canadian Women and Their Segregated Work*, 3rd ed., Toronto: McClelland & Stewart, 1994.
Armstrong, Pat, and M. Patricia Connelly, 'Feminism and Political Economy: An Introduction,' *Studies in Political Economy* 30 (Autumn 1989).
Aronson, Jane, and Sheila Neysmith. 'The Retreat of the State and Long-Term

Provisions: Implications for Frail Elderly People, Unpaid Family Carers and Paid Home Care Workers.' *Studies in Political Economy* 53 (Summer 1997).

Ayres, Jeffrey M. *Defying Conventional Wisdom: Political Movements and Popular Contention against North American Free Trade.* Toronto: University of Toronto Press, 1998.

Baillargeon, Denyse, 'La crise ordinaire: Les menageres montrealaises et la crise des anneees trente.' *Labour/Le Travail* 30 (1992).

Baines, Beverley, 'Women, Human Rights and the Constitution.' In *Women and the Constitution in Canada*, ed. Audrey Doerr and Micheline Carrier. Ottawa: Canadian Advisory Council on the Status of Women, 1981.

Bakker, Isabella, ed. *The Strategic Silence: Gender and Economic Policy.* London: Zed Books, 1988.

– *Rethinking Restructuring: Gender and Change in Canada.* Toronto: University of Toronto Press, 1996.

Bakvis, Herman, 'Shrinking the House of "HRIF": Program Review and the Department of Human Resources Development.' In *How Ottawa Spends 1996–97*, ed. Gene Swimmer. Ottawa: Carleton University Press, 1996.

Balbo, Laura, 'Crazy Quilts: Rethinking the Welfare State Debate from a Woman's Point of View.' In *Women and the State*, ed. Anne Showstack Sassoon. London: Unwin Hyman, 1987.

Banting, Keith G. *The Welfare State and Canadian Federalism*, 2nd ed. Kingston and Montreal: McGill-Queen's University Press, 1987.

– 'The Social Policy Review: Policy Making in a Semi-Sovereign Society,' *Canadian Public Administration* 38, no. 2 (Summer 1995).

– 'Social Policy.' In *Border Crossings: The Internationalization of Canadian Public Policy*, ed. Bruce Doern, L. Pal, and B. Tomlin. Don Mills: Oxford University Press, 1996.

Banting, Keith, and Ken Battle, eds. *A New Vision for Canada?: Perspectives on the Federal Discussion Paper on Social Security Reform.* Kingston: Queen's University School of Policy Studies, co-published by the Caledon Institute: 1994.

Banting, Keith G., and Charles M. Beach, eds. *Labour Market Polarization and Social Policy Reform.* Kingston: Queen's University School of Policy Studies, 1995.

Barrett, Michele. *Women's Oppression Today*, 2nd ed. London: Verso, 1988.

Barrett, Michele, and Mary McIntosh, 'Ethnocentrism and Socialist-Feminist Theory.' *Feminist Review* 20 (1985).

Bashkevin, Sylvia. *Women on Defensive: Living Through Conservative Times.* Toronto: University of Toronto Press, 1998.

Battle, Ken, and Sherri Torjman. 'Green Light, Red Flag: Caledon Statement on the Social Security Review.' In Caledon Institute, *Critical Commentaries on the Social Security Review.*

- 'How Finance Re-Formed Social Policy.' In *Warm Heart, Cold Country: Fiscal and Social Policy Reform in Canada*, ed. Daniel Drache and Andrew Ranachan. Ottawa: The Caledon Institute of Social Policy, 1995.
Begin, Monique, 'The Royal Commission on the Status of Women in Canada: Twenty Years Later.' In *Challenging Times: The Women's Movement in Canada and the United States*, ed. Constance Backhouse and David H. Flaherty. Montreal and Kingston: McGill-Queen's University Press, 1992.
Beneria, Lourdes. 'Globalization, Gender and the Davos Man.' *Feminist Economics* 5, no. 3 (1999).
Bergqvist, C., and S. Findlay. 'Representing Women's Interests in the Policy Process: Women's Organizing and State Initiatives in Sweden and Canada, 1960s-1990s.' In *Women's Organizing, Public Policy and Social Change in Sweden and Canada*, ed. L. Briskin and M. Eliasson. Montreal and Kingston: McGill-Queen's University Press, 1999.
Bhavnani, Kum•Kum, and Margaret Coulson. 'Transforming Socialist-Feminism: The Challenge of Racism.' *Feminist Review* 23 (June 1986).
Bleyer, Peter. 'Coalitions of Social Movements as Agencies for Social Change: The Action Canada Network.' In *Organizing Dissent: Contemporary Social Movements in Theory and Practice*, 2nd ed., ed. William K. Carroll. Toronto: Garamond Press, 1997.
Bock, Gisela, and Susan James, eds., *Beyond Equality and Difference: Citizenship, Feminist Politics and Female Subjectivity*. London: Routledge, 1992.
Boismenu, Gerard, and Daniel Drache, eds. *Politique et regulation: Modele de developpement et trajectoire canadienne*. Montreal: Meridien, 1990.
Borschorst, Anette, and Mirte Siim. 'Women and the Advanced Welfare State – A New Kind of Patriarchal Power?' In *Women and the State*, ed. Anne Showstack Sassoon. London: Unwin Hyman, 1987.
Boyd, Monica, and Edward Pryor, 'The Cluttered Nest: The Living Arrangements of Young Canadian Adults.' *Canadian Journal of Sociology and Anthropology* 14, no. 4 (1989).
Bradbury, Bettina. *Working Families: Age, Gender and Daily Survival in Industrializing Montreal*. Toronto: McClelland & Stewart, 1993.
Bradbury, Bettina, ed., *Canadian Family History*. Mississauga: Copp Clark Pitman, 1992.
Brand, Dionne. '"We Weren't Allowed to Go into Factory Work until Hitler Started the War" The 1920s to the 1940s.' In *'We're rooted here and they can't pull us up': Essays in African Canadian Women's History*, ed. Peggy Bristow et al. Toronto: University of Toronto Press, 1994.
- 'Black Women and Work: The Impact of Racially Constructed Gender Roles on the Sexual Division of Labour.' In *Scratching the Surface: Canadian Anti-*

*Racist, Feminist Thought*, ed. Enakshi Dua and Angela Robertson. Toronto: Women's Press, 1999.

Brandt, Gail Cuthbert. '"Pigeon-Holed and Forgotten": The Work of the Subcommittee on the Post-war Problems of Women, 1943.' *Histoire sociale/Social History* 15, no. 29 (May 1982).

Brenner, Johanna. 'The Best of Times, The Worst of Times: US Feminism Today.' *New Left Review* 200 (July/August 1993).

– 'Intersections, Locations and Capitalist Class Relations: Intersectionality from a Marxist Perspective.' In *Women and the Politics of Class*. New York: Monthly Review Press, 2000.

– *Women and the Politics of Class*. New York: Monthly Review Press, 2000.

Brenner, Robert, and Mark Glick. 'The Regulation Approach: Theory and History.' *New Left Review* 188 (July/August 1991).

Briskin, L., and M. Eliasson. *Women's Organizing Public Policy and Social Change in Sweden and Canada*. Montreal and Kingston: McGill-Queen's University Press, 1999.

Brodie, Janine. *Politics on the Margins: Restructuring and the Canadian Women's Movement*. Halifax: Fernwood, 1995.

– 'Restructuring and the Politics of Marginalization.' In *Women and Political Representation in Canada*, ed. Manon Tremblay and Caroline Andrew. Ottawa, University of Ottawa Press, 1998.

Brodie, Janine, ed. *Women and Canadian Public Policy*. Toronto: Harcourt Brace, 1996.

Brown, Ray, 'Unemployment Insurance and the National Employment Service,' *Labour Gazette* (September 1950).

Burstyn, Varda, 'Masculine Dominance and the State,' in *Socialist Register*. (London: Merlin Press, 1983).

Burt, Sandra. 'Women's Issues and the Women's Movement in Canada Since 1970.' In *The Politics of Gender, Ethnicity and Language in Canada*, ed. Alan Cairns and Cynthia Williams. Toronto: University of Toronto Press, 1986.

– 'Organized Women's Groups and the State.' In *Policy Communities and Public Policy in Canada: A Structural Approach*, ed. William D. Cole-man and Grace Skogstad. Mississauga: Copp Clark Pitman, 1990.

Burt, Sandra, and Sonya Lynn Hardman. 'The Case of Disappearing Targets: The Liberals and Gender Equality.' In *How Ottawa Spends, 2001–2002*, ed. Leslie A. Pal. Don Mills: Oxford University Press, 2001).

Caledon Institute. *Critical Commentaries on the Social Security Review*. Ottawa: The Caledon Institute of Social Policy, 1995.

Campbell, Robert Malcolm. *Grand Illusions: The Politics of the Keynesian Experience in Canada, 1945–1975*. Toronto: Broadview Press, 1987.

– 'The Full-Employment Objective in Canada in the Postwar Period.' In *Canadian Unemployment: Lessons from the 80s and Challenges for the 90s*, ed. Surendra Gera. Ottawa, Minister of Supply and Services Canada, 1991.

Carty, Linda. 'African Canadian Women and the State: "Labour only, please."' In *'We're rooted here and they can't pull us up': Essays in African Canadian Women's History*, ed. Peggy Bristow et al. Toronto: University of Toronto Press, 1994.

Chawla, Raj K. 'The Changing Profile of Dual-Earner Families.' In *Perspectives on Labour and Income*, published by Statistics Canada. Summer 1992.

Chaykowski, Richard P., and Lisa M. Powell. 'Women and the Labour Market: Recent Trends and Policy Issues.' *Canadian Public Policy* 25, Supplement, 1 (1999).

Clarke, Simon. 'Capitalist Crisis and the Rise of Monetarism.' In *Socialist Register*, Richard Miliband, Les Panitch, and John Seville, eds. London: Merlin Press, 1987.

Clayton, Richard, and Jonas Pontusson. 'Welfare State Retrenchment Revisited: Entitlement Cuts, Public Sector Restructuring, and Inegalitarian Trends in Advanced Capitalist Societies.' *World Politics* 51 (October 1998).

Clement, Wallace and John Myles. *Relations of Ruling: Class and Gender in Postindustrial Societies*. Montreal and Kingston: McGill-Queen's University Press, 1994.

Cohen, Gary. 'Then and Now: The Changing Face of Unemployment.' *Perspectives on Labour and Income*, Statistics Canada (Spring 1991).

Cohen, Marjorie. *The Macdonald Report and its Implications for Women*. National Action Committee on the Status of Women, 1985.

– *Women's Work, Markets and Economic Development in Nineteenth-Century Ontario*. Toronto: University of Toronto Press, 1988.

Collins, Patricia Hill. *Black Feminist Thought: Knowledge, Consciousness and the Politics of Empowerment*, 2nd ed. New York: Routledge, 2000.

Coutts, Jim. 'Expansion, Retrenchment and Protecting the Future: Social Policy in the Trudeau Years.' In *Towards a Just Society: The Trudeau Years*, ed. Thomas S. Axworthy and Pierre Elliott Trudeau. Markham: Viking, 1990.

Creese, Gillian. *Contracting Masculinity: Gender, Class and Race in a White-Collar Union, 1944–1994*. Don Mills: Oxford University Press, 1999.

Crenshaw, Kimberle Williams. 'Mapping the Margins: Intersectionality, Identity Politics and Violence Against Women of Color.' *Stanford Law Review* 43, no. 6 (1991).

Cuneo, Carl. 'State, Class and Reserve Labour: The Case of the 1941 Canadian Unemployment Insurance Act.' *Canadian Review of Sociology and Anthropology* 16, no. 2 (1979).

- 'State Mediation of Class Contradictions in Canadian Unemployment Insurance, 1930–1935.' *Studies in Political Economy* 3 (1980).
- 'Restoring Class to State Unemployment Insurance.' *Canadian Journal of Political Science* 19 (1986).
Cuthbert Brandt, Gail. '"Pigeon-Holed and Forgotten": The Work of the Subcommittee on the Post-war Problems of Women, 1943.' *Histoire sociale/ Social History* 15, no. 29 (May 1982).
Davis, Mike. '"Fordism" in Crisis: A Review of Michel Agietta's *Regulation et crises: L'experience des Etats-Unis.' Review* 2, no. 2 (Fall 1978).
- 'The Political Economy of Late Imperial America.' In *Prisoners of the American Dream*. London: Verso, 1986.
Dickinson, James, and Bob Russell, eds. *Family, Economy and the State: The Social Reproduction Process under Capitalism*. Toronto: Garamond Press, 1986.
Dingledine, Gary. *A Chronology of Response: The Evolution of Unemployment Insurance from 1940 to 1980*. Prepared for Employment and Immigration Canada. Ottawa, 1981.
Docquier, Gerard, Hugh Mackenzie, and Richard Shillington. *Victimizing the Unemployed: How UI Cuts Will Promote Poverty in Canada*. Ottawa, Canadian Centre for Policy Alternatives, 1989.
Doern, Bruce, L. Pal, and B. Tomlin, eds. *Border Crossings: The Internationalization of Canadian Public Policy*. Don Mills: Oxford University Press, 1996.
Doerr, Audrey, and Micheline Carrier, eds. *Women and the Constitution in Canada*. Ottawa, Canadian Advisory Council on the Status of Women, 1981.
Drache, Daniel, and Duncan Cameron. *The Other Macdonald Report*. Toronto: Lorimer, 1985.
Drache, Daniel, and Andrew Ranachan, eds. *Warm Heart, Cold Country: Fiscal and Social Policy Reform in Canada*. Ottawa, North York. Caledon Institute of Social Policy, Robarts Centre for Canadian Studies, 1995.
Drainville, Andre. 'Monetarism in Canada and the World Economy.' *Studies in Political Economy* 46 (Spring 1995).
Duffy, Ann, and Norene Pupo. *Part-Time Paradox: Connecting Gender, Work and Family*. Toronto: McClelland & Stewart, 1992.
Dulude, Louise. 'The Status of Women Under the Mulroney Government.' In *Canada under Mulroney: An End of Term Report*, ed. Andrew B. Gollner and Daniel Salee. Montreal: Vehicule Press, 1988.
Eberts, Mary. 'Women and Constitutional Renewal.' In *Women and the Constitution in Canada*, ed. Audrey Doerr and Micheline Carrier. Ottawa, Canadian Advisory Council on the Status of Women, 1981.
Eichler, Margrit. '"Family Income" – A Critical Look at the Concept.' *Status of Women News* 6, no. 2 (Spring 1980).

Eisenstein, Zillah. *Feminism and Sexual Equality*. New York: Monthly Review Press, 1984.

Elson, Diane. 'The Economic, the Poolitical and the Domestic: Business, States and Households in the Organization of Production.' *New Political Economy* 3, no. 2 (1998).

Esping-Andersen, Gosta. *Three Worlds of Welfare Capitalism*. Cambridge: Polity Press, 1990.

– 'After the Golden Age? State Dilemmas in a Global Economy.' In *Welfare States in Transition: National Adaptations in Global Economics*, ed. Gosta Esping-Andersen. London: Sage, 1996.

– *Social Foundations of Postindustrial Economies*. Oxford: Oxford University Press, 1999.

Evans, Patricia M. 'Single Mothers and Ontario's Welfare Policy: Restructuring the Debate.' In *Women and Canadian Public Policy*, ed. Janine Brodie. Toronto: Harcourt Brace, 1996.

– 'Divided Citizenship? Gender, Income Security and the Welfare State.' In *Women and the Canadian Welfare State: Challenges and Change*, ed. Patricia M. Evans and Gerda R. Wekerle. Toronto: University of Toronto Press, 1997.

Evans, Patricia M., and Gerda R. Wekerle, eds. *Women and the Canadian Welfare State: Challenges and Change*. Toronto: University of Toronto Press, 1997.

Evans, Peter, Dietrick Reuschemeyer, and Theda Skocpol, eds. *Bringing the State Back In*. Cambridge: Cambridge University Press, 1985.

Featherstone, Dennis C. *Married Female Labour Force Participation: A Micro Study*. Special Labour Force Study, Series B, No. 4. Ottawa, Dominion Bureau of Statistics, 1970.

Ferree, Myra Marx, Judith Lorber, and Beth B. Hess, eds. *Revisioning Gender*. Walnut Creek, CA: AltaMira Press, 2000.

Ferguson, Derek. 'Acrimony Rises on All Sides over Social Reforms.' *Toronto Star* (17 December 1994).

Fernandez-Kelly, M. Patricia, and S. Sassen. 'Recasting Women in the Global Economy: Internationalization and Changing Definitions of Gender.' In *Women in the Latin American Development Process*, ed. C. Bose and E. Acost-Belen. Philadelphia: Temple University Press, 1995.

Findlay, Sue. 'Facing the State: The Politics of the Women's Movement Reconsidered.' In *Feminism and Political Economy*, ed. Heather Jon Maroney and Meg Luxton. Toronto: Methuen, 1987.

Finkel, Alvin. *Business and Social Reform in the Thirties*. Toronto: Lorimer, 1979.

Folbre, Nancy. *The Invisible Heart: Economic and Family Values*. New York: The New Press, 2001.

Fox, Bonnie, ed. *Hidden in the Household: Women's Domestic Labour Under Capitalism*. Toronto: The Women's Press, 1980.

Fraser, Nancy. 'After the Family Wage: Gender Equity and the Welfare State.' *Political Theory* (November 1994).

Fraser, Nancy, and Linda Gordon. 'Contract versus Charity: Why is there no social citizenship in the United States?' *Socialist Review* 22, no. 3, (1992).

*From the Double Day to the Endless Day: Proceedings from the Conference on Homeworking, November 1992*. Ottawa, Canadian Centre for Policy Alternatives, 1994.

Glenn, Evelyn Nakano. 'The Social Construction and Institutionalization of Gender and Race.' In *Revisioning Gender*, ed. Myra Marx Ferree, Judith Lorber, and Beth B. Hess. Walnut Creek, CA: AltaMira Press, 2000.

Glucksman, M. 'In a Class of Her Own? Women Workers in the New Industries in Inter-War Britain.' *Feminist Review* 24 (1986).

Gollner, Andrew B., And Daniel Salee, eds. *Canada under Mulroney: An End of Term Report*. Montreal: Vehicule Press, 1988.

Golz, Annalee. 'Family Matters: The Canadian Family and the State in the Postwar Period,' *Left History*. 1, no. 2 (Fall 1993).

Gordon, Linda, 'The Welfare State: Towards a Socialist-Feminist Perspective.' In *Socialist Register*, ed. Ralph Miliband and Leo Panitch. London: Merlin Press, 1990.

Green, Christopher and Jean-Michel Cousineau. *Unemployment in Canada: The Impact of Unemployment Insurance*. Ottawa, Economic Council of Canada, 1976.

Grinspun, Ricardo, and Robert Kreklewich. 'Consolidating Neoliberal Reforms: "Free Trade" as a Conditioning Framework.' *Studies in Political Economy* 43 (Spring 1994).

Grubel, Herbert G., And Michael A. Walker. 'Moral Hazard, Unemployment Insurance and the Rate of Unemployment.' In *Unemployment Insurance: Global Evidence of Its Effects on Unemployment*. Vancouver: The Fraser Institute, 1978.

Guest, Dennis. *The Emergence of Social Security in Canada*, 2nd ed. Vancouver: University of British Columbia Press, 1985.

Gunderson, Morley. 'Work Patterns.' In *Opportunity for Choice: A Goal for Women in Canada*, ed. Gail C.A. Cook. Ottawa, Statistics Canada in association with the C.D. Howe Research Institute, 1976.

Hall, Karen. 'Hours Polarization at the End of the 1990s.' *Perspectives*. Statistics Canada, Summer 1999.

Hartmann, Heidi. 'The Unhappy Marriage of Marxism and Feminism: Towards a More Progressive Union.' In *Women and Revolution*, ed. Lydia Sargent. Boston: South End Press, 1981.

Hassfeld, Karen. '"Their Logic Against Them": Contradictions in Sex, Race and Class in Silicon Valley.' In *Women Workers and Global Restructuring*, ed. Katheryn Ward. Ithaca: IRL Press, 1990.

Hernes, Helga Maria. *Welfare State and Woman Power: Essays in State Feminism.* Oslo: Norwegian University Press, 1987.

Heron, Craig, and Robert Storey, eds. *On the Job: Confronting the Labour Process in Canada.* Montreal and Kingston: McGill-Queen's University Press, 1986.

Hirst, Paul, and Grahame Thompson. *Globalization in Question: The International Economy and the Possibilities of Governance,* 2nd ed. Cambridge: Polity Press, 1999.

Hobson, Barbara, and Marika Lindholm. 'Collective Identities, Women's Power Resources, and the Making of Welfare States.' *Theory and Society* 26 (1997).

Huckle, Patricia. 'The Womb Factor: Pregnancy Policies and Employment of Women.' In *Women, Power and Policy*, ed. Ellen Boneparth. New York: Permanon Press, 1982.

Institute for Research on Public Policy. 'Commentaries on the Axworthy Green Paper.' *Choices* 1, no. 2 (1995).

– 'The IRPP Position: Axworthy Proposals: Too Timid, Reforms Should Go Further.' *Choices* 1, no. 1 (1995).

Ismael, Jacqueline, S., ed. *The Canadian Welfare State: Evolution and Transition.* Edmonton: University of Alberta Press, 1987.

Issalys, Pierre, and Gaylord Watkins. *Unemployment Insurance Benefits: A Study of Administrative Procedure in the Unemployment Insurance Commission.* Law Reform Commission of Canada, 1977.

Jean, Dominique. 'Family Allowances and Family Autonomy: Quebec Families Encounter the Welfare State, 1945–1955.' In *Canadian Family History*, ed. Bettina Bradbury. Mississauga: Copp Clark Pitman, 1992.

'Jean-Claude Parrot: An Interview.' *Studies in Political Economy* 11 (Summer 1983).

Jenson, Jane. 'Gender and Reproduction, or Babies and the State.' *Studies in Political Economy.* 20 (Summer 1986).

– 'The Talents of Women, the Skills of Men: Flexible Specialisation and Women.' In *The Transformation of Work? Skill, Flexibility and the Labour Process*, ed. Stephen Wood. London: Unwin Hyman, 1989.

– 'Different But Not Exceptional: The Feminism of Permeable Fordism.' *New Left Review* 184 (November/December 1990).

Jenson, Jane, Elisabeth Hagen, and Ceallaigh Reddy, eds. *Feminization of the Labor Force: Paradoxes and Promises.* New York: Oxford University Press, 1988.

Jessop, Bob. *State Theory: Putting the Capitalist State in Its Place*. London: Polity Press, 1990.

– 'The Welfare State in the Transition from Fordism to Post-Fordism.' In *The Politics of Flexibility: Restructuring State and Industry in Britain, Germany and Scandinavia*, ed. Bob Jessop et al. England: Edward Elgar, 1991.

– 'Towards a Schumpeterian Workfare State? Preliminary Remarks on Post-Fordist Political Economy.' *Studies in Political Economy* 40 (Spring 1993).

Johnson, Andrew F. 'A Minister as an Agent of Policy Change: The Case of Unemployment Insurance in the Seventies.' *Canadian Public Administration* 24, no. 4 (Winter 1981).

– 'Political Leadership and the Process of Policy-Making: The Case of Unemployment Insurance in the 1970s.' PhD diss., McGill University, 1983.

– 'Canadian Social Services Beyond 1984: A Neo-Liberal Agenda.' In *Canada under Mulroney: An End of Term Report*, ed. Andrew B. Gollner and Daniel Salee. Montreal: Vehicule Press, 1988.

Johnson, Andrew F., Stephen McBride, and Patrick J. Smith, eds. *Continuities and Discontinuities: The Political Economy of Social Welfare and Labour Market Policy in Canada*. Toronto: University of Toronto Press, 1994.

Kelly, Laurence A. 'Unemployment Insurance in Canada: Economic, Social and Financial Aspects.' PhD diss., Queen's University, 1967.

Korpi, Walter, 'Faces of Inequality: Gender, Class and Patterns of Inequality in Different Types of Welfare States,' *Social Politics* (Summer 2000).

Krahn, Harvey. 'Non-standard Work Arrangements.' *Perspectives on Labour and Income*. Statistics Canada, Winter 1991.

– 'Non-standard Work on the Rise.' *Perspectives on Labour and Income*. Statistics Canada, Winter 1995.

Kuhn, Annette, and Ann Marie Wolpe, eds. *Feminism and Materialism*. London: Routledge and Kegan Paul, 1978.

Land, Hilary. 'Who Still Cares for the Family? Recent Developments in Income Maintenance, Taxation and Family Law.' In *Women's Welfare, Women's Rights*, ed. Jane Lewis. London: Croom Helm, 1983.

Langille, David. 'The Business Council on National Issues and the Canadian State.' *Studies in Political Economy* 24 (Autumn 1987).

Levesque, Jean-Marc. 'Unemployment and Unemployment Insurance: A Tale of Two Sources.' *Perspectives on Labour and Income*. Statistics Canada, Winter 1989.

Lewis, Jane. 'Dealing with Dependency: State Practices and Social Realities, 1870–1945.' In *Women's Welfare, Women's Rights*, ed. Jane Lewis. London: Croom Helm, 1983.

– 'Gender and the Development of Welfare Regimes.' In *Power Resources*

*Theory and the Welfare State*, ed. Julia S. O'Connor and Gregg M. Olsen. Toronto: University of Toronto Press, 1998.

Lewis, Jane, and Gertrude Astrom. 'Equality, Difference and State Welfare: Labor Market and Family Policies in Sweden.' *Feminist Studies* 18, no. 1 (1992).

Leys, Colin. *Market-driven Politics: Neoliberal Democracy and the Public Interest*. London: Verso, 2001.

Little, Margaret. 'The Blurring of Boundaries: Private and Public Welfare for Single Mothers in Ontario.' *Studies in Political Economy* 47 (Summer 1995).

– *'No Car, No Radio, No Liquor Permit': The Moral Regulation of Single Mothers in Ontario, 1920–1997*. Toronto: Oxford University Press, 1998.

Livingstone, David, and Meg Luxton. 'Gender Consciousness at Work: Modification of the Male Breadwinner Norm.' In *Recast Dreams: Class and Gender Consciousness in Steeltown*, ed. David Livingstone and J. Marshall Mangan. Toronto: Garamond Press, 1996.

Livingstone, David, and J. Marshall Mangan, eds. *Recast Dreams: Class and Gender Consciousness in Steeltown*. Toronto: Garamond Press, 1996.

Luxton, Meg. *More Than a Labour of Love: Three Generations of Women's Work in the Home*. Toronto: The Women's Press, 1980.

– 'Two Hands for the Clock: Changing Patterns in the Gendered Division of Labour in the Home.' In *Through the Kitchen Window: The Politics of Home and Family*, by Meg Luxton and Harriet Rosenberg. Toronto: Garamond Press, 1986.

MacDonald, Martha. 'Post-Fordism and the Flexibility Debate.' *Studies in Political Economy* 36 (Autumn 1991).

– 'Restructuring, Gender and Social Security Reform in Canada.' *Journal of Canadian Studies* 34, no. 2 (Summer 1999).

MacDonald, Martha, and M. Patricia Connelly. 'Class and Gender in Fishing Communities in Nova Scotia.' *Studies in Political Economy* 30 (Autumn 1989).

Mahon, Rianne. 'From Fordism to ?: New Technology, Labour Markets and Unions.' *Economic and Industrial Democracy* 8 (1987).

– 'From "Bringing" to "Putting": The State in Late Twentieth-Century Social Theory.' *Canadian Journal of Sociology* 16, no. 2 (1991).

– 'Child Care in Canada and Sweden: Policy and Politics,' *Social Politics* (Fall 1997).

Maroney, Heather Jon, and Meg Luxton. 'From Feminism and Political Economy to Feminist Political Economy.' In *Feminism and Political Economy: Women's Work, Women's Struggles*, ed. Heather Jon Maroney and Meg Luxton. Toronto: Methuen, 1987.

– 'Gender at Work: Canadian Feminist Political Economy since 1988.' In

*Understanding Canada: Building on the New Canadian Political Economy*, ed. Wallace Clement. Montreal and Kingston: McGill-Queen's University Press, 1997.

Marsden, Lorna. 'Unemployment among Canadian Women: Some Sociological Problems Raised by Its Increase.' In *The Working Sexes*, ed. Patricia Marchak. Vancouver: Institute of Industrial Relations, 1977.

Marsh, Leonard. *Report on Social Security for Canada, 1943*. Reprinted Toronto: University of Toronto Press, 1975.

Martin, Sheilah L. 'Persisting Equality Implications of the "Bliss" Case.' In *Equality and Judicial Neutrality*, ed. Sheilah L. Martin and Kathleen E. Mahoney. Toronto: Carswell, 1987.

McBride, Stephen. *Not Working: State, Unemployment and Neo-Conservatism in Canada*. Toronto: University of Toronto Press, 1992.

McDowell, Linda. 'Life without Father and Ford: The New Gender Order of Post-Fordism.' *Transactions of the Institute of British Geographers* 16 (1991).

McIntosh, Mary. 'The State and the Oppression of Women.' In *Feminism and Materialism*, ed. Annette Kuhn and Ann Marie Wolpe. London: Routledge and Kegan Paul, 1978.

McKeen, Wendy. 'The Shaping of Political Agency: Feminism and the National Social Policy Debate, the 1970s and early 1980s.' *Studies in Political Economy* 66 (2001).

McKeen, Wendy, and Ann Porter. 'Politics and Transformation: Welfare State Restructuring in Canada.' In *Changing Canada: Political Economy as Transformation*, ed. Wallace Clement and Leah F. Vosko. Montreal and Kingston: McGill-Queen's University Press, 2003.

Mies, M. *Patriarchy and Accumulation on a World Scale*. London and New York: Zed Books Ltd, 1986, 1998.

Milkman, Ruth. *Gender at Work: The Dynamics of Job Segregation by Sex during World War II*. Carbondale: University of Illinois Press, 1987.

Mohanty, Chandra Talpade. 'Women Workers and Capitalist Scripts: Ideologies of Domination, Common Interests, and the Politics of Solidarity.' In *Feminist Genealogies, Colonial Legacies, Democratic Futures*, ed. M. Jacqui Alexander and Chandra Talpade Mohanty. New York: Routledge, 1997.

Morissette, Rene, John Myles, and Garnett Picot. 'Earnings Polarization in Canada, 1969–1991.' In *Labour Market Polarization and Social Policy Reform*, ed. Keith Banting and Charles Beach. Kingston: Queen's University School of Policy Studies, 1995.

Morris, Cerise. '"Determination and Thoroughness": The Movement for a Royal Commission on the Status of Women in Canada,' *Atlantis* 5, no. 2 (1981).

Moscovitch, Allan, and Jim Albert, eds. *The Benevolent State: The Growth of Welfare in Canada*. Toronto: Garamond Press, 1987.

Moscovitch, Allan, and Glen Drover. *Inequality: Essays on the Political Economy of Social Welfare*. Toronto: University of Toronto Press, 1981.

Myles, John. 'Decline or Impasse? The Current State of the Welfare State.' *Studies in Political Economy* 26 (1988).

Myles, John, and Paul Pierson. 'Friedman's Revenge: The Reform of "Liberal" Welfare States in Canada and the United States.' *Politics and Society* 25, no. 4 (December 1997).

Nelson, Barbara. 'The Origins of the Two-Channel Welfare State: Workmen's Compensation and Mother's Aid.' In *Women, the State and Welfare*, ed. Linda Gordon. Madison: University of Wisconsin Press, 1990.

Noel, Alain, Gerard Boismenu, and Lizette Jalbert. 'The Political Foundations of State Regulation in Canada.' In *Production, Space, Identity: Political Economy Faces the 21st Century*, ed. Jane Jenson, Rianne Mahon, and Manfred Bienefeld. Toronto: Canadian Scholars' Press, 1993.

Offe, Claus. *Contradictions of the Welfare State*. Cambridge, MA: MIT Press, 1984.

O'Connor, James. *The Fiscal Crisis of the State*. New York: St Martin's Press, 1973.

O'Connor, Julia. 'Gender, Class and Citizenship in the Comparative Analysis of Welfare State Regimes: Theoretical and Methodological Issues,' *British Journal of Sociology* 44, no. 3 (1993).

O'Connor, Julia S., and Gregg M. Olsen, eds., *Power Resources Theory and the Welfare State*. Toronto: University of Toronto Press, 1998.

O'Connor, Julia S., Ann Shola Orloff, and Sheila Shaver. *States, Markets, Families: Gender, Liberalism and Social Policy in Australia, Canada, Great Britain and the United States*. Cambridge: Cambridge University Press, 1999.

Orloff, Ann Shola. 'Gender and the Social Rights of Citizenship: The Comparative Analysis of Gender Relations and Welfare State,' *American Sociological Review* 58 (1993).

Ostry, Sylvia. *The Female Worker in Canada*. 1961 Census monograph program. Ottawa: Dominion Bureau of Statistics, 1968.

– *Unemployment in Canada*. Ottawa: Dominion Bureau of Statistics, 1968.

Pal, Leslie. *State, Class and Bureaucracy: Canadian Unemployment Insurance and Public Policy*. Montreal and Kingston: McGill-Queen's University Press, 1988.

– 'Relative Autonomy Revisited: The Origins of Canadian Unemployment Insurance,' *Canadian Journal of Political Science* 19, no. 1 (1986).

Pal, Leslie A., and F.L. Morton. '*Bliss v. Attorney General of Canada*: From Legal Defeat to Political Victory.' *Osgoode Hall Law Journal* 24, no. 1 (1986).

Panitch, Leo. 'Globalisation and the State.' In *Socialist Register, 1994*, ed. Ralph Miliband and Leo Panitch. London: Merlin Press, 1994.

Parent, Madeleine. 'Women in Unions: Past, Present and Future.' In *Strong Women, Strong Unions: Speeches by Union Women*. Canada Employment and Immigration Union/Participatory Research Group, 1985.

Pascall, Gillian. *Social Policy: A Feminist Analysis*. London: Routledge, 1991.

Pateman, Carole. 'Feminism and Democracy.' In *The Disorder of Women*. Cambridge: Polity Press, 1989.

– 'The Patriarchal Welfare State.' In *Democracy and the Welfare State*, ed. Amy Gutmann. Princeton: Princeton University Press, 1988.

– 'The Fraternal Social Contract.' *Civil Society and the State*, In ed. John Keane. London: Verso, 1988.

– 'Equality, Difference, Subordination: The Politics of Motherhood and Women's Citizenship.' In *Beyond Equality and Difference*, ed. Gisela Bock and Susan James. London: Routledge, 1992.

Pearce, Diana. 'Welfare Is Not *For* Women: Why the Way on Poverty Cannot Conquer the Feminization of Poverty.' In *Women, the State and Welfare*, ed. Linda Gordon. Wisconsin: University of Wisconsin Press, 1990.

Peck, Jamie. *Workfare States*. New York: Guildford Press, 2001.

Phipps, Shelley, Martha MacDonald, and Fiona MacPhail. 'Gender Equity within Families versus Better Targeting: An Assessment of the Family Income Supplement to Employment Insurance Benefits,' *Canadian Public Policy* 27, no. 4 (2001).

Piche, Lucie. 'Entre l'acces a l'egalite et la preservation des modeles: Ambivalence du discours et des revendications du Comite Feminin de la CTCC-CSN, 1952–1966.' *Labour/Le Travail* 29 (Spring 1992).

Picot, G., and A. Heisz. 'The Labour Market in the 1990s.' *Canadian Economic Observer* (January 2000).

Picot, Garnett, John Myles, and Ted Wannell. *Good Jobs, Bad Jobs and the Declining Middle: 1967–1986*. Ottawa: Statistics Canada, 1990.

Pierson, Paul. 'The New Politics of the Welfare State.' *World Politics* 48 (January 1996).

– ed. *The New Politics of the Welfare State*. Oxford: Oxford University Press, 2001.

Pierson, Ruth Roach. 'Gender and the Unemployment Insurance Debates in Canada, 1934–1940,' *Labour/Le Travail* 25 (Spring 1990).

– *'They're Still Women After All': The Second World War and Canadian Womanhood*. Toronto: McClelland & Stewart, 1986.

Pold, Henry. 'Jobs! Jobs! Jobs!' *Perspectives on Labour and Income*. Statistics Canada, Autumn 1994.

Pollert, Anna. 'Dismantling Flexibility.' *Capital and Class* 34 (Spring 1988).

Prentice, Alison et al. *Canadian Women: A History*. Toronto, Harcourt Brace Jovanovich, 1988.

Pulkingham, Jane. 'Remaking the Social Divisions of Welfare: Gender. "Dependency" and UI Reform.' *Studies in Political Economy* 56 (Summer 1998).

Pulkingham, Jane, and Gordon Ternowetsky, eds., *Remaking Canadian Social Policy*. Halifax: Fernwood Publishing, 1996.

Rai, Shirin M. *Gender and the Political Economy of Development*. Cambridge: Polity Press, 2002.

Razack, Sherene. *Canadian Feminism and the Law*. Toronto: Second Story Press, 1991.

Reynolds, Elisabeth B., ed. *Income Security in Canada: Changing Needs, Changing Means*. Montreal: Institute for Research on Public Policy, 1993.

Rice, James J. 'Redesigning Welfare: The Abandonment of a National Commitment.' In *How Ottawa Spends, 1995–96*, ed. Susan Phillips. Ottawa: Carleton University Press, 1995.

Rice, James J., and Michael J. Prince. *Changing Politics of Canadian Social Policy*. Toronto: University of Toronto Press, 2000.

Riches, Graham, and Gordon Ternowetsky. *Unemployment and Welfare: Social Policy and the Work of Social Work*. Toronto: Garamond Press, 1989.

Robindaine-Saumure, Elsie. *Maternity Leave and Benefits*. Ottawa: Canadian Advisory Council on the Status of Women, 1976.

Rosen, Elise. *A Report on the Comprehensive Review of the Unemployment Insurance Program in Canada*. Ottawa: The Advisory Council on the Status of Women, October 1977.

Rowbotham, Sheila, and S. Mitter, eds., *Dignity and Daily Bread*. London and New York: Routlege, 1994.

Roy, F. 'Unemployment and Unemployment Insurance: An Update.' *Canadian Economic Observer* (January 1994).

Rubery, Jill, ed. *Women and Recession*. London: Routledge and Kegan Paul, 1988.

Sainsbury, Diane. 'Women's and Men's Social Rights: Gendering Dimensions of Welfare States.' In *Gendering Welfare States*, ed. D. Sainsbury. London and Thousand Oaks: Sage, 1994.

– *Gender, Equality and Welfare States*. Cambridge, New York: Cambridge University Press, 1996.

Sangster, Joan. 'Doing Two Jobs: The Wage-Earning Mother, 1945–70.' In *A Diversity of Women: Ontario, 1945–1980*, ed. Joy Parr. Toronto: University of Toronto Press, 1995.

Saywell, John, ed. *Canadian Annual Review*. Toronto: University of Toronto Press, 1960 to 1990.

Scott, Joan Wallach. 'Gender: A Useful Category of Historical Analysis.' In
   *Gender and the Politics of History*. New York: Columbia University Press,
   1988.
– 'The Sears Case.' In *Gender and the Politics of History*. New York: Columbia
   University Press, 1988.
– 'Some Reflections on Gender and Politics.' In *Revisioning Gender*, ed. Myra
   Marx Ferree, Judith Lorber, and Beth B. Hess. Walnut Creek, CA: AltaMira
   Press, 2000.
Scott, Katherine. 'The Dilemma of Liberal Citizenship: Women and Social
   Assistance Reform in the 1990s.' *Studies in Political Economy*. 50 (Summer
   1996).
Seccombe, Wally. *A Millenium of Family Change: Feudalism to Capitalism in
   Northwestern Europe*. London: Verso, 1992.
– *Weathering the Storm: Working Class Families from the Industrial Revolution to
   the Fertility Decline*. London: Verso, 1993.
Seccombe, Wally, and D.W. Livingstone. '"Down to Earth People": Revising a
   Materialist Understanding of Group Consciousness.' In *Recast Dreams: Class
   and Gender Consciousness in Steeltown*, ed. David Livingstone and J. Marshall
   Mangan. Toronto: Garamond Press, 1996.
Shaw, Rosa L. *Proud Heritage: A History of the National Council of Women of
   Canada*. Toronto, Ryerson Press, 1957.
Showstack Sassoon, Anne. 'Women's New Social Role: Contradictions of the
   Welfare State.' In *Women and the State*, ed. Anne Showstack Sassoon. Lon-
   don: Unwin Hyman, 1987.
– ed. *Women and the State*. London: Unwin Hyman, 1987.
Siim, Birte. 'Towards a Feminist Rethinking of the Welfare State.' In *The
   Political Interests of Gender*, ed. Kathleen B. Jones and Anna G. Jonasdottir.
   London: Sage, 1988.
Smith, Dorothy. 'Women's Inequality and the Family.' In *Inequality: Essays on
   the Political Economy of Social Welfare*, ed. Allan Moscovitch and Glen Drover.
   Toronto: University of Toronto Press, 1981.
– *The Everyday World as Problematic*. Toronto: University of Toronto Press,
   1987.
– 'Feminist Reflections on Political Economy.' *Studies in Political Economy* 30
   (Autumn 1989).
Strong-Boag, Veronica. *The Parliament of Women: The National Council of Women
   of Canada, 1893–1929*. History Division Paper no. 18. Ottawa, National
   Museums of Canada, 1976.
– 'Keeping House in God's Country: Canadian Women at Work in the Home.'
   In *On the Job: Confronting the Labour Process in Canada*, ed. Craig Heron and

Robert Storey. Montreal and Kingston: McGill-Queen's University Press, 1986.
- 'Canada's Wage-Earning Wives and the Construction of the Middle-Class, 1945–60,' *Journal of Canadian Studies* 29, no. 3 (Autumn 1994).
Struthers, James. *No Fault of Their Own: Unemployment and the Canadian Welfare State, 1914–1940*. Toronto: University of Toronto Press, 1983.
Sugiman, Pamela. 'Privilege and Oppression: The Configuration of Race, Gender and Class in Southern Ontario Auto Plants, 1939 to 1949.' *Labour/Le Travail* 47 (Spring 2001).
Sunter, Deborah, and Rene Morissette. 'The Hours People Work.' *Perspectives on Labour and Income*. Statistics Canada, Autumn 1994.
Symes, Beth. 'Equality Theories and Maternity Benefits.' In *Equality and Judicial Neutrality*, ed. Kathleen E. Mahoney. Toronto: Carswell, 1987.
Tangri, Beverly. 'Women and Unemployment,' *Atlantis* 3, no. 2, part II (Spring 1978).
Teeple, Gary. *Globalization and the Decline of Social Reform*. Toronto: Garamond Press, 1995.
Timpson, Annis May. *Driven Apart: Women's Employment Equality and Child Care in Canadian Public Policy*. Vancouver: UBC Press, 2001.
Townson, Monica. 'Research Notes: The Social Security Review and Its Implications for Women: #4 Unemployment Insurance.' Ottawa: The Council, 1994.
Trembley, Manon, and Caroline Andrew, eds., *Women and Political Representation in Canada*. Ottawa: University of Ottawa Press, 1998.
Ursel, Jane. 'The State and the Maintenance of Patriarchy: A Case Study of Family, Labour and Welfare Legislation in Canada.' In *Family, Economy and the State: The Social Reproduction Process Under Capitalism*, ed. James Dickinson and Bob Russell. Toronto: Garamond Press, 1986.
- *Private Lives, Public Policy: 100 Years of State Intervention in the Family*. Toronto: Women's Press, 1992.
Vickers, Jill, Pauline Rankin, and Christine Appelle. *Politics as if Women Mattered: A Political Analysis of the National Action Committee on the Status of Women*. Toronto: University of Toronto Press, 1993.
Vosko, Leah. 'Irregular workers, New Involuntary Social Exiles: Women and UI Reform.' In *Remaking Canadian Social Policy: Social Security in the Late 1990s*, ed. J. Pulkingham and G. Ternowetsky. Halifax: Fernwood, 1996.
- 'Recreating Dependency: Women, Unemployment and Federal Proposals for UI Reform.' In *Warm Heart, Cold Country: Fiscal and Social Policy Reform in Canada*, ed. Daniel Drache and Andrew Ranachan. Ottawa, North York:

Caledon Institute of Social Policy, Robarts Centre for Canadian Studies, 1995.

Walby, Sylvia. 'Flexibility and the Changing Sexual Division of Labour.' In *The Transformation of Work?: Skill, Flexibility and the Labour Process*, ed. Stephen Wood. London: Unwin Hyman, 1989.

Waring, Marilyn. *Counting for Nothing: What Men Value and What Women are Worth*. Toronto: University of Toronto Press, 1999.

Warskett, Rosemary. 'Women and Clerical Work: Revisiting Class and Gender.' *Studies in Political Economy* 30 (Autumn 1989).

Watson, Sophie, ed. *Playing the State: Australian Feminist Interventions*. London: Verso, 1990.

White, Julie. *Mail and Female: Women and the Canadian Union of Postal Workers*. Toronto: Thompson Educational Publishing, 1990.

– *Sisters and Solidarity: Women and Unions in Canada*. Toronto: Thompson Educational Publishing, 1993.

Whitfield, Dexter. *Public Services or Corporate Welfare: Rethinking the Nation State in the Global Economy*. London: Pluto Press, 2001.

Williams, Fiona. 'Race/Ethnicity, Gender and Class in Welfare States: A Framework for Comparative Analysis.' *Social Politics* (Summer 1995).

Wilson, Elizabeth. *Women and the Welfare State*. London: Tavistock Publications, 1977.

Wolfe, David. 'The Rise and Demise of the Keynesian Era in Canada: Economic Policy, 1930–1982.' In *Modern Canada, 1930–1980s*, ed. Michael S. Cross and Gregory S. Kealey. Toronto: McClelland & Stewart, 1984.

Woodsworth, Sheila. *Maternity Protection for Women Workers in Canada*. Ottawa: Canada Department of Labour, Women's Bureau, 1967.

# Index

under, 132–7; and discrimination, 133–6; and UI Act, 141

Canadian Congress of Labour (CCL), 49–50, 53–4, 78–9

Canadian Construction Association, 47–8

Canadian Federation of Business and Professional Women's Clubs (BPW), 56, 121; and married women's regulation, 55, 58; and maternity benefits, 80–1, 84; and part-time work, 96; and UI restructuring, 101, 102; and working women, 255n44, 267n88, 277n78

Canadian Human Rights Commission (CHRC), 121; and maternity benefits, 140–1, 148; and UI Act, 140–1, 174; and UI restructuring, 207

*Canadian Labour*, 85

Canadian Labour Congress (CLC): and Gill Committee, 101; and married women's regulation, 55, 58; and maternity benefits, 79, 85; and UI restructuring, 169, 171, 198, 219, 226; and women's issues, 109, 171

Canadian Manufacturers' Association, 47–8, 290n47

Canadian Medical Association, 87

Canadian Textile and Chemical Union, 141

Canadian Union of Postal Workers (CUPW), 143–4, 148

capitalism, 18–19, 26; women's position in, 15–16, 26–7

casual work. *See* temporary work

CCF, 46

Census of Canada (1971), 154–5

Charter of Rights and Freedoms

(1982), 121, 137, 142; equality under, 142, 180, 191, 236; and parental benefits, 194, 198

childbirth: and job security, 87; and maternity benefits, 126; UI disqualification after, 72, 76–7

childcare: assistance with, 226; difficulty arranging for, 95, 176, 201–2; as right, 22; state and, 20–1, 180, 191, 193; and UI eligibility, 130–1, 158–9; as UI requirement for women, 72, 76, 101, 128, 130–1, 138–40

childrearing: attitudes toward, 62, 67, 89–90; and labour force participation, 94; state and, 140, 147–8, 192

children, 39, 86, 89–90

Child Tax Benefit, 223

Chrétien, Jean, 309n21

citizenship, 21–2, 39–40

civil service. *See* public sector

Clark, Joe, 177

class, 15–19; economic structures and, 16–17, 23–4; and pregnancy, 66, 69

Cohen, Marjorie, 138

collective bargaining, 88

Commissions of Inquiry: into Part-Time Work (Wallace Commission), 191–2; on Unemployment Insurance (Forget Commission), 180, 185, 186–9

Common Front, 143

Communist Party of Canada, 255n44

*Comprehensive Review of the Unemployment Insurance Program in Canada* (UIC), 165, 169, 170, 173

Connelly, M. Patricia, 16, 17

Conservative governments: and

deficit reduction, 179–81, 208; UI restructuring by, 98–102, 173–7, 189–90, 195–209, 215; unemployment policies of, 184–90, 208–9; and women's interests, 121, 191, 210, 240
consumption, 24, 26
contingent work: EI program and, 224; growth of, 93, 119, 214–15, 237–8; women in, 95, 116, 202–4. *See also* part-time work; temporary work
Cooke Child Care Task Force, 191, 193
Co-operative Commonwealth Federation (CCF), 46
cost of living, 52, 59–60, 94
counselling, 96, 103
Cousineau, Jean-Michel, 161–2
Crease, Gillian, 41
Crevier, Etienne, 274n37
Cullen, Bud, 145, 165, 167, 168, 170, 173
cumulative employment account, 187–8, 189

daycare, 40, 80
deficit reduction, 150, 167, 179–81, 204–5, 208, 212; and equality, 214; by Liberal governments, 215–16, 217; UI program and, 235
Denmark, 20–1
Department of Employment and Immigration, 145–6, 173, 199
Department of Finance: policy role of, 121–2, 213, 229; and UI restructuring, 218–19
Department of Labour: and Gill Committee, 101, 102; and maternity benefits, 58, 64, 77, 82–9; and

part-time work, 95, 96; and UI program reform, 102–5, 106, 108; Working Party Committee on maternity leave, 85–7
Department of Labour Women's Bureau, 58, 121; and maternity leave, 64, 82–5, 87–8; and part-time work, 95, 103; and training needs, 104
Department of Manpower and Immigration, 182–4
dependants, 39, 177; and Family Income Supplement, 228–9; two-tier system and, 172, 175, 215, 277n89; and UI benefits, 42, 110–13, 164–5; women with, 39, 44–5. *See also* family income
dependency, 41; in feminist literature, 16, 20; social programs as creator of, 43, 213; and state policies, 62, 161; unemployment insurance and, 21–2, 37, 44–5, 169; of women in welfare state, 9, 20, 33, 39, 53, 232
Depression, 40
Deutch, John, 274n37
Diefenbaker, John, 96, 102
Diefenbaker government, 56–7
difference, 63, 82–5
disability benefits, 87, 140
discrimination: attitudes toward, 57; pregnancy and, 120, 123–4, 141; by sex, 56, 58; studies of, 191–4; in UI program, 37, 101, 110–11, 114–15, 169–75; women's organizations and, 128, 169–70, 191
divisor, 221–2
Docquier, Gerard, 299n46
domestic ideal, 41, 59, 60, 62, 78
domestic labour, 18; and capitalism,

Studies in Comparative Political Economy and Public Policy